Macintosh Pascal

Macintosh Pascal

Robert Moll
University of Massachusetts, Amherst

Rachel Folsom

In Conjunction with THINK Technologies, Inc.

Consultant: Mary Elting

Houghton Mifflin Company
Boston   Dallas   Geneva, Illinois
Hopewell, New Jersey   Palo Alto

Printed in the U.S.A.
Library of Congress Catalog Card Number: 84-81937
ISBN: 0-395-37574-6

ABCDEFGHIJ-H-8987654

Contents

3 Syntax, Interactive Programs, and Real Numbers   79

4 Assignment Statements and More on Looping   117

5   Conditional Statements, Rectangles, and Bar Graphs   153

6   Problem Solving with Procedures   191

Preface

Macintosh Pascal is an introductory programming textbook written specifically for Macintosh Pascal. Developed for Apple's Macintosh computer, MacPascal includes a number of improvements on the standard language, which make it far easier to use than traditional versions of Pascal.

Macintosh Pascal is more than a generic Pascal text with additional sections that explain MacPascal features. Working closely with THINK Technologies, the software firm that developed the language for Apple, we sought to create a book that would take maximum advantage of the features that make MacPascal so easy to learn and so exciting.

The book has been designed for a one-semester introductory course in Pascal programming. It is suitable for students who have no experience in computing. Some high school algebra is needed, but nothing more. The book is also suitable for students who have some programming experience.

Organization Of The Book

The book divides into two parts. The first five chapters cover in detail a core of programming fundamentals: looping, graphics, interactive programming, conditional statements, and program design. Chapters 6–11 cover more advanced topics: procedures, types, arrays, strings, functions, random numbers, records, and random-access files.

Chapter 1 explains how to type in, edit, execute, save, and print programs. We use the Instant window to introduce the *writeln* statement and graphics commands. Then, using simple examples, we present the rudiments of program structure. Finally we demonstrate how the **for** loop works with a program that rolls a "ball" across the Drawing window. Because looping is the single most important part of programming, it is taught as early as possible and is examined in great detail throughout the first five chapters.

In Chapter 2 we discuss how a computer executes a Pascal program, and we show how to use the Observe window to "view" program execution. The second half of the chapter is devoted to the principles of top-down programming.

Chapter 3 introduces Pascal syntax, interactive programs, and real numbers. The chapter ends with two detailed examples of program planning.

We complete our presentation of elementary Pascal concepts in Chapters 4 and 5. Chapter 4 explains assignment statements, the **while** loop, and the **repeat-until** loop. Chapter 5 discusses conditional statements and introduces bar graphs, which play an important part in many applications later in the book. The chapter ends with a carefully developed debugging example.

Chapter 6 is the central chapter of the book. Here we introduce procedures and incorporate them into our program planning method. We illustrate the role procedures play in top-down programming with two elaborate examples.

In Chapter 7 we present enumerated types, type *char*, and more material on procedures. We also introduce the MacPascal standard procedure *getmouse*, which reports the location of the pointer on the screen. *Getmouse* is the basis for the more ambitious mouse-driven applications presented in Chapter 11.

Chapter 8 is devoted to type *boolean*. After discussing boolean variables and flags, we present a program that checks for matched parentheses. The chapter ends with a section that discusses the relationship between programming and mathematical logic.

Chapter 9 provides an unusually thorough presentation of arrays and strings, topics that often give beginners trouble. We demonstrate the use of arrays with a street survey application, and then develop a number of variations on the street survey theme to illustrate important array ideas.

Chapter 10 discusses functions. We demonstrate the use of functions in two large programs dealing with textual analysis: a letter frequency program, which graphs the relative frequency of letters in a text; and a word frequency program, which imitates an early computer study done to determine the authorship of the *Federalist Papers*. The chapter ends with a discussion of random numbers that includes elementary material on simulations, Monte Carlo methods, and program testing using randomly generated data.

Chapter 11 presents a complex program called MiniPaint, which is modeled on the Macintosh application program MacPaint. MiniPaint creates a mouse-operated menu in the Drawing window that is used to control program execution. We then discuss records and, finally, files. The file section culminates in an electronic phone book program that reuses MiniPaint's mouse and menu "front end."

Special Features of the Text

- **Emphasis on Problem Solving and Top-Down Design.** The text develops a systematic method for problem solving and presents detailed solutions for ten large programming problems using top-down design.

- **Graphics.** Extensive use is made of MacPascal's graphics procedures so that even the simplest programs produce interesting output.

- **The Mouse.** Mouse commands are used frequently in the second half of the book to augment traditional Pascal input and output instructions.

- **Private Pascal.** The book develops the idea of a "private" Pascal—a library of procedures and functions that a programmer creates, which can be used repeatedly in a variety of programs. The menu and mouse "front end" used in programs MiniPaint and PhoneBook illustrate the private Pascal concept.

- **Problems and Exercises.** *Macintosh Pascal* includes almost 200 programming problems, some of which are quite challenging. Many problems involve graphics and others are applicable to everyday life. Numerous short exercises are also sprinkled throughout the text. Solutions to selected problems and exercises are included at the end of the book.

- **History of Computing.** From time to time the book includes notes on the history of computing that put into perspective the material on Pascal.

- **Glossary.** A comprehensive glossary explains Pascal terms and concepts as well as those terms specific to Macintosh Pascal.

Acknowledgments

We would like to thank Andrew Singer and Frank Sinton of THINK Technologies for proposing that we write *Macintosh Pascal* and for giving us early access to the language. Special thanks go to Dennis Lauro for coordinating the project. Thanks also to Fleet Hill for her support. We greatly appreciate the technical help we got from Terry Lucas and Peter Mahunic, the implementors of Macintosh Pascal.

Sandy Pratcher, Don Enns, Mary Alice Wilson, Felicia DeMay, and Clem Wang read portions of the manuscript and gave us many thoughtful comments. Jon Butah, Meg Beeler, and Peggy Redpath of Apple reviewed the manuscript and made particularly helpful suggestions about organization and style. The following people reviewed the manuscript in detail, providing many useful recommendations: Howard V. Carson, Ralph DeBoard, James Gips, William B. Jones, Helene Kershner, Thomas W. Osgood, Rita Ann Richards, Lynn Arthur Steen, Bernard Taheny, and Philip Tucker. The contributions of all of these people are gratefully acknowledged.

We also are indebted to Martin Robbins and Albert Meyer for teaching us a great deal about writing. We would like to thank Karen Strickholm, Susan Dunnington, and Ron Feintech for their help and moral support. Finally, we are grateful to Franklin Folsom, who ate out of the freezer for months while his wife, Mary Elting, worked on *Macintosh Pascal*.

R.M.
R.F.
M.E.

Macintosh
Pascal

A First Look at Pascal

Welcome to Macintosh Pascal!

Macintosh Pascal, or MacPascal for short, is a language for giving instructions to the Macintosh. In this book we'll show you how to write MacPascal programs to make an electronic phonebook; calculate electric bills; invent your own version of the Macintosh application program MacPaint that you can use for drawing pictures on the screen; tabulate the results of surveys; chart the time you spend each day jogging (or sleeping or working); and even make animated "cartoons" of shapes that move across the screen.

The first program you'll write will produce an animated "cartoon." The program will create a ball on a line and then roll it across the screen.

A *program* is simply a list of instructions that you give to a computer. In a Pascal program, some instructions tell the computer to print messages on the screen. Others are commands for doing arithmetic. Still others can make the computer draw lines or circles. And some instructions tell a computer to repeat other instructions over and over again.

MacPascal is itself just a very large program. It tells the computer what to do in response to the words and symbols you use when you write programs in Macintosh Pascal. MacPascal interprets the instructions in a program and passes these commands along to the computer.

1.1 Getting Started

If you've never used the Macintosh before, you need to learn some fundamentals before tackling the rest of this chapter. The best way to begin is by listening to the cassette tape that comes with the machine: "A Guided Tour of Macintosh." A disk that goes with the tape demonstrates on the computer screen how to use the

1

Figure 1.1 When you roll the mouse on a flat surface, the pointer on the screen follows its every move. Courtesy of Apple Computer, Inc.

Macintosh, and it gives you some practice with the *mouse*—the gadget, attached by a wire to the Macintosh, that moves a pointer around on the screen. (See Figure 1.1.)

If you don't have the tape and the disk, you can find out what you need to know by referring to the manual that comes with the Macintosh and to the reference manual that comes with the MacPascal disk. The Glossary at the end of this book will also answer many of your questions.

To understand what will happen in a moment when you insert the Mac-Pascal disk, you have to know something about how the Macintosh (and almost every other computer) works. The Macintosh stores information in two places: main memory and secondary memory. Main memory is located on tiny computer chips inside the computer itself. You never see it. Floppy disks make up secondary memory. (The Macintosh floppy disks don't look floppy because they come in hard covers.)

The computer can get to main memory quickly. But there is only a limited amount of main memory, and it is already partially filled with the program that runs the machine itself. The MacPascal program and the programs you write go in the empty part of main memory.

Secondary memory on floppy disks can store a huge amount of information, but the computer can't use this information directly. It can use only what has been stored in main memory. So you must copy the information from a floppy disk into the empty part of main memory when you want the Macintosh to use it.

MacPascal, the language you will use to give instructions to the Macintosh, is stored on the floppy disk. Now let's see how to copy or *load* it into main memory.

Loading MacPascal

■ *First switch on the Macintosh.* In a moment you will see, in the middle of the screen, a little picture of a disk with a blinking question mark.

■ *Insert the MacPascal floppy disk in the slot at the front of the machine.* The *electronic desktop* will now appear on your screen. It's called a desktop because it's the place where the computer's work will appear. (See Figure 1.2.)

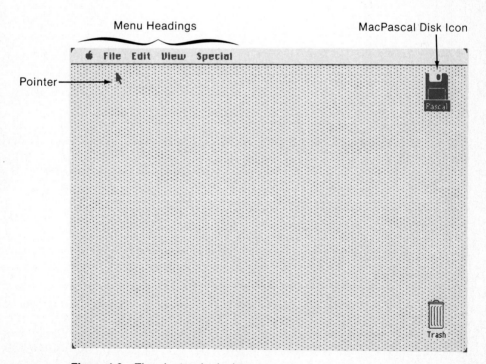

Figure 1.2 The electronic desktop.

■ *To load the MacPascal language into main memory, you must first open the MacPascal* disk window. Note that the MacPascal *disk icon*—the little picture of a disk in the upper-right corner of the desktop—is already *highlighted*. That is, it is black and is labeled with white letters. This means that the MacPascal disk window is ready to be opened.

■ *Using the mouse, move the pointer, which is in the shape of an arrow, to the word* File *at the top of the screen.*

■ *Now press the mouse button.* A box will appear right under the word *File*. Because the words in the box offer you a choice of commands that you can give to the computer, the box is called a *menu*. (See Figure 1.3.)

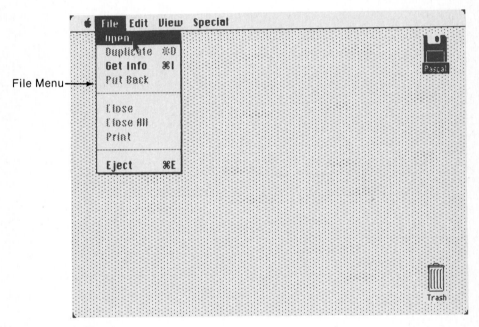

File Menu ──➤

Figure 1.3   Screen with File menu open.

■ *With the mouse button held down, move the pointer to the row in the menu labeled "Open."* Moving the pointer with the button held down is called *dragging* the pointer.

■ *Next release the button.* This opens the MacPascal disk window.

The File menu will disappear, and the MacPascal disk window will appear on top of your desktop (see Figure 1.4). In the disk window you will see several other icons. The *MacPascal icon* is the one we are interested in. Note that this icon is different from the MacPascal disk icon on the desktop.

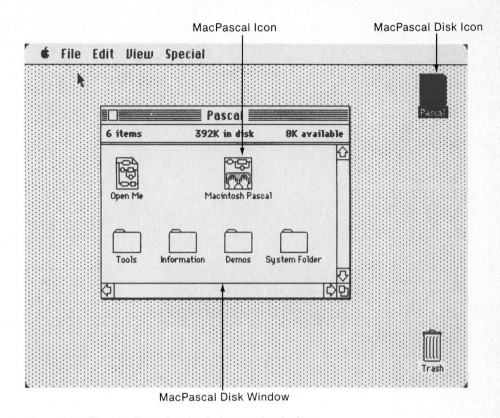

Figure 1.4   The MacPascal disk window on the desktop.

Now you are ready to load MacPascal. There are two ways to do this.

Loading—Choice 1

■ *Select MacPascal by moving the pointer to the MacPascal icon in the MacPascal disk window and clicking the mouse button.* To *click* the mouse button is to press and release it quickly. This will highlight the icon.

■ *Next move the pointer to the File menu again and choose* Open. That is, hold down the mouse button, drag the pointer to Open, and release.

Loading—Choice 2

■ *Move the pointer to the MacPascal icon.*

■ *Then quickly click the mouse button* twice.

Once you are used to the mouse, you will probably use the second method most of the time because it's faster. Both methods give the load command, which instructs the computer to copy the MacPascal program from the floppy disk into the empty part of main memory. The program is still stored on the disk as well; it's there permanently. Later, when you turn off the computer, MacPascal will vanish from main memory. You will have to load it again the next time you want to use the language.

The noises you hear come from the floppy disk spinning like a phonograph record. When the whirring stops, the disk window will disappear and your screen will display the picture shown in Figure 1.5.

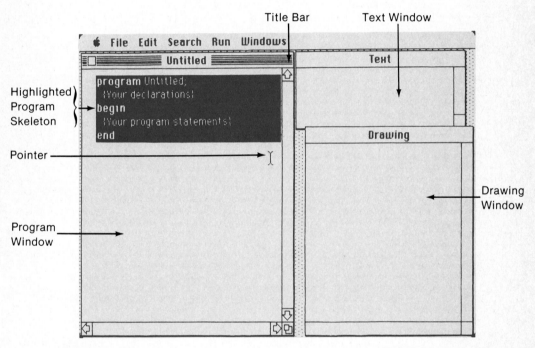

Figure 1.5 Here is what you will see when you have finished loading MacPascal.

1.2 Taking a Look at Windows

Your screen now has three windows: the Program window, the Text window, and the Drawing window.

The big window on the left is the *Program window*. When you type in a program at the keyboard, it will appear there. The highlighted material in that window is a skeleton of a Pascal program that will be useful when you start programming. Right now the Program window is labeled "Untitled," because you don't have a program there yet.

Note that, when the windows appeared on the screen, the pointer changed shape. The arrow became something like the capital letter I. When it is in this shape, the pointer is called the *I-Beam.* If you move the pointer up to the top of the screen, it turns into an arrow again.

When you *run,* or *execute,* a program, something happens in one of the two windows on the right. Either a picture appears in the *Drawing window,* or words or numbers appear in the *Text window.* What appears in these two windows is called *output,* so they are both *output windows.*

Right now the Program window is the *active* one, the one in which something either is happening or is about to happen. You can tell it is active because it has horizontal lines that run across the title bar. Using the mouse, you can make a different window the active one. Just move the pointer inside that window and click. As soon as you do this, the title bar of that window will have horizontal lines across it.

The windows you see are not completely fixed. With a few moves of the mouse, you can drag a window around on the screen, change its size, and even make it completely disappear. Try moving the Drawing window.

- *First activate it by positioning the pointer in that window and clicking.*

- *Then place the pointer on the Drawing window title bar, and drag the pointer.* The window will follow the pointer around.

It is also possible to change a window's size. First activate it, and then place the pointer on the *size box,* the square in the lower-right corner of the window. Try this with the Text window. (See Figure 1.6.)

- *Drag the pointer to the left or toward the top of the screen.* The window gets smaller.

- *Now drag the pointer toward the lower-right corner of the screen.* The window gets larger.

Suppose you want to fill the screen completely with a window,

- *First move the window to the upper-left corner of the screen.*

- *Then drag the size box to the lower-right corner.* Try this with the Drawing window.

Suppose you want to make the Drawing window disappear and reappear.

- *Move the pointer to the* close box *in the upper-left corner of the Drawing window, and click the mouse.* The window will disappear. Don't worry. It's easy to make it reappear.

- *Now open the* Windows menu *(see Figure 1.6), and choose the Drawing window. The Drawing window will reappear.*

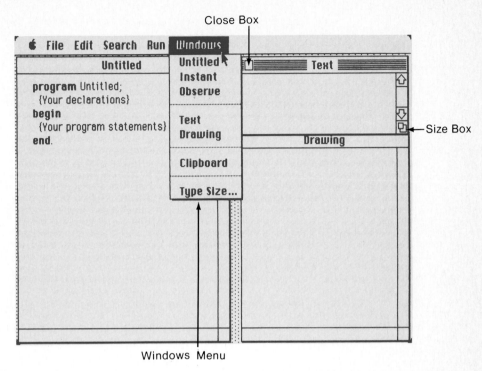

Figure 1.6   The Windows menu open. Note that only the active window has a close box and a size box.

We will show you how to use the Observe window in the next chapter, and an explanation of the Clipboard is coming up soon. The Type Size row in the Windows menu lets you use smaller or larger type in your programs and your output.

1.3 The Instant Window

There is another window, which you can't see right now—the *Instant window*. Using the Instant window is a great way to get acquainted with MacPascal. You can use it to try out individual MacPascal instructions.

- *To open the Instant window, move the pointer to the Windows menu and press the button to open the menu.*

- *Now choose the row labeled "Instant."*

The Instant window will appear, overlapping the Program window (see Figure 1.7). The Instant window became the active window when you brought it up. Inside the Instant window is a box labeled *"Do It."*

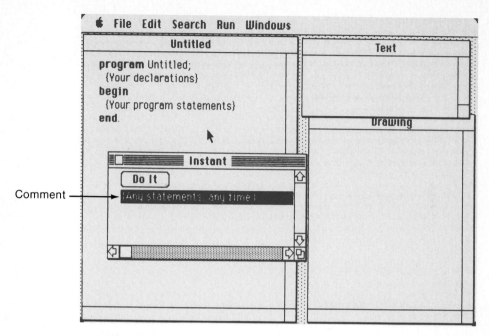

Figure 1.7   The Instant window.

In addition, the Instant window contains the following highlighted message inside braces:

```
{Any statements, any time.}
```

This is called a *comment*. Comments are *not* instructions in Pascal for your computer to follow. They are simply notes in English about the instructions you have written. Macintosh Pascal will ignore your comments as long as you remember to type them inside the braces. The foregoing comment shows up automatically in the Instant window.

Now let's try out some Pascal instructions in the Instant window.

■ *First type a space (press the space bar).* The highlighted comment in the Instant window will disappear. Whenever you want to get rid of any highlighted text on the screen, just type a space. Note the blinking vertical line that appears under the Do It box. This is the *insertion point*. Whatever you type at the keyboard will show up at the insertion point.

■ *Next type the following instruction exactly as you see it here:*

```
writeln('Hi there!')
```

These words will show up in the Instant window just to the left of the insertion point. As each new letter or symbol appears, the insertion point moves along so that it is always to the right of the last character you have typed.

■ *Now move the pointer to the Do It box and click.*

This executes the *writeln* (pronounced "write line") *instruction*, or *statement*. The message Hi there! will appear in the Text window. The *writeln* instruction commands the computer to print in the Text window whatever is written between the single quotation marks.

Writeln also tells the computer to start printing the next message (if there is one) on a new line. This is what the *ln* part of *writeln* means.

To see how this works, let's type in two new *writeln* statements. First delete the *writeln* statement you've just written. There are two ways to do this.

Deleting—Choice 1

■ *First make sure the insertion point is to the right of the right parenthesis in the* writeln *statement.* If it isn't, place the I-Beam to the right of the semicolon and click. The insertion point will show up where you clicked.

■ *Then backspace until the whole statement disappears.*

Deleting—Choice 2

■ *Depress the mouse button, drag the pointer through the instruction to highlight it, and release the button.* Learning to highlight exactly what you want takes some practice. If you highlight the wrong words, don't worry. Just click the mouse button anywhere in the window and the highlighting will disappear. Now you can try again.

■ *After you've highlighted the whole line, type a space or a backspace.* At this point, *writeln*('Hi there!') will disappear.

Now you are ready to add two new *writeln* statements.

■ *Type this in the Instant window:*

```
writeln('Hello');
```

■ *Then press the return key and type this:*

```
writeln('world')
```

Don't forget the semicolon between the two statements! The semicolon shows up a lot in Pascal. It is a *separator* symbol. It tells the computer that one instruction is over and another is about to begin.

■ *Now click on Do It.* Here's what will show up in the Text window:

```
Hello
world
```

The Macintosh prints *world* underneath *Hello* because each *writeln* statement prints its message on a separate line.

A Bug—A Missing Semicolon

Suppose you forget the semicolon between the two statements. What happens? Try taking out the semicolon and see.

- *Place the I-Beam to the right of the semicolon, and click.* This will position the insertion point just to the right of the semicolon.
- *Now backspace to get rid of the semicolon.*
- *Now try Do It.*

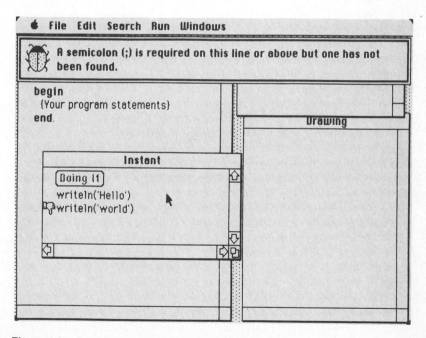

Figure 1.8   Error message for a missing semicolon.

The Macintosh will protest with three electronic beeps. Then you will get an *error message* to help you locate the *bug*, or mistake, in your program. With this kind of bug, the error message consists of two clues: A hand with its thumb down appears in the Instant window. And a box with a picture of a bug in it appears at the top of the screen, giving you a message about what's wrong. (See Figure 1.8.)

If you run into a bug, don't panic.

■ *Read the error message carefully, and use the clues to figure out what went wrong. Then move the pointer inside the error message box, and click.* This makes the error message box disappear.

Now fix the mistake. In this case you have to insert a semicolon. Here's how:

■ *First move the I-Beam to the place where the semicolon belongs, and click.* This deposits the insertion point where you need it.

■ *Now type the semicolon.* It will appear at the insertion point.

The insertion point will remain to the right of the semicolon until you move it again by placing the I-Beam somewhere else and clicking. If you don't depress the mouse button, the insertion point always stays put while you move the pointer around.

Important: Note that MacPascal actually points a finger at the line *after* the one where the missing semicolon should go. Because there was no semicolon MacPascal interprets the two commands as though they were one:

```
writeln('Hello')writeln('world')
```

But there is no such command. Macintosh Pascal "discovers" that these two *writeln* statements, taken together, aren't an acceptable command only after the second one has been read. Therefore the hand points to the second *writeln* statement when your bug is reported.

You will find that the hand often points to the line after the error. If you get an error message that you can't figure out, always look back one line to see whether that's where the problem is.

Another Bug—A Missing Quotation Mark

What happens when you leave out a quotation mark inside a *writeln* statement? Let's see.

■ *Delete what's in the Instant window, and try typing this:*

```
writeln('Go for it!)
```

You seem to get away with it—for a moment.

■ *Now press the return key.* MacPascal catches the missing quotation mark and signals you by changing the typeface in the instruction, as shown in Figure 1.9.

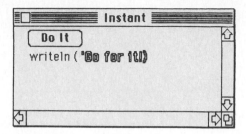

Figure 1.9   This is how MacPascal signals you that a quotation mark is missing.

- *Fix the bug by placing the I-Beam between the ! and the right parenthesis, clicking the mouse, and typing in the single quotation mark.*
- *Click on Do It.* The typeface will return to normal and then the Macintosh will execute the statement.

1.4 Quitting

If you are ready to end your programming session, here's how to do it:

- *First open the File menu and choose* Quit. *This takes you back to the electronic desktop with the Pascal window open.*
- *Now click in the close box to close the Pascal icon window.*
- *Next open the File menu again and choose* Eject. *Your disk will pop out.*
- *Finally, turn off the machine.*

1.5 Your First Program

In this chapter we want to create a "cartoon" of a ball rolling along a line across the middle of the Drawing window (see Figure 1.10). So let's start by writing a program that will print in the Text window a caption for the cartoon. It will say

```
The First Cartoon!
```

We could make the caption appear in the Text window just by typing this instruction in the Instant window:

```
writeln('The First Cartoon!')
```

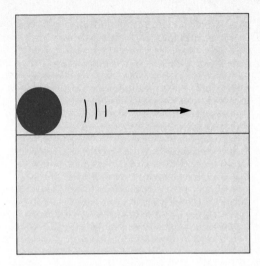

Figure 1.10   The First Cartoon!

But this time we want to write the following complete MacPascal program:

```
program Cartoon;
begin
 writeln('The First Cartoon!')
end.
```

Let's look carefully at the four lines in this program.

```
program Cartoon;
```

This line is the *program heading line*. It consists of the word **program** followed by the name of the program—and it always ends with a semicolon. Here the semicolon says the heading line is over.

The next three lines are the *body* of the program. The body is also called the *main program*, and its official name is the *statement* part of the program. The body must start with the word **begin** and end with the word **end**, followed by a period. If you forget the **begin**, the **end**, or the period, you will get an error message.

In between **begin** and **end**, you can put any number of instructions. In our first program there is only one:

```
writeln('The First Cartoon!')
```

Parentheses and single quotation marks surround the message to be printed. Here, too, you'll get an error message if you leave any of them out. The single quotation marks tell the Macintosh to print exactly what appears between them.

The words **program, begin,** and **end,** which are printed in boldface, are called *reserved words.* These are part of the basic vocabulary of Pascal, and they have special meanings. There are many other reserved words, which we have listed inside the front cover of the book.

Writeln has a special meaning in Pascal, too, but it is not a reserved word. It's called a *standard procedure.* A procedure is an instruction that does some special job, such as write a message, draw a line, or paint a circle.

We have worked out this program for you, so all you need to do is type it in the Program window.

Typing in Program Cartoon

■ *If your machine is off, you will need to turn it on and load MacPascal again.* See page 3 if you forget how.

■ *Make sure the Program window (the one labeled "Untitled") is active.* If it isn't, move the pointer into the window and click.

We want to type this program in from scratch. So let's get rid of the high-lighted program skeleton first.

■ *Press the space bar or the backspace key.* The whole block of highlighted text will disappear.

■ *Now type the first line, press the return key, and see what happens.* You type

```
program Cartoon;
```

and you get

```
program Cartoon;
```

■ *Next type*

```
begin
```

followed by a return. Then type the command

```
writeln('The First Cartoon!)
```

followed by another return. Again, what you type is not what you get. The word **begin** appears in boldface. And the Macintosh automatically indents the *writeln* statement one space. This rearrangement of the lines in a program is called *pretty printing.* It makes your program more readable.

■ *Type in the word **end** followed by a period.* You have a complete program. Now you're ready to run it.

■ *Move the pointer to the word* Run *at the top of the screen and open the* Run menu. (See Figure 1.11.)

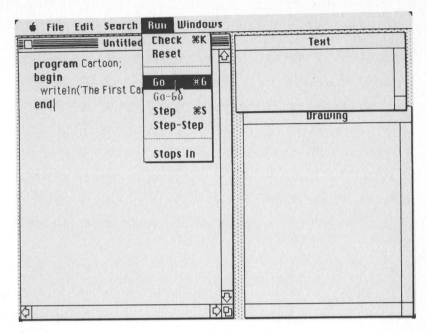

Figure 1.11   The Run menu open, with Go highlighted.

■ *Choose the row labeled "Go."* The Macintosh will run your program. This message will appear in the Text window:

    The First Cartoon!

You have run your first complete Pascal program.

1.6 Points, Lines, and the Drawing Window

Now that we've printed the caption, we can write the part of the program that actually draws the cartoon. Remember, the program will roll a ball along a line in the Drawing window. So we'll start by drawing the line. This is easy in MacPascal. But first you need to know how the Drawing window is laid out.

The standard-size Drawing window that shows up on the screen when you load MacPascal is a 201-unit-by-201-unit square made up of more than 40,000 invisible points. You can locate any point in the window using two numbers. The first number tells how far the point is from the left side of the window, and the second number tells how far it is from the top. The upper-left corner is the point (0,0). (See Figure 1.12.) Note that this convention differs from usage that is common in mathematics. In geometry, the origin point (0,0) is positioned at the lower-left corner.

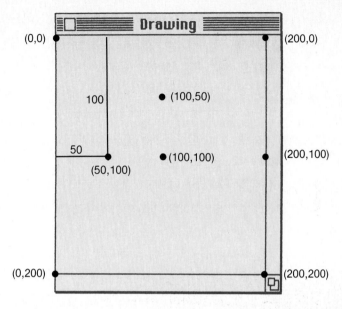

Figure 1.12 The point (50,100) is located 50 units over from the left side and 100 units down from the top.

If you have trouble remembering which number tells you the horizontal position and which tells you the vertical position, just remember that the numbers come in alphabetical order: *horizontal* then *vertical*.

If you enlarge the Drawing window, the same system of locating points still applies. When you make it fill the whole screen, the Drawing window is 500 units wide and 300 units from top to bottom. The point (500,300) would lie at the lower-right corner. When we talk about the *standard Drawing window*, we mean the 201-by-201 Drawing window that comes up when you load Mac-Pascal.

EXERCISE 1   **a.** Which point is higher, (100,100) or (100,200)?

b. Examine the accompanying picture. In which region does each of the following points fall? (50,50), (50,120), (150,150), (180,0)

Drawing Window

A	B
D	C

Answer: A, D, C, B ▬

Now you know enough about the Drawing window to start drawing lines. There is a single MacPascal instruction for this, *drawline*. The instruction

```
drawline(50,0,200,175)
```

tells the computer to draw a line from the point (50,0) to the point (200,175). Try it out in the Instant window.

■ *Bring up the Instant window by choosing Instant on the Windows menu.*

■ *Clear any text you see in the Instant window by highlighting it and then backspacing.*

■ *Next open the Run menu and choose* Reset. *This clears the output windows.*

■ *Now type in the* drawline *instruction, and then click on Do It.* Figure 1.13 shows the picture it will produce in the Drawing window.

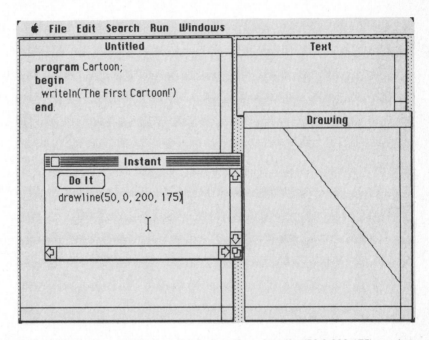

Figure 1.13   Here is the picture that the instruction *drawline(50,0,200,175)* produces in the Drawing window. By the way, the instruction *drawline(200,175,50,0)* draws exactly the same line.

EXERCISE 2   What kind of line does each of the following instructions draw? Make a sketch for each on a piece of paper, and then use the Instant window to determine whether your guess is right.

a. *drawline(0,0,200,200)*

b. *drawline(0,200,200,0)*

c. *drawline(100,0,100,200)*

d. *drawline(0,100,200,100)*

e. *drawline(0,0,200,100)* ▬

Now let's add to **program** Cartoon an instruction that will draw a horizontal line.

- *First make the Program window active by clicking in that window.*

- *Next move the insertion point to the end of the* writeln *statement, and type a semicolon to separate the* writeln *statement from the* drawline *statement.*

- *Press the return key. This will push the word* **end** *down one line.*

- *Now type the following instruction in the blank line:*

  ```
  drawline(0,100,200,100)
  ```

- *Try running this new version of* **program** *Cartoon.*

The Drawing window will clear when you choose Go, as it prepares for a new run. This time it will print the caption in the Text window and then draw a line across the Drawing window. The screen should look like this:

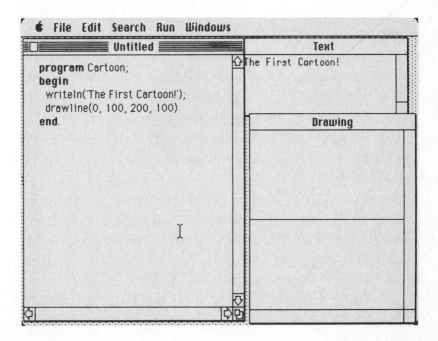

1.7 Circles

We are finally ready to work on the part of the cartoon that rolls the ball. To create the ball, we will use MacPascal's *paintcircle* instruction. Suppose we want to draw a circle that has a radius of 45 and has its center located at the point (50,80). The following statement will make it appear in the Drawing window:

```
paintcircle(50,80,45)
```

This *paintcircle* instruction tells the Macintosh to paint a black circle. The numbers in the parentheses tell the Macintosh that the center of the circle should be at horizontal position 50 and vertical position 80 and that the radius of the circle should be 45. Let's see how this works by running the *paintcircle* instruction using the Instant window.

- *Open the Windows menu, and choose Instant.*
- *Then, after clearing the Instant window, type in the* paintcircle *instruction.*
- *Next clear the output windows by opening the Run menu and choosing Reset.*
- *Now click on Do It.* The screen will then look as shown in Figure 1.14.

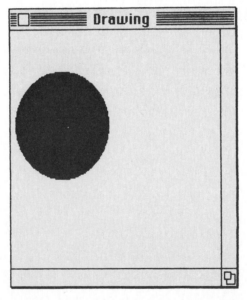

Figure 1.14   The circle's center is 50 units from the left wall and 80 units from the top, and its radius is 45 units.

EXERCISE 3   What instruction would you type in the Instant
window to make the accompanying picture?

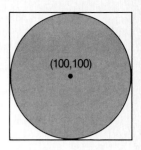

Choose Reset from the Run menu. Now type in the *paintcircle* instruction
and see whether you get the right circle. ■

Suppose we want to draw a circle of radius 20 like the one shown in Figure
1.15.

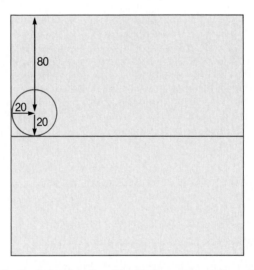

Figure 1.15   A circle of radius 20 with its center at the point (20,80).

This instruction will do the job:

```
paintcircle(20,80,20)
```

The numbers mean that the center of the circle is 20 units from the left wall
and 80 units from the top and that the circle has a radius of 20. Before going on,
make sure you understand why 20, 80, and 20 are the right numbers.

■ *Now insert the foregoing* paintcircle *instruction in* **program** *Cartoon to get this new program:*

```
program Cartoon;
begin
  writeln('The First Cartoon!');
  drawline(0,100,200,100);
  paintcircle(20,80,20)
end.
```

■ *Run it.* You will see the cartoon's first frame:

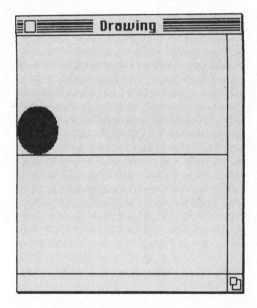

1.8 Stepping

When a computer runs a program, it carries out the instructions one at a time, usually in order. Ordinarily this happens so quickly that the output appears all at once. But MacPascal allows you to run programs slowly, one step at a time, so that you can watch each instruction doing its job. This is called *stepping*.

■ *To make your Macintosh step, open the Run menu, but this time choose* Step *instead of Go.* A little hand will appear next to the word **begin**.

■ *Then hold down the* command *key.* (The command key is the one with the symbol ⌘ on it.)

■ *Next, with the command key still down, press the S key.* The little hand will jump down to the *writeln* statement.

■ *Next, still holding the command key down, press the S key again.* The computer will execute the *writeln* instruction, and the caption will appear in the Text window. At the same time the hand will advance to the *drawline* instruction (see Figure 1.16).

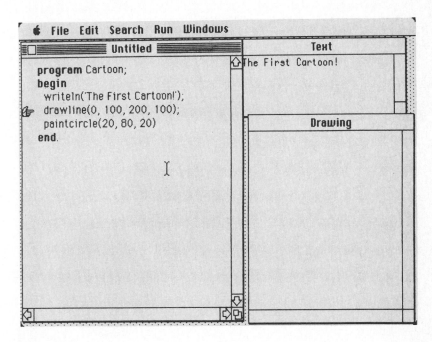

Figure 1.16   The *drawline* statement is about to be executed.

■ *Once more, hold the command key down and press the S key.* The line will be drawn across the Drawing window and the hand will advance to the *paintcircle* instruction. The finger always points to the instruction that will be done next. Each time you press, the hand advances to the next instruction. And with each advance of the hand, one more piece of the program is executed.

1.9 How to Move the Ball

Next we're going to show you the best part—how to animate your cartoon. You can do this by making the circle appear and then disappear over and over again very quickly, each time shifting its center a little bit to the right. The circle will appear to be a rolling ball, and it will flicker like an old-time movie.

To make the circle dissappear, we will use the MacPascal command *invertcircle*. The *invertcircle* instruction paints a black circle if the background is white, and it paints a white circle if the background is black. If an *invertcircle* overlaps a black region, the overlapping part will be white and the rest will be black. For example, these two instructions

```
paintcircle(70,70,50);
invertcircle(130,130,50)
```

produce in the Drawing window the picture shown in Figure 1.17.

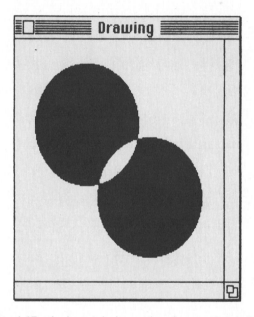

Figure 1.17   An invertcircle overlapping a paintcircle.

Try it out:

- *First use the Reset command from the Run menu to clear the output windows.*
- *Then bring up the Instant window, and after clearing it, type in the two foregoing commands.* See what happens when you click on Do It.

Now suppose you've written a program with a *paintcircle* instruction, and you add an *invertcircle* instruction with the same radius and location. The program will paint a black circle, and immediately it will reverse the color of that circle from black to white, making the circle disappear. This is exactly what we want for **program** Cartoon.

■ *So now add an* invertcircle *command to the program.* This is what the program will look like:

```
program Cartoon;
begin
 writeln('The First Cartoon!');
 drawline(0,100,200,100);
 paintcircle(20,80,20);
 invertcircle(20,80,20)
end.
```

■ *Step it and see what happens.* What you see in the Drawing window is the first frame of the animated cartoon.

Now let's add a few more statements to extend the cartoon with new frames. Don't type these in yet: We're going to show you a shortcut for adding the four new instructions.

```
program Cartoon;
begin
 writeln('The First Cartoon!');
 drawline(0,100,200,100);
  {FRAME 1}
 paintcircle(20,80,20);
 invertcircle(20,80,20);
  {FRAME 2}
 paintcircle(21,80,20);
 invertcircle(21,80,20);
  {FRAME 3}
 paintcircle(22,80,20);
 invertcircle(22,80,20)
end.
```

The three pairs of *paintcircle* and *invertcircle* instructions will draw the first three frames of the cartoon by painting and erasing circles along the line. Frame 2 is almost identical to frame 1, except that the horizontal position of the circle has been shifted one unit to the right. In frame 3, it has been shifted one more unit to the right.

Shortcuts—Copy and Paste, Cut and Paste

Because the instructions for frames 2 and 3 are so similar to the commands in frame 1, we can use a shortcut to add the new text. Our shortcut employs the Macintosh *Copy* and *Paste* commands.

■ *First highlight the* paintcircle *and* invertcircle *lines in the program.*

```
program Cartoon;
begin
 writeln('The First Cartoon!');
 drawline(0,100,200,100);
 paintcircle(20,80,20);
 invertcircle(20,80,20)
end.
```

■ *Then go to the Edit menu and choose Copy.* The Copy command instructs the Macintosh to make a copy of the highlighted text.

■ *Position the pointer after the right parenthesis in the* invertcircle *instruction and click.* The insertion point will appear there.

■ *Next open the Edit menu and choose Paste.* Copies of the two instructions you highlighted will appear right under the original ones. The reason why the new text does not show up at the insertion point is that the MacPascal prettyprinter moves it down a line.

■ *Now position the pointer just after the first* invertcircle *command, and type a semicolon.* Because you have just added more instructions, you need a semicolon here to separate the old *invertcircle* instruction from the new *paintcircle* instruction.

■ *Now move the insertion point so that it is just to the right of the last* invertcircle *instruction. You do this by positioning the I-Beam there and clicking the mouse.*

■ *Next open the Edit menu, and choose Paste again.* Another copy of the two instructions will show up beneath the others.

■ *Once again, add the missing semicolon.*

■ *Now, to get the program to move the ball, all you have to do is change the first 20 in each of the new instructions. Change the first pair of 20's to 21 and the second pair to 22.*

■ *To see what these new statements do, run the program.* (Don't step it this time.) The ball should seem to flicker and to roll along the line, just like an animated cartoon.

But there's one problem. The ball rolls only a little way, and the program is already 8 instructions long. It would take *another 316 instructions* to get the ball to roll all the way across the screen. This would be tedious even if you used Copy and Paste. There must be a better way!

And there is. Like most computer languages, Pascal has a *looping command,* a command that tells the computer to execute an instruction, or a group of instructions, over and over again.

The Clipboard: Cut and Copy

There is another command in the Edit menu: *Cut.* If you highlight a line and choose Cut, the line disappears from the text. Now you can Paste that line anywhere you want.

When you highlight text and choose either Cut or Copy, the Macintosh stores the text in the electronic Clipboard. It stays there until you highlight something else and choose Copy or Cut again. You can actually see what is in the Clipboard by opening the Windows menu and choosing Clipboard.

Before we begin looping, let's set aside the version of **program** Cartoon we've written so far by *saving* it—that is, by making a permanent copy of the program on the MacPascal disk.

1.10 Saving Your Program

When you save a program, you put it in a MacPascal document on the MacPascal disk. Here's how:

- *Click on the Program window to make it active.*
- *Open the File menu, and choose* Save As. This will open a *dialog* box, which appears on the screen like this:

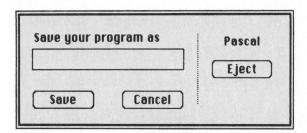

- *Now type the name you want to use for this document.* It's best to use the name of your program, Cartoon, so that you can find it again. But any name will do.
- *Then click on* Save.

Your program will be stored on the MacPascal disk, and the dialog box will disappear. But your program will still be on the screen for you to work on. Only one thing will be different. The Program window will be labeled "Cartoon" instead of "Untitled."

Saving on a Separate Disk

You may want to store your program on a separate disk so that it doesn't take up space on the MacPascal disk. Here's how to do it.

- *Open the File menu and choose Save As.*
- *When the dialog box comes up, type in the name of the program and then click on Eject.* The disk will pop out.
- *Now insert the other disk, and click on Save.* The computer will copy the program onto that disk and then eject it. After that a message will appear, telling you to insert the original disk.
- *Insert the original disk.* **Program** Cartoon will appear on the screen again, ready to be run.

Quitting

You may want to end your programming session now. If you do, here's how:

- *Go to the File menu and choose Quit.*

MacPascal windows will disappear, and the desktop will appear with the MacPascal disk window open on top of it. The MacPascal window will hold a new icon—the icon labeled "Cartoon." (See Figure 1.18.)

- *Now choose Eject from the File menu.* The disk will pop out.
- *Don't forget to turn off the machine.*

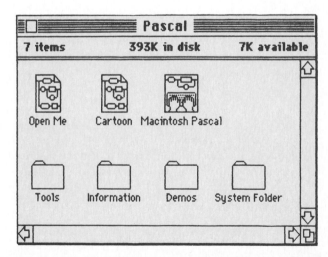

Figure 1.18   The MacPascal disk window with the Cartoon document icon.

1.11 Looping

We'll get back to the rolling ball in a moment, but first we'll show you how to loop with a much simpler example.

Suppose we want to print this column of numbers:

```
1
2
3
4
```

One way to do this is to make a column of *writeln* statements. (Note that, in the following *writeln* statements, there are no single quotation marks inside the parentheses. We'll explain why in a moment.)

```
program NumberList:
begin
 writeln(1);
 writeln(2);
 writeln(3);
 writeln(4)
end.
```

This is tedious. A more efficient way to print the list would be to use a Pascal instruction called the *for statement* to create a loop, like this:

```
program FirstLoop;
 var
  Number : integer;
begin
 for Number := 1 to 4 do
  begin
   writeln(Number)
  end
end.
```

There are several new things in **program** FirstLoop. We'll look at the **for** statement first. The for statement in this program has two parts: a *control line:*

```
for Number := 1 to 4 do
```

and a *body:*

```
begin
 writeln(Number)
end
```

The control line tells the computer, "For each Number from 1 to 4, do the instructions listed in the body." The control line advances Number from 1 to 4, so the *writeln* instruction in the body is executed four times.

Program FirstLoop tells the computer:

1. First substitute the integer 1 for the word Number in the *writeln* statement. The symbol := tells the Macintosh to make this substitution, or *assignment*, and then do the *writeln* statement, which prints a 1 in the Text window. (*Note:* There is never a space between the colon and the equal sign.)
2. Then substitute 2 for the word Number, and do the *writeln* statement.
3. Next substitute 3 for the word Number, and do the *writeln* statement.
4. Finally, substitute 4 for the word Number, and do the *writeln* statement.

Note that there are no quotation marks inside the parentheses in the *writeln* statement. Quotation marks tell the computer to print out exactly what is between them. When we leave out the quotation marks we are telling the computer to print out the *value* of Number instead of the *word* Number. And each time the **for** loop is executed, this value is different. First it is 1, then 2, then 3, then 4.

What about the words **begin** and **end** surrounding the *writeln* statement? They tell the Macintosh that the statements between them are the instructions in the body of the loop.

Because the value of Number changes in the program, Number is a *variable*. In Pascal you must tell the computer the names of the variables that you will use in a program. You put this information at the beginning of the program in the *variable declaration* part. The variable declaration in **program** FirstLoop is

```
var
 Number : integer;
```

In addition to telling the computer that Number is a variable, this declaration says that Number must be an *integer*. (Integers are whole numbers; they can be either positive or negative. For example: −1, 2, 3, −4, 5, and 0 are integers. A fraction, such as 22/7, isn't an integer. Neither is a real number with a decimal point, such as 3.1416.)

Number is a special kind of variable in **program** FirstLoop. Because it is used in the control line of the **for** statement to determine the number of times the loop is executed, it is called a *control variable*.

Loops give programs their power. You can't do much programming without them. Writing a program to print out long lists of numbers, for example, would be an overwhelming task if you didn't use a loop. Take the following program:

```
program SecondLoop;
 var
  Number : integer;
begin
 for Number := 500 to 1000 do
  begin
   writeln(Number)
  end
end.
```

Program SecondLoop prints out a column of 501 numbers in the Text window, beginning with 500 and ending with 1000.

What do you think the next program does?

```
program OverAndOver;
 var
   PledgeNumber : integer;
begin
 for PledgeNumber := 1 to 500 do
   begin
    writeln('I will not talk in class.')
   end
end.
```

Program OverAndOver is interesting because the control variable in the **for** loop—PledgeNumber—does not appear anywhere in the *writeln* instruction. So the program prints the *same* line 500 times:

```
I will not talk in class.
```

_____ 1.12 Let's Get the Ball Rolling_____

Now that you know about loops and variables, we can get on with our cartoon. We want to create a loop that will shift the center of the circle to the right, one unit at a time, until the circle reaches the right wall of the window.

The center of the ball starts at position (20,80). As the ball rolls, the position of the center changes to (21,80), (22,80), (23,80), and so on until it reaches (180,80), where the ball just touches the right wall of the Drawing window. The vertical position of the center stays the same (80), but the horizontal position varies (see Figure 1.19).

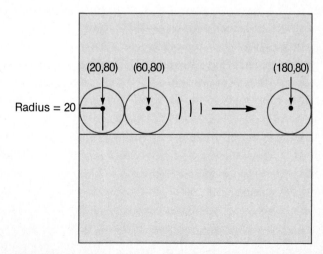

Figure 1.19   Three steps in the ball's journey from left to right.

So let's invent a variable called Position to stand for the horizontal position of the circle's center as the ball rolls. Our program must include the following declaration:

```
var
  Position : integer;
```

This declaration says we have a variable called Position, which must be an integer.

Now let's do the **for** loop. We want circles to be drawn from horizontal position 20 to horizontal position 180. And we want the body of the loop to include the instruction *paintcircle*, followed by *invertcircle*. Here is the loop that will make the ball flicker and roll across the screen:

```
for Position := 20 to 180 do
  begin
    paintcircle(Position,80,20);
    invertcircle(Position,80,20)
  end
```

Now let's put this loop in **program** Cartoon. First you must *bring up* program Cartoon.

Bringing up Program Cartoon

■ *If your Macintosh is off, turn it on, insert the disk, and open the MacPascal Disk icon.* In the MacPascal window you will see not only the MacPascal icon but also an icon labeled "Cartoon."

■ *To bring up **program** Cartoon, double click on the Cartoon icon.* You don't have to load MacPascal, because the Macintosh does this for you automatically when you bring up a MacPascal program.

■ *Now change **program** Cartoon so that it looks like this:*

```
program Cartoon;
  var
    Position : integer;
begin
  writeln('The First Cartoon!');
  drawline(0,100,200,100);
  for Position := 20 to 180 do
    begin
      paintcircle(Position,80,20);
      invertcircle(Position,80,20)
    end
end.
```

The first cartoon program is now complete!

■ *Try running it.* Watch the ball roll all the way across the Drawing window.

1.13 Saving Your Revised Program

Now that you have a running cartoon program, you will probably want to save your final version of the program so that you can run it later. Here's how to re-place the permanent copy you stored on the disk with the new version on the screen.

- *Make sure the program window is active.* If you forget to do this, you won't be able to save your new version.
- *Open the File menu, and choose Save instead of Save As.* (If you have for-gotten to activate the program window, the word *Save* in the menu will be dimmed—that is, printed in grey—and it will be impossible to choose Save.) You won't get a dialog box this time. The Macintosh will just replace the old version on the disk with a copy of the new version on the screen.

Save and Save As

Use *Save As* when you save something for the first time and you need to give the document a name. Use *Save* when you want to save a different version of a document that already has a name. But be careful here. When you use Save, the old version is lost forever.

1.14 Printing Program Cartoon

If you have a printer, you will probably want to print out your program. Here's how.

- *First make sure the Program window is active.*
- *Then turn on your printer and choose* Print *from the File menu.* A dialog box will appear (see Figure 1.20), asking you some questions about how you want your document printed.
- *Just click on* OK. The printer will print out your program.

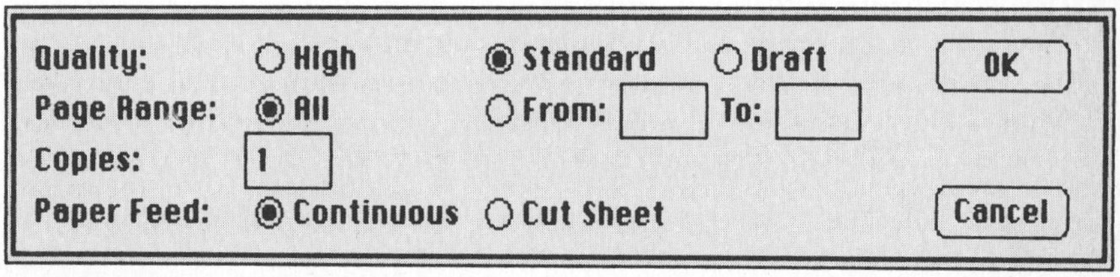

Quality:	○ High	● Standard	○ Draft	OK
Page Range:	● All	○ From:	To:	
Copies:	1			
Paper Feed:	● Continuous	○ Cut Sheet		Cancel

Figure 1.20 A print dialog box.

What if you want to print out the picture in your Drawing window or the caption in the Text window?

- *First activate the window you want to print.*
- *Then, holding down the shift and command keys, press the 4 key.* The entire active window will be printed.

You can also print out the entire screen.

- *Press the* caps lock *key.*
- *Then, holding down the shift and command key, press the 4 key.* This will give you a *screen dump*, or print-out, of the entire screen.

_____ 1.15 The Nuts and Bolts of Programs_____

All MacPascal programs use the same simple building blocks. The first building blocks you have met are the *reserved words*, which are always printed in boldface in MacPascal. The reserved words that appear in **program** Cartoon are **program, var, for, to, do, begin,** and **end.** A complete list of the reserved words in MacPascal appears inside the front cover of this book.

A word you pick out yourself to use as a name for a program or a variable is called an *identifier.* **Program** Cartoon has two identifiers: Cartoon (the name of the program) and Position (the name of the control variable in the **for** loop).

The identifiers you make up can use either capital or lowercase letters in any combination. The Macintosh doesn't care whether you write Cartoon or cartoon or even cARTOON. And it doesn't even mind if you mix things up and use capital letters the first time and lowercase the next time you use a name in the same program. In this book we will generally capitalize identifiers to make them easier to read.

What about the word integer in this line?

```
var
   Position : integer;
```

In Pascal the word integer is called a type. A *type* in a variable declaration tells what type of value the variable can have. This variable declaration says that the variable Position can have only an *integer* value.

Program Cartoon also has certain instructions called *standard procedures.* A procedure is an instruction that does some complicated special job. The standard procedures in the cartoon program are *writeln, drawline, paintcircle,* and *invertcircle.* There is a complete list of the MacPascal standard procedures in the reference manual. We list the standard procedures used in this book inside the front cover.

Finally, MacPascal has *punctuation*. In our first program we've used semicolons, commas, parentheses, single quotation marks, a colon, a colon followed by an equal sign, and a period.

MacPascal has very definite rules for building a program from reserved words, identifiers, types, standard procedures, and punctuation. Here are the rules that we've seen so far.

1. The program heading line must end with a semicolon.
2. Two statements next to each other must be separated by a semicolon. A statement followed by the reserved word **end** does not need to be followed by a semicolon, however. And there should be no semicolon following the word **do** in a **for** statement control line.
3. A program must end with a period.
4. The body of a Pascal program must begin with the word **begin** and end with the word **end**.
5. Variables must be declared at the beginning of the program.

1.16 Pascal and Macintosh Pascal

The programming language known as Pascal was developed in Europe in the early 1970's by Niklaus Wirth. Since then it has become very popular in the United States, and it is now widely used as a teaching language in American colleges and universities. There are a number of different versions of the language, but most of them closely conform to the description of the language Wirth gave in 1974.

For the most part, Macintosh Pascal conforms to this standard, too. But MacPascal has some spectacular additions. Because it runs on the Macintosh, it includes instructions for controlling the mouse, for drawing lines and circles, and for working with menus and windows. If you learn MacPascal, you should have little trouble using other versions of the language.

In the past, Pascal systems have required a program called a *compiler*, which prepares a program you've typed in so that a computer can execute it. With a compiled Pascal, you must instruct the computer to compile your program before the program can be executed.

Compiling takes time—as much as several minutes for a big program. And you must use the compiler every time you make a change in a program. This means that experimenting with a lot of changes in your programs can become quite tedious. What's more, learning to use a compiler is sometimes complicated.

MacPascal doesn't have a compiler. A different kind of program, called an *interpreter*, prepares a MacPascal program for execution. Because interpreters work much faster than compilers, a MacPascal program is ready to run as soon as you type it in.

There is a price to pay, however, for an interpreter's quickness. A program that has been prepared for execution with a compiler will run about ten times faster than the interpreted version of the same program. This is a significant speed-up that can be important if your program will be used repeatedly in some scientific or business application. But if you are just learning Pascal, you will spend most of your time writing, testing, and debugging small practice programs. You will barely notice an interpreted Pascal's slower execution speed.

The Instant window is a unique feature of MacPascal. Compiled versions of Pascal allow you to run only complete programs. In MacPascal, you can run one or several instructions that aren't in a program by using the Instant window.

In this book, when we talk about Pascal, we are referring to an instruction or idea that is part of all versions of Pascal. When we say *MacPascal*, we are talking about something peculiar to Macintosh Pascal that you probably won't find in other versions of the language.

TEST YOURSELF

1. Before you turn on the Macintosh, where is MacPascal stored?
2. Where is the point (0,100) in the Drawing window?
3. What are two synonyms for the word instruction?
4. How many units wide is the standard Drawing window? And how long is it from top to bottom?
5. What kind of word is **begin**? What kind of word is *writeln*?
6. What happens to main memory when you load MacPascal?
7. Which three words must be in every program?
8. What punctuation mark must come at the end of the heading line of a program?
9. What punctuation mark must come after the word **end** at the very end of a program?
10. What is stepping?
11. What does a loop do?
12. What is an identifier?
13. What does the semicolon do in MacPascal?
14. What's wrong with each of these programs? Find *all* of the errors.

    a. ```
program Bad
  begin
   writeln('This will not work)
   writeln('Why not?')
  end.
```
    b. ```
program NoGood
  begin.
   writeln("No way!")
  end.
```

    Hint: There are a total of three errors in **program** Bad and four errors in **program** NoGood.

___PROBLEMS___

1. Use the mouse to lay out the MacPascal windows in the following arrangements:

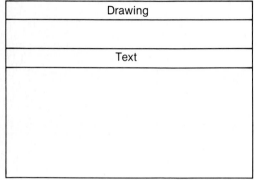

Screen 1

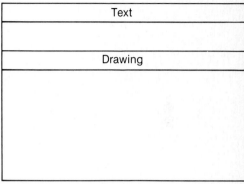

Screen 2

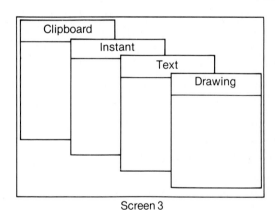

Screen 3

2. What is the output of each of the following programs?

a.
```pascal
program OuchOne;
  var
    Throb : integer;
  begin
    for Throb := 1 to 250 do
      begin
        writeln('Have I got a headache!')
      end
  end.
```

b.
```pascal
program OuchTwo;
  var
    Throb : integer;
  begin
    for Throb := 1 to 250 do
      begin
        writeln('Have I got');
        writeln('a');
        writeln('headache!')
      end
  end.
```

3. Suppose the Drawing window is divided into four parts, as shown in the accompanying figure. In which regions do the following points fall?

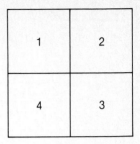

1	2
4	3

a. (101,20)
b. (101,150)
c. (50,70)
d. (150,70)
e. (150,170)

4. Read the following program and try to figure out what it does. Now run it and test your hypothesis.

```pascal
program Whoosh;
  var
   HDistance : integer;
begin
 for HDistance := 20 to 100 do
   begin
    paintcircle(HDistance,100,HDistance);
    invertcircle(HDistance,100,HDistance)
   end
end.
```

5. What do you think this program does? After you decide, type it in, run it, and see.

```pascal
program Explode;
  var
   Radius : integer;
begin
 for Radius := 1 to 100 do
   begin
    paintcircle(100,100,Radius)
   end
end.
```

6. a. What does this program do? Figure it out; then type it in and run it.

```pascal
program WhoKnows;
  var
   Position : integer;
begin
 for Position := 0 to 200 do
   begin
    paintcircle(Position,Position,20);
    invertcircle(Position,Position,20)
   end
end.
```

b. What happens when you change the *paintcircle* and *invertcircle* commands in **program** WhoKnows to the following pair?

```
paintcircle(Position,Position,Position);
invertcircle(Position,Position,Position)
```

7. What do you think **program** Implode does? Before you run it, see if you can figure out what will happen.

```
program Implode;
 var
  Radius : integer;
begin
 for Radius := 100 downto 1 do
  begin
   paintcircle(100,100,Radius);
   invertcircle(100,100,Radius)
  end
end.
```

8. Can you guess what shape this program prints out? Try it.

```
program Zag;
begin
 drawline(0,200,50,0);
 drawline(50,0,100,200);
 drawline(100,200,150,0);
 drawline(150,0,200,200)
end.
```

9. Can you figure out what shape this program draws? Now try it.

```
program WhatShape;
begin
 drawline(100,50,150,150);
 drawline(150,150,50,150);
 drawline(50,150,100,50)
end.
```

10. Using the *drawline* instruction, write programs to draw the following shapes.

a.   **b.**   **c.**   **d.**   **e.**

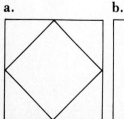
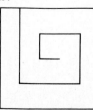
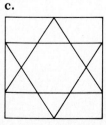
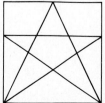
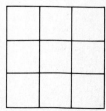

11. Write your initials using the *drawline* instruction.

12. What do you think this program does? Now try it.

```pascal
program Mystery;
  var
    Number : integer;
  begin
   for Number := 2 to 5 do
     begin
      writeln(Number + 10)
     end
  end.
```

13. Can you figure how to use *invertcircle* commands to draw the following pictures? Remember that *invertcircle* paints a white circle if the background is already black and that it paints a black circle if the background is white.

a.

b.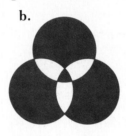

c.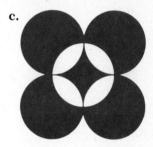

14. Change **program** OverAndOver in Section 1.11 so that it prints out this:

```
      1
I will not talk in class.
      2
I will not talk in class.
      3
I will not talk in class.
```

and so on, for 50 repetitions.

15. Now try some variations on **program** Cartoon.

a. Change **program** Cartoon so that the ball rolls along a line that goes down the middle of the screen like this:

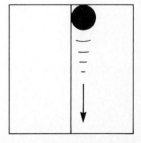

b. Next create two balls that roll perpendicular to each other, like this:

Hint: Put all four circle instructions and the two *drawline* instructions in one loop.

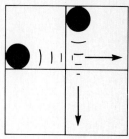

c. Now redo part (b), only this time put the *invertcircle* instruction before the *paintcircle* instruction.

Machine Organization and Program Planning

2

This chapter begins with a look at what really goes on when the Macintosh is running a MacPascal program. Then we'll discuss a four-step technique for problem solving with Pascal.

2.1 Binary Numbers and Memory

You've been using the decimal system for so long that it may seem like the only imaginable way to do arithmetic. For computers, though, it turns out to be much more practical to use the binary number system. In the binary system the only digits are 0 and 1. Here's a table that shows how binary and decimal numbers correspond.

Decimal	Binary
1	1
2	10
3	11
4	100
5	101
6	110
7	111
8	1000
9	1001
10	1010
11	1011
12	1100

The Macintosh's memory is made up of hundreds of thousands of rows of tiny electronic switches. Each row has eight switches and is called a *byte* of memory. Each switch is called a *bit*. While the Macintosh is running, some switches are open and some are closed. This is where the binary number system comes in. If you think of an open switch as the digit 0 and a closed switch as the digit 1, then a pattern of open and closed switches can stand for a binary number (see Figure 2.1). For example, 10100010 stands for the number 162.

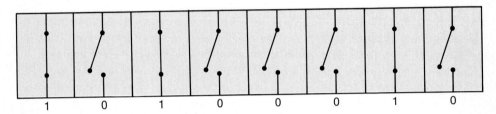

Figure 2.1   Open and closed switches.

The same pattern of switches can also have other meanings. The sequence 10100010 also stands for the symbol ¢. So one byte of memory, with its eight switches, can hold the symbol ¢ or the number 162. Larger numbers require more than one byte.

A binary pattern can also stand for a particular computer instruction, such as *writeln* or *paintcircle*. This point is very important. The computer's memory can hold not only *data*—that is, numbers and characters such as letters and punctuation marks—but also instructions, which you type on your keyboard in the form of words. Here is the binary pattern for an instruction that adds the numbers 2 and 3:

0111	1010	1001	0001	the addition instruction
1000	0000	0000	0010	the number 2
1000	0000	0000	0011	the number 3

You may find it strange that the same binary pattern can stand for a number, a letter, or an instruction. But a part of the computer that's separate from memory—the *central processing unit*—has been programmed to tell which is which.

The central processing unit, or CPU for short, is the computer's brain. The CPU doesn't really "know" whether a particular binary sequence is a number, a letter, or an instruction. But it has been programmed to expect instructions in certain parts of a program and numbers in other parts of a program. For example, the CPU always interprets the first byte after the word **begin** in the body of a program as part of an instruction.

2.2 Where Does MacPascal Fit In?

MacPascal is a giant master-program that works like the director of a theatrical production. You are the script writer, and the CPU is the actor. After you have written a script (a program), you give it to the director (MacPascal). MacPascal translates what you've written so that the actor (the CPU) can follow the instructions in your script. The CPU then performs its part by carrying out your instructions, and you see your play on one of the output windows.

The translation step is absolutely necessary, because the CPU does not understand anything except instructions written in patterns of ones and zeros. This is called *machine language.*

If you wanted to talk directly to the CPU, you would have to write your instructions in machine language—long sequences of zeros and ones. This is far too tedious and time-consuming. If you wrote the following simple instruction

```
writeln(2 + 3)
```

in machine language, it would look something like this:

```
0000 0001 0000 1010
0010 0010 0010 1100
0111 1010 1001 0001
1000 0000 0000 0010
1000 0000 0000 0011
```

As you can see, machine language is nearly incomprehensible. It takes many machine-language commands to do one *writeln* instruction, because machine-language commands are very primitive. "Fetch the byte at memory location 1024 and move it to memory location 1036" is a typical machine-language instruction translated into English.

The beauty of Pascal is that you can create your program using instructions that closely resemble phrases in English. And once you've typed these in, Mac-Pascal will see to it that the CPU gets a faithful, machine-language translation.

2.3 How Program Cartoon Is Stored in Memory

Programs are translated into machine language in two steps. First as you type in each command, the Macintosh converts the instruction into a binary code that is not actually machine language and stores the code in main memory. Later, when you run the programs, each coded command is translated into machine language and then executed.

What happens when you type in **program** Cartoon? First you type in the heading line, and MacPascal stores the name of the program in memory. The next thing you type in is the declaration for the variable Position.

This declaration directs the CPU to set aside a location in memory for the variable you have named Position. (The location is two bytes long.) When you run the program, this location in memory holds a number that represents the value of the variable. Usually this number changes as the program runs. For the moment no number is stored there, because the program isn't running.

Then the word **begin** alerts MacPascal to convert into binary code the body of the program—all the instructions you type in between the first **begin** and the final **end.** MacPascal puts the binary form of each instruction into consecutive rows of memory in the order in which the instructions appear in the program. MacPascal also tells the CPU to record where in memory the first instruction is stored. Then, when you run the program, MacPascal "knows" where to find the first statement of the body.

2.4 What Happens When You Run Program Cartoon

The CPU starts execution of the program by translating the *writeln* statement into machine language and then executing it. This prints "The First Cartoon!" in the Text window. Next the CPU translates and executes the *drawline* statement, which draws a line across the Drawing window.

Now the CPU comes to the **for** statement. First it goes to the location set aside in memory for the value of the variable Position, and it puts a value there—the integer 20.

```
┌────┐
│ 20 │
└────┘
Position
```

The statement *paintcircle*(Position,80,20) is translated next. The CPU looks up what number has been stored in the location labeled "Position." It finds the integer 20. So it executes the machine-language translation of the instruction *paintcircle*(20,80,20).

Then the CPU does the same with the instruction *invertcircle*(Position, 80,20).

Now comes the complicated part. In most cases the CPU simply goes to the next instruction when it finishes a command. But here it recognizes that it is doing a **for** statement, and it must take a special action: Before executing the instructions in the body of the loop, it must determine whether looping is over. To do this, it checks to see whether the current value of Position (20) equals the upper limit of the loop (180). Because 180 is larger than 20, the Macintosh continues looping. It increases the value of Position by 1, replacing the number 20 with the number 21 at the location labeled "Position."

```
┌────┐
│ 21 │
└────┘
Position
```

Each time the body of the **for** loop

```
begin
  paintcircle(Position,80,20);
  invertcircle(Position,80,20)
end
```

is executed, the value of Position is increased by 1 until 180 is reached. When that happens, the CPU sees that the number at location Position equals the value that is the upper limit of the loop. This terminates the loop. And, because there are no more instructions, program execution ends.

2.5 The Value of a Variable

What do we mean when we say "the value of the variable Position?" We mean that the value of a variable is the number in the location in memory assigned to that variable.

The value of a variable is very concrete; it is the number that has been written down inside memory next to the variable's name. Usually a variable's value changes during program execution. When execution of **program** Cartoon starts, the value of Position is *undefined:* No value has been copied into Position's location yet. At the beginning of the **for** loop, Position's value is set at 20. Then it becomes 21, then 22, and so on up to 180.

If you get confused by the idea of the value of a variable, just think of a little box in memory with a number written inside and a name written underneath:

```
┌─────┐
│ 180 │
└─────┘
Position
```

2.6 Watching Variables with the Observe Window

Now let's take a closer look at program execution, using MacPascal's *Observe window*. When the computer runs **program** Cartoon, it executes the instructions one by one. The value of the variable Position is undefined until the **for** loop is executed. Then its value advances from 20 to 180. With each change in the value of Position, the circle is painted and erased a little farther to the right.

Using the Observe window, you can get step-by-step reports on the value of Position as the ball rolls across the screen. To get these reports, you have to open the Observe window and identify Position as the variable you want to watch. Then you must deposit *stops* inside the program. Stops tell the Macintosh where to stop and make reports.

X's, *Y*'s, and *Z*'s—The History of Variables

After printing with movable type appeared in Europe, about 550 years ago, printers began to turn out bibles, playing cards—and books on mathematics. Some math books were in Latin, others were in the language of the writer, and each writer had his own way of handling variables in algebra problems. Some used the Latin word *res,* meaning "thing." Italians used *cosa,* also meaning "thing." And Germans used *zahl,* the word for "number." In a big book, the repeated use of the same three- or four-letter word could cause trouble: Type was expensive and printers often had limited supplies of the letters.

Then, in 1637, the French mathematician René Descartes came up with a new idea. He started using the single letters *x, y,* and *z* for variables. But toward the end of his book, the letters *y* and *z* appeared less and less often. Why?

Most books in France at that time were written in French or Latin, and words in those languages have more *x*'s in them than *y*'s or *z*'s. The French printers who set the type for Descartes's book used up all the *y*'s and *z*'s they had in stock in the early chapters. Probably they told the author to finish his book using *x* as often as possible. Descartes's book was very popular, and his use of letters for variables caught on.

When computers were first invented, programmers often used single letters to name the variables in their programs. Computer memory was very limited, and a single letter takes up less memory than a complete word. But names for variables in programs have started to get longer and longer. Since the cost of computer memory has come down, saving a few bytes by calling a variable *x* instead of Position has become foolish. Computer people recognize that a good program must be a *clear* program, and using descriptive names for variables makes programs much easier to understand. So you won't find many *y*'s or *z*'s—or even *x*'s—in this book.

Let's observe the value of Position every time the *invertcircle* command is about to be executed.

■ *First type in* **program** *Cartoon, or, if you saved a copy, bring it up.* If you don't remember how to bring up a program, see page 32 in Chapter 1.

Setting up the Observe Window

■ *Now open the Observe window, and move it to the lower-left corner of the screen.* This prevents it from blocking the text in the Program window (see Figure 2.2).

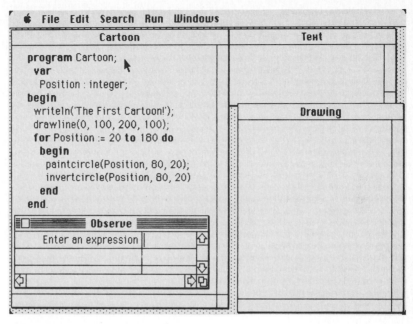

Figure 2.2   The Observe window.

■ *Type "Position" in the upper-right box in the Observe window, where the insertion point is located.* This tells the Macintosh you want to watch the variable Position.

Putting in Stops

Now you must indicate exactly where in the program you want to watch Position. Because you want to watch Position between the *paintcircle* and the *invertcircle* commands, you must put a stop to the left of the *invertcircle* instruction. To deposit a stop, take the following steps:

■ *First make the Program window active by clicking in that window.* The Observe window will disappear behind the Program window.

■ *Next open the Run menu and choose* Stops In. This adds a *Stop column* at the left of the Program window with a tiny *stop sign* at the bottom (see Figure 2.3). Now you are ready to insert a stop.

■ *Move the pointer to the Stop column.* Something peculiar happens when you do this. The pointer changes shape from an arrow to a stop sign.

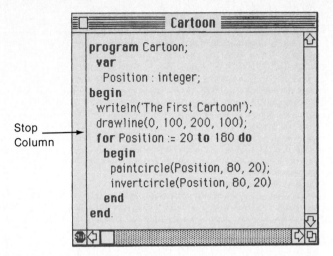

Stop
Column

Figure 2.3   Program window with Stop column.

■ *To deposit a stop sign,* move the stop sign pointer opposite the invertcircle *command, and click the mouse.* When you slide the pointer away from this position, the deposited stop sign will remain (see Figure 2.4).

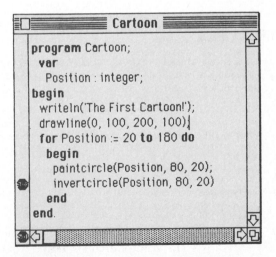

Figure 2.4   A stop sign next to *invertcircle.*

Running Program Cartoon with Stops

Now let's see what happens when you run the program with a stop in it.

- First open the Windows menu and bring up the Observe window again.

- *Run the program by choosing Go.* The program will execute until it runs into the stop sign. When it stops, you will see on the screen the caption, the line, and the first frame of the cartoon—a black circle. A little hand will be pointing to the next line to be executed—the *invertcircle* instruction. And the Observe window will report the value of the variable Position—20.

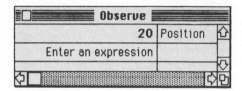

- *Choose Go again.* The Macintosh will go through the stop and continue executing until it reaches that stop sign again one loop later. Now the value of Position is 21, as you can see in the Observe window.

- *Choose Go two or three more times.* Each time, the ball will move one unit to the right and the Observe window will report the new value of Position. This is too slow! Let's start over and observe Position in a speedier way.

- *Open the Run menu and choose Reset.* Reset clears the output windows and readies the Macintosh for another run.

Running with Go-Go

There's another way to watch a variable change after you have inserted stops. When you run the program by choosing *Go-Go*, the cartoon runs in slow motion.

- Open the Run menu and choose Go-Go. As the program executes, it pauses momentarily at the stop, prints the new value of Position in the Observe window, and then resumes execution. Using Go-Go, you get a step-by-step report on the value of Position as the ball rolls slowly across the screen.

Pause and Halt

Note that, whenever you run a program, a new menu heading called *Pause* appears at the top of the screen (see Figure 2.5). You can use the two commands in that menu to stop program execution. Now get ready to use Pause in the middle of execution.

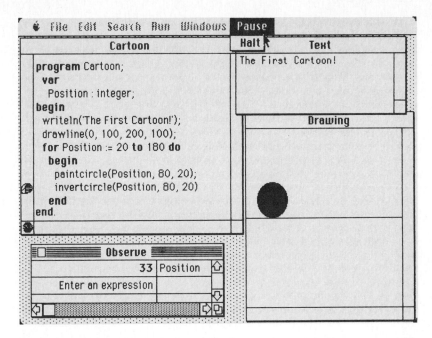

Figure 2.5   Pausing during execution with the value of Position equal to 33.

- *Try Go-Go again and, when Position gets to 100, move the pointer to Pause and hold down the mouse button.* This stops the program temporarily.

- *Release the button.* Execution will start up again, and the program will run to completion. Next get ready to freeze the program with *Halt.*

- *Try Go-Go once more, and this time, when Position gets to 100, open the Pause menu and choose Halt.* This stops program execution. The cartoon in the Drawing window is in suspended animation, and the current value of Position is reported in the Observe window.

- *Choose Go-Go again.* You will see the rest of the cartoon. If you don't want to watch the rest of the cartoon, you can Halt once more and then open the Run menu and choose Reset.

Taking Out the Stops

When you want your program to run normally again, you must remove the stops.

- First activate the Program window.

- *Move the pointer to the stop sign, and click.* The unwanted stop will disappear. (Note: This step is optional.)

■ *Now eliminate the Stop column from your program by choosing* Stops Out *on the Run menu.*

Right now the Observe window is useful only because it helps you understand how variables work. Its real use comes when programs aren't working right—that is, when you have a bug. Then you can use the Observe window to see whether the way you think the program is working squares with what's really going on. We will show you how to do this later.

Our next topic is Pascal arithmetic. First we'll look at how Pascal handles simple arithmetic. Then we'll show you how the arithmetic operations can affect looping—sometimes with spectacular results.

2.7 Arithmetic with Integers in MacPascal

Adding, subtracting, and multiplying are easy in Pascal. You use the plus sign (+) to add, the minus sign (−) to subtract, and the asterisk (*) to multiply. For example, if you type

```
writeln((5 + 2) * (6 − 4))
```

in the Instant window and click on Do It, the integer 14 will show up in the Text window.

Doing division is a little trickier; there are two different ways to divide in Pascal. One way uses the symbol /. This is the kind of division you are used to:

```
10/4 = 2.50
9.0/3.0 = 3.0
```

The other kind of division uses the symbol **div**, which means "divided by." **Div** works only with *integers*, or whole numbers. With **div**, you must always divide one integer by another integer, and the answer will always be an integer. For example,

```
5 div 3 = 1
```

This is so because 5 divided by 3 = 1 2/3, and **div** discards the fraction, leaving the integer 1 as the answer. Using **div** is like doing long division and throwing out the remainder. For example, if you wanted to calculate how many whole weeks there are in March, you would divide 31 by 7, like this:

$$
\begin{array}{r}
4 \\
7{\overline{)31}} \\
\underline{28} \\
3
\end{array}
$$

```
31 div 7 = 4   (throw out the remainder of 3)
```

Because we're working only with integers in this chapter, we'll be using only **div**. Here are some other examples of how **div** works:

```
6 div 3 =  2
7 div 3 =  2
8 div 3 =  2
9 div 3 =  3
-9 div 3 = -3
3 div 9 =  0
-9 div 4 = -2
```

Note: A smaller number divided by a larger one (both integers) always comes out zero: Smaller **div** Larger = 0. And one more thing: 6 **div** 0 doesn't make sense, because we are never allowed to divide by 0. If you try to, your program will *bomb*. That is, program execution will stop dead and you will get an error message.

At first glance, **div** might seem weird and useless to you. But there are lots of situations that require a whole-number answer.

Take these problems, for example: How many dozen eggs does your hen lay a year, if she lays an egg a day? The answer is 365 **div** 12, or 40 dozen. How many days has an astronaut been in orbit if she's been up for 115 hours? The answer is 115 **div** 24, or 4 days.

EXERCISE 1   What is the value of each of these expressions?

    a.   9 `div` 2

    b.   3 `div` 4

    c.   3 `div` (-4)   (*Answer:* 0)

    d. -20 `div` 8   (*Answer:* −2)

    e. -10 `div` -3   (*Answer:* 3) ▬

What happens when you use several operators in a single statement, like this?

```
writeln(2 + (3 * 4) - (5 div 6))
```

Try it with pencil and paper. You should get 14, because 5 **div** 6 = 0.

But what does the computer print when you type in the following instruction?

```
writeln(5 + 4 * 2)
```

Does Pascal add 5 and 4 first and then multiply by 2, giving 18? Or does it multiply 4 and 2 first and then add 5, giving 13? You can get either answer if you use parentheses. The Macintosh will print 18 if you place the parentheses like this:

```
writeln((5 + 4) * 2)
```

And it will print 13 if you place the parentheses like this:

```
writeln(5 + (4 * 2))
```

But if you leave out parentheses, Pascal has a rule that tells which operations are done first. Pascal does multiplications and divisions first, in the order in which they appear left to right. Then it does the additions and subtractions, also in the order in which they appear. This means that

```
5 + 4 * 2 = 5 + 8 = 13
```

and

```
8 – 3 div 5 = 8 – 0 = 8
```

How about this?

```
5 + 3 – 2 * 6 div 4
```

In this case, 2 * 6 is done first (because * comes before **div**), leaving

```
5 + 3 – 12 div 4
```

Next 12 **div** 4 is done, leaving

```
5 + 3 – 3
```

And then the addition is done, followed by the subtraction. So the answer is 5.

The Rules of Arithmetic in MacPascal

1. First do all the multiplications and divisions from left to right.
2. Then do all the additions and subtractions from left to right.

EXERCISE 2   What should these statements print out? Work out the answers with pencil and paper. You can check yourself using the Instant window.

a. `writeln(2 + 4 div 6 * (8 – 10))`

b. `writeln(100 div 5 div 4 div 3 div 2)`

c. `writeln(10 div 2 * 10 – 10 div 3)` ▬

2.8 Arithmetic and Looping

The real power of arithmetic in programming comes when you do arithmetic inside a loop. To see how this works, let's take a look at **program** FirstLoop, which prints the numbers 1 through 4 in a column.

```
program FirstLoop;
  var
    Number : integer;
  begin
  for Number := 1 to 4 do
    begin
      writeln(Number)
    end
  end.
```

If we make this change in the *writeln* statement

```
writeln(Number + 1)
```

We'll get this column of numbers instead:

```
2
3
4
5
```

And if we change it to

```
writeln(Number - 3)
```

the column will look like this:

```
-2
-1
 0
 1
```

To print out the first four even integers,

```
2
4
6
8
```

we need to use this *writeln* statement:

```
writeln(Number * 2)
```

And with

```
writeln(Number div 2)
```

in the loop, we'll get

```
0
1
1
2
```

One last example. The MacPascal standard procedure *sysbeep* commands the Macintosh to make an electronic beep. The instruction *sysbeep*(10) produces a beep that lasts for 10 * .022 seconds. *Sysbeep*(20) sounds the beep for 20 * .022 seconds. What do you think the following program does?

```
program Beep;
 var
  Number : integer;
begin
 for Number := 10 to 20 do
  begin
   sysbeep(5 * Number)
  end
end.
```

EXERCISE 3   **a.** What does this version of **program** FirstLoop print?

```
program FirstLoop;
 var
  Number : integer;
begin
 for Number := 1 to 4 do
  begin
   writeln(Number * Number div 5)
  end
end.
```

Answer: 0–0–1–3 in a column

b. Change **program** FirstLoop so that it prints out each of the following columns of numbers.

```
 3   0   -2   -8
 6   3    0   -6
 9   6    2   -4
12   9    4   -2
```

_____ **2.9 Solving Arithmetic Problems** _____

Now you know enough about using arithmetic in Pascal to write programs that will solve problems. Let's see how to solve this one: Print out all the years from 1901 to 1999 that end in zero.

To write this program, you need to know that there are nine years between 1901 and 1999 that end in zero. This means that there will be nine repetitions of the loop.

```pascal
program Tens;
 var
  TenYearPeriod : integer;
begin
 for TenYearPeriod := 1 to 9 do
  begin
   writeln(1900 + (10 * TenYearPeriod))
  end
end.
```

If you want to print out all the years from 1900 to 1999 that end in 9, you can write the program in two different ways (at least). Here is one way.

```pascal
program NinesOne;
 var
  TenYearPeriod : integer;
begin
 for TenYearPeriod := 1 to 10 do
  begin
   writeln(1899 + (10 * TenYearPeriod))
  end
end.
```

Here is another.

```pascal
program NinesTwo;
 var
  TenYearPeriod : integer;
begin
 for TenYearPeriod := 0 to 9 do
  begin
   writeln(1909 + (10 * TenYearPeriod))
  end
end.
```

EXERCISE 4   How about printing the leap years in the twentieth century? Leap years are years that are divisible by 4, except for some century years such as 1900. Because there are 24 leap years from 1900 to 1999, the program looks like this:

```
program Leap;
 var
  LeapYear : integer;
begin
 for LeapYear := 1 to 24 do
  begin
   writeln(1900 + ⬚)
  end
end.
```

What expression should go in the box to instruct the computer to print out all the leap years in the twentieth century? ■

2.10 Using Arithmetic in Program Explode

Now let's use what we've just learned to do some fancy geometry programs, starting with a variation of **program** Explode (Problem 5 at the end of Chapter 1). Let's use multiplication in the **for** loop to make this program more exciting. Here's the original program:

```
program Explode;
 var
  Radius : integer;
begin
 for Radius := 1 to 100 do
  begin
   paintcircle(100,100,Radius)
  end
end.
```

Bring up **program** Explode, or, if you don't have a permanent copy on a disk, type the program in. Now run it. Note that the exploding circle grows slowly. This happens because, each time the *paintcircle* instruction in the **for** statement is executed, the radius of the circle grows by just one unit.

To speed up the explosion, let's make the radius grow by two units each time through the loop. This means that we will need only 50 repetitions, or *iterations*, of the loop (instead of 100) to end up with a circle that has a radius of 100. The **for** statement in **program** Explode will now look like this:

```
for Radius := 1 to 50 do
 begin
  paintcircle(100,100,2 * Radius)
 end
```

Make this change and test it out. And while you're at it, play around with **program** Explode, making the explosion happen even faster—say, in 10 or 15 iterations.

2.11 Planning a Graphics Program—Drawing Diamonds

In this and the next example, we are going to explain how to write programs. Programming is a problem-solving skill that requires concentration, persistence, attention to detail, and (above all) practice.

In the first of these two examples, we want to write a program that draws a diamond like the one shown in Figure 2.6. We'll call it **program** Diamond.

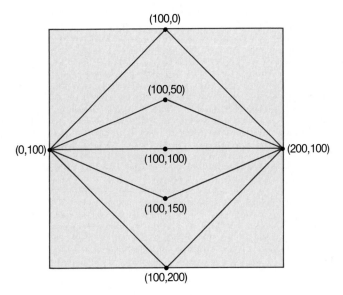

Figure 2.6   The diamond consists of 201 pairs of line segments, but only 5 are shown here.

When we solve a problem using the computer, we begin simply by thinking about the problem until we are sure we know exactly what is required. This is what we come up with:

The diamond has 201 pairs of line segments, and each pair meets halfway across the screen at horizontal position 100. The first two lines meet at the top. Each time the program draws another pair of lines, the point where the segments meet is one unit farther down. The vertical position of the meeting point of the two segments starts at 0 and goes down to 200. Because the meeting point is what varies in the picture, MeetingPoint will be a variable in our program. It will represent the vertical position of the point where the line segments meet.

Now we know enough to make a rough plan for the program. Here's the plan:

As MeetingPoint of the line segments goes from 0 to 200,
    draw the left segment
    draw the right segment

This looks promising! Now let's change the "As..." statement into a Pascal **for** statement:

> **for** MeetingPoint : = 0 **to** 200 **do**
> draw the left segment
> draw the right segment

Let's refine our plan by concentrating on how to draw the left segments. All the left segments are anchored at point (0,100), and they all end halfway across the screen (see Figure 2.7).

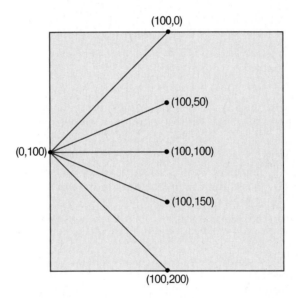

Figure 2.7 The left segments of the diamond.

In other words, the horizontal position of the right endpoints of the line segments on the left is fixed; it is always 100 units over from the left. The vertical position of the right endpoints *does* vary; with each successive line, it gets one unit farther down from the top. So with each line, the value of the variable MeetingPoint gets one unit larger. The instruction that draws each left segment should be

```
drawline(0,100,100,MeetingPoint);
```

The instruction that draws the right segments looks almost the same. The right segments are anchored at the point (200,100), so the instruction should be

```
drawline(200,100,100,MeetingPoint)
```

We're almost there. But first we'll have to write a variable declaration for MeetingPoint.

```
var
 MeetingPoint : integer
```

Now we can put the complete program together.

```
program Diamond;
 var
  MeetingPoint : integer;
begin
 for MeetingPoint := 0 to 200 do
  begin
   drawline(0,100,100,MeetingPoint);
   drawline(200,100,100,MeetingPoint)
  end
end.
```

What happens when you run **program** Diamond? **Program** Diamond draws a picture that looks pretty exciting as it appears on the screen. But there's a problem. The lines are so close together that they blend into a solid black diamond (see Figure 2.8). To fix this problem, we can spread out the lines and draw fewer of them. This means doing fewer repetitions of the **for** loop and moving the meeting point correspondingly farther down the screen with each iteration. Let's draw the picture with about one-fourth as many lines. For the upper limit of the **for** loop we'll use the expression 200 **div** 4, which equals 50. The meeting points will be four units apart. Here's how the loop should look:

```
for MeetingPoint := 0 to (200 div 4) do
 begin
  drawline(0,100,100,4 * MeetingPoint);
  drawline(200,100,100,4 * MeetingPoint)
 end
```

This time when you run **program** Diamond, you can see the individual lines. See Figure 2.9(a).

When we run the program with just one-seventh as many lines, using this loop

```
for MeetingPoint := 0 to (200 div 7) do
 begin
  drawline(0,100,100,7 * MeetingPoint);
  drawline(200,100,100,7 * MeetingPoint)
 end
```

we get the picture shown in Figure 2.9(b). This picture is a little peculiar, if you look closely, because of the way **div** works. The picture doesn't quite reach the

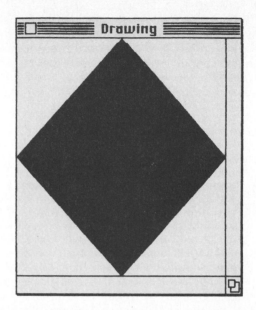

Figure 2.8.   Program Diamond's 201 pairs of lines blend together to form a completely black diamond.

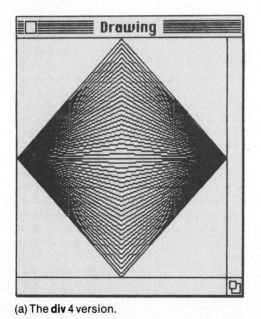

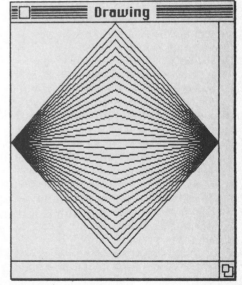

(a) The **div** 4 version.   (b) The **div** 7 version.

Figure 2.9   Program Diamond debugged.

bottom of the Drawing window, which is 200 units down from the top. This is so because the value of the upper limit in the loop is 200 **div** 7 = 28. So, at the last loop iteration, MeetingPoint has the value 28. After the loop repeats 28 times, the last meeting point is 196 units down, because 7 ∗ 28 = 196. This is 4 units short of the bottom.

For more on **program** Diamond, try Problems 6, 7, 8, and 9 at the end of this chapter.

Algorithms and the Man from Khwarizm

A little more than 1200 years ago, the Caliph of Baghdad invited a scientist named Muhammad, son of Moses, to teach and study at the House of Wisdom, an academy of learning in Baghdad. The scientist came to be known as the Man from Khwarizm, the province in Central Asia that had been his home. In Arabic his name was Al-Khwarizmi.

Al-Khwarizmi was especially interested in solving problems by using equations, and he wrote a book about his method. One of the Arabic words in the title of his book was *al-jabr.* When it was translated into Latin, that word became *algebra.* From then on, mathematicians called Al-Khwarizmi's method of solving problems algebra. In Europe his name was pronounced "Algorismus," and gradually the art of doing arithmetic came to be called algorism or algorithm. Today mathematicians use the word *algorithm* to mean a careful, step-by-step method of calculating. And in computer science, it means a detailed plan for solving a problem using the computer.

2.12 Thinking, Planning, Coding, and Testing and Debugging

Before we go on to our next example, let's summarize the steps we went through as we wrote **program** Diamond.

1. First we went through a *thinking* step, in which we described our programming problem in detail. In the thinking step it is often helpful to work the problem with pencil and paper first. Making a diagram can also be useful if the purpose of the program is to draw a picture.

2. Our second step was a *planning* step. We divided the problem into clear, understandable units and wrote them down in English phrases. After we formulated a loose plan, we refined it and converted it to a tight plan, or *algorithm.* Algorithms are written in English phrases mixed with Pascal.

3. *Coding* was our third step. In this phase we actually converted our tight program plan, or algorithm, into Pascal instructions.

4. Our final step was *testing and debugging*. We tested **program** Diamond by running it. And, when we weren't satisfied with the picture we got, we debugged the program by spreading the line segments in the Drawing window.

So there are really four separate steps to programming: thinking, planning, coding, and testing and debugging. What you probably think of as programming is actually just the coding part—writing down the MacPascal instructions that will solve your problem. But there is much more to programming than coding.

Algo-what?

You are probably wondering exactly what the word *algorithm* means. An algorithm is a list of informal instructions that will systematically get some job done. Even though you may not have heard of algorithms before, you use them every day. A pancake recipe, for example, is an algorithm. It's a step-by-step list of instructions for making pancakes. And the instruction booklet that comes with a camera includes an algorithm for changing a roll of film. Even this is an algorithm:

> You put your right foot in,
> You put your right foot out,
> You put your right foot in,
> And you shake it all about.

for doing the Hokey Pokey

2.13 An Orbiting Planet

Next we want to design and write a spectacular program called **program** PlanetIn3D. Here's what the program will do. A planet (a flickering ball) will move from the upper-left corner of the output window diagonally across the screen and will exit from the window at the lower-right corner. (See Figure 2.10.)

As it moves, the planet will also grow in size—let's say from radius 0 at the upper-left corner to radius 40 at the lower-right corner. (We've chosen 40 for the final radius of the circle for no special reason except that it looks good. The final size of the planet will be less than half the size of the standard Drawing window.)

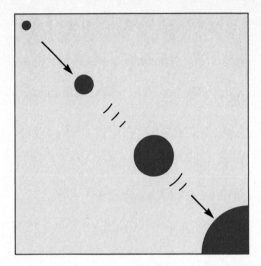

Figure 2.10   The planet will move from the upper-left-corner to the lower-right corner.

Now let's work through the four programming steps with **program** PlanetIn3D.

Thinking

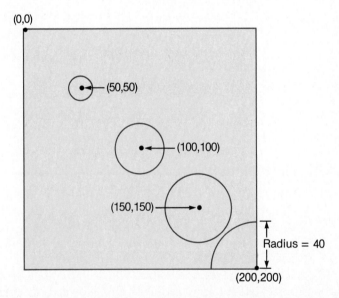

Let's look at the accompanying diagram to see what it tells us about our problem. Notice where the planet enters the window and where it leaves. It starts with its center at point (0,0). And it stops at point (200,200). In between, the center goes to $(1,1)$, then to $(2,2)$, and so on. At each position we want the planet to flicker (appear and disappear) just like the ball in **program** Cartoon. Now we understand the problem well enough to start planning the program.

Planning

Here is our first rough plan for the program.

Plan I

As the planet moves from the upper-left corner to the lower-right corner,

  make the planet flicker and grow

Now we can make the plan more specific and turn it into an algorithm.

Plan II—The Algorithm

As the horizontal and vertical positions of planet go from 0 to 200,

  make planet flicker and grow from radius 0 to radius 40.

Coding

We are now ready to translate our algorithm into Pascal. Let's look at the diagram on page 66 again. As the planet moves diagonally across the screen, it does three things: It moves across, it moves down, and it gets bigger. This might lead you to think, "Aha! Three things change so we need three variables." Luckily this isn't so. Here's why.

The center of the circle starts at $(0,0)$ and goes to $(1,1)$, then to $(2,2)$ and so on. The value of its vertical position is always the same as the value of its horizontal position. This means that we need only one variable for the horizontal and vertical positions. Let's call the variable PlanetPos.

The radius gets bigger as the value of PlanetPos increases, so let's try using PlanetPos to stand for the radius, too. (We are deliberately making an error so that we can show you how to debug later.) Here is the program:

```
program PlanetIn3D;
  var
   PlanetPos : integer;
begin
  for PlanetPos := 0 to 200 do
   begin
    paintcircle(PlanetPos,PlanetPos,PlanetPos);
    invertcircle(PlanetPos,PlanetPos,PlanetPos)
   end
end.
```

Testing and Debugging

The final step in programming involves testing the program to see whether it does what we want—and debugging it if it needs fixing. Let's test the program by running it. When you try, you'll see that . . . well, it *almost* works. The problem is that, when the circle reaches the lower-right corner, it's huge. But the problem's *specification*, or description, says that the planet's radius should be only 40 when the planet reaches the right wall of the window. The program has a bug.

Here's a pencil-and-paper trick for debugging loops. You can use it from now on, whenever you program. If a loop isn't working right (and this one isn't), see what the loop is doing at the first iteration and at the last iteration. In this case, looking at the first iteration doesn't help much. The program does the two instructions:

```
paintcircle(0,0,0);
invertcircle(0,0,0)
```

But looking at the last iteration is more promising. The program executes these two instructions:

```
paintcircle(200,200,200);
invertcircle(200,200,200)
```

And here is our bug. When the planet reaches the right side it has radius 200—and we want it to have radius 40.

Debugging with the Observe Window

This is a place where the Observe window can help us. To make use of it, we need to bring it up and enter PlanetPos as the expression to watch. Then we can deposit a stop just before the *invertcircle* command and run the program using Go-Go. We can watch the successive values of PlanetPos as the planet moves across the screen and becomes more and more oversized.

We want the radius to start at 0, growing smoothly until it reaches 40, which is exactly one-fifth of 200. We can get this to happen if we make the radius one-fifth of PlanetPos throughout the entire loop. Now the planet will be the right size when we get to the last iteration, and our bug will be fixed. Here's the new program.

```
program PlanetIn3D;
  var
   PlanetPos : integer;
begin
 for PlanetPos := 0 to 200 do
  begin
   paintcircle(PlanetPos,PlanetPos,PlanetPos div 5);
   invertcircle(PlanetPos,PlanetPos,PlanetPos div 5)
  end
end.
```

2.14 Getting the Planet to Return—Backward For Loops

Suppose we want to extend the code in PlanetIn3D so that the planet retraces its steps, as shown in Figure 2.11. This will be easy once we've mastered Pascal's backward **for** loop construction.

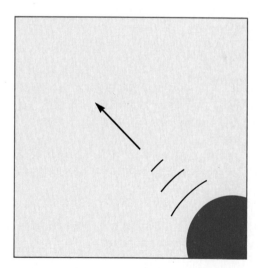

Figure 2.11   The planet retraces its steps.

The backward **for** loop makes the value of the variable go *down* by 1 with each iteration, instead of *up* by 1. Here's an easy example of how this works:

```
for Number := 4 downto 1 do
 begin
  writeln(Number)
 end;
```

This loop prints the column

```
4
3
2
1
```

With the backward **for** loop, we can get the planet to return by using the following statement:

```
for PlanetPos := 200 downto 0 do
  begin
    paintcircle(PlanetPos,PlanetPos,PlanetPos div 5);
    invertcircle(PlanetPos,PlanetPos,PlanetPos div 5)
  end
```

Here is a complete orbiting planet program:

```
program PlanetIn3D;
  var
    PlanetPos : integer;
begin
  for PlanetPos := 0 to 200 do
    begin
      paintcircle(PlanetPos,PlanetPos,PlanetPos div 5);
      invertcircle(PlanetPos,PlanetPos,PlanetPos div 5)
    end;
  for PlanetPos := 200 downto 0 do
    begin
      paintcircle(PlanetPos,PlanetPos,PlanetPos div 5);
      invertcircle(PlanetPos,PlanetPos,PlanetPos div 5)
    end
end.
```

Note: If you have already typed in the first loop and you want to add the second loop, use Copy and Paste.

2.15 Outside the Standard Drawing Window

One final touch. Note that the planet is still half on the screen at the end of the first loop. We can make it completely disappear by executing the **for** loop a few more times. Try increasing the limit in both loops from 200 to 250 and see what you get.

Something mysterious happens when you do this. The planet disappears at the lower-right corner of the window and hesitates for a while before it comes back. What's going on?

It turns out that you can write commands to draw shapes outside the limits of the standard Drawing window. When you run the program, the commands are executed, but you don't see them on the screen—that is, unless you enlarge the Drawing window. If you use the Size box to make the Drawing window larger, you will be able to see the planet go through all 250 loops.

You can write commands that will do imaginary drawings that extend way beyond the borders of the Drawing window, even when it is at its largest. Think of the Drawing window as a window that looks out onto an area that is far bigger than the actual Macintosh screen.

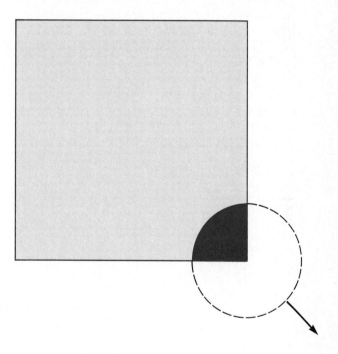

Tuning Your Planet

Unhappy with the speed of your planet as it moves across the Drawing window? Try speeding it up.

Make it move two or three times as fast by adjusting how far the planet moves between flickers. Right now it's slow because it flickers at the point (1,1), then at (2,2), then at (3,3), and so on. Make it flicker at (2,2), (4,4), (6,6), and so on.

2.16 Comments

With **program** PlanetIn3D we have reached a milestone. Our programs are now so complex that we need to include notes, or *comments*, in the program text to explain how the program works. Remember, a comment in Pascal is a message in English, enclosed in braces:

```
{THIS IS WHAT A COMMENT LOOKS LIKE.}
```

Pascal skips over whatever is inside these braces and doesn't treat it as part of the program. So we can write whatever we like inside the braces, and it won't affect the output of the program. We include comments to explain to ourselves and to others what our programs are all about. In this book we use all capital letters in comments to distinguish them from program instructions. But either capital or lowercase letters will work in comments.

To show you how helpful comments are, we've gone back and put them in our last program. With comments in place, PlanetIn3D is much more understandable for anyone who tries to read it (including *you* a couple of months from now).

Here's PlanetIn3D with comments:

```
program PlanetIn3D;
{PLANET MOVES FROM UPPER LEFT TO LOWER RIGHT AND GROWS.}
{THEN IT REVERSES ITS PATH AND SHRINKS.}
  var
   PlanetPos : integer;
begin
 {PLANET MOVES FROM UPPER LEFT TO LOWER RIGHT.}
 for PlanetPos := 0 to 200 do
  begin
   paintcircle(PlanetPos,PlanetPos,PlanetPos div 5);
   invertcircle(PlanetPos,PlanetPos,PlanetPos div 5)
  end;
 {PLANET RETURNS FROM LOWER RIGHT TO UPPER LEFT.}
 for PlanetPos := 200 downto 0 do
  begin
   paintcircle(PlanetPos,PlanetPos,PlanetPos div 5);
   invertcircle(PlanetPos,PlanetPos,PlanetPos div 5)
  end
end.
```

The first comment in a program should go right under the heading line and should summarize the purpose of the program. Often it is helpful to put in a comment that explains what a variable stands for. Each of the other comments should explain the purpose of the instructions that *follow* it.

Note that in PlanetIn3D we don't go overboard explaining what's obvious. In deciding what comments to use, you should go back and look at your plan, which tells the purpose of each step in the program.

Comments should be in English and not in Pascal. Good comments are often similar to or the same as the steps you identified in your program plan.

When have you done a good job of commenting? One way to decide is to apply the "vacation test." Imagine that you are going on vacation for a month. When you return, will you be able to understand the programs you wrote before you left?

From now on, all but the simplest programs you write should include comments. Don't be tempted to skip them. At the very least, you should put a one-line comment that states the purpose of the program just below the heading line.

2.17 Good Names, Bad Names, and Syntax Diagrams

When you make up a name for a program, it can't be just anything you think of. For example, reserved words such as **begin, end,** and **do** can't be used in a made-up name in a Pascal program. A list of the reserved words appear inside the front cover of this book.

MacPascal rules forbid us to use certain names such as 3DPlanet, although PlanetIn3D is OK. The rule says that any identifier—a name you make up and assign to a program or a variable—must begin with a letter. Digits and the underscore symbol may appear elsewhere in the name, however. This means, for example, that you could name a program R2_D2.

Pascal has lots of rules like the identifier rule, so the designers of the language use *syntax diagrams* to help make the rules clear. The syntax diagram for identifiers is shown in Figure 2.12.

How does this diagram help us? To check whether R2_D2 is OK, we start at the left and match the first symbol (R) against the first box, which is labeled "letter." R is a letter, so we can go on.

The next symbol is the digit 2. If we follow one of the loops after the first letter box, we come to a digit box, so 2 is also OK.

Then we follow the loop with the underscore box to determine whether the underscore is OK. It is.

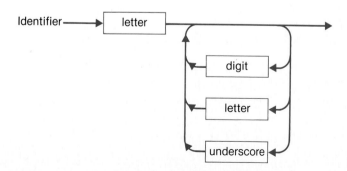

Figure 2.12 The syntax diagram for identifiers.

Next we match the D against the letter loop and the 2 against the digit box, and we're finished. The identifier R2_D2 has made it through the syntax diagram, so it's OK as an identifier.

How about 3D? As you have probably figured out, 3D is not OK. Starting at the left, the first box in the diagram is labeled "letter." Because 3 is not a letter, and because there's no alternative route to get past this part of the diagram, 3D is not allowed as an identifier. D3 is OK as an identifier, but D 3 (with a space in the middle) is not. When Pascal gets to the space in the middle, it "thinks" it has come to the end of the name. Then Pascal runs into the 3 and doesn't know what to make of it.

Here's a tip on making up identifiers: When you invent names for variables, use names that are as close as possible to the actual idea they represent. If you want a variable to represent the position of a planet as it orbits, don't call it X, or Number, or even Spot. Call it PlanetPos.

TEST YOURSELF

1. What is the CPU?
2. What do we mean when we say, "The value of the variable is of type integer"?
3. What is the value of 5 * 4 **div** 3? of 5 **div** 4 * 3? of 5 **div** (4 * 3)?
4. When you run a program using Go-Go, what happens when a stop is encountered?
5. What is an algorithm?
6. What is the "vacation test" for comments?
7. What are the four steps in programming?
8. What happens in the coding step?
9. What is a byte?
10. What is a bit?

PROBLEMS

1. a. Give the values of the following Pascal arithmetic expressions. Check yourself using the Instant window.

```
2 + 3 div 2 * 6 - 5
5 + (2 * 2)
2 + 3 - (5 * 3) div 4 + 2
```

b. Homer has 1038 eggs he wants to sell. Give a Pascal expression that tells how many full dozens of eggs Homer can take to market.

2. What picture does this program draw? Figure it out before you try it.

```
program MakeLines;
 var
   EndPoint : integer;
begin
 for EndPoint := 0 to 100 do
   begin
    drawline(0,0,200,2 * EndPoint)
   end
end.
```

3. Modify the **for** loop in **program** MakeLines so that the lines drawn are twice as far apart.

4. **a.** What does this program do?

```
program NotSure;
 var
   Point : integer;
begin
 for Point := 0 to 200 do
   begin
    drawline(0,Point,Point,Point)
   end
end.
```

b. What happens when you try **program** NotSure with this *drawline* instruction?

```
drawline(0,2 * Point,2 * Point,2 * Point)
```

c. What about this one?

```
drawline(2 * Point,0,2 * Point,2 * Point)
```

d. And this one?

```
drawline(0,Point,2 * Point,Point)
```

5. How could you change **program** NotSure to get these pictures?

a.

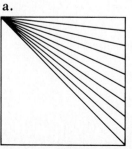

b.

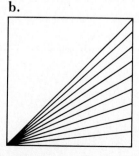

c.

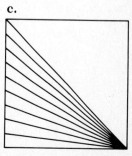

6. Change **program** Diamond so that the diamond appears on its side. Use the think-plan-code-test-and-debug method to solve this problem.

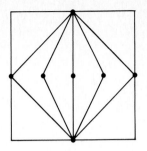

7. Change the lower and upper limits in the **for** loop of **program** Diamond so that you get a picture like this:

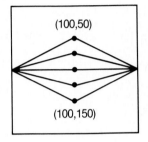

8. How could you shift the meeting point in **program** Diamond 50 units to the left so that the program draws this picture?

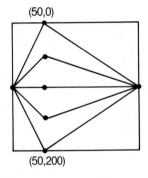

9. Change **program** Diamond so that all the left segments are drawn first and then all the right segments are drawn.

   (*Hint:* You'll need two loops).

10. Which of the following are legal identifiers?
    a. D2_R2
    b. Monkey_Business
    c. 5_Easy_Pieces
    d. Five_Dollar_Bill
    e. _NO_Way
    f. No Way

11. Look at the accompanying syntax diagram. Which of the following sentences are OK for this diagram?

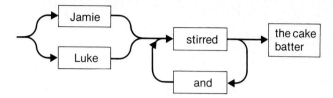

a. Jamie stirred and stirred and stirred the cake batter.
b. Luke stirred stirred the cake batter.
c. Jamie and Luke stirred the cake batter.
d. Jamie or Luke stirred the cake batter.
e. Luke stirred the cake batter.

Answer: a and e

12. Draw this picture in the Drawing window.

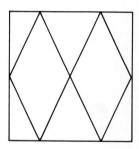

13. Write programs that print out the following columns of numbers:

a.	b.	c.	d.	e.	f.	g.
0	5	9	90	51	2	0
0	6	8	80	52	2	0
0	7	7	70	53	3	0
0	8	6	60	54	3	1
	9	5	50	55	4	1
					4	1
						2
						2
						2

14. What does this program print?

```
program Question;
  var
    Number : integer;
  begin
    for Number := 5 downto 0 do
    begin
      writeln(Number)
    end
  end.
```

15. What does this program do?

```
program What;
 var
  Position : integer;
begin
 for Position := 0 to 200 do
  begin
   invertcircle(100,Position,40);
   invertcircle(100,Position,40)
  end
end.
```

16. Try to figure out what this program does, and then run it.

```
program MoreLines;
 var
  Point : integer;
begin
 for Point := 0 to 20 do
  begin
   drawline(0,10 * Point,200,200 - 10 * Point)
  end
end.
```

Now change **program** MoreLines so that the image it produces is rotated 90 degrees and looks like a vertical hourglass.

17. Write programs that draw these pictures.

a.

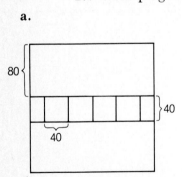

b.

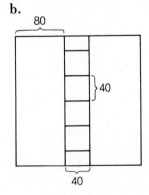

c.

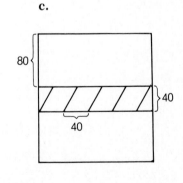

Syntax, Interactive Programs, and Real Numbers

3

Pascal has a lot of rules for arranging and punctuating programs, and we will talk about them in this chapter. You have to know them, or your programs just won't run. These rules make up the *syntax* of Pascal. When you master them, you will be able to write your own programs from scratch. The better you know the rules, the fewer bugs you'll have.

We are also going to show you how to write *interactive* programs. When you run an interactive program, it stops in the middle of execution and asks you a question about what to do next.

Finally, we'll show you how to use *real numbers*—numbers with decimal points. Real numbers are important for doing scientific calculations, working with percentages, and making calculations with money.

3.1 Pascal Syntax—How to Beat the Bugs

PlanetIn3D is the most complicated program we've seen so far. Let's use it to explore Pascal's syntax rules.

```
program PlanetIn3D; ①
 var
  PlanetPos : integer; ②
begin
 for PlanetPos := 0 to 200 do
  begin
   paintcircle(PlanetPos,PlanetPos,PlanetPos div 5); ③
   invertcircle(PlanetPos,PlanetPos,PlanetPos div 5)
  end; ④
 for PlanetPos := 200 downto 0 do
  begin
   paintcircle(PlanetPos,PlanetPos,PlanetPos div 5); ⑤
   invertcircle(PlanetPos,PlanetPos,PlanetPos div 5)
  end
end.
```

Semicolons

Placing semicolons correctly is an important part of mastering Pascal syntax. Semicolons separate statements. They also mark the end of the heading line of a Pascal program, and they end variable declarations.

Look at the five semicolons in PlanetIn3D. The first one separates the heading line from the variable declaration. The second semicolon separates the variable declaration from the body. The third and fifth semicolons separate *paintcircle* instructions from *invertcircle* instructions. And the fourth semicolon separates the two **for** statements.

The *invertcircle* instructions are not followed by semicolons. Why? Because each is followed by the reserved word **end** and not by another statement. A semicolon is never needed before an **end,** because the word **end** also serves to separate statements. (Pascal is generous here. If you put a semicolon after the *invertcircle* statements, it will not object.)

You don't need a semicolon after the word **end** in the second loop either. It's not followed by another statement. But, as before, Pascal doesn't mind if you put one in.

Let's make some changes in PlanetIn3D that illustrate another important syntax rule. We'll call the new program TwoStreaks. See Figure 3.1 for sample output.

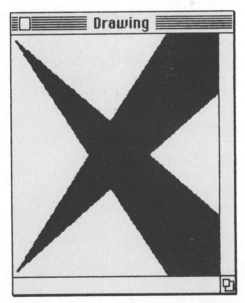

Figure 3.1   The output for **program** TwoStreaks.

```
program TwoStreaks;
 var
  PlanetPos : integer;
begin
 for PlanetPos := 0 to 200 do
  begin
   paintcircle(PlanetPos,PlanetPos,PlanetPos div 5)
  end;
 for PlanetPos := 200 downto 0 do
  begin
   paintcircle(PlanetPos,200 - PlanetPos,PlanetPos div 5)
  end
end.
```

In program TwoStreaks the *paintcircle* instructions are no longer followed by semicolons. Why? In each case the instruction is followed by the reserved word **end**, not by another statement.

Begin and End

We can simplify the form of **program** TwoStreaks by getting rid of the **begin** and the **end** inside each **for** loop:

```
program TwoStreaks;
 var
  PlanetPos : integer;
begin
 for PlanetPos := 0 to 200 do
  paintcircle(PlanetPos,PlanetPos,PlanetPos div 5);
 for PlanetPos := 200 downto 0 do
  paintcircle(PlanetPos,200 - PlanetPos,PlanetPos div 5)
end.
```

Because there is only one instruction in each **for** statement, the **begin-end** pair that usually frames the **for** body is not necessary. When the body of the **for** statement doesn't start with the word **begin**, the **for** control line applies only to the next statement and to no others.

Now that we've eliminated the **begin-end** pair, we need a semicolon after the *paintcircle* instruction in the first **for** statement, because the second **for** statement follows directly after it.

Be careful when you get rid of the **begin-end** pair in a **for** statement: If you try to include two statements instead of just one in the **for** loop, you'll get into trouble. For example, if you write the first **for** loop in **program** PlanetIn3D like this:

```
for PlanetPos := 0 to 200 do
 paintcircle(PlanetPos,PlanetPos,PlanetPos div 5);
 invertcircle(PlanetPos,PlanetPos,PlanetPos div 5);
```

the program will behave strangely. Because the **begin** and **end** have been omitted, the **for** statement will apply only to the *paintcircle* statement. This leaves the *invertcircle* command dangling—it's not in the body of the loop. But it includes the control variable PlanetPos, which gets its value from the control line.

When program execution reaches that statement, you won't actually get an error message. Something worse will happen. MacPascal will assign an arbitrary value to PlanetPos and execution will continue. You won't see what you expected, *and* you won't know where to start looking for the problem.

EXERCISE 1   On a piece of scratch paper, insert the punctuation that should appear in the following program. Then see whether your version conforms to the listing in Problem 2 of Chapter 2.

```
program MakeLines
 var
  EndPoint integer
begin
 for EndPoint  0 to 100 do
  begin
   drawline 0 0 200 2 * EndPoint
  end
end
```

What can you do to simplify the program? ▬

3.2 What Is a Statement?

Semicolons separate statements. To place them correctly, you need to understand exactly what a statement is.

In Pascal, the term *statement* is the official name for an instruction or command. So far we have seen three different kinds of statement. The simplest statements are the standard procedures: *writeln*, *paintcircle*, *invertcircle*, and *drawline*. These are called *simple statements*.

Next come *compound statements.* A compound statement is a kind of package of statements that starts with the word **begin** and ends with the word **end.** It has this form:

```
begin
  statement 1;
  statement 2;
  ...
  statement n - 1;
  statement n
end
```

Even if there's only one statement between the **begin** and the **end,** the package is considered a compound statement. In fact, it is still a compound statement if you put *nothing* between the **begin** and the **end.** We'll talk about this in a moment.

Finally there are *for statements,* which have this form:

```
for control-variable := initial-value to final-value do
  statement;
```

The body of a **for** statement is itself a statement. It can be a simple statement:

```
for Number := 1 to 5 do
  writeln(Number);
```

a compound statement:

```
for Position := 20 to 180 do
  begin
    paintcircle(Position,80,20);
    invertcircle(Position,80,20)
  end;
```

or even another **for** statement:

```
for Number := 1 to 3 do
  for PledgeNumber := 1 to 500 do
    writeln('I will not talk in class.');
```

All three of these examples are legal statements. In each case the body of the **for** statement is also a statement. In the first example, the body is a simple statement. In the second it's a compound statement. And in the third it's actually another **for** statement.

A loop that comes inside another loop is called a *nested loop.* The nested loop in the third example prints three blocks of 500 copies of "I will not talk in class." That is, the *writeln* statement is executed 1500 times. We'll tell you more about nested loops a little later.

Because **for** statements are legal statements, you need to use a semicolon to separate a **for** statement from any statement following it.

The Empty Statement

Now suppose you open the Instant window and type in

```
begin
end
```

What happens when you click on Do It? MacPascal does not complain. It happily runs this little compound statement according to the following philosophy: "If you don't want me to execute any instructions, I won't consider what you've done a mistake." However, MacPascal *does* consider there to be a statement between the **begin** and the **end.** It is called the *empty statement.*

More nonsense: Suppose you open the Instant window and type in

```
begin
  ;
end
```

Again no complaints. MacPascal sees two empty statements, one before the semicolon and one after. When you run it, this compound statement does nothing—twice!

Will Pascal accept the following program?

```
program Test;
 var
  Number : integer;
begin
 for Number := 1 to 5 do
  begin
   writeln(Number);
  end
end.
```

Yes. Each time through the loop, Pascal does the *writeln* statement. When it hits the semicolon, it thinks another statement is coming. Then it comes to the **end,** and it figures you've included an empty statement, so it just goes on about its business. In fact, it would even accept this:

```
for Number := 1 to 5 do
 begin
  writeln(Number);;
 end
```

Pascal would just figure that you've included two empty statements after the *writeln.*

3.3 Syntax Notation

You now know about four different kinds of statement: simple statements, compound statements, **for** statements, and empty statements. When we want to indicate that a statement of some kind must appear at a particular place in a program, we use this notation:

⟨statement⟩

And the syntax of a **for** statement has this general form:

for control-variable := initial-value **to** final-value **do**
 ⟨statement⟩

Pascal expects every **for** statement to have this form. For example, we have the following match-ups with the **for** loop in **program** Test which is shown on page 84.

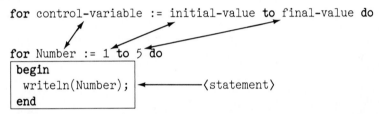

You will get an error message if your **for** statements don't conform to this general pattern.

Syntax diagrams are another way to show how the syntax of a statement works. For the **for** statement, we can draw the diagram shown in Figure 3.2.

If we trace through the **for** loop in **program** Test, we find that everything in the loop matches up with an essential feature of the **for** loop in the syntax diagram. Thus we know the syntax of the loop is correct.

In the Macintosh Pascal reference manual, syntax diagrams are the standard way of describing Pascal syntax. From time to time we will also use syntax diagrams to clarify the syntax for a particular instruction.

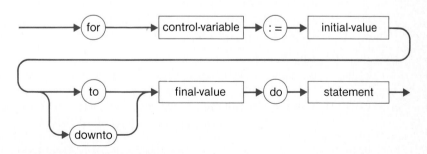

Figure 3.2 A syntax diagram.

EXERCISE 2   Use the **for**-loop syntax diagram to check the three **for** loops on page 83 to determine whether they are legal. ▬

Syntax Rules

Let's sum up what we've discovered so far about Pascal's syntax rules.

1. Every program must have a heading line, a declaration part, and a body.

2. You must use semicolons:
   a. After the heading line
   b. After each variable declaration
   c. Between statements

3. So far, we have seen four kinds of statement:
   a. Simple statements consisting of standard procedures
   b. Compound statements, which have the form

      ```
      begin
        ⟨statement⟩;
          . . .
        ⟨statement⟩
      end
      ```

   c. **For** statements, which have the form

      ```
      for control-variable := initial-value to final-value do
        ⟨statement⟩
      ```

   d. The empty statement

4. The body of a **for** statement is itself a statement. It can be:
   a. A simple statement
   b. A compound statement
   c. Another **for** statement (a nested loop)
   d. An empty statement

5. A **for** statement whose body contains a single statement does not need a **begin-end** pair.

6. You do *not* need a semicolon:
   a. After a statement if that statement is followed by the reserved word **end**
   b. After the reserved word **end** if **end** is followed by another **end**.

7. Every program ends with a period.

3.4 Nested Loops

In the third example in the previous section, we introduced something new—a loop within a loop, or a *nested loop*.

Let's look at a more interesting example of a nested loop. We will expand PlanetIn3D so that the planet makes a total of eight identical orbits. To do this, we'll use a variable called OrbitNumber, which will be the control variable of an outer loop and will count out the orbits. The OrbitNumber loop contains the other two loops, and it makes them repeat their jobs eight times.

```
program EightOrbits;
 var
  PlanetPos,OrbitNumber : integer;
begin
 for OrbitNumber := 1 to 8 do
  begin
   for PlanetPos := 0 to 200 do
    begin
     paintcircle(PlanetPos,PlanetPos,PlanetPos div 5);
     invertcircle(PlanetPos,PlanetPos,PlanetPos div 5)
    end;
   for PlanetPos := 200 downto 0 do
    begin
     paintcircle(PlanetPos,PlanetPos,PlanetPos div 5);
     invertcircle(PlanetPos,PlanetPos,PlanetPos div 5)
    end
  end
end.
```

Program EightOrbits has *two* variables. Note how they are declared. PlanetPos and OrbitNumber are separated by a comma. They could also be declared like this:

```
var
 PlanetPos : integer;
 OrbitNumber : integer;
```

Either way, you have to put in a colon before the word *integer*. But the reserved word **var** can appear only once in the declaration part of a program.

When **program** EightOrbits is executed, the outer loop starts up first. OrbitNumber starts with the value 1, and then the two **for** statements in the body of the outer loop are executed. After the first inner **for** statement goes through 200 iterations, the second inner **for** statement does its 200 iterations. This completes one repetition of the body of the outer **for** statement.

Now OrbitNumber is advanced from 1 to 2, and the inner **for** statements are executed again. This pattern repeats 8 times before the outer loop is over and execution terminates.

EXERCISE 3   What do these nested loops print?

a. for Number := 1 **to** 4 **do**
   for StatementNumber := 1 **to** 50 **do**
    writeln('Polly want a cracker?');

b. for FirstNumber := 1 **to** 2 **do**
   for NextNumber := 10 **to** 12 **do**
    writeln(FirstNumber * SecondNumber);
   Answer: 10, 11, 12, 20, 22, 24 printed in a column ▬

_____ 3.5 **Constants** _____

In Pascal, a *constant* is a quantity that is fixed throughout the program. Sometimes it is useful to give this kind of fixed quantity a name. For example, in **program PlanetIn3D**, the width of the standard Drawing window is fixed at 200. We can give the number 200 a name: WindowWidth.

```pascal
program PlanetIn3D;
 const
  WindowWidth = 200; {A CONSTANT DEFINITION}
 var
  PlanetPos : integer;
begin
 for PlanetPos := 0 to WindowWidth do
  begin
   paintcircle(PlanetPos,PlanetPos,PlanetPos div 5);
   invertcircle(PlanetPos,PlanetPos,PlanetPos div 5)
  end;
 for PlanetPos := WindowWidth downto 0 do
  begin
   paintcircle(PlanetPos,PlanetPos,PlanetPos div 5);
   invertcircle(PlanetPos,PlanetPos,PlanetPos div 5)
  end
end.
```

Constants are defined in the declaration part of the program. Constant definitions must appear immediately after the program heading and before the variable declarations. Each definition must end with a semicolon.

Constants are useful for several reasons. First of all, remember the vacation test: Imagine yourself taking a look at **program** PlanetIn3D next fall after your summer vacation. When you've been away from the computer for a few months, do you think you will remember what 200 stands for? Maybe. But if you replace 200 in the body with the constant WindowWidth, the meaning of the number will be absolutely clear.

When we use constants to clarify what certain numbers mean, we say we are using them to *document* the program. A well-named constant often eliminates the need for a comment.

You can change a program more easily if the program has been written using constants. Here is **program** Cartoon redone, using a list of constants that explains all the numerical values in the program.

```
program NewCartoon;
 const
   LineHeight = 100;
   Radius = 20;
   LeftWall = 0;
   RightWall = 200;
 var
   Position : integer;
begin
 writeln('The First Cartoon!');
 drawline(LeftWall,LineHeight,RightWall,LineHeight);
 for Position := (LeftWall + Radius) to (RightWall - Radius) do
  begin
    paintcircle(Position,(LineHeight - Radius),Radius);
    invertcircle(Position,(LineHeight - Radius),Radius)
  end
end.
```

Now suppose you want to roll a ball of radius 40 along a line 80 units from the top of this screen. You can do this simply by changing Radius to 40 and LineHeight to 80. (See Figure 3.3.)

EXERCISE 4   Add the constant definitions we have just presented to your version of **program** Cartoon. Now do the following:

a. Roll a ball of radius 30 along a line of height 175.

b. Roll a ball of radius 45 along a line of height 195. ▬

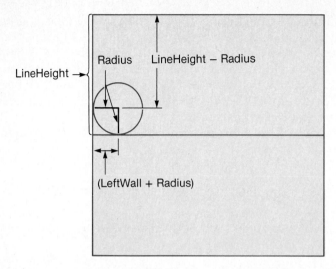

Figure 3.3 Position (the horizontal position of the center of the circle) starts at (LeftWall + Radius) and ends up at (RightWall − Radius). The vertical position of the center of the circle is always at (LineHeight − Radius).

3.6 Interactive Programs

Now we are going to show you how to write a kind of program that's much more exciting than any you have seen before: an *interactive* program. When you run an interactive program, you give the computer information while the program is running, and this information affects what the program does. Let's see how this works by transforming **program** Explode from Chapter 1 into an interactive program called **program** Blowup.

While **program** Blowup is running, it will stop and ask for a value for the speed of the explosion. After you type this value in and press the return key, the program resumes execution, exploding the circle on the screen at the speed you requested. Each time you run it, you can make the explosion happen at a different speed.

```
program Blowup;
  var
    Speed,Radius : integer;
begin
  writeln('Type in speed of explosion, an integer from 1 to 100.');
  readln(Speed);
  for Radius := 1 to (100 div Speed) do
    paintcircle(100,100,Radius * Speed)
end.
```

The program works this way. First the writeln statement prints the following message in the Text window.

```
Type in speed of explosion, an integer from 1 to 100.
```

This message is called a *prompt*. Now the Macintosh comes to the *readln* statement.

```
readln(Speed);
```

At this point, the integer variable Speed has a location assigned to it in memory, but that location is empty: Speed is undefined. When the Macintosh reaches the *readln* statement, program execution stops and waits for you to type an integer value at the keyboard. As you type in a value, the number appears in the Text window underneath the prompt:

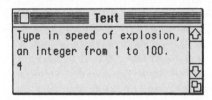

When you press the return key, the *readln* statement copies or *reads* the value you've typed into Speed's location in memory. Speed now has this value.

Then program execution resumes and the **for** loop is executed a number of times equal to 100 **div** Speed. If you type in a speed of 4, the **for** loop is executed 25 times; during each iteration the radius of the exploding circle grows by 4.

Before every *readln* statement, you should always have a *writeln* statement to serve as a prompt. The prompt should be a complete sentence and should state as clearly as possible what the person using the program should type. When you run the program, this *writeln* instruction prints a message in the Text window telling you what sort of value to type in.

The next point is very important. The *readln* statement supplies the program with a value for the input variable. You *must* place the *readln* statement *before* any statement in the program that uses the input variable, so that the variable will have a value. If you put the *readln* statement *after* an instruction containing the input variable, your program won't work properly. Take this program, for example:

```
program BadExplode;
 var
  Radius,Speed : integer;
begin
 writeln('Type in speed of explosion, an integer from 1 to 100');
 for Radius := 1 to (100 div Speed) do
  paintcircle(100,100,Radius * Speed);
 readln(Speed)
end.
```

Program BadExplode will behave strangely. First the Macintosh sets aside a location in memory for the variable Speed. Then the **for** loop is executed, but because you haven't supplied a value for Speed yet, the variable holds some arbitrary value and the program runs unpredictably.

Observing the Readln Statement

To see more clearly how *readln* works, type in **program** Blowup, bring up the Observe window, and then type Speed in the upper-right box. Now insert a stop next to the **for** statement, and run the program using Go. The program will prompt you for a value. Type one in. Then execution will resume and the program will immediately run into the stop. When this happens, you will see in the Observe window the number you supplied as the value of the variable Speed.

EXERCISE 5   What does this program do? Which statements are the prompts? Will the program run if the last statement in the body is moved to the beginning of the body? Why or why not?

```
program AddNumbers;
  var
    FirstNumber,SecondNumber : integer;
  begin
  writeln('Give me a number.');
  readln(FirstNumber);
  writeln('Give me another number.');
  readln(SecondNumber);
  writeln(FirstNumber + SecondNumber)
  end. ▄
```

Program Yoyo

Program Yoyo drops a yo-yo on a string from the top of the Drawing window and then pulls it back in (see Figure 3.4). The yo-yo is a flickering circle and the string is a line. The program does this yo-yoing a number of times equal to YoyoCount. YoyoCount has a value that you supply interactively. This value is the upper limit of the outer **for** loop, and it determines the number of times yo-yoing is done. In one iteration of the outer loop, the first inner loop lowers the yo-yo and the second inner loop raises it.

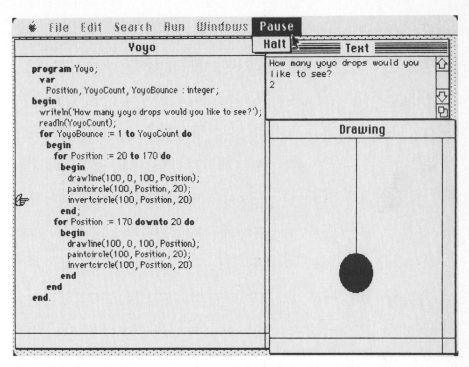

Figure 3.4 **Program** Yoyo and its output in the middle of execution.

Program VerticalLines

Suppose we want to write a program that will draw any number of vertical lines in the Drawing window. To do this, we need to read in the values for two different variables, which we will call TotalLines and Separation. We can read in both of these variables with one *readln* statement.

```
program VerticalLines;
 var
   TotalLines,Separation,LineNumber : integer;
begin
 writeln('Type in the number of lines you want to draw.');
 writeln('Then type an integer value for the separation between lines.');
 readln(TotalLines,Separation);
 for LineNumber := 1 to TotalLines do
   drawline(Separation * LineNumber,0,Separation * LineNumber,200)
end.
```

First the Macintosh will prompt you with the following message:

```
Type in the number of lines you want to draw and separation.
Then type an integer value for the separation between lines.
```

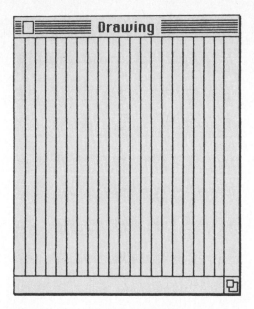

Figure 3.5   The output of **program** VerticalLines.

In response, you must type in two integers separated by a space. The first value gives the number of lines you want drawn. The second value tells the computer how far apart you want the lines to be. When you press the return key, program execution resumes. The **for** statement draws the picture, using the two values you've supplied interactively to determine the layout of the picture. (See Figure 3.5.)

3.7 More on Output—Fields and Field Widths

Now that you are acquainted with one of Pascal's input statements, *readln*, it's time to learn more about Pascal's output statement *writeln* and its companion instruction, *write*.

Just as *readln* can handle more than one input, *writeln* can handle more than one output. The statement

```
writeln('The tallest tree in the world is a ', 367,' foot redwood')
```

prints in the Text window

```
The tallest tree in the world is a    367 foot redwood
```

The *writeln* statement has three regions, or *fields*, that are separated by commas. The first region is a phrase in quotation marks. It is sometimes called a *literal field*, because the single quotation marks command the Macintosh to print literally (that is, print exactly to the letter) what is between the quotes. The middle field holds an actual number, 367, and this is what is printed. The last field is another literal field.

The output is a little peculiar, however: There is
and the "367."

```
The tallest tree in the world is a      367
```

The gap in the middle field appears because MacPa
when it prints out an integer, and it *right-justifies*
field. That is, it prints the number as far over to tl
spaces allotted to it.

If you don't like the gap, you can control the number of spaces allotted to a
field by inserting a colon followed by a positive integer. The statement

```
writeln('The tallest tree in the world is a ', 367 : 3,' foot redwood')
```

lays out the line this way

```
The tallest tree in the world is a 367 foot redwood
```

The value 3 following the colon determines the *field width* allotted to 367. Now,
instead of using the automatic or *default* width of 8, the program uses the field
width we have specified: 3.

What happens if we specify a field width of 1?

```
writeln('The tallest tree in the world is a ', 367 : 1,' foot redwood')
```

Now we have requested just 1 space, but of course the number 367 requires 3
spaces. So the Macintosh improvises: It takes the 1 space you've given it and,
when it "realizes" that it needs 2 more, it just takes them. So again you get

```
The tallest tree in the world is a 367 foot redwood
```

Now let's look at the field-width specification in **program** HeightConversion.

```
program HeightConversion;
 var
  Feet,Inches : integer;
begin
 writeln('Type in your height in feet and inches.');
 readln(Feet,Inches);
 writeln('Your height is',12 * Feet + Inches : 3,' inches.')
end.
```

Program HeightConversion reads in your height in feet and inches and
prints this quantity out in inches. If you are 6 feet, 6 inches tall, after the prompt
you must type 6 6, and the program will print out

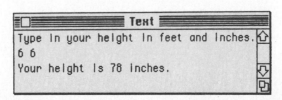

The field-width value 3 in the middle field leaves 3 spaces for your height in inches. Unless you are a giant, your height in inches will require only 2 digits. But we need the extra space because we've left no space after the word *is* in the first field to keep the two fields apart.

There is a better way to separate them, however: Leave a space at the end of the literal field after *is* and specify the exact field width that you need.

```
writeln('Height is ',12 * Feet + Inches : 2,' inches.')
```

This method is better because it leaves no chance that the first two fields will ever run together.

EXERCISE 6

Examine **program** CheckFieldWidth. Now decide which output belongs to **program** CheckFieldWidth, (a) or (b)? How can you alter **program** CheckFieldWidth to get the other output?

```
program CheckFieldWidth;
 var
  Number : integer;
begin
 for Number := 1 to 5 do
  begin
   writeln(Number : 5);
   writeln(Number : Number)
  end
end.
```

a.

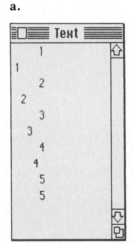

b.

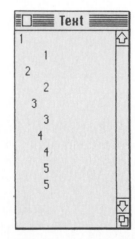

One last feature of *writeln*: If you use it with no fields—that is, with nothing after it—it causes a blank line to be printed. So **program** Numbers prints numbers on every other line, in a column.

```
program Number;
 var
  Number : integer;
begin
 for Number := 1 to 3 do
  begin
   writeln(Number);
   writeln
  end
end.
```

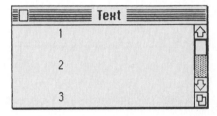

3.8 The Write Statement

The *write* statement works exactly like the *writeln* statement, except that two consecutive *write* statements print their output on the same line. For example, the two instructions

```
write('Tuna on rye, ');
write('hold the mayo.')
```

print this:

```
Tuna on rye, hold the mayo.
```

But with the two instructions

```
writeln('Tuna on rye, ');
write('hold the mayo.')
```

you get

```
Tuna on rye,
hold the mayo.
```

EXERCISE 7   What does each of the following statements print? After you decide, check your answers in the Instant window.

    a. `writeln('Be there ','or ','be square.')`

    b. `write('Be ','there ');`
       `writeln('or ','be square.')`

    c. `write('Be there ');`
       `writeln('or');`
       `write('be square.')` ■

Now that you know how to use fields and how to specify field widths, you are ready to tackle real numbers.

3.9 Real Numbers

A number with a decimal point (such as 98.6, 19.95, and −0.04) is a *real number*. Temperature, money, miles per gallon, percentages, batting averages—these quantities are ordinarily represented as real numbers with decimal points.

In Pascal, real numbers belong to a separate type called *real*, which is distinct from the type called *integer*.

Because Pascal is an important language for scientists and engineers, it uses *scientific notation* as the standard way of writing real numbers. In scientific notation, 93,000,000 is written

$$9.3 \times 10^7$$

A number in scientific notation has two parts. The first part consists of a number with a decimal point, such as 9.3. It is usually written with just one digit to the left of the decimal point. The second part is 10 raised to some power, such as 7.

To write a large number such as 93,000,000 in scientific notation, first make it a real number by adding a decimal point followed by a zero: 93,000,000.0. Now there are eight digits to the left of the decimal point. Move the decimal point to the *left* until only one digit remains to its left. Each step to the left divides the number by 10, so you must multiply by 10 for every place you move the decimal point. In the number 93,000,000.0, you move the decimal point seven places to the left.

So, to keep the value of the number the same, you multiply 9.3 by 10^7. This gives the number in scientific notation: 9.3×10^7.

For a decimal fraction such as .00025, move the decimal point to the *right* until one non-zero digit appears on the left:

$$. \underset{1\quad 2\quad 3\quad 4}{0\ \ 0\ \ 0\ \ 2}.5$$

Now count the number of places you have moved the decimal point, but this time use a *negative* exponent instead of a positive exponent. Because you have moved the decimal point four places to the right, .00025 in scientific notation is 2.5×10^{-4}.

In Pascal, scientific notation looks a little different because the computer can't print powers, which appear slightly above the line of type. Pascal uses the letter e, which stands for "exponent," followed by a plus or a minus sign, followed by a power:

```
9.3e+7
2.5e-4
```

Here are some numbers in scientific notation, with their familiar equivalents.

Quantity	Decimal Number	Scientific Notation	Pascal Notation
Hairs on head (blond)	90,000	9.0×10^4	9.0e+4 or 9e+4
Hairs on head (black)	110,000	1.1×10^5	1.1e+5 or 11e+4
Coldest recorded temperature in Canada (Snag, Yukon)	−63.0	-6.3×10	−6.3e+1
Average man's daily whisker growth in inches	.015	1.5×10^{-2}	1.5e−2 or 15e−3

Pascal requires that every real number have either a decimal point or an e. When Pascal expects a real number, you can write the number in various ways. Pascal will accept 110000.0, 1.1e5, 1.1e + 5, 11.0e4, or even 11e4. However, you have to have a digit on *both sides* of a decimal point. The numbers 110000. and .367 won't work. And one more thing. Other symbols such as dollar signs and commas are also not permitted: $64,000.00 is unacceptable.

EXERCISE 8   **a.** Which of the following numbers are legal Pascal real numbers?

123.4	−000.004
−1,234.5	−0.0
−.26	$19.95

Answer: The numbers 123.4, −000.004, and −0.0 are legal.

b. Write each of the following as a Pascal real number.

$19.95	.342
−126	1/4
0	396,000 ▬

_____3.10 **Writing Programs with Real Numbers** _____

Now let's use real numbers in a program.

```
program CircleArea;
 const
  Pi = 3.14159;
 var
  Radius : real;
begin
 writeln('How long is the radius? Type in a real number.');
 readln(Radius);
 writeln('The area of the circle is: ',Pi * (Radius * Radius) : 5 : 1)
end.
```

Program CircleArea is interactive. When you run it, the *writeln* statement prints a prompt asking you to specify the value of the radius. Then you type in how big the radius is. When you press the return key, the program reads in the value for the variable Radius, and then it calculates the area according to this familiar formula:

```
Area = π * Radius²
```

The variable Radius has type *real*. This means that the value it holds must be a real number. When the *writeln* statement prints the prompt, you are supposed to type a Pascal real number, such as 15.0 or 2e4.

What happens if you type an integer? This will work, too. Pascal automatically converts your input to type real and stores it in real number form in the location in memory that is set aside for the variable Radius.

Note that the constant Pi is written without a type declaration. Because its defined value, 3.14159, includes a decimal point, Pascal knows that Pi is a *real* constant. In Pascal the type of a constant is *never* declared.

When you run the program, you may not like the answer
will be in Pascal's form of scientific notation. If you type in 10.0 a
the program will print 3.1e+2 instead of 314.159. You don't get the an
3.14159e+2, because MacPascal's scientific notation shows you only one digit to the right of the decimal point.

If you don't want scientific notation, you *can* get the program to print out 314.159. You do this by changing the *writeln* instruction.

3.11 Getting Around Scientific Notation

The number 314.159 is 7 characters long: 6 digits and the decimal point. So, when we print out this number, we want a field width of at least 7. But it's not enough just to include " : 7" in the *writeln* statement. We also need to specify that we want 3 digits to the right of the decimal point. These two numbers, 7 and 3, are the figures we need to make the *writeln* statement print the area of a circle the way we want it.

```
writeln('Area of circle is ',Pi * (Radius * Radius) : 7 : 3 )
```

The value after the first colon tells how many spaces to allow for the number—including the digits, the decimal place, and a sign if the number is negative. The number after the second colon tells how many digits to show to the right of the decimal point.

If Pascal runs out of space, it will override your directive and use as much space as it needs, the way it does when you specify too narrow a field width for integers. For example, if Radius equals 1000.0, the foregoing *writeln* statement will print

```
Area of circle is 3141590.000
```

Pascal follows your instructions and shows 3 digits to the right of the decimal point. Then it goes ahead and uses 11 spaces for the answer, although you specified a field width of only 7.

EXERCISE 9 Give *writeln* statements for printing the values in a and b.

a. 5/7. Show 10 places to the right of the decimal point.

b. 100/7. Show 6 places to the right of the decimal point.

c. Use two fields in a *writeln* statement that will print: "My bucket of night crawlers costs $2.98" ▬

3.12 Arithmetic with Real Numbers

Arithmetic with real numbers is almost the same as arithmetic with integers. The operators +, −, and * work for real numbers in just the same way they work for integers. The only difference is that the answer is always a real number. This is true even for an expression such as 3.14 − 0.14, which gives a value of 3.00, not the integer 3.

You must use the conventional division symbol / to divide with real numbers. Division with / gives familiar answers: 1.0/4.0 = 0.25. The operator **div** won't work with real numbers: Try (1.4 **div** 7), and see what happens.

When you have a complicated expression like

    2.0 + 6.0/3.0 = 2.0 + 2.0 = 4.0

the arithmetic operators follow the rules for doing arithmetic with integers. Multiplication and division are done first in order from left to right; then addition and subtraction are done in order.

Program CrossCountryTrip

To see how arithmetic with real numbers works in a program, look at **program** CrossCountryTrip (see Figure 3.6).

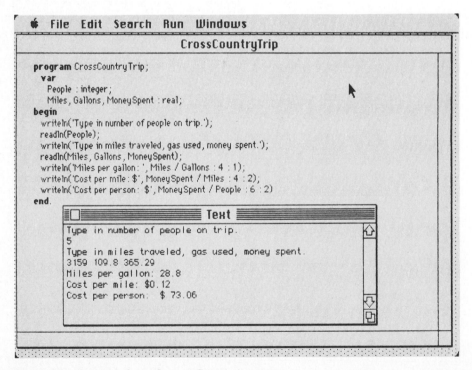

Figure 3.6   Program CrossCountryTrip and output.

Program CrossCountryTrip is an interactive program that calculates trip statistics for a cross-country trip you take with friends. First you type in the number of people on the trip who are sharing the costs. Then you type the distance traveled, the number of gallons of gasoline used, and the total amount of expenses. The program calculates and prints out miles per gallon, cost per mile, and cost per person.

When you type in the input values, you should separate them with a space, although *readln* will also accept a carriage return as a separator between input values.

Note that we have entered an integer—3159—for the miles traveled in the sample run. When the Macintosh sees this value, it immediately converts it to type *real*, because the variable Miles is declared to be of this type.

Now look at the expression MoneySpent/People. This is called a *mixed-mode* expression, because the types are mixed: MoneySpent is type *real*, and People is type *integer*. You can mix *real* and *integer* types in arithmetic expressions, and Pascal will convert integer values to *real* for you as it evaluates the expression. In the sample run, first Pascal converts 365.29/5 to 365.29/5.0. Then it does the division.

3.13 Program HockeyScore—Planning an Interactive Program

Suppose we want to keep track of the wins, ties, and losses of our hockey team, the Sharks. In North America hockey scoring usually works this way:

win: 2 points

tie: 1 point

loss: 0 points

Our program will read in the wins, ties, and losses for the Sharks. Then it will calculate the number of points accumulated, the percentage of games won, and the percentage of games won or tied.

We'll write **program** HockeyScore by adding some new ideas to our thinking, planning, coding, and testing and debugging scheme.

Thinking

First we must formulate the problem: Given figures for wins, ties, and losses, we want to calculate and print out three things: total points, percentage of wins, and percentage of wins and ties.

When we write an interactive program, we can usually organize our thinking around the following general format:

1. Read in the input data.
2. Make some calculations and print the output.

For input we will need values for number of wins, ties, and losses. For output we want a value for the number of points, as well as for percentage of games won and percentage of games won or tied.

To calculate the number of points, we will use the expression

points = 2 × wins + ties

We can calculate the percentage of games won by using the formula

Percentage won = wins/(wins + ties + losses) × 100

To get the percentage of games won or tied, we'll use

Percentage won or tied = (wins + ties)/(wins + ties + losses) × 100

Before going on, it's a good idea to collect all this information, and some other information besides, in a chart called a *data table*. A data table lists the input variables, the output variables, the program variables (variables needed for calculations and loops), the constants, the loops, and any formulas to be used in a program.

_____ DATA TABLE _____

Input Variables	Output Variables	Program Variables
Wins, Ties, Losses	none	none
Constants	**Loops**	
none	none	

Formulas
points = 2 × wins + ties
percentage won = wins/(wins + ties + losses) × 100
percentage won or tied = (wins + ties)/(wins + ties + losses) × 100

We have included space for other variables, constants, and loops in our data table, even though there aren't any in this program. In the next example we'll see a more complex data table.

It's a good idea to save your data table and keep it with the printout of your program. It will help you figure out how your program works when you shake the dust off it next year.

Planning

In the planning step, we will use a mixture of English and Pascal to state roughly what the program will do. We won't be concerned if we haven't figured out how to do all of the steps we are planning. We'll get to that later.

For this interactive program we can start with a general plan:

1. Read the input data.
2. Calculate and print the output data.

Now we can refine the plan and turn it into an algorithm:

1. Read the wins.
2. Read the ties.
3. Read the losses.
4. Print out the total points.
5. Print out the percentage won.
6. Print out the percentage won or tied.

Each of these steps is straightforward; we can move on to the coding step.

Coding

In this step we convert the pieces of our final plan into Pascal statements. For the steps that involve reading in values, we use a prompt followed by a *readln* statement. For the steps that involve printing a result, we use a *writeln* statement.

```pascal
program HockeyScore;
{READS IN WINS, TIES, AND LOSSES.}
{PRINTS TOTAL POINTS, PERCENT WON, AND PERCENT WON OR TIED.}
  var
   Wins,Ties,Losses : integer;
begin
 writeln('Type in games won.');
 readln(Wins);
 writeln('Type in games tied.');
 readln(Ties);
 writeln('Type in losses.');
 readln(Losses);
 writeln('Total points: ',2 * Wins + Ties : 5);
 writeln('Percentage of games won: ',
         Wins/(Wins + Ties + Losses) * 100 : 5 : 1,'%');
 writeln('Percentage won or tied: ',
         (Wins + Ties)/(Wins + Ties + Losses) * 100 : 5 : 1,'%')
 end.
```

Testing and Debugging

Always test an interactive program by running it with a variety of inputs. Then check your answers with pencil and paper. For **program** HockeyScore, try supplying numbers that could be actual numbers of wins, ties, and losses. It's also a good idea to try *exceptional* input values, such as 0 or even negative numbers.

3.14 Program Targets—Donuts and Bull's-eyes

Program Targets draws pictures using the *invertcircle* command. Two *invertcircle* instructions with the same center but different radii create a pattern like a donut. For example, the two instructions

```
invertcircle(100,100,25);
invertcircle(100,100,50)
```

print out this picture:

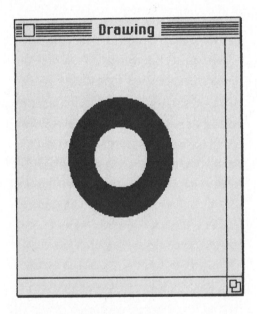

And three *invertcircle* commands, all with the same center, give you a pattern that looks like a target. The three instructions

```
invertcircle(100,100,25);
invertcircle(100,100,50);
invertcircle(100,100,75)
```

produce the picture at the top of page 107.

The program we are going to write will draw target patterns in the Drawing window. When you run **program** Targets, you will be able to draw as many

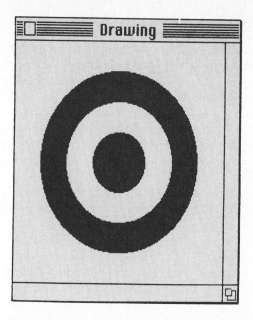

targets in the Drawing window as you like (see Figure 3.7). Again, each target will be made up of a series of concentric circles. And, in each target, each circle will be larger than the one inside it by a fixed amount. You enter data about the number of targets and the description of each target interactively.

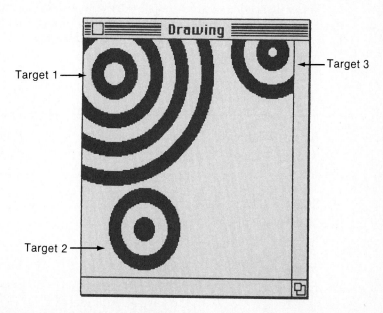

Figure 3.7 Sample output for **program** Targets. Target 2 has its center at (60,160). The BullseyeRadius is 10. There are 3 circles in the pattern, and the SizeIncrease is 12.

Thinking

Program Targets is more complicated than the other interactive programs in the chapter. A good way to approach a complex program is to think about it as if you are telling a story about what happens when you run the program. The story of **program** Targets goes like this:

First you read in the number of targets you want. Next, for each target, you read in information about the location of the center, the radius of the innermost circle, the size difference between successive circles, and the number of circles you want in that target. Then the program draws the target. Next you go through another cycle of reading in target specifications, and another target is drawn. This goes on until all the targets are drawn.

Let's see if we can use this description to fill in a data table for the program.

We won't need any output variables, because the output is all pictures. For input variables, we will use TargetCount, Hcenter, Vcenter, BullseyeRadius, SizeIncrease, and CircleCount. All are of type integer.

Program variables—the other variables in the program—are often control variables in loops. So we should try to understand looping in the program before we decide what program variables we'll need.

We'll need one loop (the main loop in the program) to gather data about a single target and then draw that target. This loop will repeat a number of times equal to TargetCount; TargetCount gives the total number of targets you want to draw. We'll use a variable called TargetNumber as a control variable for this loop.

We will need a second loop to draw a series of concentric circles using invertcircle. This loop will repeat a number of times equal to CircleCount, and the control variable for this loop will be CircleNumber.

Now we can prepare the data table.

―――――――――――――――――――――――― DATA TABLE ――――――――――――――――――――――――

Input Variables	Output Variables	Program Variables
TargetCount	none	TargetNumber
Hcenter		CircleNumber
Vcenter		
StartRadius		
SizeIncrease		
CircleCount		

Constants	Loops	Formulas
none	the TargetCount loop	none
	the CircleCount loop	

Planning

When you do the planning step, always start with the most general plan you are sure of. But don't get carried away! The one-step plan

    do everything

is a little *too* general to help out with the assignment that's due tomorrow. This two-step plan is more helpful:

    Read in the number of targets to be drawn
    Draw the targets

Now we're getting somewhere. The first step is ready to be coded: It consists of a prompt and a *readln* statement for the input variable TargetCount. So let's put off working on the first part and move on to the second part of the plan.

How many targets shall we draw? The number of them will be equal to TargetCount. So we can refine our plan to this form:

    read in TargetCount
    for TargetNumber : = 1 to TargetCount do
      draw a target

Now we need to plan how to draw a single complete target. Here's our new plan, with the "draw a target" part refined:

    read in TargetCount
    for TargetNumber : = 1 to TargetCount do
      read in center of circle
      read in radius of the bull's-eye
      read in size increase
      read in number of circles
        draw a target

And here is our final plan, or algorithm. Note that it is a mixture of English and Pascal.

    read in TargetCount
    for TargetNumber : = 1 to TargetCount do
      read in Center
      read in BullseyeRadius
      read in SizeIncrease
      read in CircleCount
      for CircleNumber : = 1 to CircleCount do
        draw an inverted circle

This concludes the planning session. There's one point we should emphasize, though. Planning involves much more trial and error than we have shown here. Don't get discouraged if you find you have to start over or make changes part of the way through the planning step. This happens to everyone.

Coding

Here is the program, with each part of the plan coded. Note that we made one small change from our final plan. The inner loop that draws a complete target has been changed so that it runs from 0 to CircleCount − 1. That way, the bull's-eye has a radius equal to BullseyeRadius.

Also, we have added a dotted line that will appear in the Text window before each new round of prompts for each target. This will help you notice that input for one target is over and that it is time to work on the next.

```pascal
program Targets;
{YOU READ IN HOW MANY TARGETS YOU WANT, WHERE THEIR CENTERS SHOULD}
{BE, HOW MANY CIRCLES PER TARGET, AND HOW MUCH BIGGER EACH CIRCLE}
{SHOULD BE THAN THE ONE INSIDE IT. PROGRAM PRINTS OUT TARGETS.}
  var
    Hcenter,Vcenter,SizeIncrease,BullseyeRadius : integer;
    CircleCount,CircleNumber,TargetNumber,TargetCount : integer;
begin
 {ENTER NUMBER OF TARGETS YOU WANT TO DRAW}
 writeln('How many targets do you want to draw?');
 readln(TargetCount);
 {GATHER INFORMATION ON EACH TARGET TO BE DRAWN. THEN DRAW TARGET.}
 for TargetNumber := 1 to TargetCount do
  begin
   writeln('------------');
   write('Type in values for the horizontal ');
   writeln('and vertical position of the center.');
   readln(Hcenter,Vcenter);
   writeln('Type in the starting radius.');
   readln(BullseyeRadius);
   writeln('Type in the number of circles in the target.');
   readln(CircleCount);
   writeln('Type in the increment in the size of the circles.');
   readln(SizeIncrease);
   for CircleNumber := 0 to (CircleCount - 1) do
    invertcircle(Hcenter,Vcenter,
            BullseyeRadius + CircleNumber * SizeIncrease)
  end
end.
```

Testing and Debugging

Try **program** Targets with all sorts of different inputs. There is no end to the variety of pictures you can draw with this program.

TEST YOURSELF

1. What do semicolons do?
2. Where can you leave out a semicolon?
3. When can you omit a **begin** and an **end** in a **for** loop?
4. Where do you have to use colons?
5. Where do you use the symbol : = ?
6. What is mixed-mode arithmetic?
7. Name one of Pascal's input statements.
8. What must a real number look like to be acceptable to Pascal?
9. What is the empty statement?
10. Which comes first, the *readln* statement or the prompt?

PROBLEMS

1. Examine **program** HockeyScore and list all of the simple statements, compound statements, **for** statements, and empty statements that you find.
2. What do you think Pascal will do with the following statement? Why? After deciding on your answer, try it in the Instant window and see whether you are right.

```
begin
begin
 ;;
end
end
```

3. Supply the missing semicolons for the following program, and then see whether it will run.

```
program Grid
  var
    LineNumber : integer
begin
for LineNumber := 1 to 20 do
  begin
    drawline(0,10 * LineNumber,200,10 * LineNumber)
    drawline(10 * LineNumber,0,10 * LineNumber,200)
  end
end.
```

4. Write an interactive program that reads in a baseball player's at-bats and number of hits and then computes the player's batting average.

5. There are 1760 yards in a mile and 0.9144 meters in a yard. Calculate, accurate to five decimal places, the number of meters a runner covers in a marathon: 26 miles, 385 yards. (You can do this in the Instant window.)

6. The Drawing window comes with an *electronic pen* that can be controlled by two commands, *lineto* and *moveto*. When you give the command *moveto*(15,75), you place the tip of the pen at the point (15,75) in the window. Then, if you follow the *moveto* instruction with the *lineto* instruction *lineto*(100,25), the pen moves from (15,75) to (100,25), drawing this line as it goes:

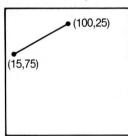

Here are some examples of *moveto* and *lineto* in action.

```
moveto(20,30);
lineto(100,190)
```

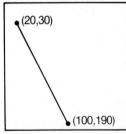

```
moveto(20,30);
lineto(100,190)
lineto(200,0)
```

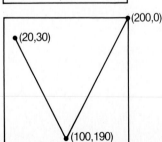

Using *moveto* and *lineto*, write a program that draws this picture:

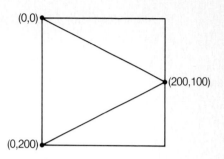

7. Now write a program that draws this picture, with the value of Vpoint supplied interactively.

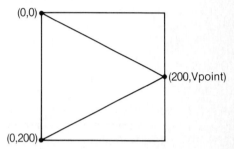

8. Write a program using *moveto* and *lineto* that draws this picture:

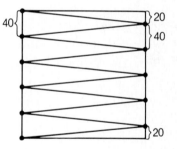

9. Which of the following are valid Pascal numbers of type real?

1.05	385
−0.003	34567.890
−3	3.0e5
3.	.943−6

10. An exam has 55 true-false questions. Write an interactive program that reads in the number of correct answers a student gets and then prints the student's percentage correct, accurate to one decimal place.

   Sample input: 48
   Output: 87.3% correct

11. Write a program that prints

1	2	3	4	5	6	7	8	9	10
2	4	6	8	10	12	14	16	18	20

12. The following loop prints out this column of numbers:

```
 4
 8
12
 5
10
15
```

```
for Number1 := Little to Big do
  for Number2 := 1 to 3 do
    writeln(Number1 * Number2)
```

What are the values of Little and Big?

13. What does this nested **for** loop print?

```
for Number1 := 7 to 9 do
  for Number2 := 3 downto 1 do
    writeln(Number1 * Number2);
```

14. Write a program that prints out the full 10×10 multiplication table. *Hint*: Use a nested loop. *Another hint*: Use the *writeln* statement

```
writeln
```

with no numbers after it to space the lines in your table.

15. Write a program that draws this picture:

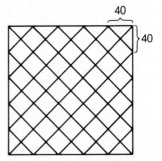

16. Redo the program in Problem 15, but this time supply the spacing between the lines interactively.

17. Look at the following program and its output. Why do the last two entries spill over on the right?

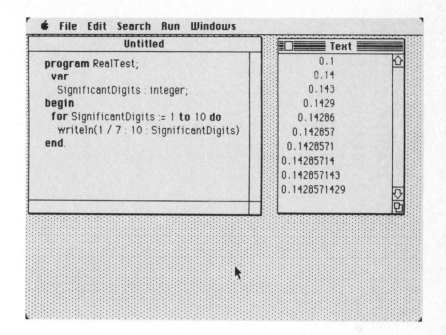

Assignment Statements and More on Looping

4

Looping is one of the most important actions in programming. So far we have worked only with the **for** loop, but Pascal has two others: the *while loop* and the *repeat-until loop*. These looping commands are more versatile than the **for** loop. But they require a new kind of statement—the *assignment* statement. We'll talk about assignment statements first. An assignment statement allows you to change the value of a variable.

4.1 Assignment Statements

The time has come for another look at variables. Remember that, when you declare a variable, you instruct the Macintosh to choose a location in memory where the variable's value will be stored. Let's keep this in mind as we look at the following program. It contains a new kind of simple statement called an *assignment statement*.

```
program AssignOne;
 var
  Number : integer;
begin
 Number := 5;
 writeln(Number)
end.
```

A colon directly followed by an equal sign makes up the assignment symbol, and the instruction

```
Number := 5
```

is an assignment statement. In words, it says, "Number is assigned the value 5" or "Number becomes 5." When Pascal translates the declaration for Number into machine language, Number is given a location in memory. Then, when the assignment statement is executed, the value 5 is copied into Number's location. So, when you run the program, it prints 5 in the Text window.

Here is a program with two assignment statements:

```
program AssignTwo;
 var
  Number : integer;
begin
 Number := 3;
 Number := Number + 3;
 writeln(Number)
end.
```

This program prints 6. First, the assignment statement

```
Number := 3
```

is executed, and a 3 is copied into Number's location in memory. Then the assignment statement

```
Number := Number + Number
```

is executed. The right side of an assignment statement is always evaluated first. So the value of Number + 3 is calculated, yielding a value of 6. Pascal calculates this sum in the central processing unit (CPU). When the calculation on the right is complete, the Macintosh transfers the answer to Number's location in memory. As this happens, the old value of Number—that is, 3—is written over and destroyed.

Finally, the *writeln* statement is executed. The value of Number is now 6, and that is what the Macintosh prints.

The statement

```
Number := Number + 3
```

may look strange to you because it seems to violate the rules of algebra. After all, the equation

Number = Number + 3

makes little sense. But there is a big difference between the equal symbol and the assignment symbol. In algebra, the symbol = means that the value on the left side equals the value on the right side.

In Pascal, the assignment symbol := stands for an action command. It says, "First calculate the value of the expression on the right side of the statement. Then copy this value into the location in memory set aside for the variable named on the left side." So it really *isn't* illogical to write Number := Number + 3.

EXERCISE 1   Before you read on, try to figure out what the next two toy programs do. Make sure you understand how to get the right answers.

a. **program** ToyOne;
   var
    Number : integer;
   begin
    Number := 3;
    Number := Number + Number + 10;
    writeln(Number)
   end.

Answer: 16

b. **program** ToyTwo;
   var
    Number1,Number2 : integer;
   begin
    Number1 := 10;
    Number2 := 100;
    Number2 := Number1 + Number2;
    Number2 := Number2 + 1;
    writeln(Number2)
   end.

Answer: 111 ▬

4.2 The Staircase Problem

Now let's write a more intriguing program. This one uses assignment statements and a **for** loop.

Suppose your Uncle Harold decides to build a staircase out of cinder blocks. The stairs will be 6 steps high and 1 block wide. How many blocks will he need? Starting from the top, step 1 has 1 block, step 2 has 2 blocks, and so on. So the loop

```
for StepNumber := 1 to 6 do
   writeln(StepNumber);
```

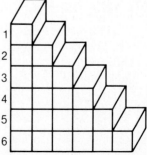

reports the number of blocks in each step: 1-2-3-4-5-6. The problem asks us to add these numbers, which we can do as follows.

First we'll create a variable called BlockCount that will keep track of the number of blocks Harold needs. We'll give it an initial value of 0:

```
BlockCount := 0;
```

Then, in each iteration of the loop, we'll add to the current value of BlockCount the value of StepNumber during that iteration:

```
BlockCount := 0;
for StepNumber := 1 to 6 do
 BlockCount := BlockCount + StepNumber;
```

These statements, which we've included in **program** BlocksNeeded, solve Harold's problem.

```
program BlocksNeeded;
{CALCULATES NUMBER OF BLOCKS NEEDED TO BUILD}
{A SIX-STEP STAIRCASE, ONE BLOCK WIDE.}
 var
  StepNumber,BlockCount : integer;
begin
 BlockCount := 0;
 for StepNumber := 1 to 6 do
  BlockCount := BlockCount + StepNumber;
 writeln('Harold needs ',BlockCount : 2,' blocks.')
end.
```

Note how the value of BlockCount accumulates. It starts at 0. Then, each time through the loop, the number of blocks in the next step—StepNumber—is added to its old value. The sixth time through, the loop is over and the *writeln* statement prints

```
Harold needs 21 blocks.
```

The assignment statement BlockCount := 0 is very important. It *initializes,* or gives an initial value to, the variable BlockCount. If we had left this instruction out, the program might behave strangely the first time through the **for** loop, when it encounters

```
BlockCount := BlockCount + StepNumber
```

This is so because Pascal tries to evaluate the expression on the right side first. Because you haven't initialized BlockCount, the variable will hold some arbitrary value, and the program will be executed with this value as BlockCount's starting value.

Suppose Harold had put the staircase on a 12-block base, like this:

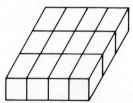

We would have initialized the variable BlockCount with the assignment statement

```
BlockCount := 12
```

EXERCISE 2   What does each of the following programs print?

a. program NumbersOne;
   var
     Number,PrintNumber : integer;
   begin
    PrintNumber := 1;
    for Number := 1 **to** 4 **do**
     begin
      writeln(PrintNumber);
      PrintNumber := PrintNumber + 1
     end
   end.

Answer: 1-2-3-4 in a column

b. program NumbersTwo;
   var
     Number,PrintNumber : integer;
   begin
    PrintNumber := 1;
    for Number := 1 **to** 4 **do**
     begin
      writeln(PrintNumber);
      PrintNumber := PrintNumber + 2
     end
   end.

Answer: 1-3-5-7 in a column

c. program NumbersThree;
   var
     Number,PrintNumber : integer;
   begin
    PrintNumber := 1;
    for Number := 1 **to** 4 **do**
     begin
      writeln(PrintNumber);
      PrintNumber := 2 * PrintNumber
     end
   end.

Answer: 1-2-4-8 in a column ▬

Three Assignment Statement Restrictions

There are three important restrictions on assignment statements that you should know about.

1. *The left side of an assignment statement must always be a single variable.* So a statement such as

   ```
   Number1 + Number2 := 3
   ```

   is not valid. Remember that an assignment statement copies a value into a variable's assigned location in memory. But in this statement there is no place to make the copy, because there are two variables on the left.

2. *An assignment statement must be consistent with respect to the types of the variables in it.* If Number is of type *integer*, then

   ```
   Number := 3.14
   ```

   will cause an error, because you are trying to copy a real number into a space reserved for an integer. *Note:* You *can* assign an integer to a real variable. Pascal will convert the integer value to type *real* for you before the assignment is done.

3. *Assignment statements cannot be used to change the value of the control variable in a **for** loop.* The following loop, for example, is invalid, and a program that uses it won't work.

   ```
   for Number := 1 to 5 do
     begin
       writeln(Number);
       Number := Number + 2
     end
   ```

4.3 Back to Money—Compound Interest

Now that we know how to use assignment statements, we can write some interesting programs about money. Let's start with a program that calculates compound interest.

Suppose you have $100.00 in a bank account that pays 9% interest, compounded yearly. At the end of 1 year you will have your $100.00 principal plus $9.00 in interest, for a total of $109.00:

$$109.00 = 100.00 + (100.00 \times 0.09)$$

Using the variables Amount and Rate we can convert this equation into a Pascal assignment statement. This statement is the key instruction in the compound interest problem that's coming up:

```
Amount := Amount + (Amount * Rate)
```

amount after one year   starting amount

If Rate is 0.19 and Amount has the value 100.00 before the statement is executed, then the value of Amount after execution is 109.00—the sum in your bank account after 1 year.

If the value of Amount is equal to 109.00 and the statement is executed again, the new value of Amount will be 118.81—the sum in your bank account after 2 years.

Now let's look at program Interest, which is interactive and will calculate how much money will accumulate in your account, given any principal, any interest rate, and any number of years.

```
program Interest;
{YOU TYPE IN PRINCIPAL, INTEREST RATE, AND YEARS IN BANK.}
{PROGRAM CALCULATES TOTAL MONEY ACCUMULATED.}
  var
    Years,TotalYears : integer;
    Principal,Amount,Rate : real;
begin
  writeln('Type in principal,interest rate and years in bank.');
  readln(Principal,Rate,TotalYears);
  Amount := Principal;
  for Years := 1 to TotalYears do
    Amount := Amount + (Amount * Rate);
  writeln('Total amount accumulated: $',Amount : 6 : 2)
end.
```

First the *readln* statement reads in values for Principal, Rate, and TotalYears. Then the statement

```
Amount := Principal;
```

is executed. It initializes the variable Amount to the value of Principal, the starting sum in your account. The loop

```
for Years := 1 to TotalYears do
  Amount := Amount + (Amount * Rate);
```

does the real work in the program. Each year, the value of Amount is increased by (Amount * Rate), and this accumulation goes on for a number of years equal to TotalYears.

Let's suppose that you type in a principal of 100.00, a rate of 0.09, and a total of 5 years. The **for** statement will loop 5 times, and the value of Amount will go successively from 100.00 to 109.00, from 109.00 to 118.81, and so on, up to 153.86.

If you want to find out how to calculate interest compounded monthly and quarterly see Problem 8 at the end of the chapter.

The Double-Your-Money Problem

If you put a sum of money in a bank account at 9% interest, compounded yearly, how many years will it take to double your money?

It is possible to solve this problem using **program** Interest, if you're willing to run the program repeatedly. Each time you run it, you'll have to read a larger number into TotalYears, until you reach a year when TotalAmount exceeds 2 * Principal. But this is awkward and time-consuming. And there's a better way, which involves using a more powerful looping command called the *while state-ment*.

4.4 The While Statement

Let's start with some simple examples that use the **while** statement. We'll come back to the double-your-money problem a little later. First, here's a program that prints a column of numbers.

```
program FirstWhile;
 var
  Number : integer;
begin
 Number := 1;
 while (Number <= 4) do
  begin
   writeln(Number);
   Number := Number + 1
  end
end.
```

This program contains a **while** statement and the symbol < = . This symbol means "less than or equal to," and it is Pascal's way of writing the mathematics symbol ≤.

The **while** statement in **program** FirstWhile includes a *test* part:

```
(Number <= 4)
```

and a *body*:

```
begin
 writeln(Number);
 Number := Number + 1
end
```

The test part is either true or false. The control line

```
while (Number <= 4) do
```

tells the computer, "Keep looping while the test is true." The test becomes false when the value of Number is greater than 4.

When you run the program, first the assignment statement initializes the variable Number to 1.

```
Number := 1
```

Then comes the **while** statement. Its test, (Number <= 4), is evaluated first. The test is true because the value of Number is 1, so the body of the loop is executed. The value of Number, 1, is printed out, and then the statement

```
Number := Number + 1
```

increases, or *increments*, the value of Number by 1, from 1 to 2.

Next the loop starts over again, beginning with the test. Again it's true, because the value of Number is 2. So the computer executes the body, printing a 2 and then incrementing Number by 1. In the same way 3 and 4 are printed out. After 4 is printed, the value of Number becomes 5, and (Number <= 4) is tested again. Because the test is false this time, execution of the **while** statement ends.

In **program** FirstWhile we initialized Number to 1. We can get the same output if we initialize Number to 0, change the test expression to

```
(Number <= 3)
```

and then increment Number by 1 *before* the *writeln* statement.

```
program SecondWhile;
  var
    Number : integer;
begin
  Number := 0;
  while (Number <= 3) do
    begin
      Number := Number + 1;
      writeln(Number)
    end
end.
```

Program FirstWhile is a little clearer, though, because the statement that initializes Number,

```
Number := 1
```

and the test expression,

```
Number <= 4
```

make it easier to see that the loop prints out the numbers from 1 to 4.

EXERCISE 3   **a.** What does the following program print?

```
program WhileOne;
 var
  Number : integer;
begin
 Number := 2;
 while (Number < 12) do
  begin
   writeln(Number);
   Number := Number + 2
  end
end.
```

Answer: These numbers in a column: 2-4-6-8-10

b. What does the following program print?

```
program WhileTwo;
 var
  Number : integer;
begin
 Number := 10;
 while (Number > 0) do
  begin
   writeln(Number);
   Number := Number - 3
  end
end.
```

Answer: These numbers in a column: 10-7-4-1

c. What expression must go in the box if **program** WhileThree is to print in a column 2-6-18?

```
program WhileThree;
 var
  Number : integer
begin
 Number := 2;
 while (Number <= 20) do
 begin
  writeln(Number);
  Number := [_____]
 end
end.
```

For the answer, see Problem 2 at the end of the chapter. ▬

The While Loop vs. the For Loop

You may have noticed that you have to do more work with a **while** statement than with a **for** statement. This two-line **for** loop

```
for Number := 1 to 4 do
  writeln(Number);
```

prints the same column of numbers as the five-line **while** loop in **program** FirstWhile on page 124. The **for** statement initializes and increments the control variable Number automatically. In **program** FirstWhile, however, you need assignment statements to initialize and increment the control variable Number.

Nevertheless, the **while** statement is much more flexible than the **for** statement because it uses assignment statements for initializing and incrementing the control variable.

For example, suppose we want to roll a ball across the screen as we did in **program** Cartoon, only this time we want it to roll 3 times as fast. To write the **for** loop that does this, you need to calculate the number of flickers required to get the ball across the screen. A total of $(180 - 20)$**div** $3 = 53$ are necessary.

```
for FlickerNumber := 0 to 53 do
  begin
    paintcircle(20 + 3 * FlickerNumber,80,20);
    invertcircle(20 + 3 * FlickerNumber,80,20)
  end;
```

If you use a **while** loop to do the fast roll, however, you don't need to calculate the number of flickers, and the loop is more straightforward.

```
Position := 20;
while (Position <= 180) do
  begin
    paintcircle(Position,80,20);
    invertcircle(Position,80,20);
    Position := Position + 3
  end;
```

Even though the **for**-loop version is shorter, you'll probably agree that the **while**-loop version is much clearer. The **while** statement is more flexible because its control variable can be incremented by any amount. With the **for** loop, you're stuck: The control variable can be increased or decreased only by 1. *Moral:* Use a **while** loop when you want to increase or decrease the control variable by more than 1 each time through the loop.

4.5 While-Loop Pitfalls

In spite of its power, the **while** loop has some pitfalls. Suppose you forget to initialize the control variable, as in **program** BadOne:

```
program BadOne;
 var
  Number : integer;
begin
 while (Number <= 4) do
  begin
   writeln(Number);
   Number := Number + 1
  end
end.
```

Your program may behave strangely as soon as the computer gets to the *writeln* statement, because Number has an arbitrary value when the Macintosh reaches this instruction.

If you forget to increment the control variable, however, you create a completely different problem.

```
program Forever;
 var
  Number : integer;
begin
 Number := 1;
  while (Number <= 4) do
   begin
    writeln(Number)
   end
end.
```

Program Forever will go on printing a column of 1's unendingly. This is called an *infinite loop*, because there is no way out. With no assignment statement to increment the variable Number, Number will have the value 1 every time the loop body is executed. So the value of Number will always be less than or equal to 4, and the test will always be true.

If you find your program is locked in an infinite loop, you can take one of the following steps.

1. Wait for a power failure.

2. Wait for the Macintosh to burn out.

3. Open the Pause menu and choose Halt. Then open the Run menu and choose Reset, which will terminate the program.

Otherwise you'll just see an unending column of 1's. To avoid strange program behavior and infinite loops, always check to make sure you've initialized and incremented your **while**-loop control variable.

4.6 Relationships and Relational Operators

Suppose Meg and Jon are sister and brother. Then the statement

Meg is the sister of Jon

is true, but the statement

Jon is the sister of Meg

is false. "Sister of" is a relationship between people. When we state that one person is the sister of another person, the statement can be true or false. In this way, we can think of the "sister of" relationship as a kind of test.

In mathematics and also in Pascal, we often use the terms *relation* and *relationship* when we compare numbers. For example, 3 < 5 is a true relationship, whereas 3 > 5 is a false one.

The symbol < is called a *relational operator* because it tests whether the relationship "less than" holds between two numbers. In Pascal there are six relational operators. These are symbols such as > and >= that give true-or-false answers about relationships between numbers. The six relational operators are listed in the following table with examples of how they work.

Operator	Name	True	False
>	greater than	5 > 3	5 > 5
>=	greater than or equal to	5 >= 3	4 >= 5
<	less than	2 < 3	3 < 2
<=	less than or equal to	2 <= 3	3 <= 2
=	equal to	5 = 5	5 = 3
<>	not equal to	3 <> 5	5 <> 5

When we use the term *test*, we mean any expression that is either true or false. So far, the only tests we have seen involve relational operators. For example, the expression

(3 < 4)

is a test. And so is

(Number >= 4)

where Number is some variable of type integer.

True and false, the answers to tests, are standard constants that make up another type, called *boolean*. True and false are actually considered *values*, so we can say that the value of a test is true or false. We will talk about type *boolean* in Chapter 8.

_____ 4.7 Longint—a Second Integer Type _____

Does the following program include an infinite loop?

```
program LongLoop;
 var
   Number : integer;
 begin
  Number := 1;
  while (Number <> 0) do
   begin
    writeln(Number);
    Number := Number + 1
   end
 end.
```

It looks as if it does. Number is initialized to 1, and the assignment statement in the loop increases the value of Number during each iteration, so Number will never equal 0.

However, the program stops running and you get an error message when the value of Number exceeds 32,767. This number is the largest value in the type *integer*, and it is called *maxint*, which is a standard constant. Unlike integers in mathematics, which are infinite in number, the integers that make up the MacPascal type *integer* are finite: They run from $-32,767$, or $-maxint$, up to *maxint*.

If you run **program** LongLoop just as you see it, you're in for a long wait before the program crashes. But there's a way to shorten the wait by choosing Halt while the program is running and then bringing up the Instant window.

When you choose Halt and stop **program** LongLoop in mid-execution, the variable Number still has an assigned location in memory, and that location holds the value it had when execution stopped. While program execution is on hold, you can actually use the Instant window to change the value of this variable.

When you type

```
Number := 32760
```

in the Instant window and then click on Do It, the assignment changes the value of Number to 32,760. Now, when you click on Go, the program will run for just a few more loops, until the value of Number reaches 32,767. Because (Number <> 0) is still true, the loop is executed one more time. The *writeln* statement prints the value of Number—32767—and then the assignment statement is reached. The right side is evaluated first. When you add 32,767 and 1, *maxint* is exceeded by 1.

This doesn't make the program crash, though. The program crashes when it tries to copy 32,768 into the variable Number. Number's location in memory is too small to hold that value. See Figure 4.1.

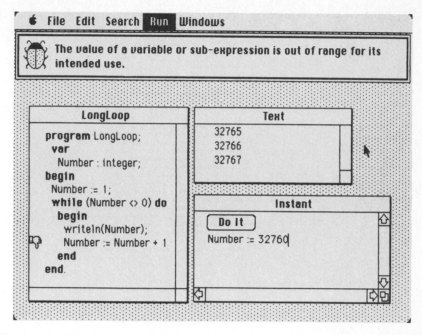

Figure 4.1   When **program** LongLoop crashes, this is what you see on the screen.

Fortunately, MacPascal has an additional integer type called *longint*, which runs from −2,147,483,647 to +2,147,483,647. The second number is called *maxlongint*, and it is also a standard constant. If you expect computations in your program to use values larger than 32,767, use *longint* instead of *integer* variables.

Of course the type *longint* is finite, too, and the following program will eventually crash as well.

```
program LongLongLoop;
 var
  Number : longint;
begin
 Number := 1;
 while (Number <> 0) do
  begin
   writeln(Number);
   Number := Number + 1
  end
end.
```

EXERCISE 4   Watch **program** LongLongLoop crash. (*Hint:* Unless you have a lot of time to kill, use the Instant window to change the value of Number after you have brought the program to a halt.) ▬

Because every member of type *integer* also belongs to type *longint*, the two types are closely related. If Number has type *integer* and LongNumber has type *longint*, then the assignment statement

```
LongNumber := Number
```

will always work, and

```
Number := LongNumber
```

is acceptable if the value of LongNumber is small enough to be an integer.

4.8 While-Loop Syntax

For any Pascal expression that can have a true or false value, we will use this notation

```
⟨test⟩
```

so the general form of a Pascal **while** statement is

```
while ⟨test⟩ do
 ⟨statement⟩;
```

The **while** statement is itself one kind of statement. Hence it is possible to put **while** loops inside **while** loops or **for** statements.

The notation ⟨statement⟩ now stands for simple statements, compound statements, **for** statements, **while** statements, or the empty statement.

EXERCISE 5   **a.** What happens in the following program?

```
program SimpleThree;
 var
  Number : integer;
begin
 Number := 2;
 while (Number <= 8) do
  begin
   writeln(Number);
   Number := Number + 2
  end
end.
```

b. What happens in the following program?

```
program SimpleFour;
 var
   Number : integer;
begin
 Number := 2;
 while (Number <> 16) do
  begin
   writeln(Number);
   Number := 2 * Number
  end
end.  ▬
```

4.9 The Natural Superiority of the While Statement

We have already seen one way in which the **while** statement outshines the **for** statement: If you want to advance the control variable of a loop by increments larger than 1, the **while** statement is much more convenient and versatile.

But there is a second, more important reason to prefer the **while** loop to the **for** loop. The **for** loop is actually rather limited. Once the lower and upper limits are fixed, the number of iterations is completely determined, and the Macintosh must execute the loop exactly that many times.

This is not true with **while** statements. A **while** statement loops until the test condition of the loop is false, and this can be an indefinite number of iterations. So the **while** statement can help us solve problems when we don't know how many loops we need. To see how useful indefinite looping can be, let's return to the double-your-money problem.

4.10 Back to Double-Your-Money

The double-your-money problem asks this question: If you put $100.00 in the bank at 9% interest, compounded yearly, how many years must you wait until your money doubles?

Here's one way to solve the problem using a **while** loop:

```
program DoubleMoney;
{CALCULATES NUMBER OF YEARS IT TAKES FOR A $100}
{DEPOSIT TO DOUBLE IF THE INTEREST RATE IS 9%}
 const
  Principal = 100.00;
  Rate = 0.09;
 var
  MoneyInBank,NewMoney : real;
  Years : integer;
```

(continued)

```
begin
 Years := 0;
 MoneyInBank := Principal;
 while (MoneyInBank < 2 * Principal) do
  begin
   NewMoney := MoneyInBank * Rate;
   MoneyInBank := MoneyInBank + NewMoney;
   Years := Years + 1
  end;
 writeln('Money doubles in ',Years : 1,' years.')
end.
```

This is an important program, so let's study it carefully. The body begins with two initialization statements:

```
Years := 0;
MoneyInBank := Principal;
```

These two statements make sense. They say that, at 0 years, the money in your account is your starting principal, $100.00.

The test part of the **while** statement,

```
(MoneyInBank < 2 * Principal)
```

says, "Keep looping as long as the money in your account is less than twice your starting principal."

Every time you loop, the NewMoney earned (MoneyInBank * Rate) is added to the balance in the account:

```
MoneyInBank := MoneyInBank + NewMoney
```

And the number of years in the bank is incremented by 1:

```
Years := Years + 1
```

Finally, after 9 years, the money accumulated exceeds twice the principal, so the looping ends and the value 9 is reported.

Program DoubleMoney is unlike any we've seen so far because it doesn't report the most obvious value that it calculates—the final value of MoneyInBank. Instead, it reports the number of loops required to increase MoneyInBank to the value 2 * Principal. Because we've used the variable Years to count the number of iterations in the loop, Years is called a *counter*.

EXERCISE 6   What does the following program print?

```
program FirstPuzzle;
 var
  Stepper,Counter : integer;
```

```
begin
  Stepper := 2;
  Counter := 0;
  while (Stepper < 20) do
   begin
     Stepper := Stepper * Stepper;
     Counter := Counter + 1
   end;
  writeln(Counter)
end.
```

Answer: 3 ▬

4.11 Tests and Counters

Let's get back to Uncle Harold's staircase. Suppose Harold has 8 blocks, and he decides to build a new staircase (1 block wide) as high as he possibly can. How many steps high can he make it?

Here, we've turned Harold's problem around: Earlier we wanted to know how many blocks he would need to build 6 steps. Now we want to know how many steps (that is, how many loop iterations) he can fit in before his 8 blocks are used up.

This situation is similar to the circumstances in the double-your-money problem. We want to count the number of loops until a certain value is reached. This kind of problem can't be solved easily with a **for** loop, because we don't know ahead of time how many loops we will need. So, using **program** DoubleMoney as a model, let's attempt a **while**-loop solution with the variable StepNumber as a counter.

```
program HowManySteps;
{CALCULATES HOW MANY STEPS CAN BE BUILT WITH 8 BLOCKS,}
{BUT GETS THE WRONG ANSWER}
  var
    StepNumber,BlockCount : integer;
begin
  StepNumber := 0;
  BlockCount := 0;
  while (BlockCount <= 8) do
   begin
     StepNumber := StepNumber + 1;
     BlockCount := BlockCount + StepNumber
   end;
  writeln('With 8 blocks, Harold can build ',StepNumber : 1,' steps.')
end.
```

Because this program is trickier than it looks, let's build a chart that shows the values of BlockCount and StepNumber at the beginning and end of each loop.

	StepNumber	BlockCount	Test: BlockCount <= 8
Loop 1			
at **begin**	0	0	test is true
at **end**	1	1	test is true
Loop 2			
	1	1	test is true
	2	3	test is true
Loop 3			
	2	3	test is true
	3	6	test is true
Loop 4			
	3	6	test is true
	4	10	test is false

Loop 4 is the final loop, so the program reports that Harold can build a staircase with 4 steps, which will require 10 blocks. But wait a minute—Harold has only 8 blocks! What went wrong?

The Countess and the Machine

Ada, Countess Lovelace, was the daughter of the British poet Lord Byron. She was also the first computer programmer—almost a century and a half before anyone had heard of the personal computer. The story of the Countess and the computer began around 1834 when teenager Ada met Charles Babbage, an inventor, mathematician, and great party-giver. Babbage had devised a calculating machine, and at one of his parties he spent an evening explaining to the countess how this, the world's first computer, was going to work. Immediately Lovelace was hooked on computing. She studied the math and mechanics of Babbage's machine and gave Babbage advice on how to get rid of bugs. Along the way she invented a kind of repetitive calculating—what today is called looping.

Unfortunately neither Lovelace nor Babbage ever got to see the machine perform. Its elaborate parts were extremely difficult to make, and before one version of the machine was working, Babbage had thought of some improvements. When he changed one part, other parts had to be changed. The process went on and on. Finally Babbage ran out of money, and both he and Lovelace died before their calculating machine was perfected.

At the beginning of the fourth and last loop, the value of StepNumber is 3 and the value of BlockCount is 6. So the test is still true, and the last loop is executed. The last loop pushes the value of StepNumber to 4 and the value of BlockNumber to 10, which is 2 more blocks than Harold actually has.

The program has overshot Harold's supply of blocks. Instead of reporting the number of complete steps possible, the program reports the number of complete steps *plus* the one extra step where Harold runs out of blocks.

This means that **program** DoubleMoney is not a completely accurate model for Harold's problem. In **program** DoubleMoney, we are interested in the number of years it takes to go *over* the doubled principal. But in the staircase problem, we want to know how many steps we can build *without going over* the number of blocks on hand.

Here's a correct solution to Harold's problem:

```
program HowManyStepsTwo;
{CALCULATES HOW MANY STEPS CAN BE BUILT WITH 8 BLOCKS.}
  var
    StepNumber,BlockCount : integer;
begin
  StepNumber := 0;
  BlockCount := 0;
  while (BlockCount + (StepNumber + 1) <= 8) do
    begin
      StepNumber := StepNumber + 1;
      BlockCount := BlockCount + StepNumber
    end;
  writeln('With 8 blocks, Harold can build ',StepNumber : 1,' steps.')
end.
```

Now the test

```
BlockCount + (StepNumber + 1) <= 8
```

checks *before* the loop is executed to determine whether adding in the next step—that is, StepNumber + 1—will put BlockCount over the limit.

When the value of BlockCount gets to 6 and the value of StepNumber reaches 3, BlockCount and (StepNumber + 1) are added together in the test and compared with 8. Because they add up to 10, the test is false, and the Macintosh advances to the *writeln* statement without changing the value of StepNumber again. So the *writeln* statement prints the correct answer, 3.

When a counter holds the answer you are looking for in a program with a **while** loop, be sure to check whether you've coordinated it properly with the loop test. If you're interested in the number of loops needed to put some value "over the top," as in **program** DoubleMoney, the test will probably be simple and straightforward. But if looping is supposed to put some number just *under* a certain value—say, the number of blocks on hand—then you must create a test that anticipates what will happen one loop ahead.

4.12 Yet Another Way to Loop: Repeat-Until

We've talked about two looping commands so far: the **for** statement and the **while** statement. Pascal has one more looping command, the **repeat-until** instruction. Like the **while** statement, the **repeat-until** statement has a test part and a body. But in the **repeat-until** statement, the test comes *after* the body and looping continues until the test becomes true.

Here is a simple program using a repeat loop. What does it do?

```
program NumberColumn;
 var
   Number : integer;
begin
 Number := 1;
 repeat
   writeln(Number);
   Number := Number + 1
 until(Number > 4)
end.
```

It prints out the 1-2-3-4 column.

Program NumberColumn begins by initializing Number to 1. Then comes the loop. The statements between **repeat** and **until** make up its body, and the loop ends with a test:

```
(Number > 4)
```

In a repeat loop, the test always comes at the end, after the reserved word **until**. This means that the body of the **repeat-until** loop is *always* executed at least once. This can create some problems that we will discuss in a minute.

The general form of the **repeat-until** statement is

```
repeat
 ⟨statement⟩
until ⟨test⟩
```

Because **repeat-until** is a kind of statement, we will add it to our growing list of ⟨statement⟩s.

Repeat-until has one peculiarity. Because the reserved words **repeat** and **until** frame the body of the loop, Pascal allows you to leave out the **begin** and the **end** even if the body includes more than one instruction, as we did in **program** NumberColumn.

Note that there is no semicolon in **program** NumberColumn after the statement Number := Number + 1. This is so because the *writeln* statement is followed by the reserved word **until**, not by another statement. Like the reserved word **end**, **until** works as a separator, so a semicolon isn't needed.

It's easy to get a **repeat-until** loop to work backward. **Program** Backward prints 4-3-2-1 in a column.

```
program Backward;
 var
  Number : integer;
begin
 Number := 4;
 repeat
  writeln(Number);
  Number := Number -1
 until (Number = 0)
end.
```

EXERCISE 7

a. What does this program do?

```
program PuzzleOne;
 var
  Number : integer;
begin
 Number := 3;
 repeat
  writeln(Number);
  Number := Number + 3
 until(Number > 15)
end.
```

b. And what will this program do? (There's a trick here.)

```
program PuzzleTwo;
 var
  Number : integer;
begin
 Number := 3;
 repeat
  writeln(Number);
  Number := Number + 3
 until (Number = 14)
end.
```

Answer: It will bomb when Number gets large enough. Can you see why? What will the value of Number be at the time of the crash? How would you fix the program so that it prints just five numbers?

c. What does this program draw?

```
program PuzzleThree;
 var
  Vertical : integer;
begin
 Vertical := 0;
 repeat
  drawline(0,Vertical,200,Vertical);
  Vertical := Vertical + 10
 until (Vertical > 200)
end.
```

Program AngleRoll

Here's another program that uses a **repeat-until** loop. **Program** AngleRoll allows you to roll a ball across the screen at an angle, like this:

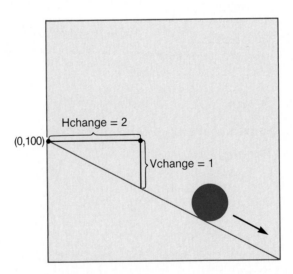

The input variables Hchange (for horizontal change) and Vchange (for vertical change) determine the slope of the path of the ball as it moves across the screen. When Hchange = 2 and Vchange = 1, for example, the ball drops down 1 unit for every 2 units it moves across.

```
program AngleRoll;
 const
   Hstart = 0;
   Vstart = 100;
   Radius = 20;
 var
   H,V,Hchange,Vchange : integer;
begin
 H := Hstart;
 V := Vstart;
 writeln('Type in horizontal change and vertical change.');
 writeln('Horizontal change must be a positive integer.');
 writeln('Vertical change can be a positive or negative integer.');
 readln(Hchange,Vchange);
 repeat
   paintcircle(H,V,Radius);
   invertcircle(H,V,Radius);
  H := H + Hchange;
  V := V + Vchange
 until (H > 180)
end.
```

Program AngleRoll does something we haven't seen before. It increments two different variables inside the loop, H and V. But only one of these variables—H—serves as a control variable.

EXERCISE 8
    a. What happens if Hchange is 0?

    b. Where does the ball leave the window if Hchange < Vchange?

    c. What values must Hchange and Vchange have for the ball to leave the Drawing window at the upper-right corner? ■■

4.13 The Pitfalls of the Repeat Loop

The test in a **repeat-until** statement comes at the end of the loop, and this can cause trouble if you aren't careful. To see why this is so, let's look at an interactive program that solves Uncle Harold's cinder block problem using a **repeat** loop.

In **program** InteractiveHowManySteps, you read in the number of blocks Harold has, and the program calculates the number of steps he can build.

```
program InteractiveHowManySteps;
{YOU READ IN NUMBER OF BLOCKS. PROGRAM}
{CALCULATES HOW MANY STEPS CAN BE BUILT.}
  var
    StepNumber,BlockCount,BlocksUsed : integer;
  begin
  writeln('How many blocks does Harold have?');
  readln(BlockCount);
  StepNumber := 0;
  BlocksUsed := 0;
  repeat
    StepNumber := StepNumber + 1;
    BlocksUsed := BlocksUsed + StepNumber
  until ((BlocksUsed + (StepNumber + 1)) > BlockCount);
  writeln('With ',BlockCount : 1,' blocks, Harold can build ',
          StepNumber : 1,' steps.')
  end.
```

The value you type in for the number of blocks Harold has becomes the value of BlockCount. After StepNumber is initialized to 0, the **repeat** statement is executed. First StepNumber is increased by 1. Then StepNumber is added to BlocksUsed.

Next the test is made. If BlocksUsed plus the number that will be needed for the next step (StepNumber + 1) is greater than 0, there aren't enough blocks for another step, so the loop ends.

The program works fine *unless* you specify that Harold has 0 blocks. In that case, one loop of the **repeat** statement is executed anyway (although there aren't any blocks), because the test *follows* the **until** at the end of the statement. So StepNumber is incremented to 1 in the body before the test is done, and the program prints

```
With 0 blocks, Harold can build 1 steps.
```

which is the wrong answer!

*When you use the **repeat-until** statement, make sure that at least one loop will always be needed to solve the problem. If you are not sure, use a **while** statement.*

4.14 Math Formulas and Functions

In mathematics a *function* is some operation that gives, or *returns*, a single answer. For example, when you square a number, you are applying the squaring function to that number. The answer you get back is the value of that number times itself.

Pascal has some built-in functions, such as squaring, that allow you to do important math calculations easily. The squaring function is written *sqr*. If you type

```
writeln(sqr(3))
```

in the Instant window, you will get 9 for an answer in the Text window. The *sqr* function works equally well with *real* or *integer* inputs. *Writeln(sqr(3.0))* will print 9.0e + 0 instead of 9 for its output.

There is also a square root function, *sqrt*, which always returns a real number for an answer. You can apply *sqrt* to either a real number or an integer, but the input cannot be a negative number. The expression *sqrt(2)* returns the value 1.414, and *sqrt(sqrt(2))* returns the square root of the square root of 2, or 1.189. You can get standard decimal notation instead of scientific notation with more than one place to the right of the decimal point, if that's what you want:

```
writeln(sqrt(2) : 5 : 3)
```

prints 1.414, and

```
writeln(sqrt(sqrt(2)) : 8 : 6)
```

prints 1.189207.

Let's look at a third Pascal function, *round*, which rounds off a real number to the nearest integer. Here are some examples of how *round* works:

```
round(3.14) = 3
round(3.5) = 4
round(3.6) = 4
round(-1.2) = -1
round(-1.5) = -2
```

There are two other functions related to *round*, which we'll need later on. The function *trunc*, which is short for "truncate," returns the integer part of any real number: *trunc(3.95) = 3*, *trunc(-3.9) = -3*, and *trunc(4.111) = 4*.

The function *abs*, which is short for "absolute value," makes any number positive: *abs(-4) = 4*, *abs(-4.1) = 4.1*, and *abs(3.14) = 3.14*.

Now look at this expression:

```
sqr(round(sqrt(2)))
```

What is its value? When functions are applied to other functions in this way, Pascal evaluates the expression from the inside out. First *sqrt(2)* is calculated, yielding the value 1.414. Then this number is rounded, and the resulting value is the integer 1. Finally 1 is squared, giving the integer 1 as a result, which is the value of the entire expression.

EXERCISE 9   What are the values of the following expressions? They are easier than they look. Just remember that *sqrt* (2) is about 1.4 and that *sqrt*(3) is about 1.7.

a. `trunc(sqrt(2))`

(*Answer:* 1)

b. `sqr(round(sqrt(3)))`

(*Answer:* 4)

c. `abs(trunc(sqrt(2)))`

d. `trunc(sqrt(abs(-3.14)))`

e. `trunc(sqrt(round(sqrt(3))))` ■

Program CalcDistance

Let's use what we've learned about functions in two short examples. Our first example, **program CalcDistance**, draws a line between two points in the Drawing window—the points (H_1, V_1) and (H_2, V_2)—and then calculates the distance between them.

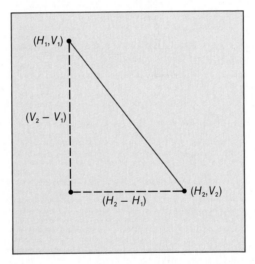

To solve this problem we will use the Pythagorean theorem: In a right triangle, the square of the hypotenuse is equal to the sum of the squares of the other two sides. This equation will be useful because, unless the points determine a horizontal or a vertical line, the distance between our two points will be the hypotenuse of a right triangle. Using the Pythagorean relationship, we can write this formula for the distance between the two points:

$$\text{Distance apart} = \sqrt{(H_2 - H_1)^2 + (V_2 - V_1)^2}$$

And when we use this formula in a Pascal program, this is what we get:

```
program CalcDistance;
  var
   H1,V1 : integer; {THE FIRST POINT}
   H2,V2 : integer; {THE SECOND POINT}
   DistanceApart : real;
begin
 writeln('Type in values for the first point.');
 readln(H1,V1);
 writeln('Type in values for the second point.');
 readln(H2,V2);
 drawline(H1,V1,H2,V2);
 DistanceApart := sqrt(sqr(H2 - H1) + sqr(V2 - V1));
 writeln('Distance between the 2 points is:',DistanceApart : 5 : 2)
end.
```

EXERCISE 10   What happens when the two points in **program** CalcDistance lie on a horizontal or a vertical line? ▬

Program CircleOrbit

Now let's try a more ambitious example. Suppose we want a planet or ball to move in a circle, cartoon style, around the standard Drawing window, as in Figure 4.2. We'll make the program interactive: When you run it, you supply values for OrbitRadius and PlanetRadius.

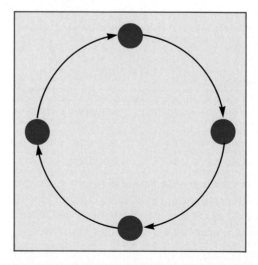

Figure 4.2   **Program** CircleOrbit will move a ball in a circular orbit around the Drawing window.

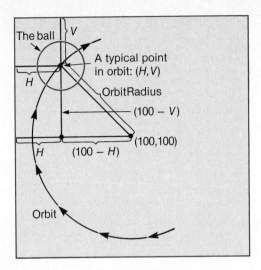

Figure 4.3   The ball at a typical point in **program** CircleOrbit.

Figure 4.3 shows the ball at typical point (H, V) as it moves around the screen in a circle with radius equal to OrbitRadius. From the right triangle in the diagram in Figure 4.3, we have the equation

$$\text{OrbitRadius}^2 = (100 - H)^2 + (100 - V)^2$$

Solving for V, we get

$$V = 100 - \sqrt{\text{OrbitRadius}^2 - (100 - H)^2}$$

Given a value for H, we can use this equation to calculate a value for V so that the point (H, V) lies on the circumference of the orbit circle. The loop below will move the ball along the upper half of the orbit when we finish coding it.

```
H := 100 - OrbitRadius;
repeat
   V := 100 - √(OrbitRadius² - (100 - H)²);
   paintcircle(H,V,PlanetRadius);
   invertcircle(H,V,PlanetRadius);
   H := H + 1
until (H = 100 + OrbitRadius)
```

To make the **repeat** loop work correctly, we must translate into proper Pascal the assignment statement that calculates a value for V. Rather than write the statement on a single line, we'll use three assignment statements. Using several statements will make the code less cumbersome.

```
OrbitRadiusSqr := sqr(OrbitRadius);
HDistanceSqr := sqr(100 - H);
V := 100 - round(sqrt(OrbitRadiusSqr - HDistanceSqr));
```

Note that it is necessary to use the function *round*. This is because *sqrt* gives an answer of type *real*, but the variable V is of type *integer*. Also, OrbitRadiusSqr and HDistanceSqr may exceed maxint, so we've declared them to be of type *longint* instead of type *integer*.

Here is the complete program. It has two loops, one for the upper semicircle and one for the lower semicircle.

```
program CircleOrbit;
{YOU READ IN RADIUS OF ORBIT AND RADIUS OF PLANET. PROGRAM MOVES}
{PLANET IN AN ORBIT AROUND THE CENTER OF THE DRAWING WINDOW.}
  var
  H,V : integer; {THE CENTER OF THE PLANET}
  OrbitRadius,PlanetRadius : integer;
  OrbitRadiusSqr : longint; {SQUARE OF THE RADIUS OF THE ORBIT}
  HDistanceSqr : longint; {SQUARE OF THE HORIZONTAL DISTANCE}
    {BETWEEN THE CENTER OF THE ORBIT AND THE CENTER OF THE PLANET}
begin
  writeln('Type in radius of orbit and radius of planet.');
  readln(OrbitRadius,PlanetRadius);
  H := 100 - OrbitRadius;
  OrbitRadiusSqr := sqr(OrbitRadius);
  {DRAWS THE UPPER HALF OF THE ORBIT.}
  repeat
   HDistanceSqr := sqr(100 - H);
   V := 100 - round(sqrt(OrbitRadiusSqr - HDistanceSqr));
   paintcircle(H,V,PlanetRadius);
   invertcircle(H,V,PlanetRadius);
   H := H + 1
  until(H = 100 + OrbitRadius);
  {DRAWS THE LOWER HALF OF THE ORBIT.}
  repeat
   HDistanceSqr := sqr(100 - H);
   V := 100 + round(sqrt(OrbitRadiusSqr - HDistanceSqr));
   paintcircle(H,V,PlanetRadius);
   invertcircle(H,V,PlanetRadius);
   H := H - 1
  until (H <= 100 - OrbitRadius)
end.
```

EXERCISE 11   What does **program** CircleOrbit do if the plus sign in the assignment statement

```
V := 100 + round(sqrt(OrbitRadiusSqr - HDistanceSqr));
```

is changed to a minus sign? ▄

TEST YOURSELF

1. What does it mean to initialize a variable?
2. When can you assign a *longint* value to a variable of type *integer*?
3. What is the difference between *round* and *trunc*?
4. How can you get out of an infinite loop?
5. When is it not permitted to change the value of the control variable of a loop using an assignment statement?
6. What are the six relational operators?
7. Name two ways in which the **while** statement is superior to the **for** statement.
8. Why won't this assignment statement work?

        Number + 3 := Number

9. Explain carefully what happens when Pascal does this assignment:

        Number := trunc(sqrt(2))

10. How can you get into trouble with a **repeat-until** loop?

PROBLEMS

1. What does each of the following programs print?

    a.
    ```
    program AssignmentCheck;
      var
        M,N : integer;
    begin
      M := 2;
      N := 2 * M + 3;
      writeln(M - N)
    end.
    ```

    b.
    ```
    program WhatNumber;
      var
        BigNumber,StepNumber : integer;
    begin
      StepNumber := 0;
      BigNumber := 10;
      while (BigNumber <= 20) do
        begin
          StepNumber := StepNumber + 2;
          BigNumber := BigNumber * StepNumber - StepNumber
        end;
      writeln(StepNumber)
    end.
    ```

2. What number must be inserted in the box to make the following program print the column 1-3-9? (The loop body in this program gives the answer to part c of Exercise 3 on page 126.)

```
program TakeAGuess;
 var
  Number : integer;
begin
 Number := [_____];
 while(Number <= 20) do
  begin
   writeln(Number);
   Number := 3 * Number
  end
end.
```

3. Suppose Uncle Harold wants to build his 6-step staircase 3 blocks wide instead of just 1 block wide. Modify program BlocksNeeded so that it will do this calculation.

4. Rewrite **program** Explode (Problem 5 in Chapter 1) using a **while** loop.

5. Write programs that print the following columns of numbers, using (a) a **while** loop and (b) a **repeat-until** loop.

```
10   51 1  0   30
20   41 4  1   24
30   31 9  0   18
40   21 16 1   12
50   11 25 0   6
```

6. Suppose Number1 = 5 and Number2 = 8. What are the values of the following expressions?

   a. Number1 < Number2
   b. Number1 >= Number2
   c. (2 * Number1) <=(Number2 - 2)
   d. Number1 + 3 = Number2

7. Write an interactive program called **program Crosshairs**: You type in a point, say (50,50), and a radius, say 35, and the program draws a circle of the given radius with its center at the given point. It also draws "crosshairs"—one vertical and one horizontal line through the center of the circle. So the program output should look like this:

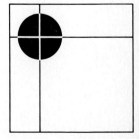

8. If a bank pays you interest at the rate of 9%, compounded quarterly, then each quarter of the year you get interest equal to 1/4 of 9%, or 2.25%. If monthly interest is paid, each month you receive 1/12 of 9% = .75% interest, and the assignment statement

```
Amount := Amount + (Amount * Rate/12)
```

calculates the new amount in your bank account each month. Write an interactive program that reads in a principal, a number of years, an interest rate, and an integer representing the number of times during a year that the interest will be compounded. For example, if the interest is compounded monthly, you type in 12. For output, the program prints the amount of money in your account when the number of years is up.

9. First National Bank pays 9.5% on its savings accounts, compounded yearly. Second National Bank pays 9%, compounded monthly. Which bank offers a better deal?

10. How many integers in the sequence 1,2,3,4,5,...must you add together before the sum exceeds 200? Write a program that makes this calculation. *Hint*: You will need a counter.

11. Successive square roots of 2 keep getting smaller:

```
sqrt(2) = 1.414
sqrt(1.414) = 1.183
```

How many successive square roots do you have to take before you get to a value smaller than 1.0000001?

12. Using **while** loops only, write a program that rolls a ball around the inside perimeter of the standard drawing window.

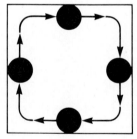

13. Hero's formula,

$$\text{Area} = \sqrt{s(s-a)(s-b)(s-c)}$$

calculates the area of a triangle, where *s* equals one-half of the perimeter and *a*, *b*, *c* are the lengths of the sides. Planning carefully, write a program that reads in the locations of three points in the Drawing window and then calculates the area of the triangle they form.

14. Change **program** AngleRoll so that you can start the ball rolling anywhere on the left wall of the Drawing window.

15. Can a program that includes **for** loops only (no **while** loops or **repeat-until** loops allowed) ever go into an infinite loop?

Conditional Statements, Rectangles, and Bar Graphs

5

"You may borrow my car on condition that you bring it back by noon." This is a *conditional statement.* It says that something will happen provided that some condition is met. Conditional statements show up in computing, too: "If the first number equals the second number, then print this message: The two numbers are equal. Otherwise, print: The two numbers are not equal."

In this chapter you will learn about Pascal's two conditional statements: the **if-then** and **if-then-else** commands. We'll also show you how to use Pascal's rectangle-drawing instructions to draw bar graphs and to create unusual graphics. Let's look at conditional statements first.

5.1 Conditional Statements—A Two-Number Sort

When you arrange a list of numbers in numerical order, or when you alphabetize a list of names, you are *sorting* the list. **Program** TwoSort sorts two numbers by putting the larger one first. It is our first illustration of an **if-then** statement.

```pascal
program TwoSort;
 var
   FirstNumber,SecondNumber,Larger,Smaller : integer;
begin
 writeln('Type in two integers.');
 readln(FirstNumber,SecondNumber);
 Larger := FirstNumber;
 Smaller := SecondNumber;
 if (Larger < Smaller) then
  begin
   Larger := SecondNumber;
   Smaller := FirstNumber
  end;
 writeln('The larger number is ',Larger : 1);
 writeln('The smaller number is ',Smaller : 1)
end.
```

When you run **program** TwoSort, you type in two integers, which are read into the variables FirstNumber and SecondNumber. Then the program assigns the value of FirstNumber to a variable called Larger, and it assigns the value of SecondNumber to another variable called Smaller.

These assignments might be mixed up: Suppose the second number is the larger of the two. For example, the first number might be 3 and the second number 5.

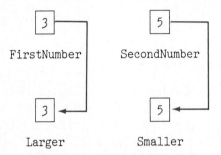

This is where the **if-then** statement comes in:

```
if (Larger ⟨ Smaller) then
  begin
   Larger := SecondNumber;
   Smaller := FirstNumber
  end;
```

This statement says, "If Larger is less than Smaller, then do the two actions that will reassign the numbers, putting the larger one in Larger and the smaller one in Smaller."

The **if** part is a test: (Larger < Smaller). If the result of the test is true, the program goes on to execute the body of the **then** part. If the result of the test is false, the program skips over the rest of the **if-then** statement and goes on to the next instruction.

What happens when FirstNumber = SecondNumber? For example, what if they are both 5? In that case, the test (Larger < Smaller) is false. So the **then** part is not executed, and the program prints

```
The larger number is 5
The smaller number is 5
```

If this bothers you, add the following **if-then** statement at the end of the program:

```
if (Larger = Smaller) then
  writeln('The numbers are equal.')
```

If-Then Statement Syntax

The general form of the **if-then** statement is

```
if ⟨test⟩ then
  ⟨statement⟩
```

The statement in the **then** part can be a simple statement, a compound statement, or any other kind of Pascal statement. We get these match-ups for the **if-then** statement in **program** TwoSort:

```
if (Larger ⟨ Smaller) then        ⟨test⟩
begin
  Larger := Second;  ←——⟨statement⟩
  Smaller := First
end;
```

The body of the **then** part in **program** TwoSort is a compound statement.

The **if-then** statement is called a *conditional statement*, because the **then** part is executed on condition that the test in the **if** part is true. When the test is false, the **then** part is skipped over.

5.2 A Better Two-Number Sort—The Scratchpad Principle

Program TwoSort works fine, but there is a more efficient way of sorting two numbers. In **program** BetterTwoSort, we'll use FirstNumber and SecondNumber as our input variables once again. But instead of using the output variables Larger and Smaller, we will reuse FirstNumber and SecondNumber for output. To help with the sort, we'll include a program variable called Scratchpad, which will hold a value temporarily during program execution.

```
program BetterTwoSort;
  var
    FirstNumber,SecondNumber,Scratchpad : integer;
begin
  writeln('Type in two integers.');
  readln(FirstNumber,SecondNumber);
  if (FirstNumber ⟨ SecondNumber) then
    begin
      Scratchpad := FirstNumber;
      FirstNumber := SecondNumber;
      SecondNumber := Scratchpad
    end;
  writeln('The larger number is ',FirstNumber : 1);
  writeln('The smaller number is ',SecondNumber : 1)
end.
```

When you run this program, you type in a value for FirstNumber and a value for SecondNumber. If FirstNumber is greater than or equal to SecondNumber, the **if** part of the loop is false and execution skips to the *writeln* statement.

But suppose FirstNumber is smaller; let's say FirstNumber is 3 and SecondNumber is 5.

   FirstNumber   SecondNumber   Scratchpad

In this case, the **then** part of the **if-then** statement switches the two values. First it copies the value of FirstNumber into Scratchpad.

   FirstNumber   SecondNumber   Scratchpad

Then it copies the value of SecondNumber into FirstNumber.

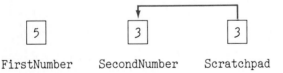

   FirstNumber   SecondNumber   Scratchpad

And finally it copies the value of Scratchpad into SecondNumber, completing the swap.

        5   3   3

   FirstNumber   SecondNumber   Scratchpad

Now FirstNumber holds the larger number and SecondNumber holds the smaller number.

The variable Scratchpad plays a special role in **program** BetterTwoSort: It holds a number temporarily so that the values in the two other variables can be swapped. This technique will show up again and again in programming, so it is important that you thoroughly understand how it works.

Program BetterTwoSort is a more efficient way to sort two numbers than **program** TwoSort. It uses three variables and three assignment statements instead of four variables and four assignment statements. This may not seem like a big advantage, but in a large program that sorts thousands of names or numbers, executing up to 25% fewer assignment statements means the program will run much faster.

In Chapter 10 we'll see how to use the Scratchpad principle in sorting long lists of names and numbers.

EXERCISE 1   **a.** What would **program** BetterTwoSort do if you used the condition (FirstNumber > SecondNumber) in the **if-then** test?

b. Suppose the **then** part of **program** BetterTwoSort didn't use Scratchpad, but simply looked like this:

```
begin
  FirstNumber := SecondNumber;
  SecondNumber := FirstNumber
end;
```

What would the program print if FirstNumber = 3 and SecondNumber = 5?

c. What would happen if the **then** part of **program** BetterTwoSort looked like this?

```
begin
  Scratchpad := FirstNumber;
  SecondNumber := FirstNumber;
  SecondNumber := Scratchpad
end;
```

Hint: Draw a diagram with three cells named Scratchpad, FirstNumber, and SecondNumber. Put sample values in the cells and then "execute" the statements with pencil and paper. ■

5.3 If-Then-Else: Pascal's Other Conditional Statement

An **if-then-else** statement works a lot like an **if-then** statement. An **if-then-else** tells the computer, "If something is true, do this, or else if it's not true, do that." Let's illustrate how the **if-then-else** works with a few examples.

Program Tuna

A supermarket ad includes a coupon that entitles you to a can of tuna for 29 cents if the cost of your other purchases is $7.50 or more. Otherwise the can costs 89 cents. **Program** Tuna adds the cost of the can of tuna to the cost of the other items you buy to give a total cost.

```pascal
program Tuna;
 const
  RegTunaPrice = 0.89;
  CheapTunaPrice = 0.29;
 var
  OtherItems : real;
  Cost : real;
begin
 writeln('Type in cost of other items.');
 readln(OtherItems);
 if (OtherItems )= 7.50) then
  Cost := OtherItems + CheapTunaPrice
 else
  Cost := OtherItems + RegTunaPrice;
 writeln('Total cost is $',Cost : 4 : 2)
end.
```

An **if-then-else** statement is appropriate here, because there is one action to be taken if the test is true and another action to be taken if the test is false.

If-Then Statement Syntax

The **if-then-else** statement has this general form:

```pascal
if ⟨test⟩ then
 ⟨statement1⟩
else
 ⟨statement2⟩
```

Statement1 and Statement2 represent the actions taken on each of the two branches of the **if-then-else.**

There is one absolutely firm syntax rule for **if-then** and **if-then-else** statements: *Never put a semicolon immediately before a **then** or an **else.***

Now let's look at a more complicated **if-then-else** program.

Program Average

Program Average reads in a list of positive integers and prints out their average. When you run the program, you type positive integers until you are ready to quit, and then you type a zero. The program adds up the integers and stores their sum in a variable called Sum. Meanwhile, a variable called NumberCount tallies the number of positive integers you have entered. Then the program calculates the average,

```pascal
Average := Sum/NumberCount
```

and prints it out.

Program Average is not quite so straightforward as it seems. We want the program to treat different kinds of input in different ways. So we've handled the *special-case* inputs with **if-then** and **if-then-else** statements.

```pascal
program Average;
{YOU READ IN POSITIVE INTEGERS, PROGRAM CALCULATES THE AVERAGE.}
 var
  Sum,Number,NumberCount : integer;
  AverageValue : real;
begin
 Number := 1;
 Sum := 0;
 NumberCount := 0;
        {READ IN NUMBERS.}
 while (Number <> 0) do
  begin
   writeln('Type in a positive integer.');
   writeln('Type zero to quit.');
   readln(Number);
   if (Number < 0) then
    writeln('Bad input -- type another value.')
   else
    begin
     Sum := Sum + Number;
     if (Number > 0) then
      NumberCount := NumberCount + 1
    end
  end;
        {CALCULATE AVERAGE.}
 if (NumberCount > 0) then
  begin
   AverageValue := Sum/NumberCount;
   writeln('The average of the ',NumberCount : 1,
          ' numbers you entered is ',AverageValue : 3 : 1)
  end
 else
  writeln('No values submitted -- no average reported.')
end.
```

First of all, the program tells you to type in a positive number or a zero. But you might absentmindedly type a negative number. The first **if-then-else** statement checks for this error: If the number you have entered is less than zero, the **then** part of the statement informs you of your mistake.

If the number isn't negative, the **else** part is executed. But here, too, there is something to check for. In this program, the number zero doesn't really figure in the average. It is a signal that you don't want to enter any more numbers. So NumberCount is incremented only when Number is greater than zero.

What happens if the first number you type is zero? This input terminates the **while** loop, and so NumberCount, which has been initialized to zero, won't be incremented and will remain at zero for the rest of the program. But, because you can't divide by zero, the average value

```
Average := Sum/NumberCount
```

cannot be computed. Hence we have included a final **if-then-else** statement to avoid the possibility of dividing by zero. Had we left it out, the program would crash if the first value entered were a zero. This is called a *run-time* error, because the bug shows up while the program is running.

The **if-then-else** statement that complains when you type a negative number has a special function. It protects you against bad input values. This is called *idiot-proofing*. If you make a mistake when you are entering data, the **if-then-else** statement keeps your bad input from producing invalid output.

MacPascal does some idiot-proofing of its own. Suppose you type a letter instead of an integer. The program won't accept it, and the Macintosh will beep when you press the key. And if you type a real number, MacPascal will read into the variable Number only the integer part of what you type. It ignores the decimal point and the digits that follow it.

Program ElectricBill

Here is a more practical **if-then-else** example. Your electric company, Podunk Power and Light, has a *life-line* rate of 2.30 cents per kilowatt hour (KWH) for customers who use less than 250 KWH's of electricity per month. A customer who uses more than 250 KWH's, however, is charged 4.20 cents per KWH on *all* electricity used.

Program ElectricBill will compute your electric bill using an **if-then-else** statement that splits the program into two parts. If you use less than 250 KWH's of electricity per month, the **then** part of the program calculates your bill at the life-line rate. If you use more electricity, the **else** part does the calculation at the regular rate.

```
program ElectricBill;
{READS IN KILOWATT HOURS USED AND CALCULATES ELECTRIC BILL}
{BASED ON TWO-TIERED RATE SYSTEM.}
  const
    LifeLineRate = 0.023;
    RegRate = 0.042;
  var
    Cost : real;
    KWH : integer;
```

```
begin
 writeln('Type in the number of kilowatt hours used -- an integer.');
 readln(KWH);
 if (KWH < 250) then
  Cost := LifeLineRate * KWH
 else
  Cost := RegRate * KWH;
 writeln('Your electric bill is $',Cost : 4 : 2)
end.
```

Now suppose Podunk Power and Light changes its rates to a three-tiered system. Customers who use less than 250 KWH's of electricity still pay 2.30 cents per kilowatt hour. But a customer who uses 250 KWH's or more pays 4.20 cents per KWH on the first 0 to 499 Kilowatt hours and 5.35 cents per kilowatt hour for any additional power. Here is the revised program.

```
program ElectricBillTwo;
{READS IN KILOWATT HOURS USED AND CALCULATES ELECTRIC BILL}
{BASED ON THREE-TIERED RATE SYSTEM}
 const
  LifeLineRate = 0.023;
  LowRegRate = 0.042;
  HighRegRate = 0.053;
 var
  Cost,PartialCost : real;
  KWH,KWHsLeft : integer;
begin
 writeln('Type in the number of kilowatt hours used -- an integer.');
 readln(KWH);
 if (KWH < 250) then
  Cost := LifeLineRate * KWH
 else if (KWH < 500) then
  Cost := LowRegRate * KWH
 else
  begin
   PartialCost := LowRegRate * 499;
   KWHsLeft := KWH - 499;
   Cost := PartialCost + (KWHsLeft * HighRegRate)
  end;
 writeln('Your electric bill is $',Cost : 4 : 2)
end.
```

To handle the three-way split in the cost of electricity, **program ElectricBillTwo** has an **if-then-else** statement as the **else** part of another **if-then-else**. This is called a *nested* **if-then-else** statement. Make sure you understand this program completely by tracing how it will run on inputs of 249, 250, and 500 kilowatt hours.

5.4 The Case of the Dangling Else

Now look at **program** Dangle, keeping an eye on the final **else**.

```
program Dangle;
 var
   Number : integer;
begin
 writeln('Type in an integer.');
 readln(Number);
 if (Number > 0) then
   if (Number > 10) then
   Number := 100
   else  ←──────────────── The dangling else
   Number := 50;
 writeln(Number)
end.
```

What does **program** Dangle print out when you type in 1? (Make a guess!) To figure out the answer, you must know which **if-then** the final **else** is a part of—the outer **if-then** or the inner **if-then**. If the final **else** belongs to the inner or nearest **if-then**, the program prints 50. If it belongs to the outer **if-then**, the program prints 1.

In Pascal, an **else** statement always goes with the *nearest* **if-then** that isn't followed by another **else**. And so **program** Dangle prints 50. The **else** part of an inner **if-then-else** statement is called a *dangling else.*

Once you type a program in, pretty-printing will clarify where the dangling **else** goes; it will line up with the **if** it belongs to. But when you first create a program with pencil and paper, you may be tempted to hook the **else** up with the outer or farthest **if-then**. Pascal won't see it this way. It uses the "nearest **if-then** rule," and you must, too.

5.5 The Mod Operator

When we talked about arithmetic with integers, we introduced **div**, the operator that does integer division.

$5 \div 3 = 1\ 2/3$
$5\ \mathbf{div}\ 3 = 1$

Pascal has another operator that is a companion to the **div** operator. It's called **mod**. The **mod** operator does division, too—but the answer it gives is the *remainder* that's left after the division is done. For example, 5 divided by 3 equals 1 with a remainder of 2, so

$5\ \mathbf{mod}\ 3 = 2$

Whereas the expression 31 **div** 7 gives you the number of full weeks in March, the expression 31 **mod** 7 gives the number of days left in March after 4 full weeks have passed.

$$\begin{array}{r} 4 \\ 7\overline{)31} \\ \underline{28} \\ 3 \end{array}$$

31 **div** 7 = 4

31 **mod** 7 = 3

Here are some examples of division using ÷, **div**, and **mod**.

3 ÷ 3 = 1	3 **div** 3 = 1	3 **mod** 3 = 0
4 ÷ 3 = 1 1/3	4 **div** 3 = 1	4 **mod** 3 = 1
10 ÷ 7 = 1 3/7	10 **div** 7 = 1	10 **mod** 7 = 3
5 ÷ 6 = 5/6	5 **div** 6 = 0	5 **mod** 6 = 5

Note that with **mod,** if the second number divides the first evenly, the answer is zero. And if the second number is bigger than the first, the answer is the same as the first number.

EXERCISE 2   **a.** Figure out the answers to these problems. Then check your answers in the Instant window.

11 **mod** 6 = ?
2 **mod** 5 = ?
111 **mod** 10 = ?
5 **mod** 5 = ?
8 **mod** 5 = ?

b. What does this program print?

```
program ModQuestion;
 var
   Number : integer;
 begin
  for Number := 11 to 20 do
   writeln(Number mod 5)
 end. ▬
```

5.6 A Math Puzzle

Now let's use the **mod** function to write a program that solves an intriguing math puzzle. First, recall that, to cube a number, you multiply it by itself three times:

$$3^3 = 3 \times 3 \times 3 = 3 * 3 * 3 = 27$$

The following table gives the cubes of the numbers from 0 to 9.

Number	Cube
0^3	0
1^3	1
2^3	8
3^3	27
4^3	64
5^3	125
6^3	216
7^3	343
8^3	512
9^3	729

EXERCISE 3   Figure out the sums of the cubes of the digits of these numbers.

a. 121

Answer: 10

b. 567

Answer: 684 ▬

Now here's a strange fact: The number 153 equals the sum of the cubes of its digits.

$$153 = 1^3 + 5^3 + 3^3 = 1 + 125 + 27 = 153$$

Question: Are there other three-digit numbers that equal the sums of the cubes of their digits? To find out, let's write a program called **program** CubeSum that will test each number from 100 to 999 for this peculiar property. Let's tackle this problem with our think-plan-code-test-and-debug method.

Thinking

The problem asks us to examine all three-digit numbers—that is, all numbers from 100 to 999—and report back if we find any that satisfy the cube-sum property. So a piece of our program will have to *generate* all these numbers. We can do this with a loop.

There aren't any input or output variables. The program merely steps through the integers from 100 to 999 and reports any with the cube-sum property.

How about program variables? We'll need a control variable for the loop that generates each number from 100 to 999. Let's call it TestNumber. And we'll need a variable called SumOfCubes to hold the value of the sum of the cubes of the digits.

We will also have to keep track of the separate digits for each value of TestNumber. Three-digit numbers have a hundreds place, a tens place, and a ones place. So let's use Hundreds, Tens, and Ones as the names for these variables.

Given a number, we need a way to calculate its digits. The operators **div** and **mod** will do the job. To see how, let's look first at a two-digit number—say, 47. In the two-digit case, **div** and **mod** give us the answers we want directly:

47 **div** 10 = 4
47 **mod** 10 = 7

The first digit is 4 and the second digit is 7. Using **div** 10 and then **mod** 10, we can produce the two digits that make up any two-digit number.

A similar strategy works for three-digit numbers. Let's look at 567.

567 **div** 100 = 5   (This gives us the first digit.)
567 **mod** 100 = 67
67 **div** 10 = 6   (This gives us the second digit.)
67 **mod** 10 = 7   (This gives us the third digit.)

We can shorten these calculations by writing them this way:

567 **div** 100 = 5
(567 **mod** 100) **div** 10 = 6
(567 **mod** 100) **mod** 10 = 7

These **div** and **mod** calculations give us the digits if TestNumber is *any* three-digit number:

digit in hundreds place = TestNumber **div** 100
digit in tens place   = (TestNumber **mod** 100) **div** 10
digit in ones place   = (TestNumber **mod** 100) **mod** 10

Here is our data table for **program** CubeSum:

───────────────────────── **DATA TABLE** ─────────────────────────

Input Variables	**Output Variables**	**Constants**
none	none	none

Program Variables	**Formulas**
TestNumber	Hundreds = TestNumber **div** 100
Hundreds	Tens = (TestNumber **mod** 100) **div** 10
Tens	Ones = (TestNumber **mod** 100) **mod** 10
Ones	
SumOfCubes	

Loops
one loop generates all three-digit numbers

The problem asks us to test each number after it has been generated to determine whether the cube-sum property holds. So we can solve this problem by using a method that can be applied to a great many programming problems: the *generate-and-test* method.

Planning

Our starting plan looks like this:

> *generate* numbers from 100 to 999
> > *test* to see if a number satisfies cube-sum
> > property, and report the number if it passes the test

We can refine our plan, using the variables from the data table:

> step TestNumber in a loop from 100 to 999
> > calculate SumOfCubes for TestNumber
> > if SumOfCubes = TestNumber then print TestNumber

Now we can turn our plan into a more concrete algorithm by working out the looping structure. There are three possibilities—a **for** loop, a **while** loop, or a **repeat-until** loop. Using a **for** loop:

```
for TestNumber : = 100 to 999 do
   begin
      calculate sum of cubes of digits in TestNumber
      if sum = TestNumber, then print TestNumber
   end
```

Using a **while** loop:

```
TestNumber : = 100;
while TestNumber < = 999 do
   begin
      calculate sum of cubes of digits in TestNumber
      if sum = TestNumber, then print TestNumber
      TestNumber : = TestNumber + 1
   end
```

Using a **repeat-until** loop:

```
TestNumber : = 100;
repeat
   calculate sum of cubes of digits in TestNumber
   if sum = TestNumber, then print TestNumber
   TestNumber : = TestNumber + 1
until TestNumber = 1000
```

All three looping plans will solve the problem. The **for**-loop solution will work out just fine, because we already know the lower and upper limits of the loop. The **repeat** plan is OK too, because the loop will execute at least once, so having the looping test at the end of the loop will cause no problems. And the **while** loop will also work. It's the most versatile looping command.

Coding

Now we have the machinery to code **program** CubeSum. We'll use a **while** statement for the loop that generates each TestNumber, and we'll use an **if-then** statement to do the test part of the generate-and-test scheme. Here's the program:

```
program CubeSum;
{REPORTS EVERY INTEGER FROM 100 TO 999}
{THAT EQUALS THE SUM OF THE CUBES OF ITS DIGITS.}
 var
   Hundreds,Tens,Ones,SumOfCubes,TestNumber : integer;
begin
 TestNumber := 100;
 while (TestNumber <= 999) do
  begin
   Hundreds := TestNumber div 100;
   Tens := (TestNumber mod 100) div 10;
   Ones := (TestNumber mod 100) mod 10;
   SumOfCubes := Hundreds * Hundreds * Hundreds +
       Tens * Tens * Tens + Ones * Ones * Ones;
   if (SumOfCubes = TestNumber) then
    writeln(TestNumber : 1,
       ' equals the sum of the cubes of its digits.');
   TestNumber := TestNumber + 1
  end
end.
```

Are there any other of these strange numbers besides 153? We're not telling!

5.7 Drawing Rectangles

Next we're going to show you four MacPascal instructions for drawing rectangles. The Macintosh Pascal instruction *framerect* draws the outline of a rectangle in the Drawing window. For example, the instruction

```
framerect(30,40,150,100)
```

creates the picture shown in Figure 5.1. The values 30, 40, 150, and 100 determine the top, left, bottom, and right sides of the rectangle. So *framerect* works this way:

```
framerect(top,left,bottom,right)
```

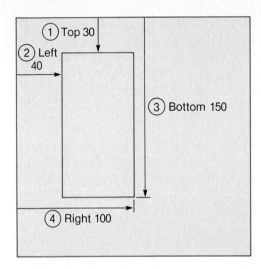

Figure 5.1   The rectangle drawn by *framerect*(30,40,150,100).

To keep straight which number determines which side of the rectangle, re-member to start at the top and go *counterclockwise* around the rectangle: top, left, bottom, right.

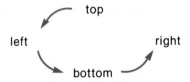

The width of a rectangle is equal to the fourth number minus the second number, or right minus left. Its height is equal to the third number minus the first number, or bottom minus top. So the dimensions of the rectangle shown in Figure 5.1 are 100 − 40 = 60 by 150 − 30 = 120. When you use a rectangle com-mand, top must be smaller than bottom, and left must be smaller than right. If you frame a rectangle with left larger than right or top larger than bottom, the figure will have negative width or height and nothing will be printed out.

EXERCISE 4   **a.** What *framerect* command draws a square that is 50 units on a side with its upper-left corner at the point (100,100)?

Answer: framerect(100,100,150,150)

b. What *framerect* command draws a rectangle that is exactly 10 units in-side the border of the standard Drawing window?

Answer: framerect(10,10,190,190) ■

MacPascal has three other rectangle commands: *paintrect, invertrect,* and *eraserect. Paintrect* works like *framerect,* only instead of drawing just an outline, it paints the whole rectangle black. *Invertrect* works the way *invertcircle* does. It reverses the color of everything inside the rectangle's boundary. *Eraserect* completely "whites out" the area inside the rectangle's borders.

EXERCISE 5   **a.** Paint the entire Drawing window black.

b. Which two *invertrect* commands will create this picture?

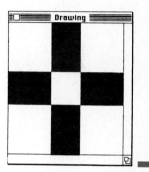

Using rectangle commands and loops, we can create dramatic graphics in the Drawing window. For example, **program** ExplodeRect works like **program** Explode from Chapter 2—only it explodes a rectangle instead of a circle, and then it erases the rectangle from the inside out with an "exploding" *eraserect* command. See Figure 5.2.

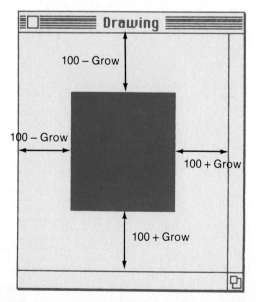

Figure 5.2   ExplodeRect when Grow = 50 in the first loop.

```
program ExplodeRect;
{EXPLODES AND THEN ERASES A RECTANGLE}
 var
  Grow : integer;
begin
 Grow := 0;
 {EXPLODES A RECTANGLE}
 while (Grow <= 100) do
  begin
   Grow := Grow + 1;
   paintrect(100 - Grow,100 - Grow,100 + Grow,100 + Grow)
  end;
 Grow := 0;
 {ERASES THE RECTANGLE}
 while (Grow <= 100) do
  begin
   Grow := Grow + 1;
   eraserect(100 - Grow,100 - Grow,100 + Grow,100 + Grow)
  end
end.
```

Here is another spectacular program that uses a rectangle command (see Figure 5.3).

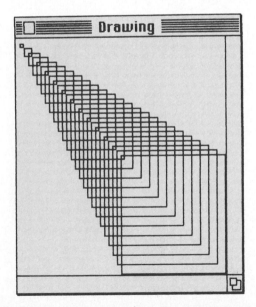

Figure 5.3 Output for **program** StackOfRectangles.

```
program StackOfRectangles;
 const
  Spacing = 4;
 var
  Grow : integer;
begin
 Grow := 0;
 repeat
  framerect(Grow,Grow,2 * Grow,2 * Grow);
  Grow := Grow + Spacing
 until (Grow > 100)
end.
```

If you substitute an *invertrect* command for the *framerect* command in **program StackOfRectangles**, you will get the picture at the beginning of this chapter, on page 153. Try it and see.

5.8 Bar Graphs

Bar graphs help you compare the sizes of things. You can draw bar graphs that give you all sorts of information in picture form, from the consumer price index during the last twelve months to the amount of money you will accumulate in your savings account over the next ten years. Figure 5.4 and Figure 5.5 are examples of typical bar graphs.

A bar is just a black rectangle. To print out a sequence of bars, we will put a *paintrect* command inside a loop.

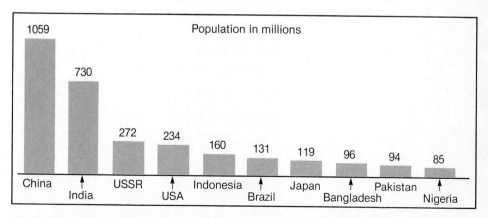

Figure 5.4   A bar graph of the populations of the world's ten most populous countries.

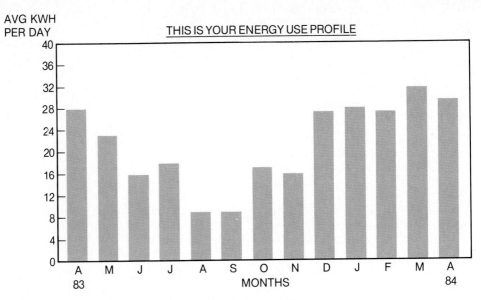

Figure 5.5   A bar graph that comes with an electric bill.

Program BarGraphOne

Our first bar graph program will print a picture that is barely a bar graph at all (see Figure 5.6).

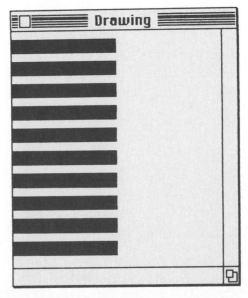

Figure 5.6   Output for **program** BarGraphOne.

The bars are identical except that each one has a different vertical position. All have the same left boundary, the same right boundary, and the same thickness. And the gaps between the bars are all the same size.

```
program BarGraphOne;
{PRINTS 10 HORIZONTAL BARS ON LEFT SIDE OF DRAWING WINDOW}
 const
   Left = 0;
   Right = 100;
   Separation = 7;
   Thickness = 12;
   BarCount = 10;
 var
   BarNumber,Top,Bottom : integer;
begin
{BOTTOM IS INITIALIZED TO 0, WHICH IS THE TOP OF THE WINDOW}
 Bottom := 0;
 BarNumber := 1;
 while (BarNumber <= BarCount) do
  begin
    Top := Bottom + Separation;
    Bottom := Top + Thickness;
    paintrect(Top,Left,Bottom,Right);
    BarNumber := BarNumber + 1
  end
end.
```

After Bottom and BarNumber are initialized, the **while** loop is executed, and the bars are drawn.

In order to paint a rectangle, we must determine the values of Top, Left, Bottom, and Right. In this program Left and Right are fixed, so we need to determine values only for Top and Bottom.

Top has for its value the previous or initial value of Bottom plus the separation between the bars.

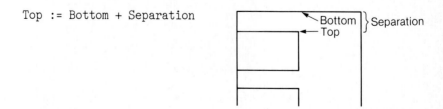

```
Top := Bottom + Separation
```

In the first iteration of the loop, Top is assigned the initial value of Bottom, 0, plus the separation between the bars, which is a constant.

Once we know the value for the top of a rectangle, we can calculate the value for its bottom by adding the thickness of a rectangle:

```
Bottom := Top + Thickness
```

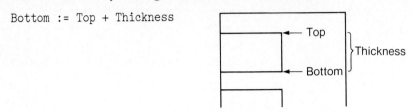

Each loop iteration draws one bar, and, because the number of loops equals BarCount, we will get BarCount (in this case 10) bars.

EXERCISE 6   a. How would you change **program** BarGraphOne so that there are twelve bars separated by eight units?

b. Change the program so that the bars start at the right instead of at the left. ■■

BarGraphTwo

Next let's rotate the graph so that the bars are vertical, which is the traditional way of displaying bar graphs (see Figure 5.7). **Program** BarGraphTwo on page 175 does the trick.

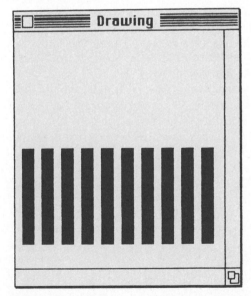

Figure 5.7 Output for **program** BarGraphTwo.

```
program BarGraphTwo;
{PRINTS 10 VERTICAL BARS NEAR BOTTOM OF DRAWING WINDOW}
 const
   Bottom = 180;
   Top = 100;
   Separation = 7;
   Thickness = 12;
   BarCount = 10;
 var
   BarNumber,Left,Right : integer;
begin
{BOTTOM IS INITIALIZED TO 0, WHICH IS THE TOP OF THE WINDOW}
 Right := 0;
 BarNumber := 1;
 while (BarNumber <= BarCount) do
  begin
   Left := Right + Separation;
   Right := Left + Thickness;
   paintrect(Top,Left,Bottom,Right);
   BarNumber := BarNumber + 1
  end
end.
```

This time Left and Right are variables, and Top and Bottom are constants. We have made Bottom 180 instead of 200 so that there will be room underneath the bars for labels. We will show you how to add the labels in a moment. Inside the loop we calculate Left first, adding the previous (or initial) value of Right to the constant value for Separation.

5.9 Writing in the Drawing Window

In order to create a real bar graph, we need to be able to label the bars. We can't use *write* or *writeln*, because they print text in the Text window. To print text or numbers in the Drawing window, we'll use the MacPascal instructions *writedraw* and *moveto*. *Moveto* tells MacPascal where in the Drawing window you want your words and numbers to appear.

Imagine that the Drawing window comes with a pen. The *moveto* instruction places the tip of the pen at the point where you want something printed in the Drawing window. The *writedraw* command prints text at the pen position. Figure 5.8 illustrates how *moveto* and *writedraw* work.

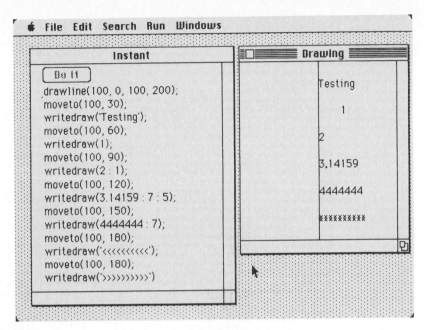

Figure 5.8 The *writedraw* command, along with the *moveto* command, prints words and numbers in the Drawing window. The word Testing starts at point (100,30). Note that a decimal point takes up less space than a full character.

We're almost ready to draw a real bar graph with labels. But first we need to make the typeface of the print on the screen smaller so that the labels will fit under the bars. This is done by opening the Windows menu and choosing Type-Size.

Program GraphOfSquares

Program GraphOfSquares draws a series of bars that represent the squares of the integers 1 through 10 (see Figure 5.9). It also labels the bars with their heights.

```pascal
program GraphOfSquares;
{GRAPHS THE SQUARES OF THE INTEGERS FROM 1 TO 10.}
 const
  Bottom = 180;
  Separation = 7;
  Thickness = 12;
  BarCount = 10;
 var
  BarNumber,Left,Right,Top,Height : integer;
```

```
begin
{BOTTOM IS INITIALIZED TO 0, WHICH IS THE TOP OF THE WINDOW}
Right := 0;
BarNumber := 1;
while (BarNumber <= BarCount) do
 begin
   Left := Right + Separation;
   Right := Left + Thickness;
     {CALCULATE HEIGHT}
   Height := BarNumber * BarNumber;
     {CALCULATE TOP}
   Top := Bottom - Height;
     {DRAW BAR}
   paintrect(Top,Left,Bottom,Right);
     {LABEL BAR}
   moveto(Left,Bottom + 10);
   writedraw(Height : 1);
     {INCREMENT BAR NUMBER}
   BarNumber := BarNumber + 1
 end
end.
```

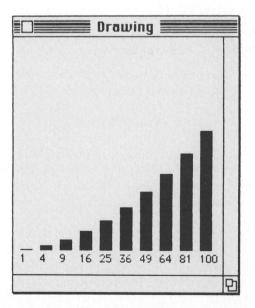

Figure 5.9   The output for **program** GraphOfSquares.

In **program** GraphOfSquares the height of the bar is the value of the variable Height. Once we know the value of Height, we can calculate Top:

```
Top := Bottom - Height
```

This calculation looks backward, but it isn't. As the bars get bigger, the values of Top get smaller, because a small value for Top means that the top of the bar is closer to the top of the window.

Each time the loop is executed, the program draws a bar and then inserts a label. The *moveto* instruction starts the label 10 units below the left corner of each bar. Then *writedraw* prints out the height of the bar. Like *writeln*, *writedraw* allots an 8-space field width for integers, which you can override using colon notation.

5.10 A Compound-Interest Bar Graph Program

Now we are ready to draw a much fancier bar graph. **Program** InterestGraph will show how compound interest makes a sum of money grow in your bank account year by year. You enter any principal, any interest rate, and any number of years in the account, and the program prints a bar graph that shows how the balance in your account will increase. Each bar represents the amount of money in the account at the beginning of a year.

Program InterestGraphOne includes some code from **program** Interest in Chapter 4. It's always a good idea to see whether you can borrow pieces of old programs when you're writing new ones. Doing so can save you a lot of time and energy. This is not cheating; it's being economical.

After **program** InterestGraphOne reads in values for Principal, Rate, and TotalYears, a figure is calculated for the variable Scale:

```
Scale := FirstBar/Principal
```

FirstBar is a constant that gives the height of the first bar, which we have set at 80. If Principal = $1000.00, Scale = .08. This means that one dollar = .08 units in the Drawing window. When we print a bar, we multiply Scale times MoneyInBank and round off the product to get the Height of a bar:

```
Height := round(MoneyInBank * Scale)
```

After MoneyInBank is initialized to Principal, the main loop in the program draws labels and bars. Then it calculates MoneyInBank for the next year. Here is the program.

```
program InterestGraphOne;
{READS IN PRINCIPAL, INTEREST RATE, AND YEARS IN BANK.}
{PRINTS OUT GRAPH OF MONEY ACCUMULATED IN BANK.}
 const
  Separation = 30;
  Thickness = 30;
  Bottom = 190;
  FirstBar = 80; {FIRSTBAR REPRESENTS PRINCIPAL}
 var
  MoneyInBank,NewMoney,Principal,Rate : Real;
  Scale : real; {ADJUSTS HEIGHT OF BARS}
  Left,Right,Top,Height,Year,TotalYears : integer;
begin
 writeln('Type in principal, interest rate, and years in bank.');
 readln(Principal,Rate,TotalYears);
 if (Principal <> 0.0) then
  Scale := FirstBar / Principal
 else
  Scale := 0.0;
 Year := 0;
 Left := 0;
        {INITIALIZE MONEY IN BANK}
 MoneyInBank := Principal;
 while (Year <= TotalYears) do
  begin
        {CALCULATE AND PAINT RECTANGLE}
   Right := Left + Thickness;
   Left := Right + Separation;
   Height := round(MoneyInBank * Scale);
   Top := Bottom - Height;
   paintrect(Top,Left,Bottom,Right);
        {DRAW TOP LABEL, 3 UNITS ABOVE BAR}
   moveto(Left,Top - 3);
   writedraw(MoneyInBank : 5 : 2);
        {DRAW BOTTOM LABEL}
   moveto(Left,Bottom + 13);
   writedraw(Year : 1);
        {CALCULATE NEXT YEAR'S MONEY}
   Year := Year + 1;
   NewMoney := MoneyInBank * Rate;
   MoneyInBank := MoneyInBank + NewMoney
  end
end.
```

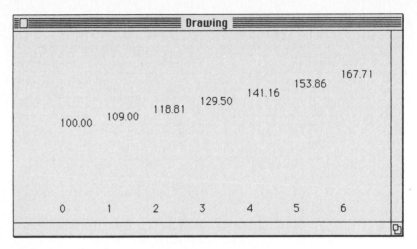

Figure 5.10   The output for **program** InterestGraphOne.

Now let's look at Figure 5.10 for the output.

As you can see, something is drastically wrong with this bar graph—no bars! Let's try to figure out where the bug is.

Debugging Program InterestGraphOne with the Observe Window

The Observe window is a terrific debugging tool, but it is no substitute for careful thinking on your part. When you run into a bug, study your code carefully and learn as much as you can just from reading before you turn to the Observe window. You may be completely stumped when you start out, but simple reasoning will often enable you to make progress isolating the problem. If you still can't locate the bug, go to the Observe window.

If we think about the bug in **program** InterestGraphOne, we'll come up with this: The error has to do with the *paintrect* command. Either it is not being executed at all, or there is something wrong with the values of Top, Left, Bottom, and Right. But we are not sure which, so it's time to turn to the Observe window.

After we open the Observe window, let's identify Top, Left, Bottom, and Right as the variables we want to watch and then place a stop next to *paintrect*.

Now we'll run the program using Go. Go-Go wouldn't help much here, because we can find out what we need to know by watching the very first iteration of the loop. Here's what we need to know: Why wasn't the first bar drawn? Was *paintrect* ever executed? And if it was, what were the values of its variables?

When we run the program, here's what we get:

```
╔══════════ Observe ══════════╗
║              100 │ Top        ⇧║
║               49 │ Left       ▯║
║              180 │ Bottom      ║
║               24 │ Right      ⇩║
╚═══════════════════════════════╝
```

The Observe window gives us a big clue. We can tell that *paintrect was* executed in the original program run, because the stop next to the *paintrect* command brings the program to a halt. But the values of the variables were faulty. Top is smaller than Bottom, which is correct. But Right is smaller than Left—that is, *Right is to the left of Left*. The rectangle has negative width, which is why it didn't appear on the screen.

To finish debugging, we need to reason backward: How were the values of Left and Right determined? Left is initialized to 0—the left wall. Then, inside the loop, Right is assigned Left + Thickness = 0 + 24 = 24. Now Left is assigned another value: Right + Separation = 49. So Left > Right, and this is our bug.

The statement

```
Left := Right + Separation
```

must come *before* the statement

```
Right := Left + Thickness
```

This will guarantee that Right is larger than Left by an amount equal to the thickness of a bar. If the two assignment statements come in this order, Right must be defined initially, because the other calculations depend on the initial value of Right. So, instead of using the initialization Left := 0 just before the loop, we'll use

```
Right := 0
```

Here is the corrected program, and Figure 5.11 gives a sample of output for this program.

```
program InterestGraphTwo;
{READS IN PRINCIPAL, INTEREST RATE, AND YEARS IN BANK.}
{PRINTS OUT GRAPH OF MONEY ACCUMULATED IN BANK.}
 const
   Separation = 30;
   Thickness = 30;
   Bottom = 190;
   FirstBar = 80; {FIRSTBAR REPRESENTS PRINCIPAL}
```

(continued)

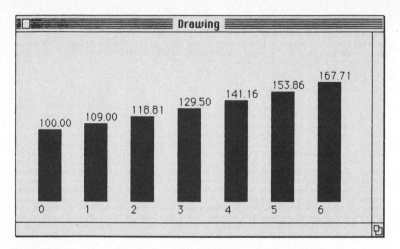

Figure 5.11   Typical output for **program** InterestGraphTwo.

```
var
  MoneyInBank,NewMoney,Principal,Rate : Real;
  Scale : real;  {ADJUSTS HEIGHT OF BARS}
  Left,Right,Top,Height,Year,TotalYears : integer;
begin
writeln('Type in principal, interest rate, and years in bank.');
readln(Principal,Rate,TotalYears);
if (Principal <> 0.0) then
  Scale := FirstBar / Principal
else
  Scale := 0.0;
Year := 0;
Right := 0;
    {INITIALIZE MONEY IN BANK}
MoneyInBank := Principal;
while (Year <= TotalYears) do
  begin
    {CALCULATE AND PAINT RECTANGLE}
  Left := Right + Separation;
  Right := Left + Thickness;
  Height := round(MoneyInBank * Scale);
  Top := Bottom - Height;
  paintrect(Top,Left,Bottom,Right);
    {DRAW TOP LABEL, 3 UNITS ABOVE BAR}
  moveto(Left,Top - 3);
  writedraw(MoneyInBank : 5 : 2);
    {DRAW BOTTOM LABEL}
```

```
moveto(Left,Bottom + 13);
writedraw(Year : 1);
   {CALCULATE NEXT YEAR'S MONEY}
Year := Year + 1;
NewMoney := MoneyInBank * Rate;
MoneyInBank := MoneyInBank + NewMoney
   end
end.
```

With InterestGraphTwo, the usefulness of our programs has taken a quantum leap. Give it a try, using a few different values and see how it does.

5.11 Oval Graphics

MacPascal has four more standard procedures for drawing pictures. The commands *frameoval*, *paintoval*, *invertoval*, and *eraseoval* draw ovals in the Drawing window. When you create an oval on the screen, it is inscribed inside an imaginary rectangle. The top, left, bottom, and right values for this rectangle determine the shape and position of the inscribed oval. These two instructions

```
framerect(10,15,180,70);
frameoval(10,15,180,70)
```

draw a rectangle with an oval inside it (see Figure 5.12).

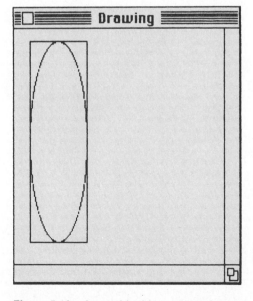

Figure 5.12 An oval inside a rectangle.

EXERCISE 7   Draw these pictures.

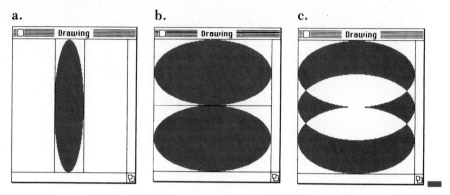

Program Cone

Program Cone draws 100 ovals, each a little lower on the screen and a little narrower than the one before. You have to see the program running to appreciate it. Figure 5.13 shows the final picture that is produced.

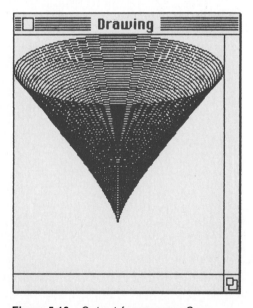

Figure 5.13   Output for **program** Cone.

```
program Cone;
 const
  Rate = 2;
 var
  Top,Left,Bottom,Right,ConeNumber : integer;
begin
 Top := 0;
 Left := 0;
 Bottom := 60;
 Right := 200;
 ConeNumber := 1;
 repeat
  frameoval(Top,Left,Bottom,Right);
  Top := Top + Rate;
  Bottom := Bottom + Rate;
  Left := Left + Rate;
  Right := Right - Rate;
  ConeNumber := ConeNumber + 1
 until (ConeNumber > 100)
end.
```

Program OvalsAndRecs

Program OvalsAndRecs uses an **if-then-else** statement to draw alternating ovals and rectangles. Whenever the variable Grow is odd, the program paints an oval; otherwise it paints a rectangle (see Figure 5.14).

```
program OvalsAndRecs;
 var
  Grow : integer;
begin
 Grow := 10;
 repeat
  if odd(Grow) then
   invertoval(Grow,2 * Grow,2 * Grow,4 * Grow)
  else
   invertrect(Grow,2 * Grow,2 * Grow,4 * Grow);
  Grow := Grow + 11
 until (Grow > 100)
end.
```

In **program** OvalsAndRecs we use the function *odd*. *Odd* is an unusual function. Unlike *sqrt*, *sqr*, and *round*, which return numerical answers, *odd* returns

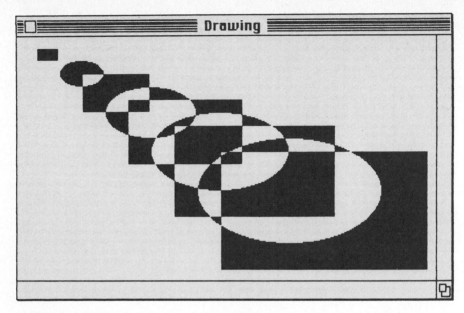

Figure 5.14   Output for **program** OvalsAndRecs.

an answer that is either true or false. Because *odd* gives a true or false answer, it can appear in the ⟨test⟩ position of a conditional statement, and that's how it is used in this program.

EXERCISE 8   What does **program** OvalsAndRecs do if the assignment statement Grow := Grow + 11 is changed to Grow := Grow + 10? ▬

Program Globe

Using two **repeat-until** loops, **program** Globe draws a globe in the standard Drawing window with the vertical, longitude lines drawn in first (See Figure 5.15). If you change the value of the constant GrowthRate, you can build other dramatic versions of the output.

```
program Globe;
 const
  GrowthRate = 6;
 var
  Top,Left,Bottom,Right : integer;
```

```
begin
 Top := 0;
 Left := 0;
 Bottom := 200;
 Right := 200;
     {DRAWS LONGITUDE LINES.}
 repeat
  frameoval(Top,Left,Bottom,Right);
  Left := Left + GrowthRate;
  Right := Right - GrowthRate
 until (Left )= 100);
 Top := 0;
 Left := 0;
 Bottom := 200;
 Right := 200;
     {DRAWS LATITUDE LINES}
 repeat
  frameoval(Top,Left,Bottom,Right);
  Top := Top + GrowthRate;
  Bottom := Bottom - GrowthRate
 until (Top )= 100)
end.
```

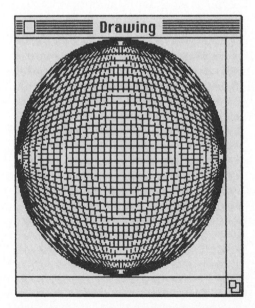

Figure 5.15 Output for **program** Globe.

TEST YOURSELF

1. What are Pascal's conditional statements?
2. What is a dangling **else**?
3. What is the "nearest **if-then**" rule?
4. What is idiot-proofing?
5. Describe the Scratchpad principle.
6. What MacPascal instruction writes text in the Drawing window?
7. Explain the generate-and-test method.
8. What does the instruction *moveto* do?
9. What Pascal arithmetic operation gives remainders?
10. What MacPascal instruction whites out the standard Drawing window?
11. What is a run-time error?
12. What instruction inverts everything in the standard Drawing window?

PROBLEMS

1. Would **program** BetterTwoSort work differently if the **if-then** statement used the test (FirstNumber < = SecondNumber)?
2. **a.** Type in **program** ExplodeRect to see how it works. Now speed it up so that the explosion happens faster.
   b. Rewrite **program** ExplodeRect using a **repeat-until** loop.
3. Write a program that will draw a cube like this in the Drawing window. *Hint:* Use two *framerect* instructions and four *drawline* instructions.

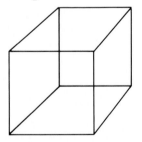

4. Homer has 1038 eggs. Write a Pascal expression that tells how many eggs he will have left after he sells as many complete dozens as he can.
5. Using the equation 8 **mod** 7 = 1, you can figure out that, if today is Tuesday, 8 days from now will be 1 day later in the week, or Wednesday. Suppose that this year isn't a leap year and that January 22 falls on a Tuesday. On what day of the week does January 22 fall next year? What if this year *is* a leap year?

6. Modify **program** GraphOfSquares so that it graphs the cubes of the numbers from 1 to 10. Be sure to scale the heights of the bars so that the graph fits in the Drawing window.

7. Write an interactive program in which you supply the coordinates of a point in the Drawing window: horizontal then vertical. The program draws and labels the point. For example, if you type in 50,50, it will respond with

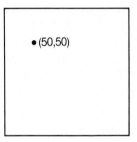

(*Hint:* To draw the point, use *paintcircle* with a small value for the radius.)

8. Write an interactive program that reads in the horizontal and vertical coordinates of a point in the Drawing window and also the top, left, bottom, and right values representing the borders of a rectangle. The program determines whether the point lies inside the rectangle and prints its answer in the Text window.

9. Write an interactive program, similar to the one in Problem 8, that determines whether a point lies inside a circle. The circle should be represented by three integers: the horizontal and vertical coordinates of the center and the radius.

10. Write an interactive program that reads in the top, left, bottom, and right values of a rectangle and yields as output the rectangle flipped over on its right side. For example,

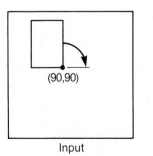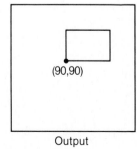

11. Write an interactive program that reads in the top, left, bottom, and right values of a rectangle. Instead of drawing that rectangle, the program should draw a square with the same area as the rectangle. The square should appear in the lower-left corner of the standard Drawing window. Make the area of the square as close as possible to the area of the rectangle.

12. Are there any two-digit numbers that equal the sum of the squares of their digits?

13. In what percentage of two-digit numbers does the sum of the squares of the digits *exceed* the number?

14. Write an interactive program that reads in the coordinates of the center of a circle and a radius. If the radius is less than or equal to zero, the program tells you it has received a bad input. Otherwise it draws the outline of a circle, using the *frameoval* command.

15. Using the generate-and-test method, write a program that reads in a positive integer and prints out all positive integers that evenly divide the one you typed. (*Hint: b* divides *a* evenly if and only if (*a* mod *b*) = 0.)

16. Podunk Power and Light has a new rate schedule. Customers now pay the life-line rate for the first 249 kilowatt hours, the low regular rate for the next 250 kilowatt hours, and the high rate on all additional power used. Modify **program** ElectricBillTwo to handle this rate change. Idiot-proof your program so that if a negative number is typed, the program responds with "Bad input—start over."

Problem Solving with Procedures

6

We have come to the most important chapter in the book. Here you'll learn about a method for attacking any complicated problem without getting lost in the details.

This method is called *top-down programming*. When you use it to solve a big problem, you divide the problem into small, easy-to-code pieces. Then you deal with each piece separately. This "divide and conquer" strategy relies on Pascal's all important procedure command.

We've seen procedure commands before—the standard procedures such as *writeln*, *paintcircle*, and *drawline*. These instructions are built into MacPascal, and each does some special job. Now we are going to show you how to write your own procedures. From here on, when we say *procedure* we mean the kind you make up yourself. We'll refer to the built-in procedures as *standard procedures*.

6.1 Creating Your Own Procedures

Like a standard procedure, any procedure you make up yourself does some special job. Let's consider a simple example of how procedures work. Suppose we want to write a program that prints out the first verse of "Old MacDonald." We can create a procedure called Refrain that will print out the refrain. Wherever the word *Refrain* appears in the body of the program, the program will print "Ei, ei, o."

```
program OldMac;
{PRINTS THE FIRST VERSE OF OLDMACDONALD}

{THE PROCEDURE DECLARATION}
procedure Refrain;
begin
 writeln('Ei, ei, o.')
end;
```

(continued)

```
{THE BODY OF THE PROGRAM}
begin
 writeln('Old MacDonald had a farm,');
 Refrain;  {THE PROCEDURE STATEMENT}
 writeln('And on that farm he had some pigs,');
 Refrain   {THE PROCEDURE STATEMENT}
end.
```

Like all procedures, **procedure** Refrain has two parts: a procedure declaration and a procedure statement. The *procedure declaration* comes in the declaration part of the program between the variable declarations and the body. The declaration looks almost like a program: It has a heading line followed by a body. The body of a procedure declaration consists of a statement or a series of statements sandwiched between a **begin** and an **end.**

The *procedure statement* is simply the name of the procedure, Refrain. When the statement Refrain is executed in the body of the program, it commands the computer to follow the instruction in the procedure declaration.

6.2 Executing Procedure Refrain

When you run **program** OldMac, Pascal first takes note of the declaration for **procedure** Refrain. Then it goes to the body of the program and executes the first *writeln* statement, printing

```
Old MacDonald had a farm,
```

Next comes the procedure statement Refrain. This statement tells the computer to follow the instructions listed in the procedure declaration. So it prints out

```
Ei, ei, o.
```

Now the computer returns to the body of the program and executes the next statement, printing

```
And on that farm he had some pigs,
```

Another Refrain statement is next. Once again the Macintosh jumps to the declaration for Refrain, printing out

```
Ei, ei, o.
```

Finally the Macintosh returns to the main program. There are no more instructions, so execution ends.

If you type in **program** OldMac and step it, you can see how the Macintosh executes the procedure statement. The stepper hand jumps to the declaration portion of the program when the computer is carrying out the instructions for the procedure.

When the computer executes the instructions in a procedure declaration, we say it is doing a *procedure call*. The main program *calls* the procedure to do the job that the procedure is dedicated to. When the procedure call is finished, the computer goes on to the next instruction in the main program. This is called a *return* from the procedure call.

You can think of the main program as a general contractor who is building a house and calls up a carpenter to do the carpentry work. The procedure is like the carpentry work. And the instructions in the procedure are like the specific steps the carpenter follows. When the carpentry work is finished, the contractor calls another worker to do some other special job.

6.3 Program SquashedGlobe

Next let's look at a more ambitious program called **program** SquashedGlobe that uses three procedures to draw the flattened globe shown in Figure 6.1. Here's a tip on how to read programs with procedures: Always read the body of the main program first. It will tell you about the program *as a whole*. Once you understand what the big pieces of the program do, you can go back and look at the details of the procedures.

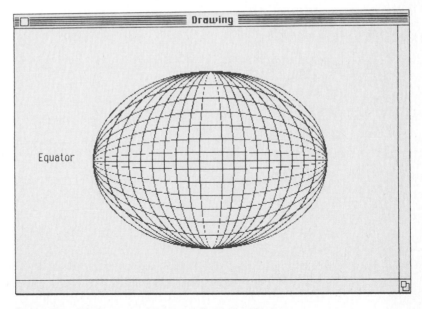

Figure 6.1   The output of **program** SquashedGlobe.

Learning to read programs is an important skill. Don't sell it short! The best programmers learn a lot from reading other people's programs.

```
program SquashedGlobe;
```

```
procedure DrawLatitudeLines;
{DRAWS THE HORIZONTAL LINES}
 const
  LatitudeSpread = 15;
  Left = 100;
  Right = 400;
 var
  Top,Bottom : integer;
 {BODY OF PROCEDURE}
begin
 Top := 50;
 Bottom := 250;
 repeat
  frameoval(Top,Left,Bottom,Right);
  Top := Top + LatitudeSpread;
  Bottom := Bottom - LatitudeSpread
 until (Top >= Bottom)
end;
```

```
procedure DrawLongitudeLines;
{DRAWS THE VERTICAL LINES}
 const
  LongitudeSpread = 15;
  Top = 50;
  Bottom = 250;
 var
  Left,Right : integer;
 {BODY OF PROCEDURE}
begin
 Left := 100;
 Right := 400;
 repeat
  frameoval(Top,Left,Bottom,Right);
  Left := Left + LongitudeSpread;
  Right := Right - LongitudeSpread
 until (Left >= Right)
end;
```

```
procedure DrawEquator;
{DRAWS STRAIGHT HORIZONTAL LINE}
begin
 drawline(100,150,400,150);
 moveto(30,150);
 writedraw('Equator')
end;
```

```
{MAIN PROGRAM}
begin
 DrawLatitudeLines;
 DrawLongitudeLines;
 DrawEquator
end.
```

The main program tells a great deal about what **program** SquashedGlobe does. It draws the horizontal latitude lines, then the vertical longitude lines, then the equator line with its label. These three actions form the flattened globe in the Drawing window.

When you run **program** SquashedGlobe, execution begins in the main program. First comes a call to **procedure** DrawLatitudeLines. The computer jumps to the declaration for this procedure and carries out the instructions listed there. When it comes to a constant such as Left or to a variable such as Top, it uses the value it finds inside the procedure. Because they are declared inside the procedure, Left is called a *local constant* and Top is called a *local variable*.

When execution of DrawLatitudeLines is complete, the computer returns to the main program and executes the next instruction, which is the procedure statement DrawLongitudeLines. Again the computer jumps to the declaration part of the program—this time to the declaration for DrawLongitudeLines. It follows these instructions, drawing the vertical lines on the globe, and then returns to the main program.

Finally, **procedure** DrawEquator is executed. The computer jumps one more time to the declaration part, executes the instructions that add the equator line and its label, and then returns to the main part, where program execution ends.

Procedure Syntax

Procedure syntax and program syntax are practically the same. **Procedure** DrawLatitudeLines, for example, starts with a heading line, includes a declaration part, and has a body that's surrounded by a **begin-end** pair. The declaration has its own constants and variables, and the body includes a loop.

So far we have seen just two differences between procedure syntax and program syntax. A procedure heading line starts with the word **procedure** instead of the word **program**, and procedures end with a semicolon instead of a period.

This brings us to an important point. A procedure is a self-contained unit. *Constants and variables that are declared locally can be used only in the instructions within that procedure.* In **program** SquashedGlobe, **procedure** DrawLatitudeLines and **procedure** DrawLongitudeLines seem to have conflicting declarations: Top is a variable in DrawLatitudeLines and a constant in DrawLongitudeLines. But there is no conflict. The constants and variables declared in DrawLatitudeLines are inaccessible to instructions in DrawLongitudeLines, and vice versa. No instruction in the main program can include them, either.

6.4 Flexible Procedures—Procedures with Parameters

The **procedure** DrawLatitudeLines has one job: drawing the latitude lines in a picture of a squashed globe. But a procedure does not have to be limited to a single job. We can invent a procedure that is flexible—a procedure with a parameter. A *parameter* is like an input variable in an interactive program. For each value of the parameter, the procedure does a somewhat different job.

Program HorizontalLines

To show how parameters work, let's invent a procedure called DrawHLine that can draw *any* horizontal line across the Drawing window. When **procedure** DrawHLine appears in the body of a program, it must be followed by a number or expression that stands for the vertical position of the line. This number is the parameter for DrawHLine. The procedure statement

```
DrawHLine(100)
```

draws a line at height 100.

Program HorizontalLines includes the declaration for DrawHLine and two DrawHLine procedure calls. When you run it, you get the output shown in Figure 6.2.

```
program HorizontalLines;

{THE PROCEDURE DECLARATION}
procedure DrawHLine(Height : integer);
begin
  drawline(0,Height,200,Height)
end;

{THE BODY OF THE PROGRAM}
begin
  DrawHLine(100);
  DrawHLine(130)
end.
```

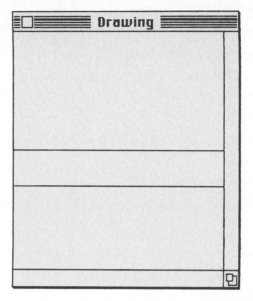

Figure 6.2   Output for **program** HorizontalLines.

The heading line for the procedure

```
procedure DrawHLine(Height : integer);
```

names the procedure and then lists the procedure's *formal parameter*, Height, along with its type. A formal parameter is sometimes called a *dummy parameter*, because it is simply a place-holder inside the declaration. It does nothing until a procedure call gives, or *passes*, a value to take its place. Height holds two places in the body of the procedure. Both places are in the *drawline* statement:

```
drawline(0,Height,200,Height)
```

The procedure statement in the body of the program,

```
DrawHLine(100)
```

passes the value 100 to the procedure declaration. This value is called the *actual parameter.*

When the statement

```
DrawHLine(100)
```

is executed, the procedure call first assigns the value 100 to Height. So the *drawline* statement in the procedure,

```
drawline(0,Height,200,Height)
```

is executed as though it looked like

```
drawline(0,100,200,100)
```

The type of the actual parameter must match the type declaration of the formal parameter given in the heading line. The heading line for DrawHLine,

```
procedure DrawHLine(Height : integer);
```

dictates that the quantity passed to Height must be an integer. The procedure statement

```
DrawHLine(98.6)
```

won't work. You'll get an error message if you try it.

Program HorizontalLinesTwo

Once you've included a procedure declaration in a program, the procedure statement can be used in the main program like any other statement. **Program** HorizontalLinesTwo uses DrawHLine in a **while** loop to fill the standard Drawing window with horizontal lines 10 units apart (see Figure 6.3).

```
program HorizontalLinesTwo;
{FILLS DRAWING WINDOW WITH HORIZONTAL LINES 10 UNITS APART.}
 const
  Separation = 10;
 var
  LineHeight : integer;

{THE PROCEDURE DECLARATION}
procedure DrawHLine(Height : integer);
begin
 drawline(0,Height,200,Height)
end;

{THE BODY OF THE PROGRAM}
begin
 LineHeight := 0;
 while (LineHeight < 200) do
  begin
   DrawHLine(LineHeight); {THE PROCEDURE STATEMENT}
   LineHeight := LineHeight + Separation
  end
end.
```

Program HorizontalLinesTwo contains a new idea: The actual parameter in the procedure call is a variable, not simply a fixed integer value.

When the computer executes the procedure call

```
DrawHLine(LineHeight);
```

it assigns the *value* of the actual parameter LineHeight to the formal parameter Height. Then it does the instruction in the body of the procedure. Each time the

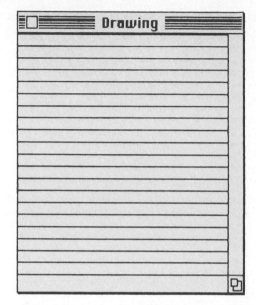

Figure 6.3 Output for **program** HorizontalLinesTwo.

procedure is called, the value of LineHeight is greater by 10, and a line is drawn 10 units farther down in the Drawing window.

Don't confuse the formal parameter Height with the variable LineHeight. LineHeight is the actual parameter for DrawHLine in this program. When the procedure is called, the *value* of the actual parameter LineHeight gets assigned to the formal parameter Height.

The program uses separate locations or cells in memory for the values of Height and LineHeight. When DrawHLine is called, the value of the actual parameter LineHeight is copied into the cell assigned to the formal parameter Height (see Figure 6.4).

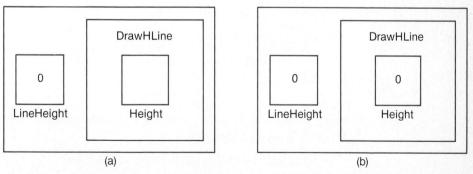

Figure 6.4 The actual and formal parameters for **procedure** DrawHLine (a) just before and (b) just after the procedure call.

Suppose you make this procedure call:

```
DrawHLine(LineHeight + 1)
```

This will work fine. Now the actual parameter is a complex expression, LineHeight + 1, not simply a variable. If the value of LineHeight is 0, the value of LineHeight + 1 is 1, and this is the value the computer copies into Height's cell in memory.

When you write a program, you can give the formal parameter the same name that you give the variable used as the actual parameter. You can also give them similar names, as we did here, or you can give them names that are completely different from each other. In this book we will generally use names that are similar, in order to remind you that one is a formal parameter and that the other is a variable used as the actual parameter.

EXERCISE 1   **a.** What does **program** Lines do?

```
program Lines;
 const
  Separation = 10;
 var
  LineHeight : integer;

{THE PROCEDURE DECLARATION}
procedure DrawSLine(Height : integer);
begin
 drawline(0,Height,200,Height - 20)
end;

{THE BODY OF THE PROGRAM}
begin
 LineHeight := 0;
 while (LineHeight <= 200) do
  begin
  DrawSLine(LineHeight);
  LineHeight := LineHeight + Separation
  end
end.
```

b. What would **program** Lines do if the *drawline* instruction in **procedure** DrawSLine looked like this?

```
drawline(0,Height,100,Height - 200) ■
```

Procedure DrawVLine

Now let's invent a companion procedure for DrawHLine called DrawVLine, which draws vertical lines. Here is the declaration for **procedure DrawVLine**:

```
procedure DrawVLine(HDistance : integer);
begin
  drawline(HDistance,0,HDistance,200)
end;
```

The formal parameter, HDistance, determines the distance from the line to the left wall of the Drawing window. Using this declaration, the procedure statement

```
DrawVLine(100)
```

will draw a vertical line 100 units from the left wall of the window.

Program Grid—a Program with Two Procedures

We can put DrawHLine and DrawVLine together in a program that draws grids in the standard Drawing window. **Program** Grid draws a grid of horizontal and vertical lines. It allows you to determine the spacing between the lines in the grid.

```
program Grid;
{YOU SPECIFY THE SPACING BETWEEN THE HORIZONTAL LINES}
{AND BETWEEN THE VERTICAL LINES. PROGRAM DRAWS A GRID.}
  var
    Position,HSpacing,VSpacing : integer;

  procedure DrawHLine(Height : integer);
  begin
    drawline(0,Height,200,Height)
  end;

  procedure DrawVLine(HDistance : integer);
  begin
    drawline(HDistance,0,HDistance,200)
  end;

{MAIN PROGRAM}
begin
  writeln('Type in horizontal and vertical spacing between lines.');
  readln(HSpacing,VSpacing);
```

(continued)

```
{DRAWS HORIZONTAL LINES}
Position := 0;
while (Position <= 200) do
 begin
  DrawHLine(Position);
  Position := Position + HSpacing
 end;

{DRAWS VERTICAL LINES}
Position := 0;
while (Position <= 200) do
 begin
  DrawVLine(Position);
  Position := Position + VSpacing
 end
end.
```

Program Grid has two loops. One uses **procedure** DrawHLine to draw the horizontal lines. The other uses **procedure** DrawVLine to draw the vertical lines. The variables HSpacing and VSpacing determine the spacing between the lines. Position is the control variable used to increment each loop, and it is also the actual parameter in both procedure calls.

When you type in a value of 10 for HSpacing and a value of 40 for VSpacing, this is what happens: The first time DrawHLine is executed, the value of the actual parameter, Position, is 0, and a line is drawn along the top of the

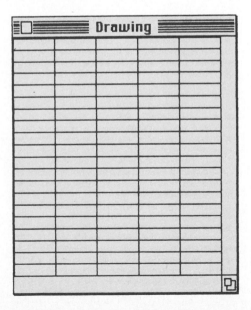

Figure 6.5   Output for **program** Grid.

window. Then Position is incremented by 10, and a line is drawn 10 units down. Each successive line is drawn 10 units lower than the line before.

After the first loop is over, Position is re-initialized to zero and the same process happens for DrawVLine. The first vertical line is drawn at the left wall, and each successive line is drawn 40 units over (see Figure 6.5).

6.5 Procedures with Several Parameters

Just as an interactive program can have any number of input variables, a Pascal procedure can have any number of parameters. These parameters can be of different types. To see how this works, let's look at some procedures with several parameters.

Program ElectricBill

We've modified **program** ElectricBill from Chapter 5 so that you can now enter the electric rates interactively. The program uses a procedure called CalcCost to calculate the cost of electricity. It has three parameters, one of type *integer* and two of type *real*.

```pascal
program NewElectricBill;
{YOU READ IN THE RATES AND THE KILOWATT HOURS USED.}
{PROGRAM CALCULATES THE BILL.}
 var
   LifeLineRate,RegRate : real;
   KWHUsed : integer;

 procedure CalcCost(LifeLine,Reg : real;
         KWH : integer);
  const
   LifeLineCutOff = 250; {LOCAL CONSTANT}
  var
   Cost : real; {LOCAL VARIABLE}
 begin
  if (KWH < LifeLineCutOff) then
   Cost := LifeLine * KWH
  else
   Cost := Reg * KWH;
  writeln('Your electric bill is $',Cost : 5 : 2)
 end;

{BODY OF THE PROGRAM}
 begin
  writeln('Type in lifeline rate, regular rate, and KWH used.');
  readln(LifeLineRate,RegRate,KWHUsed);
  CalcCost(LifeLineRate,RegRate,KWHUsed)
 end.
```

Procedure CalcCost has a parameter *list*—that is, a list of the formal parameters, along with their types. The syntax for declaring parameters of different types is the same as the syntax for declaring variables of different types in a program: Parameters of the same type may be grouped together, separated by commas. A semicolon separates declarations for parameters of different types.

Note that once again we have called the formal parameters and the actual parameters by similar but different names. Remember: Only the *values* of the actual parameters matter to the procedure. The names we choose make no difference.

The actual parameters in a procedure call are matched with the formal parameters in the formal parameter list *by position:*

```
procedure CalcCost(LifeLine,Reg : real;KWH : integer);

CalcCost(LifeLineRate,RegRate,KWHUsed);
```

If the call to CalcCost had listed the actual parameters this way:

```
CalcCost{RegRate,LifeLineRate,KWHUsed};
```

the program would have run to completion, but it would have given the wrong answer. The formal parameter LifeLine would have been assigned the value of RegRate, and Reg would have been assigned the value of LifeLineRate. With this mix-up in the actual parameters, Podunk Power and Light would charge a lower rate for people who waste electricity!

On the other hand, if the call had been made this way:

```
CalcCost(LifeLineRate,KWHUsed,RegRate)
```

the program wouldn't have run at all, because the formal and actual parameters don't match up by type.

Procedure Flicker

Here is another example of a procedure with several parameters: **procedure** Flicker. **Procedure** Flicker is quite versatile. You can use it in any program in which you want a ball to flicker and roll across the screen. **Procedure** Flicker paints and then inverts a circle of fixed radius at any point on the Drawing window.

```
program RollBall;
{ROLLS A BALL ACROSS THE DRAWING WINDOW}
  var
   Position : integer;
```

```
procedure Flicker(Horizontal,Vertical : integer);
  const
    Radius = 20;
begin
  paintcircle(Horizontal,Vertical,Radius);
  invertcircle(Horizontal,Vertical,Radius)
end;
```

```
{BODY OF THE PROGRAM}
begin
  for Position := 20 to 180 do
    Flicker(Position,80)
end.
```

Here we have used **procedure** Flicker in a program called RollBall, which rolls a ball horizontally across the Drawing window. To show how useful **procedure** Flicker is, we'll make several changes in the body of **program** RollBall to produce a number of different cartoons.

First, suppose we substitute this **for** statement for the body of **program** RollBall:

```
for Position := 20 to 180 do
  Flicker(Position,Position);
```

If we run the program, we will get the ball to roll like this:

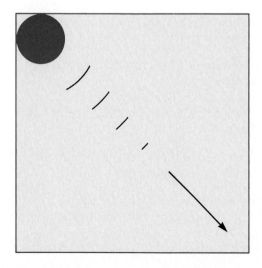

Now suppose we add two new variables, HPosition and VPosition, and replace the body of **program** RollBall with this code:

```
begin
 HPosition := 0;
 VPosition := 100;
 while (HPosition <= 200) do
  begin
   Flicker(HPosition,VPosition);
   HPosition := HPosition + 1;
   VPosition := 100 + (HPosition div 2)
  end
end.
```

We will get a ball rolling downhill. It starts at the point (0,100) and ends at the point (200,200). For every 2 units the ball rolls horizontally, it drops 1 unit vertically.

EXERCISE 2   **a.** Change the body of **program** RollBall so that it makes the ball roll down the left wall.

b. Change the body of **program** RollBall so that it makes the ball roll along the top wall, left to right. ▬

In **procedure** Flicker, Radius is a constant. We can create a procedure that's more flexible than Flicker, however, by making Radius a third formal parameter. This procedure, which we'll call BigFlicker, will make a circle *of any radius* flicker anywhere in the Drawing window. Here is the declaration for our new procedure.

```
procedure BigFlicker(Horizontal,Vertical,Radius : integer);
begin
 paintcircle(Horizontal,Vertical,Radius);
 invertcircle(Horizontal,Vertical,Radius)
end;
```

If we use BigFlicker to rewrite **program** PlanetIn3D from Chapter 2, the body of the program becomes

```
for Position := 0 to 200 do
 BigFlicker(Position,Position,Position div 5);
for Position := 200 downto 0 do
 BigFlicker(Position,Position,Position div 5)
```

EXERCISE 3   Use **procedure** BigFlicker to write a
program that will make a planet move
like this:

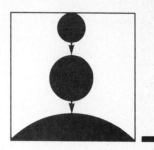

6.6 Procedures and Program Planning

We have now arrived at a key section of the book. Here we are going to show you a method for tackling even the most complex problems by reducing them to a series of procedures. When you have mastered the next few pages, you will no longer be a beginner!

This problem-solving technique is called *top-down programming*. When you use it, along with Pascal's procedure instruction, you will be able to organize, and then solve, even the most mind-boggling programming problems.

Top-Down Programming

In top-down programming, you apply the "divide and conquer" method. That is, you break a complicated problem into a number of smaller sub-problems. If a sub-problem is especially complex, you solve it using a procedure.

When you do top-down programming, you concentrate first on the main program, which is also called the *top level* of the program. You postpone working out the details of the procedures, which are considered *lower-level* parts of the program. Coding the procedures is the last thing you do.

This approach helps you think clearly about the problem without getting bogged down in the details. The top level of a well-written program should be very simple. It might not be much more than a list of procedure statements like the top level of **program** SquashedGlobe:

```
DrawLatitudeLines;
DrawLongitudeLines;
DrawEquator
```

Now let's use top-down design and the procedure command to solve a sample problem.

6.7 The Thermometer Problem

We want to write a program that converts a temperature given in degrees Fahrenheit to its equivalent in degrees Celsius. The program will also print out a picture of a thermometer. The height of the mercury will indicate the temperature, which is labeled in both scales. If you specify 32.0 degrees, for example, the program should print the picture shown in Figure 6.6.

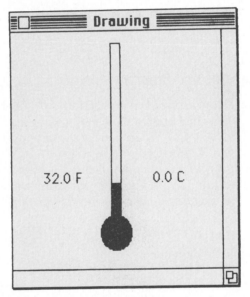

Figure 6.6 Typical output for **program** Thermometer.

Thinking

Let's brainstorm about how to solve this problem. The Fahrenheit-to-Celsius conversion is easy. We will use the formula

$$C = 5/9 \times (F - 32.0)$$

Here F is the Fahrenheit temperature and C is the Celsius equivalent. The following table gives some representative temperatures on both scales.

Degrees Fahrenheit	Degrees Celsius
32.0	0.0
212.0	100.0
−40.0	−40.0
98.6	37.0

How do we lay out the picture? We can use *framerect* for the thermometer tube, *paintrect* for the mercury, and *paintcircle* for the bulb.

We have to make some arbitrary decisions about the design of the thermometer. Let's give the bulb a radius of 15 and put its center at the point (100,160). The tube will be 10 units wide and will end 10 units from the top of the window (see Figure 6.7).

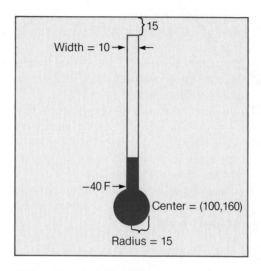

Figure 6.7 The thermometer.

We must also decide how to handle the scale on the thermometer. Let's have 1 degree Fahrenheit equal 1 vertical unit on the screen. And let's make the scale start at the bottom of the tube where the temperature will read −40 degrees Fahrenheit.

DATA TABLE

Input Variables	Output Variables	Program Variables
FTemp	FTemp, CTemp	none
Constants	**Formulas**	**Loops**
none	$C = 5/9 \times (F - 32.0)$	none

Top-Down Planning

Now we will begin planning the program, keeping our plan simple at first.

Plan I

1. Read in the Fahrenheit temperature.
2. Calculate the Celsius equivalent.
3. Draw and label the thermometer.

We have divided our problem into three simpler sub-problems. The first two are easy. We can quickly convert them to Pascal code. But the last step, drawing and labeling the thermometer, is more complicated. We will have trouble if we try to code it directly. So our strategy will be to invent a procedure to handle this step.

When you name a procedure, it's a good idea to use a phrase that captures the action the procedure performs, such as DrawLatitudeLines. Here we'll use the name DrawThermometer.

Now we come to the most important idea in the top-down programming method: We should *not* code DrawThermometer right away. Instead, we should *clarify* what DrawThermometer is supposed to do and then go on to code the body of the main program. When the top level has been completed, *then* we go back and finish DrawThermometer.

To clarify a procedure, we do two things. We write the procedure heading line, and we do a *paper check* to determine whether the heading we've come up with is what we want.

How to Clarify Procedure DrawThermometer

Our first job is writing **procedure** DrawThermometer's heading line. This means deciding on its parameter list. So we must ask ourselves the question "What quantities does DrawThermometer depend on?" DrawThermometer is supposed to draw and label a thermometer with a Fahrenheit temperature and its Celsius equivalent, so these two quantities should be named in the parameter list. Here is our proposed heading line:

```
procedure DrawThermometer(F,C : real);
```

A reminder: F and C are *dummy* parameters. Their names don't matter. We could have named them FT and CT or FTemp and CTemp.

Next let's do a paper check to determine whether we are satisfied with this choice of parameters. When we do a paper check, we draw a diagram or make a table that shows what the procedure is supposed to do when the main program passes it some typical parameters. On page 211 are diagrams for DrawThermometer(72.0,22.2) and DrawThermometer(−40.0, −40.0).

The paper check is useful because it helps us find out whether we have passed enough information to a procedure to get the answers we are looking for. In the case of DrawThermometer, we seem to have succeeded. Now let's go back to the top-level plan and finish the program at that level.

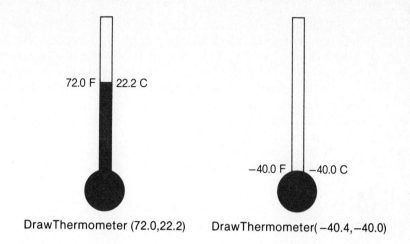

DrawThermometer (72.0,22.2)   DrawThermometer(−40.4,−40.0)

Now that DrawThermometer has been clarified, the plan looks like this:

Plan II

1. Read the Fahrenheit temperature.
2. Calculate the Celsius equivalent.
3. DrawThermometer(FTemp,CTemp).

We can now go on and code the top level.

Coding the Top Level

Here is our code for the main program:

```
begin
  writeln('Type in a Fahrenheit temperature -- a real number.');
  readln(FTemp);
  CTemp := 5/9 * (F - 32.0);
  DrawThermometer(FTemp,CTemp)
end.
```

This completes the top level. *Now* we go back and complete DrawThermometer.

Planning and Coding DrawThermometer

Plan for DrawThermometer

1. Draw the tube.
2. Draw the bulb.
3. Calculate the height of the mercury and paint it.
4. Label the Fahrenheit temperature.
5. Label the Celsius temperature.

Calculating the height of the mercury is the only complicated part. One degree Fahrenheit equals 1 unit of height. But, because we started the scale at −40.0 degrees, the height doesn't equal the Fahrenheit temperature. We need to add 40 to the Fahrenheit temperature to get the correct value for height.

The program reads in real numbers for Fahrenheit temperatures and prints out real numbers for both scales on the thermometer. But the height of the mercury must be an integer. So we must use the round function to calculate Height from the Fahrenheit temperature.

Now we can code **procedure** DrawThermometer and put the program together. Here is the complete program:

```
program Thermometer;
{YOU TYPE IN THE TEMPERATURE IN DEGREES FAHRENHEIT. THE PROGRAM DRAWS A}
{THERMOMETER AND LABELS TEMPERATURE IN FAHRENHEIT AND IN CELSIUS.}
  var
  FTemp,CTemp : real;

  procedure DrawThermometer (F,C : real);
  var
   Height,Top : integer; {LOCAL VARIABLES}
  begin
   {DRAW TUBE}
   framerect(10,95,160,105);
   {DRAW BULB}
   paintcircle(100,170,15);
   {ROUND OFF F TEMP AND CALCULATE HEIGHT OF MERCURY}
   Height := round(F) + 40;
   {DRAW MERCURY}
   Top := 200 - Height;
   if (Top > 160) then
    Top := 160; {KEEP LABELS FROM GOING TOO LOW}
   paintrect(Top,95,160,105);
   {LABEL TEMPERATURE IN FAHRENHEIT}
   moveto(30,Top);
   writedraw(F : 4 : 1, 'F');
   {LABEL TEMPERATURE IN CELSIUS}
   moveto(130,Top);
   writedraw(C : 4 : 1, 'C')
  end;

{BODY OF PROGRAM}
begin
 writeln('Type in a Fahrenheit temperature -- a real number.');
 readln(FTemp);
 CTemp := 5 / 9 * (FTemp - 32.0);
 DrawThermometer(FTemp,CTemp)
end.
```

When you run **program** Thermometer, you type in FTemp and the program calculates CTemp. Then the main program passes to **procedure** DrawThermometer the values of the actual parameters FTemp and CTemp. Finally the procedure draws and labels the thermometer. The **if-then** statement in the procedure guarantees that, when the temperature falls below −40F, the labels will be even with the bottom of the tube.

Testing and Debugging Program Thermometer

To test **program** Thermometer, try running it on a variety of temperatures. What happens when you type in a high temperature? You've got a problem. The mercury zips up too far, goes right out of the thermometer, and hits the top of the window. How would you fix this bug? *Hint:* Use a conditional statement like the one that keeps the labels from going too low.

EXERCISE 4   Fix **program** Thermometer so that the mercury remains in the thermometer tube even at very high temperatures. ■■

The Structure of Program Thermometer

Let's look at the structure of **program** Thermometer from a different angle. Here is a diagram that shows how we handled the problem.

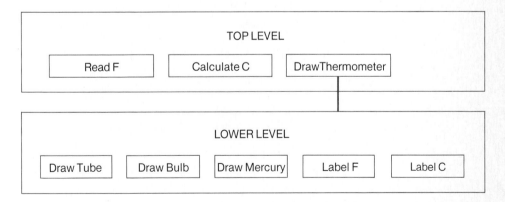

At the very top we divided the program into three pieces. The first two pieces were easy to convert to code, and we did this directly. The last part was harder. We *specified* what **procedure** DrawThermometer was supposed to do, but we did not code it until we had finished coding the top level. Then we descended to the next level, where we planned and then coded the five separate pieces of **procedure** DrawThermometer. This is top-down programming.

Procedure DrawThermometer, like **procedure** CalcCost in **program** New-ElectricBill, has its own private or *local* variables, Height and Top. Because Height and Top are declared inside the procedure, they make sense only for instructions inside the procedure. You would get an error if you referred to Top or Height in the body of the program.

6.8 Creating a Checkerboard

Let's work through another top-down programming example. This time let's write a program that creates in the Drawing window a checkerboard like the one shown in Figure 6.8. First we'll paint a series of black horizontal stripes, using *paintrect* commands alternating with *framerect* commands. Then we'll paint a series of vertical stripes, using *invertrect* and *framerect*.

Figure 6.8   Typical output for **program** Checkerboard.

Superimposing the inverted stripes over the painted stripes creates the checkerboard effect. *Invertrect* turns to black the white horizontal stripes it crosses, while turning the black stripes it crosses to white. We'll make the program interactive so we can read in any number of stripes. This problem is harder than it looks, so we must plan carefully.

Thinking

What really happens in this program? First we read in the total number of black and white stripes. There will be an equal number of horizontal and vertical ones, because the standard Drawing window is square. The program calculates how wide to make each stripe. Then the first loop alternately paints and outlines a series of rectangles to create the horizontal stripes. For example, if we read in five stripes, the first loop will draw this picture:

Next the second loop uses *invertrect* and *framerect* to create the vertical stripes. When *invertrect* is used, it reverses the colors of the stripes it crosses, and we get our checkerboard.

Because the number of horizontal stripes and the number of vertical stripes are the same, we need only one variable for the number of stripes. Let's call it NumOfStripes. We won't need any output variables, because our output is a drawing.

But we will need a program variable for the width of the stripes, which we'll call StripeWidth. We can determine StripeWidth by dividing the size of the window by the number of stripes. So we'll need this formula:

```
StripeWidth = window size div NumOfStripes
```

While we're at it, let's make WindowSize a constant.

From this information we can create our data table:

DATA TABLE

Input Variables	Output Variables	Constants
NumOfStripes	picture	WindowSize = 200

Program Variables	Loops	
StripeWidth	one to draw the horizontal stripes	
	one to draw the vertical stripes	

Formulas

StripeWidth = WindowSize **div** NumOfStripes

Planning

Now we know enough to do a rough first plan.

Plan I
1. Type in the number of stripes.
2. Calculate the width of the stripes.
3. Draw the horizontal stripes.
4. Draw the vertical stripes.

Step 1 is easy. In step 2, we can calculate the width of the stripes, using the formula

StripeWidth = WindowSize div NumOfStripes

So both of these steps can be coded without difficulty—a task we'll put off for the time being.

Steps 3 and 4 (drawing the stripes) are the hard parts. So let's make each of these steps into a procedure and call them DrawHStripes and DrawVStripes. This will make the top level of our program very simple. It will look a lot like Plan I.

Our next step is to clarify what **procedure** DrawHStripes and **procedure** DrawVStripes are supposed to do. We must propose heading lines for the two procedures and then do paper checks to determine whether they will behave properly.

Clarifying Procedure DrawHStripes

To clarify DrawHStripes we must first determine the quantities that DrawHStripes depends on. To draw any particular stripe, we must have values for its top, left, bottom, and right boundaries. In this procedure, the left and right boundaries are constant; they are the left and right boundaries of the Drawing window.

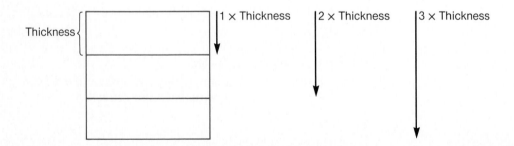

The bottom of the first (or highest) stripe has a value equal to the thickness of one stripe. The bottom of the second stripe has a value equal to twice the thickness of one stripe. Similarly, the bottom of each additional stripe is a multiple of the stripe thickness. And the top of each stripe is the bottom of the stripe above it. So the data that the procedure needs, in order to draw all the stripes in its loop, are

1. The thickness, or *Width*, of a stripe
2. The number of stripes to be drawn, or *StripeCount*

And so we propose this heading line for DrawHStripes:

```
procedure DrawHStripes(Width,StripeCount : integer);
```

Let's do a paper check to find out whether these two quantities are sufficient, given that the left and right boundaries of the rectangle are the left and right sides of the window.

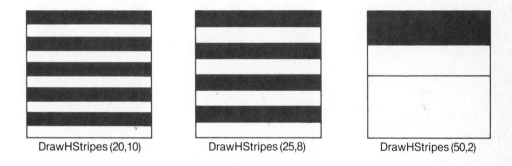

DrawHStripes (20,10)   DrawHStripes (25,8)   DrawHStripes (50,2)

EXERCISE 5   Sketch what you think **procedure** DrawHStripes(45,4) will do. ▬

Here's something peculiar. The first two examples we've drawn fit the problem: They completely fill the window with stripes. The third paper check, however, fills only about half of the window. Does this irregularity make **procedure** DrawHStripes incorrect? Not at all. It simply means that the procedure is capable of drawing other patterns beside the ones that the main program will call for.

The main part of the program does the job of stripe bookkeeping—reading in the number of stripes needed and figuring out how wide each should be to fill the window. And **procedure** DrawHStripes does the job of drawing the stripes—any number of them, of any thickness.

This is the "divide and conquer" method in action: One tough job has been split into two easy ones—a bookkeeping job and a stripe-drawing job.

Clarifying Procedure DrawVStripes

DrawVStripes can be clarified by the same reasoning we used for DrawHStripes. DrawVStripes, too, depends on the width of a stripe and on the number of stripes, so we get this heading line, which has the same parameters as DrawHStripes:

```
procedure DrawVStripes(Width,StripeCount : integer);
```

And here are some examples of a DrawVStripes paper check.

DrawVStripes (40,5)   DrawVStripes (25,8)   DrawVStripes (50,2)

Because we have done our paper check against an all-white background, our diagrams for **procedure** DrawVStripes are misleading. In the actual program, DrawVStripes draws stripes, using *invertrect*, against the background prepared by DrawHStripes. When the vertical stripes are drawn, they reverse the background pattern, and we get our checkerboard.

Coding the Top Level

Now that we understand the procedures and have written their heading lines, we can code the top level of the program:

```
begin
  writeln('How many stripes do you want?');
  readln(NumOfStripes);
  Width := WindowSize div NumOfStripes;
  DrawHStripes(StripeWidth,NumOfStripes);
  DrawVStripes(StripeWidth,NumOfStripes)
end.
```

We can now go on to tackle the procedures.

Thinking, Planning, and Coding Procedure DrawHStripes

Thinking

What exactly will **procedure** DrawHStripes do? It will alternately paint a rectangle and then frame a blank rectangle until it has drawn NumOfStripes number of rectangles. We want DrawHStripes to draw a series of stripes, so it will need a loop.

DrawHStripes receives as input the parameters in its parameter list: Width and StripeCount. These are its input data. It needs a control variable to keep track of which stripe it is drawing. Let's call this control variable CurrentStripe.

Planning

Now we can start sketching out the loop for drawing the stripes. Here is a first plan. (Look back at **program** Grid and see how similar this loop is to the **while** loop we used there.)

Plan I

```
while (CurrentStripe < = StripeCount) do
   begin
      draw a stripe
      increment CurrentStripe
   end
```

Now we come to something a bit tricky—how to get the loop to paint a stripe and then frame a stripe. We can distinguish between the painted stripes and the blanks by using the standard function *odd*. If CurrentStripe is odd, a *paintrect* command will paint a rectangle across the screen. For the even stripes, a *framerect* instruction will leave the rectangle white.

Plan II

```
while (CurrentStripe < = StripeCount) do
   begin
      if odd(CurrentStripe) then paint a stripe
      else frame a stripe
      increment CurrentStripe
   end
```

Before we move on to the coding phase, we should think through what *paintrect* and *framerect* need in order to do their jobs. They need values for the top, left, bottom, and right sides of a rectangle. Left and right are constant, so we will define them as constants inside the procedure. Top and bottom vary with each stripe, so we will declare them as variables within the procedure. We can get the value of Bottom by multiplying CurrentStripe by Width. And we can get the value of Top by subtracting Width from Bottom.

Coding DrawHStripes

Knowing all this, we can begin to code. As always, it is important to remember to initialize the variables.

```pascal
procedure DrawHStripes(Width,StripeCount : integer);
 const
  Left = 0;
  Right = 200;
 var
  CurrentStripe,Top,Bottom : integer;
begin
 CurrentStripe := 1;
 while (CurrentStripe <= StripeCount) do
  begin
   Bottom := CurrentStripe * Width;
   Top := Bottom - Width;
   if odd(CurrentStripe) then
    paintrect(Top,Left,Bottom,Right)
   else
    framerect(Top,Left,Bottom,Right);
   CurrentStripe := CurrentStripe + 1
  end
end;
```

Procedure DrawVStripes

Procedure DrawVStripes is like **procedure** DrawHStripes, with this important difference: To create the alternating black and white squares, it uses *invertrect* instead of *paintrect*. Also Top and Bottom are constants here instead of Left and Right. The local variable Right equals CurrentStripe times Width. And the variable Left equals Right minus Width. The variables and constants in **procedure** DrawVStripes are completely independent of the variables and constants in DrawHStripes and are not affected by them.

Here is the complete program:

```pascal
program Checkerboard;
 const
  WindowSize = 200;
 var
  NumOfStripes,Width : integer;

 procedure DrawHStripes(Width,StripeCount : integer);
  const
   Left = 0;
   Right = 200;
```

```
var
  CurrentStripe,Top,Bottom : integer;
begin
 CurrentStripe := 1;
 while (CurrentStripe <= StripeCount) do
  begin
   Bottom := CurrentStripe * Width;
   Top := Bottom - Width;
   if odd(CurrentStripe) then
    paintrect(Top,Left,Bottom,Right)
   else
    framerect(Top,Left,Bottom,Right);
   CurrentStripe := CurrentStripe + 1
  end
end;
```

```
procedure DrawVStripes(Width,StripeCount : integer);
 const
  Top = 0;
  Bottom = 200;
 var
  CurrentStripe,Left,Right : integer;
begin
 CurrentStripe := 1;
 while (CurrentStripe <= StripeCount) do
  begin
   Right := CurrentStripe * Width;
   Left := Right - Width;
   if odd(CurrentStripe) then
    invertrect(Top,Left,Bottom,Right)
   else
    framerect(Top,Left,Bottom,Right);
   CurrentStripe := CurrentStripe + 1
  end
end;
```

```
{MAIN PROGRAM}
begin
 writeln('How many stripes do you want?');
 readln(NumOfStripes);
 Width := WindowSize div NumOfStripes;
 DrawHStripes(Width,NumOfStripes);
 DrawVStripes(Width,NumOfStripes)
end.
```

Testing and Debugging

Now try running **program** Checkerboard, reading in three or four stripes. The program draws a fairly symmetrical checkerboard. But when you read in a larger figure for the number of stripes, the picture is distorted. This happens because the black line around the white stripes takes up proportionally more of the white space as the white stripes get smaller. You can correct this distortion by making the white stripes completely blank instead of creating them using *framerect*.

EXERCISE 6   How would you alter **procedure** DrawHStripes and **procedure** DrawVStripes so that the white stripes are blank instead of being outlined? ▬

That was a challenging program! But it is an important one to master. You should read and reread it until you are sure you understand it. Remember: The whole point of top-down programming is to give you a framework for transforming one complicated problem into several easy ones. That is what we did here. Pascal's procedure instruction enabled us to program the pieces of the problem separately and then put them together into a single working program.

_____TEST YOURSELF _____

1. What is a procedure call?
2. What is a formal parameter?
3. What is an actual parameter?
4. What is the top level of a program?
5. What is a local variable?
6. What part of a complex program should you read first?
7. Why is a formal parameter called a dummy?
8. What happens when program execution returns from a procedure call?
9. How does the syntax of a procedure differ from the syntax of a program?
10. How do you clarify a procedure?

_____PROBLEMS _____

1. Using a procedure, write a program that prints the verse of the Hokey Pokey given on page 64 of Chapter 2.
2. Create your own *drawline* procedure from scratch, using the *moveto* and *lineto* instructions. (See Problem 6 in Chapter 3.) Call this **procedure**

DrawLineTwo. DrawLineTwo(a,b,c,d) should draw a line from the point (a,b) to the point (c,d), where a, b, c, and d are integers. Use **procedure** DrawLineTwo in a program that draws a tic-tac-toe board in the standard Drawing window.

3. Use the *frameoval* instruction to create a procedure called FrameCircle. The command FrameCircle(H,V,Radius) should draw the outline of a circle with its center at the point (H,V) and its radius equal to Radius. Use FrameCircle in a program that draws this picture:

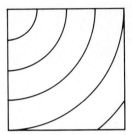

4. Write an interactive program that divides the Drawing window into vertical "cells." Use a procedure called VertDivide, which has the heading line

```
procedure VertDivide(Cells : integer);
```

Procedure VertDivide divides the standard Drawing window into Cells number of cells:

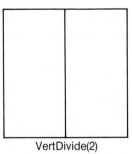   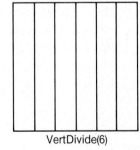

VertDivide(2)   VertDivide(6)

When Cells ≤ 1, the program should leave the Drawing window empty.

5. Rewrite **program** CircleOrbit from Chapter 4, using **procedure** Flicker.

6. Rewrite **program** YoYo from Chapter 3, using **procedure** Flicker.

7. Rewrite **program** Targets from Chapter 4, using a procedure called DrawTarget with parameters HCenter, VCenter, StartRadius, SizeIncrease, and CircleCount.

8. Using **procedure** Flicker, write a program called PerimeterRoll that rolls a ball all around the perimeter of the Drawing window.

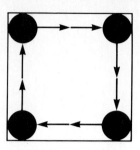

9. Modify **program** Grid so that it draws a picture like the one at the right.

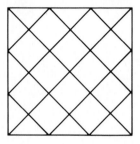

10. Using procedures, write **program** OneBounce, which makes the following cartoon appear in the Drawing window:
    a. A ball falls down the center of the Drawing window.
    b. When it reaches the bottom, it "squashes" so that it becomes an oval twice as wide as it is high.
    c. Then it resumes its normal shape and bounces back to the top of the window.

11. Write an interactive program that will brick up the Drawing window with bricks of any size. The picture on the right shows typical output.

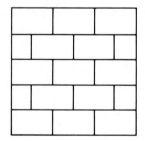

This is quite a hard problem. Don't get discouraged if you have to change your original plan several times.

Enumerated Types, the Type Char, and More on Procedures

7

So far in our introduction to Pascal, we have seen just two types of data: integer and real. They are built into the language and are two of Pascal's standard data types. Now we want to show you how to invent new types that aren't standard—*enumerated types*. We'll also introduce another standard type—type *char*. Type *char* is made up of the characters you type at the keyboard.

In this chapter we'll also show you how a different kind of formal parameter can make the procedure command more flexible.

7.1 Enumerated Types

Pick almost any subject for a computer program—days of the week, months of the year, New England states, clothes, planets, meals—and Pascal gives you the power to turn that subject into a made-up *enumerated type*. This type gets its name from the fact that it lists, or enumerates, related things one after another.

When you invent an enumerated type, you write a definition for it in the declaration part of your program. Here are definitions of some enumerated types.

```
type
 DaysOfWeek = (Mon,Tue,Wed,Thur,Fri,Sat,Sun);
type
 YearAtSchool = (Freshman,Sophomore,Junior,Senior);
type
 meals = (breakfast,lunch,dinner,midnightsnack);
type
 Directions = (North,NorthEast,East,SouthEast,
        South,SouthWest,West,NorthWest);
```

Here's how you can use an enumerated type in a program. **Program** Days (see Figure 7.1) lists the days of the week in order in a column, exactly as they are named in the type definition.

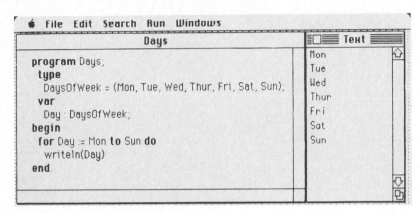

Figure 7.1   Program Days and its output.

You also can list consecutive members of a type in reverse order with a backward **for** loop, as illustrated in **program** Class (see Figure 7.2).

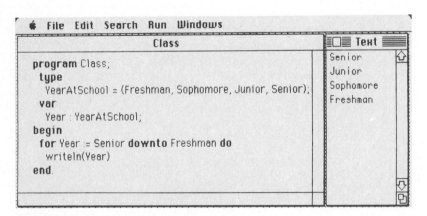

Figure 7.2   Program Class and its output.

EXERCISE 1   Write a program that lists the elements of the enumerated type meals, from lunch to midnightsnack. Use the type definition given on page 225. ▬

Whenever you define an enumerated type, you list the elements of that type in a specific order. Each element holds a numbered position in the type, beginning with 0. In the type DaysOfWeek, for example, the position of Mon is 0, that of Tue is 1, that of Wed is 2, and so on.

Pascal has a standard function called *ord* that gives you the position of any member of an enumerated type.

```
ord(Mon) = 0
ord(Tue) = 1
ord(Wed) = 2
```

If you make the following change in the *writeln* statement in **program** Days:

```
writeln(Day,ord(Day))
```

it will print out

```
Mon   0
Tue   1
Wed   2
Thur  3
Fri   4
Sat   5
Sun   6
```

Because members of an enumerated type hold fixed positions in the type definition, you can use the relational operators with them. For example, the *value* of the expression (Wed ⟨ Thur) is true, just as the value of the expression (5 ⟨ 6) is true.

Variables that go with an enumerated type behave just like variables of type *integer* or type *real*. The declaration

```
var Day : DaysOfWeek;
```

creates a location in memory for the variable Day. The only kind of value this location may hold is a day of the week—one of the seven values listed in the type definition. When the computer executes the assignment statement

```
Day := Thur
```

Thur becomes the *value* of Day, and this value is copied into the location or cell in memory set aside for the variable Day:

```
┌──────┐
│ Thur │
└──────┘
Day
```

Day has the value Thur in the same way in which the integer variable Number has the value 3 after this assignment statement is executed:

```
Number := 3          ┌───┐
                     │ 3 │
                     └───┘
                     Number
```

When you include more than one enumerated type in a program, you must be sure that there is no overlap in the names of the elements. You will get an error message if you put the following two definitions in the same program:

```
type
  HeavenlyBodies = (sun,moon,stars);
  DaysOfWeek = (Mon,Tue,Wed,Thur,Fri,Sat,Sun);
```

Because the Macintosh ignores capital letters when it compares the names of identifiers, sun is the same as Sun and the definitions overlap.

7.2 Successor and Predecessor

Two standard Pascal functions are often used with enumerated types: *successor* and *predecessor*. These functions allow you to step through the elements of a type. The successor function, *succ*, gives the next element in the type:

```
succ(Tue) = Wed
succ(lunch) = dinner
```

The predecessor function, *pred*, works just like *succ*, only it goes backward:

```
pred(Sat) = Fri
pred(lunch) = breakfast
```

What happens when you write *succ*(Sun)? You're in trouble. Because Sun is the last element in the type, it has no successor. So the value of *succ*(Sun) is undefined, and you will get an error message if you include this kind of expression in a program. For example, this program won't run properly:

```
program Time;
  type
    TimeZone = (Eastern,Central,RockyMt,Pacific);
  var
    Zone : TimeZone;
begin
  Zone := Eastern;
  while (Zone <= Pacific) do
    begin
      writeln(Zone);
      Zone := succ(Zone)
    end
end.
```

After the **while** loop increments the value of Zone to Pacific, Pacific is printed out. Then Pascal tries to evaluate the right side of this statement:

```
Zone := succ(Zone)
```

But Pacific—the value of Zone—has no successor, so the program crashes.

Just as *succ* doesn't work with the last element in a type, *pred* doesn't work when it is applied to the first element. *Pred*(Mon), for example, is undefined.

Question: Does **program** Months do what the comment says it's supposed to do?

```
program Months; {LISTS THE MONTHS OF THE YEAR}
  type MonthsOfYear = (Jan,Feb,Mar,April,May,June,July,
                                Aug,Sept,Oct,Nov,Dec);

  var
    Month : MonthsOfYear;
begin
  Month := Jan;
  repeat
    writeln(Month);
    Month := Succ(Month)
  until (Month = Dec)
end.
```

The answer is no. You cannot use a **repeat-until** loop to step *all the way through* an enumerated type. The loop will end before it prints the last member of the type. So **program** Months never prints Dec.

Looping Through an Enumerated Type

Let's summarize what we have learned about looping and enumerated types. The function *succ* allows you to step forward through a type, and the function *pred* allows you to step backward. But if you use *pred* or *succ*, you will not be able to loop all the way through a type. With the **while** statement, you step past the last element in the type and get an error message. With **repeat-until**, you undershoot by one and don't cover the entire type.

Moral: Use a **for** statement when you want to loop *all the way through* an enumerated type. The control line of the **for** loop can name the first and last members of the type, so there is no problem stepping all the way to the end.

7.3 Program WeekPlan—Using a Global Constant

Next let's look at a program that prints out a weekly planning sheet using an enumerated type (see Figure 7.3).

Program WeekPlan uses the enumerated type DaysOfWeek. **Procedure** VertDivide, which we assigned as Problem 4 of Chapter 6, divides the Drawing window into 7 columns, and **procedure** LabelColumns writes a day of the week at the top of each column.

Before you run the program, enlarge the Drawing window so that it fills the entire screen. The dimensions of the enlarged window are 500 units by 300 units.

```
program WeekPlan;
{PRINTS OUT A WEEKLY PLANNING SHEET}
 const
  HeightOfLabels = 15; {GLOBAL CONSTANT}
  WindowWidth = 500; {GLOBAL CONSTANT}
 type
  DaysOfWeek = (Mon,Tue,Wed,Thur,Fri,Sat,Sun);
 var
  Hpos : integer; {HORIZONTAL POSITION OF DAY LABELS}


procedure VertDivide(Cells : integer);
{DIVIDES THE DRAWING WINDOW INTO EQUAL-SIZED COLUMNS}
  const
   Top = 0;
   Bottom = 300;
  var
   Left,Right,Width,CellNumber : integer;
begin
 CellNumber := 1;
 if (Cells > 0) then
  begin
   Width := WindowWidth div Cells;
   while (CellNumber <= Cells) do
    begin
     Right := CellNumber * Width;
     Left := Right - Width;
     framerect(Top,Left,Bottom,Right);
     CellNumber := CellNumber + 1
    end
  end
end;


procedure LabelColumns;
 var
  Day : DaysOfWeek;
  Width : integer;
begin
 Width := WindowWidth div 7;
 for Day := Mon to Sun do
  begin
   Hpos := ord(Day) * Width;
   moveto(HPos + 5,HeightOfLabels);
   writedraw(Day)
  end
end;
```

```
begin
   VertDivide(7);    {DIVIDES DRAWING WINDOW INTO 7 COLUMNS}
                     {DRAWS LINE UNDER DAY LABELS}
   drawline(0,HeightOfLabels + 5,WindowWidth,HeightOfLabels + 5);
   LabelColumns      {LABELS COLUMNS WITH DAYS OF WEEK}
end.
```

There's one new idea in **program** WeekPlan. Both VertDivide and
LabelColumns use the width of the Drawing window to make calculations. So
we've defined the constant WindowWidth *in the declaration part of the main
program* instead of putting it in the declaration part of each procedure. This
makes WindowWidth a *global constant*.

When the Macintosh executes VertDivide and comes to the statement

```
Width := WindowWidth div Cells
```

it checks the declaration part of the procedure to determine whether there is a
constant or a variable by that name. When it finds none, it searches one level up,
in the main program, for a value for WindowWidth. WindowWidth is defined
there, and this is the value the Macintosh uses.

The same process goes on during execution of **procedure** LabelColumns. No
value for WindowWidth can be found inside the procedure, so the computer
looks for the value of WindowWidth one level up in the main program.

The constant HeightOfLabels is also a global constant. When the Macintosh
executes **procedure** LabelColumns, no definition of the constant can be found in
the procedure, so the computer uses the definition that appears in the declaration
part of the main program.

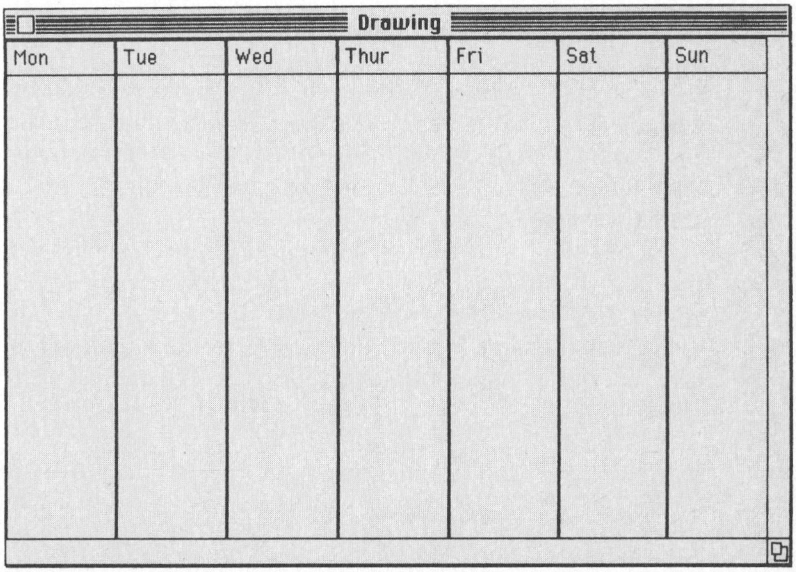

Figure 7.3   Program WeekPlan's output.

EXERCISE 2   **a.** Explain what the procedure call VertDivide(0) does.

b. How would you change **procedure** LabelColumns so that the name of each day starts at the middle of each cell? ▬

7.4 The Case Statement

Suppose you want a program to help you keep track of your weekly activities. It might work this way: You read in a day of the week, and the program responds with your planned activities for the day, according to a schedule such as this:

Monday	work in cafeteria
Tuesday	basketball
Wednesday	Outing Club meeting
Thursday	basketball
Friday	none
Saturday	shopping and laundry
Sunday	none

You *could* write the program using a giant **if-then-else** statement that begins

```
if Day = Mon then
 writeln('work in cafeteria')
else if Day = Tue then
 writeln('basketball')
else if Day = Wed then
 writeln('Outing Club meeting')
```

But you can do the same thing more efficiently using Pascal's *case statement* (see Figure 7.4).

The case statement is bracketed by the reserved words **case** and **end.** The variable Day is called the *case selector*. When you type in a day of the week, the case statement looks down the list of days, which are called *case labels*. When it finds the label—that is, the day you have typed in—it executes the instructions after the colon.

The action named after the colon can be any Pascal statement. Note that, in the case of Saturday, it is a compound statement with two instructions sandwiched between a **begin** and an **end.**

When the same instruction is to be executed in more than one case, you can list those days on one line, followed by a colon and the instruction.

```
Tue,Thur : writeln('basketball');
```

However, you can't use the same label twice. This will cause an error:

```
Sat : writeln('wash car');
Sat : writeln('mow lawn');
```

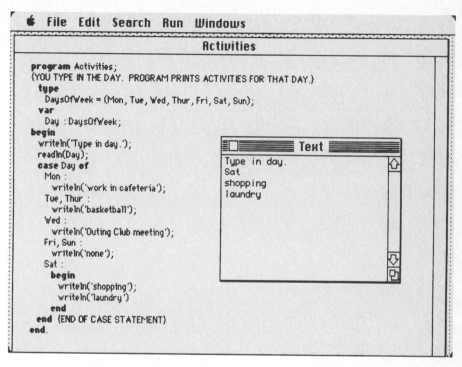

Figure 7.4 **Program** Activities and its output.

Case statements can also include an **otherwise** clause. We can use one in **program** Activities for Friday and Sunday, which have the same instruction —*writeln*('none').

```
case Day of
 Mon :
  writeln('work in cafeteria');
 Tue,Thur :
  writeln('basketball');
 Wed :
  writeln('Outing Club meeting');
 Sat :
  begin
   writeln('shopping');
   writeln('laundry')
  end;
 otherwise
  writeln('none')
end
```

Note that there is no colon after **otherwise** in this statement. In fact, **otherwise** is *never* followed by a colon. Note also that there is no semicolon at the end of the case statement because it is followed by the word **end.** (If you do put one in, however, Pascal won't object.)

Case Statement Syntax

We can summarize case statement syntax as follows:

```
case ⟨selector⟩ of
  label1 : ⟨statement1⟩;
            ⋮
  labeln : ⟨statementn⟩;
  otherwise ⟨statement⟩
end;
```

Program Equipment

Here is another example that uses an enumerated type in a case statement. **Program** Equipment is a crude version of the kind of program used by computerized cash registers.

Suppose you work in a ski equipment store. Every time a customer makes a purchase, you type in the items, and the program adds up the cost and prints out the total bill, including the tax. **Program** Equipment is shown on page 235. Figure 7.5 shows some sample output of **program** Equipment.

```
▤▭ Text ▭
Type in boots, skis, poles, bindings, or done.
>boots
How many pairs of boots purchased?
>2
The 2 pairs of boots cost $ 69.90.
Type in boots, skis, poles, bindings, or done.
>skis
How many pairs of skis purchased?
>2
The 2 pairs of skis cost $147.90.
Type in boots, skis, poles, bindings, or done.
>done
The total cost is $217.80.
```

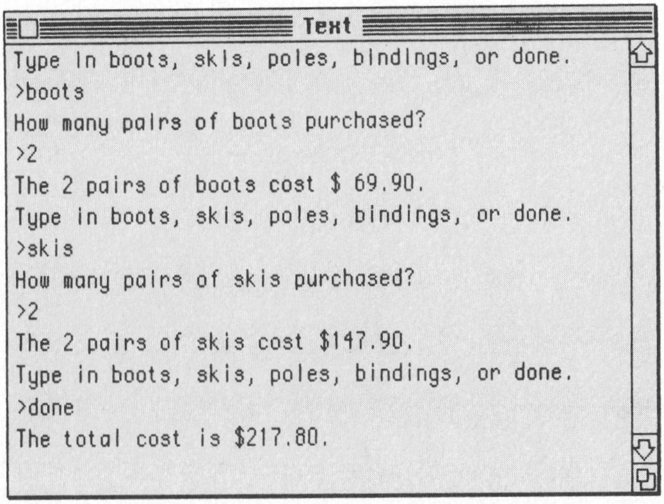

Figure 7.5   Some sample output of **program** Equipment.

```pascal
program Equipment;
  const
   TaxRate = 0.05;
   Discount = 10.00;
  type
   SkiEquipment = (boots,skis,poles,bindings,done);
  var
   Number,Count : integer;
   Tax,Cost,TotalCost : real;
   Item : SkiEquipment;
begin
 TotalCost := 0.00;
 Cost := 0.00;
 repeat
  writeln('Type in boots,skis,poles,bindings,or done.');
  write('>');
  readln(Item);
  if (Item <> done) then
   begin
    writeln('How many pairs of ',Item,' purchased?');
    write('>');
    readln(Number);
         {CASE STATEMENT}
    case Item of
     poles :
      begin
       Tax := 12.95 * TaxRate;
       Cost := (12.95 + Tax) * Number
      end;
     bindings :
      begin
       Tax := 19.95 * TaxRate;
       Cost := (19.95 + Tax) * Number
      end;
     boots :
      Cost := 34.95 * Number; {NO TAX ON CLOTHING}
     skis :
      begin
       Tax := 79.95 * TaxRate;
       Cost := (79.95 - Discount + Tax) * Number
      end
    end; {END OF CASE STATEMENT}
    TotalCost := TotalCost + Cost;
    writeln( 'The ',Number : 1,' pairs of ',Item,' cost $',
            Cost : 6 : 2,'.')
   end {END OF IF STATEMENT}
 until (Item = done);
 writeln('The total cost is $',TotalCost : 6 : 2,'.')
end.
```

The prompt in the **repeat-until** loop in **program** Equipment asks you to type in either the name of a piece of ski equipment or the word *done*. If you type in *done*, no action is taken and the loop is terminated.

But if you type in *poles*, for example, the loop continues and another prompt asks you how many pairs of poles are being purchased. Then you type in an integer, say 2.

Poles is now the value of the case selector variable, which is called *Item*. So the computer searches for the label *poles* among the list of case labels. When it finds this label among the case labels, it calculates the cost of the two pairs of poles.

Then execution returns to the beginning of the loop, and you can read in the name of another item of ski equipment. This process continues until you enter, *done*. Finally the total cost is printed, and program execution ends.

In **program** Equipment, we've added a new feature to our style of writing interactive programs. We've included the statement

```
write('>')
```

before each *readln* statement. The symbol ⟩ serves here as a second prompt. It signals you to enter data. This symbol makes the Text window display easier to read, as you can see from the sample output in Figure 7.5.

Made-up enumerated types come in handy when you are writing programs about every-day topics such as days of the week and ski equipment. Now let's look at another type—the standard type *char*.

7.5 The Type Char

Pascal's third standard type is the type *char*, which is pronounced like the syllable *car-* in carrot. Char is short for "character," and the type includes letters, numbers, punctuation, and every other symbol on the keyboard. Even the blank space you get when you press the space bar is an element of type *char*.

Char is laid out like an enumerated type. This means that there are a limited number of items in the type and that they are arranged in a definite order. But you don't need to define type *char* at the beginning of a program, because it is built into Pascal.

In this and later chapters, we will be looking at many programs that use type *char* to process text. Some of these form the basis of *word-processing programs* such as MacWrite that allow you to type in, edit, and print out letters, papers, and other documents.

Let's begin with a very simple example. **Program** StandardKeyboard (see Figure 7.6) lists in the Text window the elements of type *char* that appear on many standard typewriter keyboards, beginning with a blank space and ending with ⁓, which is called a *tilde*. (There are actually other members of the type, which we will tell you about later.)

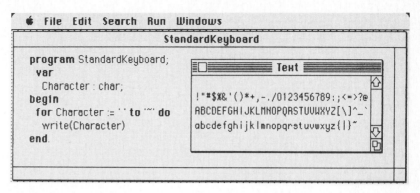

Figure 7.6   Program StandardKeyboard and its output.

In this program, Character is a variable of type *char*. The declaration

```
var Character : char;
```

sets aside a location in memory for the variable Character. This location holds the *value* of the variable Character, which is one character. A character is a value of type *char* in the same way in which a whole number is a value of type *integer* and Thur is a value of type DaysOfWeek.

Initially, the value of Character in the **for** loop of **program** PrintCharacters is a space—the character that is typed when you press the space bar. The **for** statement advances through the members of the type that follow the space symbol until it reaches the tilde.

The symbols that serve as the lower and upper limits of the loop (the space and the ˜) are surrounded by single quotation marks. The single quotation marks tell the computer to treat the symbol between them as a character and not as a variable or some other kind of symbol. If you leave out the quotation marks, the computer will "assume" that you typed in a variable rather than a character, and you will get an error message.

Because the members of type *char* are arranged in a specific order, you can use *succ* and *pred* with members of the type. For example,

```
succ(A) = B
pred(z) = y
```

You can also use the relational operators to compare the positions of the characters. For example,

```
'a' < 'b' is true
```

And you can use *ord* to find out the position of a character in the type. For example,

```
ord(' ') = 32
```

This equation means "a blank space holds the thirty-second place in the list of characters in the type *char*."

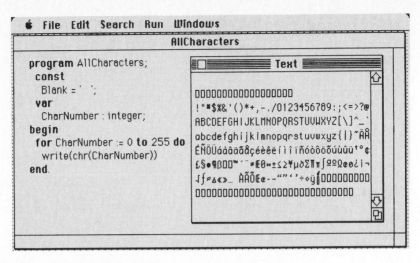

Figure 7.7   **Program** AllCharacters and its output.

The characters in the type that hold positions 0 through 31—such as escape, carriage return, and backspace—are part of type *char*, but they are not standard printing characters. They are called *non-printing control characters*. There are also characters beyond the tilde. You can find out more about these additional characters in Appendix E of the Macintosh Pascal *Technical Appendix*.

Pascal has a function *chr* (pronounced "cur"), which is the inverse of the function *ord* for type *char: ord*('!') = 33, and *chr*(33) = !. The *chr* function works only for integer values from 0 to 255, because there are 256 characters available on the Macintosh. **Program** AllCharacters (see Figure 7.7) uses the *chr* function to step through all 256 character positions. Non-printing control characters appear as blanks or as the symbol ☐.

The capital letters come before the lowercase letters in type *char*. But the distance between 'A' and 'a' or 'B' and 'b' is 32 positions, not 26, as you might suspect, because there are 6 symbols between the capitals and the lowercase letters. We will use this fact later in programs that convert capital (uppercase) letters to lowercase letters, or vice versa.

EXERCISE 3   Examine the output of **program** AllCharacters to figure out the answers to the following questions.

     a. true or false?   'A' = 'a'
     b. true or false?   '5' ⟨ '7'
     c. *succ*('@') = ?

         Answer: A

     d. *succ*(*succ*('@')) = ?
     e. true or false?   *pred*('1') ⟩ *succ*('A') ▬

The next point is very important. The integer 2 and the character 2 (that is, '2') are *not* the same. The character 2 is merely a name for a number, and you *cannot* add it to the number 2 or to another character 2 to get the answer 4. Hence the following program *will not work:*

```
program VeryBad;
  var Character : char;
    Number : integer;
begin
  Character := '2';
  Number := 2;
  Number := Number + Character;
  writeln(Number)
end.
```

The plus sign and the other arithmetic operators work only for numeric data—that is, for values of type *integer* or type *real.* In **program** VeryBad we are trying to add a character to a number, and this makes no sense to Pascal.
· To understand the difference between the integer 2 and the character 2, think about the following riddle:

What is the longest word in the world?

Answer: Smiles—there is a mile between the two *s*'s.

This riddle is based on the difference between the *quantity* one mile and the *name* for this quantity—the word *mile.* The two kinds of 2 differ in the same way. The integer 2 is a quantity. The character 2 is a name for this quantity. The computer expects you to keep them separate by using single quotation marks when you refer to the character 2 in a program.

7.6 Writedraw and Drawchar

You have already seen two of Macintosh Pascal's instructions for writing in the output windows—*writeln* and *writedraw. Writeln* prints in the Text window and *writedraw* prints in the Drawing window. MacPascal has a third command for printing text—*drawchar.* Like *writedraw, drawchar* prints in the Drawing window, so it must be preceded by a *moveto* statement that positions the electronic pen. Unlike both *writeln* and *writedraw, drawchar* can print only one character at a time. When the Macintosh executes the following commands

```
moveto(100,100);
drawchar('o');
drawchar('x');
```

it first sets the pen at position (100,100). Then it prints the letter o at that position. Next it advances the pen the width of one character. The second *drawchar* statement prints out the o, and you see

```
ox
```

in the Drawing window.

_____7.7 Echoing in the Drawing Window—Read and Readln_____

Now let's look at a program that uses *drawchar*. **Program** ReadlnEcho reads in a character in the Text window and then prints the character in the Drawing window. When the computer prints in one of the output windows a duplicate of a character or phrase you have just typed, we say that it is *echoing* your input.

In this example and others to come, we will use the name Ch (pronounced "see H") for a variable of type *char*.

```
program ReadlnEcho;
  var
    Ch : char;
  begin
    writeln('Type in one character.');
    write('>');
    readln(Ch);
    moveto(100,100);
    drawchar(Ch)
  end.
```

When you run **program** ReadlnEcho, the prompt is printed in the Text window, and the prompt symbol ⟩ appears on the next line. Now the program comes to the *readln* statement. To execute it, you must type a character and then type a carriage return. The *readln* statement isn't finished until a carriage return is typed. Then *moveto* positions the pen, and *drawchar* prints the character you've typed in the Text window at the pen tip.

Now look at this program:

```
program ReadEcho;
  var
    Ch : char;
  begin
    writeln('Type in one character.');
    write('>');
    read(Ch);
    moveto(100,100);
    drawchar(Ch)
  end.
```

Program ReadEcho is exactly the same as **program** ReadlnEcho, except that we have replaced the statement *readln*(Ch) with the statement *read*(Ch). Unlike *readln*, the *read* statement is over as soon as you type a character. No carriage return is needed to finish executing the *read* statement. After you type a character, the Macintosh goes immediately to the next statement.

In character-processing programs, we use the *read* statement to read whole phrases or sentences a character at a time, because we don't want to type carriage returns between characters. If we used *readln* in a character-processing program, each letter would show up on a different line, because we would have to include a carriage return after each letter.

7.8 Echoing a Whole Sentence to the Drawing Window

Now let's look at a program that echoes a whole sentence to the Drawing window (see Figure 7.8).

Program DrawEcho contains several new ideas. First of all, it has a constant of type *char* called Period, which we use to make the test in the **while** loop easier to read:

```
while (Ch <> Period) do
```

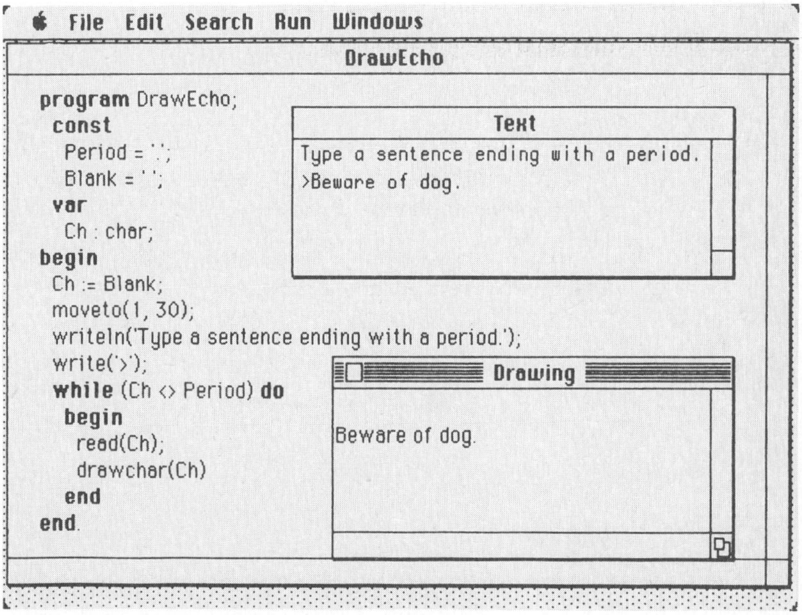

Figure 7.8   Program DrawEcho and its output.

We could have written it as

```
while (Ch <> '.') do
```

but the statement would have been harder to understand. In the constant definition, the quotation marks around the period symbol are absolutely necessary. They tell the Macintosh that you mean the character period, not a decimal point.

We have also included a constant definition for a blank space, and we've called this constant Blank. We wrote the definition by typing a single quotation mark, a space, and then another single quotation mark.

In the body of the program we have initialized Ch to Blank. This makes the value of Ch the blank symbol.

The *value* blank space is not an *undefined* value. When we say the value of a variable is undefined, we mean that the variable has not yet been assigned any value and that the location for that variable in memory is empty.

Now look at the **while** loop in **program** DrawEcho. It loops as long as the value of Ch is not a period.

What happens when you type this?

```
Beware of dog.
```

Each time through the loop, one character is processed, beginning with the B and ending with the period. After each character is printed in the Drawing window, *drawchar* automatically advances the tip of the electronic pen.

EXERCISE 4   **a.** How would you change **program** DrawEcho so that the echo is printed in doubled characters? That is, if you typed

```
Bye.
```

it would respond

```
BByyee..
```

b. How would you change **program** DrawEcho so that the echo printed a space between characters? That is, if you typed

```
Bye.
```

it would respond

```
B y e .  ▬
```

Program AdEcho

Here is one more character-processing program. Sometimes the cost of a want ad in a newspaper is figured by the character—two cents per character, for example. So ads are often placed with all the vowels removed, except for those that come at the beginning of a word. For example,

Student seeks apartment for summer.

would become

Stdnt sks aprtmnt fr smmr.

Program AdEcho (see Figure 7.9) reads in a full one-sentence ad in the Text window, and then prints the abbreviated form in the Drawing window.

After the *read* statement is executed inside the **while** loop, a case statement processes each character that has been read. If you read in a vowel, the a-e-i-o-u-A-E-I-O-U case is selected. If the previous character is a blank, the **if-then** test is true and the vowel gets printed in the Drawing window. But if the previous character is not a blank, the **if-then** case is false, so the program prints nothing in the Drawing window.

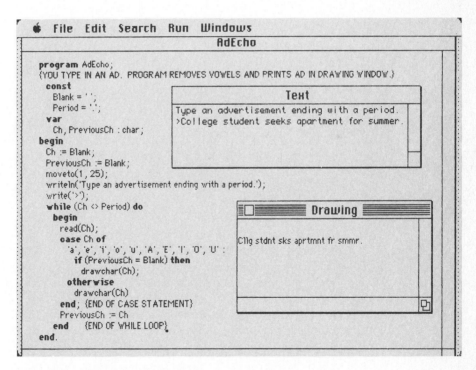

Figure 7.9 **Program** AdEcho with some sample output.

7.9 The Standard Function Chr

Let's look at a special application for the functions *chr* and *ord*. Because (*ord*('A') + 32) gives the *position* of 'a' in type *char*, the following relationship holds:

```
'a' = chr(ord('A') + 32)
```

This relationship holds for *all* letters: 'w' = *chr*(*ord*('W') + 32), and so on. Thus we can use it to convert capital letters to lowercase letters. **Program** ChangeToLowercase reads in a sentence, converts all the capital letters to lowercase letters, and then echoes the output back to the Drawing window:

```
program ChangeToLowercase;
{YOU TYPE IN A SENTENCE. PROGRAM CHANGES CAPITAL LETTERS TO}
{LOWERCASE AND ECHOES THE SENTENCE IN THE DRAWING WINDOW.}
  const
    Blank = ' ';
    Period = '.';
    OffSet = 32; {LOWERCASE LETTERS COME 32 POSITIONS AFTER UPPERCASE.}
  var
    Ch : char;
begin
  Ch := Blank;
  moveto(1,50);
  writeln('Type in a sentence,ending with a period.');
  write('>');
  while (Ch <> Period) do
    begin
      read(Ch);
      if (Ch >= 'A') and (Ch <= 'Z') then
       Ch := chr(ord(Ch) + OffSet);
      drawchar(Ch)
    end
end.
```

The **if-then** statement in the **while** loop first checks to determine whether the value of Ch is a capital letter. If it is, the *ord* function calculates the position of this value in type *char*. Then an Offset of 32—the gap between the position of a capital letter and the position of its corresponding lowercase letter—is added in. This calculation gives the position of the lowercase version of Ch's value. Next the function *chr* looks up the character at this position and assigns it to Ch.

Now we want to use **program** ChangeToLowercase to illustrate a very important idea in Pascal.

7.10 Variable Parameters

Changing uppercase letters to lowercase letters turns out to be something we will frequently want to do in character-processing programs. So it would be useful to turn **program** ChangeToLowercase into a procedure called MakeLowercase that we can insert into a program. Let's do this conversion. In the process we'll discover a new and more powerful way to write procedures.

How do we want **procedure** MakeLowercase to work? First the main program should pass a character to the procedure. If the character is an uppercase letter, the procedure should change it to lowercase. Otherwise it should leave the character unchanged. Then the procedure should pass the character back to the main program.

$$G \longrightarrow \boxed{\begin{array}{c} \textbf{procedure} \\ \text{MakeLowercase} \end{array}} \longrightarrow g$$

Here is the procedure inside a program called **program** Lowercase.

```
program Lowercase;
 const
  Blank =' ';
  Period ='.';
 var
  Ch : char;

  procedure MakeLowercase(ThisChar : char);
   const
    OffSet = 32; {LOWERCASE LETTERS COME 32 POSITIONS AFTER UPPERCASE.}
   begin
    if (ThisChar >= 'A') and (ThisChar <= 'Z') then
     ThisChar := chr(ord(ThisChar) + OffSet)
   end;

{MAIN PROGRAM}
begin
 Ch := Blank;
 moveto(1,50);
 writeln('Type in a sentence,ending with a period.');
 write('>');
 while (Ch <> Period) do
  begin
   read(Ch);
   MakeLowercase(Ch);
   drawchar(Ch)
  end
end.
```

When you type in the letter *G*, it is stored in the cell set aside for the variable Ch. The actual parameter Ch is passed to MakeLowercase, and the computer sets aside a location in memory for the formal parameter ThisChar. *G* is assigned to ThisChar and copied into that location:

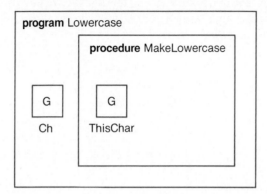

Next the commands in the procedure are executed, changing *G* to *g*.

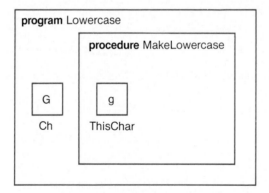

Now comes the crucial part. The Macintosh returns from the procedure call and does the *writeln* statement. It looks up the value of Ch, *which is still G*, and prints out this value—a capital *G*. But *G* is *not* what we wanted. What's going on here?

The procedure changes the value of ThisChar from *G* to *g*. But the main program doesn't print out a lowercase *g* because the value of the formal parameter ThisChar is completely isolated from the instructions in the main program. The new value of ThisChar has absolutely no effect on the value of the actual parameter for **procedure** MakeLowercase, or on any variable in the main program.

This example illustrates an important limitation of the kind of parameter we have been using in procedures. With this kind of parameter, there's nothing that a procedure can do to affect the value of a variable in the main program. A procedure call can pass information in one direction only: from the main program to the procedure.

Procedures that work this way can use data from the main program to draw pictures and bar graphs, and they can print text in the output windows. They can also change the data they receive from the main program and print out the altered data. But they can't send altered data back to the main program. This one-way information flow is a serious limitation.

There is a simple way to get **procedure** MakeLowercase to do what we want. We can make ThisChar a *variable parameter.* The value of a variable parameter *can* be passed back to the main program. This will allow information to flow in two directions—from the main program to the procedure, *and* from the procedure back to the main program.

The kind of formal parameter we have been using up until now is called a *value parameter.* Value parameters cannot be passed back to the main program.

To change the formal parameter ThisChar from a value parameter into a variable parameter, all we have to do is add the word **var** to the procedure heading line:

```
procedure MakeLowercase(var ThisChar : char)
```

The word **var** identifies ThisChar as a variable parameter. Now when you run **program** Lowercase, passing parameters between the main program and the procedure works differently. When you pass the actual parameter Ch to the procedure, the value of Ch is *not* copied into a separate, private memory location reserved for ThisChar. Instead, ThisChar becomes a *second name* for the memory location reserved for the actual parameter Ch:

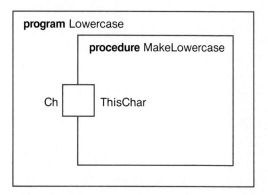

When the value of the formal parameter ThisChar is changed during the procedure call, the value of the actual parameter Ch is also changed, because ThisChar and Ch share a common cell in memory:

Ch ⬚g⬚ ThisChar

When Pascal returns from the procedure, the value stored in Ch is g, and this is what the program prints out.

When the computer is executing commands in the main program, the cell is named Ch and instructions in the main program control the value it holds. When the computer is executing commands in the procedure, the cell is called ThisChar, and its value is controlled by instructions in the procedure.

Here is our revised version of **program** Lowercase, which we have called LowercaseTwo.

```
program LowercaseTwo;
{YOU TYPE IN A SENTENCE. PROGRAM CHANGES CAPITAL LETTERS TO}
{LOWERCASE AND ECHOES THE SENTENCE IN THE DRAWING WINDOW.}
 const
  Blank = ' ';
  Period = '.';
 var
  Ch : char;

 procedure MakeLowercase(var ThisChar : char);
 {CHANGES CAPITAL LETTERS TO LOWERCASE.}
 {RETURNS OTHER CHARACTERS UNCHANGED.}
  const
   OffSet = 32; {LOWERCASE LETTERS COME 32 POSITIONS AFTER UPPERCASE.}
 begin
  if (ThisChar >= 'A') and (ThisChar <= 'Z') then
   ThisChar := chr(ord(ThisChar) + OffSet)
 end;

{MAIN PROGRAM}
begin
 Ch := Blank;
 moveto(1,50);
 writeln('Type in a sentence,ending with a period.');
 write('>');
 while (Ch <> Period) do
  begin
   read(Ch);
   MakeLowercase(Ch);
   drawchar(Ch)
  end
end.
```

A cell in memory for a variable parameter is like a mail box in which the main program and a procedure exchange messages. When a procedure is called, the main program leaves in the box a message for the procedure. The procedure takes this message, processes it, and leaves a new message in the box. When program execution returns from the procedure, the main program picks up its new message.

EXERCISE 5   What value does **program** ParameterTest print?

```
program ParameterTest;
 var
  Number : integer;
 procedure ChangeNumber(var Num : integer);
 begin
  Num := 10
 end;

{MAIN PROGRAM}
begin
 Number := 5;
 ChangeNumber(Number);
 writeln(Number)
end.
```

Answer: 10 ▬

When you use a variable parameter, the actual parameter passed in a procedure call *must* be a variable. It can't be a value such as 8, or a constant, or a complex expression. For example, in the following program, all three calls to **procedure** ChangeNumber are illegal.

```
program ParameterTestTwo;
 const
  Twenty = 20;
 var
  Number : integer;

 procedure ChangeNumber(var Num : integer);
 begin
  Num := 10
 end;

begin
 Number := 5;
 ChangeNumber(8); {ILLEGAL}
 ChangeNumber(2 * Number); {ILLEGAL}
 ChangeNumber(Twenty); {ILLEGAL}
 writeln(Number)
end.
```

This restriction makes sense. A variable formal parameter becomes a second name for the actual parameter's cell in memory. But only variables can be names for cells. Values, constants, and complex expressions such as (2 * Number) cannot be names for cells.

An actual parameter *can* be a constant, a value, or a complex expression if the corresponding formal parameter is a value parameter. With a value parameter, only the value of the actual parameter matters. First the Macintosh figures out the value of the actual parameter. Then it assigns that value to the formal parameter.

7.11 Getmouse—A MacPascal Standard Procedure

Standard procedures can have variable parameters, too. The MacPascal standard procedure *getmouse*, for example, has two variable parameters. Let's see how *getmouse* works in **program** MouseReport (see Figure 7.10), which reports in the Text window the location of the tip of the pointer.

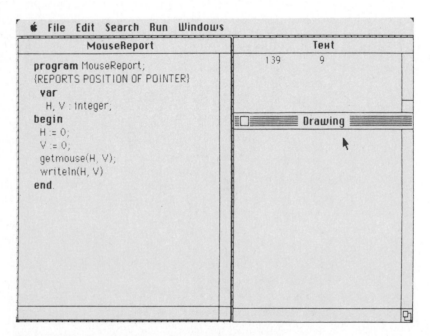

Figure 7.10   Program MouseReport and its output.

When you use **program** MouseReport, it is awkward to choose Go from the Run menu and then quickly position the pointer where you want it on the screen. Luckily there is another, mouseless way to run a program.

First place the pointer where you want it on the screen. Then hold down the command key (the one with the clover leaf), and press the G key. The program will run and report in the Text window the position of the pointer.

It is also possible to execute other commands on the Run menu using the keyboard instead of the mouse. The keyboard methods are listed alongside the commands in the menu (see Figure 7.11).

Figure 7.11   Keyboard symbols that can be used to run, step, or check a program are listed next to the items on the menu.

When the standard procedure *getmouse* is called, the procedure is passed the actual parameters H and V, which have been intialized to zero. When program execution returns from the procedure call, the variable H holds the value of the horizontal position of the tip of the pointer, and the variable V holds the value of its vertical position.

If you position the pointer outside the Drawing window, you will still get a value for H and V when you run the program. The values are calculated in relation to the upper-left corner of the Drawing window. With the pointer in the upper-left corner of the screen, for example, you will get two negative numbers for output.

The two variable parameters for *getmouse* must be of type *integer*. But no matter what values these variables hold before they are passed to the procedure, *getmouse* passes back values that correspond to the horizontal position and the vertical position of the tip of the pointer. So the values returned by the procedure are not related to the values passed to the procedure. Because it ignores the values of the actual parameters passed to it, *getmouse* is an unusual procedure.

We use *getmouse* again in the **program** WatchMouse (see Figure 7.12). This program reports the position of the tip of the pointer continuously until you move the pointer to the left of the Drawing window.

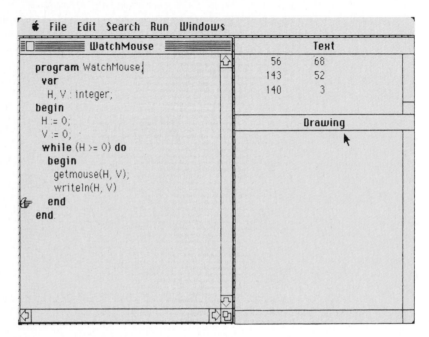

Figure 7.12   **Program** WatchMouse and its output as it runs using the Step command.

In **program** WatchMouse, the *getmouse* procedure is inside a **while** statement. The **while** statement loops continuously, reporting the current values of H and V during each iteration. When you move the mouse pointer across the left wall of the Drawing window, H becomes less than zero and you terminate the loop.

7.12 Drawing with Getmouse

Using *getmouse*, we can draw spectacular pictures in the Drawing window. **Program** OvalDraw below draws ovals 80 units high and 20 units wide all over the screen as you move the mouse (see Figure 7.13).

The *frameoval* command in **program** OvalDraw draws an oval located in an imaginary rectangle whose upper-left corner is the point (H, V).

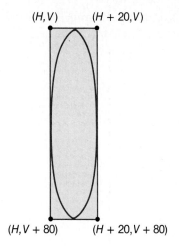

As long as you keep the pointer to the right of the left wall of the Drawing window—that is, as long as

```
H >= 0
```

the **while** statement continues to loop. During each iteration, *getmouse* reports the current position of the pointer, and the program draws an oval.

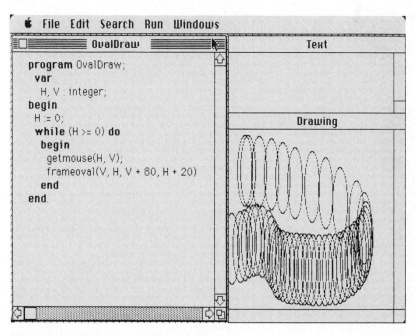

Figure 7.13   Program OvalDraw and its output.

One small change in **program** OvalDraw will make its output more dramatic. If we use this *frameoval* command

```
frameoval(V,H,V + 80,H + V)
```

ovals drawn near the bottom of the screen will be wider, and ovals drawn near the top of the screen will be narrower. With an enlarged Drawing window, your output will look something like Figure 7.14.

Figure 7.14   The output of modified **program** OvalDraw.

7.13 Cryptography

Since the Second World War, computers have become indispensable in cryptography—the science of making and breaking secret messages. But work with codes began long before the computer age.

Secret ciphers are almost as old as writing itself. About 3500 years ago, a pottery maker in Mesopotamia used a cipher to write down his private formula for putting a glaze on his pots. In most ancient civilizations, secret writing was something of a game. One could fool people with it, conceal recipes for magic potions, and use it in love letters.

The first to use cryptography for military purposes were apparently the Spartans in ancient Greece. In the fifth century B.C., they invented a cipher that worked like this: First a strip of cloth, parchment, or leather was wound around a rod. Then the message was written, one character on each loop, down the length of the rod. When the strip was unwound, the random letters made no sense. On a messenger's cloth belt they might seem like decorations, and he could go on his way unsuspected. When he delivered the belt, it was wrapped around a rod the same size as the original. Restored to their proper order, the letters spelled out the message.

In the first century B.C., Julius Caesar used a scheme called a linear substitution cipher for his secret military messages. A linear substitution cipher is created when each letter in a message is replaced with another letter that comes a fixed number of positions later in the alphabet. When each letter is shifted two positions, for example, c becomes e and z becomes b. Using this method, the message

hide immediately

becomes

jkfg koogfkcvgna

If you intercept an enciphered message that's long enough, a linear substitution cipher is easy to break using letter-frequency data. Suppose the letter g occurs most often in the message. Because the letter e is the most common letter in English (about 13 percent of all letters are e's), you will probably be right if you guess that the message has been enciphered with a shift of 2.

7.14 Creating a Secret Cipher

Now let's write a linear substitution enciphering program, which we'll call **program** Cipher. It will convert a sentence you enter at the keyboard into an enciphered message. We'll make it interactive so that you can specify a different shift and create a different cipher each time you read in a text.

Program Cipher will work this way: First you type in two letters that determine the shift. If you want the a's to become e's, for example, you type in an a and then an e. Then you type in a message ending with a period, and the program enciphers this message, shifting each letter ahead 4 letters. The enciphered message will be printed in the Drawing window. For simplicity, we'll print the enciphered output using all lowercase letters.

This is our first big program using variable parameters, so we'll go over it in detail.

Thinking

Let's begin by summarizing what **program** Cipher will do. First it reads in the two letters that determine how the letters will be shifted, and it calculates the shift. Next you type in a sentence. The program reads the sentence letter by letter, enciphering and printing each letter as it goes. Because we want lowercase output, each character will also be converted to lower case as soon as it is read.

We will use Ch1 and Ch2 as the names of the input variables that determine the shift in the cipher, and we'll read each letter of the original sentence using the variable Ch.

We'll use a loop to read each character, change it to lower case, encipher it, and print it out. To make the program easier to read, we'll define two constants: the period and the blank symbol. We'll use the blank symbol to initialize the variable Ch. And we'll use the period in the test part of the control line of the loop.

―――――――――――――――――― DATA TABLE ――――――――――――――――――

Input Variables	Output Variables	Program Variables
Ch1,Ch2,Ch : char;	Ch	Shift : integer;

Constants	Formulas	
Period, Blank	None	

Loops

Main loop reads and then enciphers letters

―――

Planning

From our initial description we can formulate this first plan for the program.

Plan I

1. Read the first character.
2. Read the second character.
3. Calculate the shift.
4. Read and encipher the message character by character until a period is reached:
    a. Read a character.
    b. Change the character to lowercase.
    c. Encipher the character.
    d. Print the enciphered character in the Drawing window.

This is a good start. Now let's turn it into a more concrete algorithm.

Plan II

ReadFirstChar(Ch1)
ReadSecondChar(Ch2)
calculate shift
while (Ch ⟨⟩ Period) do
  begin
    read(Ch)
    MakeLowerCase(Ch)
    Encipher(Ch,Shift)
    drawchar(Ch)
  end

This plan is close to the actual top-level code. It includes four procedures, which handle four of the smaller jobs the program does.

The "calculate shift" part of the plan is very simple. It's just

```
Shift := ord(Ch2) - ord(Ch1)
```

so we won't bother to put it inside a procedure. If Ch2 is an *e* and Ch1 is an *a*, then Shift will be assigned 101 − 97, or 4. Note that, if Ch2 comes before Ch1 in the alphabet, Shift will be negative.

Clarifying the Procedures

ReadFirstChar and ReadSecondChar

ReadFirstChar has the heading line

```
procedure ReadFirstChar(var Ch1 : char);
```

Ch1 is a variable parameter, because it is passed to the procedure undefined and is passed back as a character. We'll diagram its paper check this way:

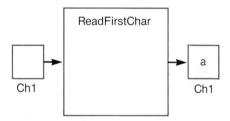

ReadSecondChar is almost identical to ReadFirstChar, and it is clarified in the same way.

MakeLowercase

We have already written this procedure. It has the heading line

```
procedure MakeLowercase(var Ch : char);
```

Encipher

Encipher is the most interesting procedure in the program. Its heading line includes both a variable parameter and a value parameter:

```
procedure Encipher(var Ch : char; Shift : integer);
```

Here are two Encipher paper checks—one for a positive shift of three characters forward and one for a negative shift of 2 characters back.

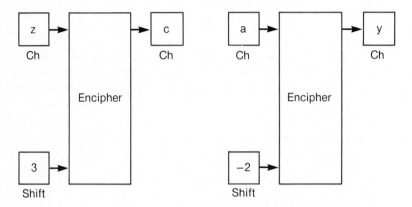

When we write a paper check for a procedure that has both a variable parameter and a value parameter, we treat all the formal parameters as inputs to the procedure, but only the variable parameters will be treated as procedure outputs. This makes sense because only variable parameters return information to the main program.

Now we know enough to code the top level.

```
begin
  ReadFirstChar(Ch1);
  ReadSecondChar(Ch2);
  Shift := ord(Ch2) - ord(Ch1);
  Ch := Blank;
  moveto(1,100);
  writeln('Type in message ending with a period.');
  write('>');
  while (Ch <> Period) do
    begin
      read(Ch);
      MakeLowercase(Ch);
      Encipher(Ch,Shift);
      drawchar(Ch)
    end
end.
```

Thinking, Planning, and Coding Procedure Encipher

Procedure Encipher is the most complicated of the four procedures, so let's look at it in detail.

The main program passes **procedure** Encipher two values—a character, Ch, and a value for Shift, which can be any integer. Encipher passes Ch back to the main program. If the character passed is a letter, Encipher passes that letter back in cipher. Otherwise it returns the character unchanged.

The tricky part of the procedure is the "wrap-around" effect, which shifts a letter at the end of the alphabet so that it becomes a letter at the beginning of the alphabet. For example, a positive shift of 3 changes z to c. We handle the wrap-around problem in two stages. First we identify each letter with a number from 0 to 25 so that 0 stands for a, 1 stands for b, and so on. Next, we add in the shift. If we add 3 to z's position, which is 25, we get 28. Then, for the wrap-around operation, we use the **mod** operator. When we calculate 28 **mod** 26 we get 2, which is c's position in the alphabet when we number the letters beginning with zero.

What happens when the shift is negative? Suppose the shift is -3 and we want to encipher b. We get the right answer by counting backward from b 3 positions and wrapping around to the end of the alphabet: a-z-y. So b becomes y. We can use the **mod** operator to calculate the negative wrap-around in the same way we used it for the positive wrap-around. With negative numbers, **mod** is defined to work as follows. Suppose Number1 and Number2 are both greater than 0. Then

    -Number1 mod Number2 = (Number2 - Number1) mod Number2

So

    -2 mod 26 = (26 - 2) mod 26 = 24 mod 26 = 24.

This formula gives the correct answer, because 24 is the position of the letter y.

To make the position of each letter equal to a number from 0 to 25, we'll subtract $ord(\text{'a'}) = 97$ from the letter's position: $ord(\text{'a'}) - 97 = 0$, $ord(\text{'b'}) - 97 = 1$, and so on. The procedure will use a constant that we'll call PositionOf_a.

We'll need a variable called ChPosition to hold the number from 0 to 25 that represents the value of Ch in terms of its distance from a. For example, for the letter c, ChPosition = 2.

We will also create a variable called EncipheredChPosition to hold the number of Ch's position after the shift has been applied. EncipheredChPosition can equal less than 0 or more than 25.

We can write this plan for the procedure:

    if Ch is a lowercase letter
    then
        calculate ChPosition from 0 to 25
        add the shift to get EncipheredChPosition
        calculate the new letter value for Ch

Now we can code **procedure Encipher:**

```
procedure Encipher(var Ch : char; Shift : integer);
 const
  PositionOf_a = 97;
 var
  ChPosition, EncipheredChPosition : integer;
begin
 if (Ch )= 'a') and (Ch <= 'z') then
  begin
  ChPosition := ord(Ch) - PositionOf_a;
  EncipheredChPosition := ChPosition + Shift;
  Ch := chr((EncipheredChPosition mod 26) + PositionOf_a)
  end
end;
```

Here's what the procedure does. Suppose the program passes the procedure the letter *z* and a shift of 3. The procedure subtracts 97 from *ord*(z) and comes up with 25. Then it adds a shift of 3 to get 28. Next it calculates 28 **mod** 26, which gives 2. Then it adds 2 to 97 and gets 99. And finally, *chr*(99) = c.

Here is the complete **program Cipher:**

```
program Cipher;
{PROGRAM ENCIPHERS A MESSAGE BY SHIFTING EACH LETTER A CERTAIN}
{NUMBER OF PLACES FORWARD OR BACKWARD IN THE ALPHABET.}
 const
  Blank = ' ';
  Period = '.';
 var
  Ch1,Ch2,Ch : char;
  Shift : integer;
procedure ReadFirstChar(var FirstChar : char);
begin
 writeln('Type in a lowercase letter.');
 write('>');
 read(FirstChar);
 writeln
end;

procedure ReadSecondChar(var SecondChar : char);
begin
 writeln('What lowercase letter do you want
          the first letter to be shifted to?');
 write('>');
 read(SecondChar);
 writeln
end;
```

```
procedure MakeLowercase(var ThisChar : char);
 const
   OffSet = 32; {THERE ARE 32 POSITIONS}
                {BETWEEN CAPITAL AND LOWERCASE LETTERS.}
begin
 if (ThisChar >= 'A') and (ThisChar <= 'Z') then
   ThisChar := chr(ord(ThisChar) + OffSet)
end;


procedure Encipher (varCh : char;
        Shift : integer);
 const
   PositionOf_a = 97;
 var
   ChPosition,EncipheredChPosition : integer;
begin
 if (Ch >= 'a') and (Ch <= 'z') then
   begin
    {CALCULATE POSITION OF CH, A NUMBER FROM 0 TO 25}
    ChPosition := ord(Ch) - PositionOf_a;
    {CALCULATE ENCIPHERED POSITION OF CH: IT MAY BE < 0 or > 25}
    EncipheredChPosition := ChPosition + Shift;
    {USE MOD TO CALCULATE THE ENCIPHERED VALUE OF CH}
    Ch := chr((EncipheredChPosition mod 26) + PositionOf_a)
   end
end;


{THE MAIN PROGRAM}
begin
 ReadFirstChar(Ch1);
 ReadSecondChar(Ch2);
 Shift := ord(Ch2) - ord(Ch1);
 Ch := Blank;
 moveto(1,50);
 writeln('Type in a message, ending with a period.');
 write('>');
 while (Ch <> Period) do
  begin
   read(Ch);
   MakeLowercase(Ch);
   Encipher(Ch,Shift);
   drawchar(Ch)
  end
end.
```

TEST YOURSELF

1. What is an enumerated type?

2. What does the Pascal function *ord* do?

3. What does *chr* do?

4. Explain the difference between 3 and '3'?

5. What does the **otherwise** part of a case statement do?

6. What is a case label?

7. What is a case selector?

8. What is a value parameter?

9. What is a variable parameter?

10. How many elements are there in type *char*?

11. Name three of Pascal's standard types.

12. What is a global constant?

PROBLEMS

1. Write a program that lists all the directions in type Directions in Section 7.1. Do the program two ways: first list the directions forward, then list them backward.

2. Make up a type called vehicles (car, truck, bus, and so on) with six elements. Then write a program that lists each element along with its position in the type.

3. Write a program that lists the capital letters *A* through *Z* across the top of the Drawing window and that lists the lowercase letters *a* through *z* across the bottom of the window.

4. Modify **program** DrawEcho so that the vowels in the sentence you type in are echoed as stars. "Pass the pepper." would become "P*ss th* p*pp*r."

5. The following procedure alters a rectangle in some way. What does it do? (*Hint:* Draw a picture. Then put the procedure in a program and run it to check your answer.)

```
procedure ChangeRec(var Top,Left,Bottom,Right : integer);
  var
   Scratchpad: integer
begin
 Scratchpad := Left;
 Left := Top;
 Top := Scratchpad;
 Scratchpad := Right;
 Right := Bottom;
 Bottom := Scratchpad
end;
```

Give an example of a rectangle that **procedure** ChangeRec leaves unchanged.

6. Write a program called **program** ThreeSort that reads in three real numbers and then prints them out, largest to smallest. In your program, use a procedure called SwapNumbers with the heading line

```
procedure SwapNumbers(var First,Second : real);
```

When your program passes SwapNumbers two numbers, it passes them back with their positions switched.

7. Write an interactive program that reads in a sentence and prints out the number of letters, both capital and lowercase, that you have typed.

8. Write an interactive program that reads in two characters and then a sentence. If the two characters appear consecutively in the sentence, the program reports this by printing out this character in the Text window.

9. Write an interactive program using the enumerated type Directions defined in Section 7.1. You type in a direction—say, SouthWest—and the program draws this picture:

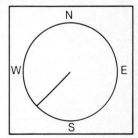

10. Write a program that reads in several sentences and then prints out the percentage of all letters in the text that come from the first half of the alphabet (*A* through *M* and *a* through *m*). In order to read in more than one sentence, you need to end the reading loop with some character other than a period. Use a dollar sign in the while statement control line:

```
while (Ch <> '$') do
```

11. Write a calendar program. You type in the name of a month, the number of days in that month, and the day of the week that the month starts on, and it prints out a calendar for that month. If you type in

```
January 31 Tue
```

the program prints out

```
                JANUARY
    Mon  Tue  Wed  Thur  Fri  Sat  Sun
          1    2    3     4    5    6
     7    8    9    10    11   12   13
    14   15   16    17    18   19   20
    21   22   23    24    25   26   27
    28   29   30    31
```

12. How would you change **program** DrawEcho so that all *a*'s in a text are replaced with *e*'s, all *e*'s with *i*'s, all *i*'s with *o*'s, all *o*'s with *u*'s, all *u*'s with *y*'s, and all *y*'s with *a*'s?

The Type Boolean and Subrange Types

8

True and False are important values in Pascal. When we say that an expression such as

```
(Number <= 4)
```

is a test, we mean that True and False are its possible values. These two values make up the type *boolean*—the major topic of this chapter.

We'll also talk about subrange types. A subrange type, which is a subtype of another type, makes a program easier to understand.

8.1 The Type Boolean: Pascal's True/False Type

The type *boolean*—Pascal's fourth standard type—is surprisingly simple. It has only two elements, the values True and False.

We can print out the elements of type *boolean* with **program** BooleanElements, which appears in Figure 8.1. It prints the elements of type *boolean* just the way **program** AllCharacters in Chapter 7 prints the Macintosh's character set.

In the type *boolean*, *ord*(False) = 0 and *ord*(True) = 1, so (False < True) just as ('A' < 'a') in type *char* and (Mon < Wed) in the enumerated type DaysOfWeek.

The variable declaration in **program** BooleanElements,

```
var
  Test : boolean;
```

sets aside a location in memory for a variable of type *boolean*. The values that can go in that location are limited to the two boolean values, True and False.

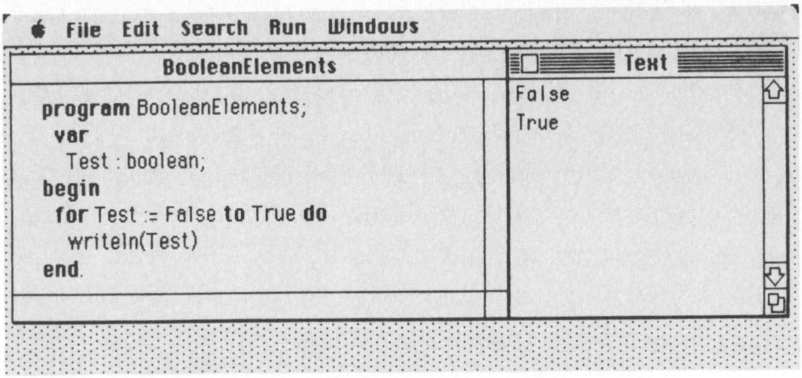

```
 ¢ File  Edit  Search  Run  Windows
┌─────────────────────────────────┬──────────────────┐
│          BooleanElements         │        Text      │
├─────────────────────────────────┼──────────────────┤
│ program BooleanElements;         │ False            │
│   var                            │ True             │
│     Test : boolean;              │                  │
│   begin                          │                  │
│    for Test := False to True do  │                  │
│      writeln(Test)               │                  │
│    end.                          │                  │
└─────────────────────────────────┴──────────────────┘
```

Figure 8.1   Program BooleanElements and its output.

Boolean variables work just like other variables. You can use boolean variables in *readln*, *writeln*, and assignment statements, as we have done in **program** BooleanDemo, which appears in Figure 8.2. If you type in True after the prompt, the program will print out True.

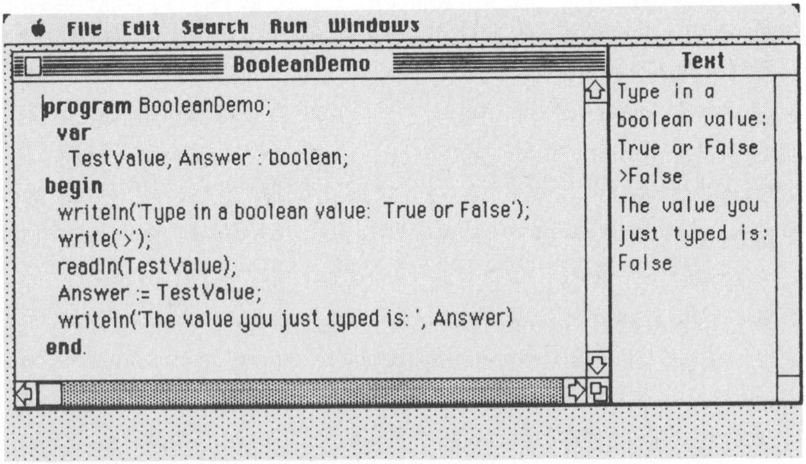

```
 ¢ File  Edit  Search  Run  Windows
┌─────────────────────────────────────────────────┬──────────────────┐
│                  BooleanDemo                      │       Text       │
├─────────────────────────────────────────────────┼──────────────────┤
│ program BooleanDemo;                              │ Type in a        │
│   var                                             │ boolean value:   │
│     TestValue, Answer : boolean;                  │ True or False    │
│   begin                                           │ >False           │
│    writeln('Type in a boolean value:  True or False'); │ The value you │
│    write('>');                                    │ just typed is:   │
│    readln(TestValue);                             │ False            │
│    Answer := TestValue;                           │                  │
│    writeln('The value you just typed is: ', Answer) │                │
│   end.                                            │                  │
└─────────────────────────────────────────────────┴──────────────────┘
```

Figure 8.2   Program BooleanDemo and its output.

The type *boolean* is important because many Pascal commands—**while, repeat-until, if-then-else**—include ⟨test⟩ slots. A ⟨test⟩ slot can be filled by any variable or expression that has a boolean value. Let's look at the connection between tests, boolean values, and boolean variables more closely.

8.2 Boolean Values and Tests

Any expression that has or returns a boolean value is a *boolean expression*. Hence *odd*(Number + 5) is a boolean expression, and so is (Number ⟨= 5). We can use a boolean expression in any ⟨test⟩ position.

Because a boolean expression has a value of True or False, we can assign its value to a boolean variable. For example, suppose MoreToPrint is a boolean variable. Then we can write the assignment

```
MoreToPrint := (Number <= 5)
```

This statement seems peculiar, but it's perfectly valid. When you run a program that includes this statement, the computer evaluates the right side of the assignment first. Because the right side is a test, the result of the evaluation is a boolean value. The type of the value on the right matches the declared type of MoreToPrint, so the assignment goes through without a hitch.

Because MoreToPrint has a boolean value, we can use it in the test position of a **while** statement, as we have in **program** NumberList.

```
program NumberList;
 var
  Number : integer;
  MoreToPrint : boolean;
begin
 Number := 1;
 MoreToPrint := True;
 while MoreToPrint do
 {WHILE MORETOPRINT IS TRUE DO}
  begin
   writeln(Number);
   Number := Number + 1;
   MoreToPrint := (Number <= 5)
   {MORETOPRINT IS TRUE IF NUMBER IS LESS THAN OR EQUAL TO 5}
  end
end.
```

The control line in the **while** loop

```
while MoreToPrint do
```

means

"While MoreToPrint is true, do the following."

Looping will continue as long as MoreToPrint is true, and MoreToPrint will remain true as long as Number is less than or equal to 5. When Number exceeds 5, MoreToPrint becomes false and looping stops.

EXERCISE 1　**a.** In **program** IfTest, what is the value of the boolean variable FirstNumberIsGreater after you type in the values 6 and 7? What does the program print?

```
program IfTest;
 var
   FirstNumberIsGreater : boolean;
   FirstNumber,SecondNumber : integer;
begin
 writeln('Type in two integers.');
 write('>');
 readln(FirstNumber,SecondNumber);
 FirstNumberIsGreater := (FirstNumber > SecondNumber);
 if FirstNumberIsGreater then
   writeln('The first number is greater than the second.')
 else
   writeln('First number is less than or equal to second.')
end.
```

b. What does **program** MoreNumbers print?

```
program MoreNumbers;
 var
   Number : integer;
   TooBig : boolean;
begin
 Number := 0;
 TooBig := False;
 repeat
   Number := Number + 2;
   writeln(Number);
   TooBig := (Number > 10)
 until TooBig
end.
```

Answer: 2-4-6-8-10-12 in a column ▬

8.3 The Logical Connectives and, or, and not

Look at the following **if-then-else** statement:

```
if (Top < Bottom) and (Left < Right) then
 paintrect(Top,Left,Bottom,Right)
else
 writeln('Sorry -- no rectangle')
```

The expression in test position includes *two* tests tied together by the reserved word **and**. The word **and**, along with the words **or** and **not**, are Pascal's *logical operators* or *logical connectives.* Using logical operators, you can build complex boolean expressions such as the one above in the ⟨test⟩ position.

Here is an example of an expression using the logical connective **or**, which we could use to idiot-proof **program** Interest from Chapter 4.

```
if (Years < 0) or (Principal < 0.0) then
  writeln('Bad input -- restart program.')
else...
```

The **then** part is executed if *either one* of the tests (Years < 0) or (Principal < 0.0) is true.

The logical operator **not** is type boolean's flip-flop connective. It changes the value of the variable or expression that comes after it. In **program** RecurringHunger, the **not** changes the value of the variable Hungry each time through the loop.

```
program RecurringHunger;
  var
   Count : integer;
   Hungry : boolean;
begin
 Hungry := False;
 for Count := 1 to 4 do
  begin
   Hungry := not(Hungry);
   writeln('Am I hungry? ',Hungry)
  end
end.
```

Here is a summary of how the logical connectives work. We've used the boolean variables p and q to illustrate the rules:

1. The expression (p **and** q) is true only if *both* parts of the expression are true. That is, if p is true and q is true, then (p **and** q) is true.

2. The expression (p **or** q) is true if *either* part of the expression is true—that is, if either p is true or q is true, or both are true.

3. The expression (**not** p) is true if p is false. And the expression (**not** p) is false if p is true. Hence the **not** operator flips the value of a boolean variable or expression.

Important: When you write a complex expression using several logical connectives, *always* use parentheses to make the meaning clear. Where you place the parentheses affects the value of the expression. For example,

```
not(p) and (q or r)
```

can have a different value from

```
not(p and (q or r))
```

EXERCISE 2   **a.** What does **program** Easy print?

```
program Easy;
 const
  EasyToDo = True;
begin
 writeln(not(EasyToDo));
 writeln(EasyToDo and not(EasyToDo));
 writeln(EasyToDo or not(EasyToDo))
end.
```

Answer: False   False   True printed in a column.

b. What does **program** TasteIt print?

```
program TasteIt;
 const
  Edible = True;
 var
  Tasty,Appealing,IMightTryIt : boolean;
begin
 Tasty := True;
 Appealing := False;
 IMightTryIt := Tasty and (Appealing and Edible);
 writeln(IMightTryIt)
end.
```

Answer: False

c. What does **program** Vote print?

```
program Vote;
 var
  Experienced,Honest,Corrupt,
   NobodyElseBetter,IWillVoteForHer : boolean;
begin
 Experienced := True;
 Honest := True;
 Corrupt := not(Honest);
 NobodyElseBetter := True;
 IWillVoteForHer := (Experienced and not(Corrupt))
                       or NobodyElseBetter;
 writeln(IWillVoteForHer)
end.
```

Answer: True ▰

8.4 Flags

Now we come to an important application of boolean variables—the flag. A *flag* is a boolean variable that causes looping to end early when some special condition is met. Let's see how flags work by looking at a program that processes text, that is, a program that works on data of type *char*.

Programs that process text often search for something—a vowel, a period, or perhaps a special pattern of characters such as a word or a combination of symbols. In this kind of program a loop is usually terminated in one of two ways: Either you reach the end of the text, or you find what you are looking for (a doubled letter, for example) and looping ends early. To end a loop early after you find what you're looking for, you need a flag.

Program DoubledChar looks for doubled characters (such as the *t*'s in Otto) in a phrase or sentence. The program includes a flag called *Found*. Initially Found is False. It changes from False to True when a doubled character is encountered.

```
program DoubledChar;
{YOU TYPE IN A SENTENCE. PROGRAM REPORTS}
{FIRST PAIR OF DOUBLED CHARACTERS.}
 const
  Period ='.';
  Blank =' ';
 var
  Ch,PreviousChar : char;
  Found : boolean; {THE FLAG}
begin
 Found := False; {THE FLAG IS INITIALIZED TO FALSE.}
 writeln('Type a sentence ending with a period.');
 write('>');
 read(Ch);
 PreviousChar := Ch;
 while (Ch <> Period) and (not(Found)) do
  begin
   read(Ch);
   if (PreviousChar = Ch) then
    Found := True; {IF FOUND BECOMES TRUE, LOOP ENDS EARLY.}
   PreviousChar := Ch
  end;
 writeln;
 if Found then
  writeln('The character ',PreviousChar,' is doubled in the sentence.')
 else
  writeln('There are no doubled characters in the sentence.')
end.
```

Program DoubledChar includes two variables of type *char*—Ch and PreviousChar. When Ch = PreviousChar, we have found a doubled character.

Before looping begins, the flag (Found) is initialized to False. Then a first value for Ch is read in and assigned to PreviousChar as well.

If the first character you type is a period, the **while** loop is skipped altogether. Because Found is initially False, when the final **if-then-else** statement is executed, the program reports that no doubled characters have been found.

If the first character is not a period, the **while** loop begins and another value is read into Ch. Now PreviousChar is one character "behind" Ch, and the two are compared to determine whether they are equal. If they are, Found is set to True.

Then PreviousChar is assigned the value of Ch, and the loop test is evaluated again.

If Found is True *or* if Ch is a period, looping is over and the final **if-then-else** statement uses the value of Found to determine which output to print. Otherwise, the loop does another iteration. See Figure 8.3 for sample output.

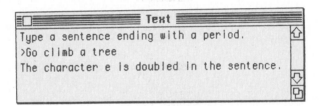

Figure 8.3   Sample output for **program** DoubledChar.

Let's alter the program slightly so that it finds a doubled lowercase letter instead of any doubled character. To do this, we will add a boolean variable called IsALetter to the program and replace the **if-then** statement inside the **while** loop with these statements:

```
IsALetter := ('a' <= Ch) and ('z' >= Ch);
if (PreviousChar = Ch) and IsALetter then
 Found := True;
```

If Ch is a lowercase letter, the variable IsALetter is set to True; otherwise it is set to False. Next the ⟨test⟩ part of the **if-then** statement, which has two parts connected by an **and**, is executed. It checks whether the current character equals the previous character *and* whether the current character is a lowercase letter. Once this **if-then** statement is added, you won't trip the flag if you type in two blank spaces or two capital letters in a row.

Note: **Program** DoubledChar finds only the first set of doubled characters in a sentence.

—8.5 Matching Parentheses—A Proofreading Program —

Suppose that you open the Instant window, type

```
writeln(2 * 2))
```

and click on Do It. Immediately you are notified of your mistake:

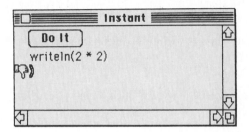

How does MacPascal "know" that you failed to match the parentheses properly in the *writeln* instruction?

As MacPascal processes your instruction, it checks the syntax of the expression in the *writeln* statement. The techniques and algorithms it uses are part of *syntactic analysis*, an important and thoroughly studied area of computer science. One small but significant part of the MacPascal program checks to determine whether parentheses match up. It is this algorithm that has complained about your *writeln* statement.

For every left parenthesis in a statement, there must be a right parenthesis. And in each pair, the left parenthesis must always come first. Here are some examples of matched and unmatched parentheses:

Matched	Unmatched
( )	((((
( ) ( )	(((( )))
(( ))	( ))
((( )) ( ))	)
( ) (( ))	( )) (( )

If the parentheses in a program are not "legally" matched, Pascal won't run your program.

Pascal checks other patterns as well. Turn back to **program** Checkerboard in Chapter 6. If you ignore all the words and symbols except **begin** and **end**, you will see the following pattern:

begin begin end end begin begin end end begin end

Begin-end pairs in a program must match up according to the same rules that determine whether parentheses are matched properly.

Many other elements of a program must also match up according to the rules for matching parentheses. In fact, the structure of matched parentheses underlies much of the syntax of Pascal and nearly every other programming language.

Let's write a program that checks whether the parentheses in a string of characters match up. To write it, we need to state precisely what is required for a string to be legal.

A string of parentheses is legal if two conditions are met. First, every parenthesis must have a partner, so there must be an equal number of left and right parentheses. Second, the left parenthesis must come first in each pair.

EXERCISE 3   Tell which of the following strings of parentheses are invalid, and explain why.

   a. ((( ))
   b. ( )) ( ) (
   c. (( ) ( )) ( ) ▬

We can use the following algorithm to spot violations of these conditions. We'll invent a variable called Counter that has an initial value of zero. As we read across the string from left to right, we will perform the following operations:

■ Add 1 to Counter for every left parenthesis.
■ Subtract 1 from Counter for every right parenthesis.

Here's how we decide whether the string of parentheses is legal:

1. If the value of Counter ever becomes negative, reject the string. (This detects a right parenthesis that comes before its partner.)
2. If Counter ends up at a value greater than zero, reject the string. (This detects left parentheses without partners.)
3. If Counter ends up at zero without ever going negative, accept the string. (This means that left and right parentheses even out and that a right parenthesis never precedes its matching left parenthesis.)

Here is an example:

```
string:    (  (  )  (  )  )
Counter:   1  2  1  2  1  0
         ***accept***
```

Here is another example:

```
string:    (  (  )  )  (  )     )  (
Counter:   1  2  1  0  1  0  -1  0
         ***reject***
```

Program ParenCheck is an interactive program that does this analysis. If you type in a string such as (( )), it will check whether the parentheses match up. And because it ignores all characters except the parentheses, you can even type in an entire program as the input to **program** ParenCheck. **Program** ParenCheck will determine whether the parentheses match up properly in the program you typed in as input.

```pascal
program ParenCheck;
{PROGRAM CHECKS WHETHER A STRING OF PARENTHESES IS MATCHED PROPERLY.}
 const
  Period = '.';
  Blank = ' ';
 var
  Counter : integer;
  Ch : char;
  Acceptable : boolean;

 procedure ProcessCharacter (Ch : char;
          var Counter : integer;
          var Acceptable : boolean);
 begin
  if Ch = '(' then
   Counter := Counter + 1;
  if Ch = ')' then
   Counter := Counter - 1;
  if (Counter < 0) then
   Acceptable := False
 end;
     {MAIN PROGRAM}
begin
 Counter := 0;
 Ch := Blank;
 Acceptable := True;
 writeln('Type in a string of symbols, ending with a period.');
 write('>');
 while Acceptable and (Ch <> Period) do
  begin
   read(Ch);
   ProcessCharacter(Ch,Counter,Acceptable)
  end;
 writeln;
 if (Counter = 0) and Acceptable then
  writeln('***accept***')
 else
  writeln('***reject***')
end.
```

Where Did the Word *Boolean* Come From?

Type *boolean* was named in honor of George Boole, an Irish mathematician. Boole's father was a poor shoemaker who couldn't afford to send his son to school. So as a boy Boole learned mathematics by himself, and by the time he was sixteen, in 1831, he was teaching math in a private academy. Later, although he had never gone to college or university, he became professor of mathematics at Queens College in Cork, Ireland.

Boole was interested not only in math but also in the process of thinking and reasoning. It seemed to him that it should be possible to set up strict rules by which one could inquire into a subject and arrive at the correct answer—the kind of reasoning that is called logic.

Boole wrote a book called *An Investigation of the Laws of Thought*. He also discovered that he could use symbols in logical thinking. This meant that logical reasoning began to look more like mathematics, and mathematicians became interested in the subject. Today Pascal uses these same rules of logic to govern how the logical operators behave when you use them in boolean expressions.

We have used a boolean variable, Acceptable, to break out of the loop if we discover early that the string is unacceptable. Acceptable is our flag. If Acceptable ever becomes False, the loop ends. Note that it is passed as a variable parameter to **procedure** ProcessCharacter. It is always True when ProcessCharacter is called (Can you explain why?) but the procedure changes the value of Acceptable if Counter becomes negative.

EXERCISE 4   What does **program** ParenCheck print if the first character is a period? ▬

Here are some sample data:

Input	Output
(()	***reject***
(a +(b + c))	***accept***
)(	***reject***

─── 8.6 The Mouse Button ───

MacPascal includes a standard function called *button* that reports True if the mouse button is down and False if it isn't. **Program** ClickPoint, which appears in Figure 8.4, shows how *button* works.

When you run **program** ClickPoint, the first **repeat-until** statement loops continuously until you press the mouse button. Pressing the button terminates

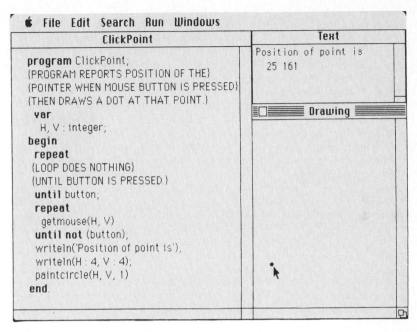

Figure 8.4 **Program** ClickPoint and its output.

the first loop. Then the second loop runs until you release the mouse button. During each iteration of the second loop, *getmouse* returns the current position of the pointer, using the variables *H* and *V*.

When you release the button, the location of the pointer (the final values of *H* and *V* in the second loop) is printed in the Text window, and a tiny circle is drawn at this location in the Drawing window.

Button is a standard function that, like the function *odd*, returns a boolean value. *Odd* takes as input the integer you put between parentheses. The input for *button* doesn't come from inside the program at all. It comes from your finger: Either you are pressing the button, and *button* returns True, or you're not, and *button* returns False.

Here is another program that uses the *button* function. **Program** RectangleInvert allows you to draw a pattern of black and inverted rectangles in the Drawing window (see Figure 8.5). To create a rectangle, you press the mouse button, drag the pointer down and to the right, and release the button. The point where you start to drag the pointer will be the upper-left corner of the rectangle, and the point where you release the button will be the lower-right corner. To stop the program, position the pointer to the left of the Drawing window and click.

EXERCISE 5 Explain why rectangles show up only when you drag the pointer from the upper left to the lower right. ■

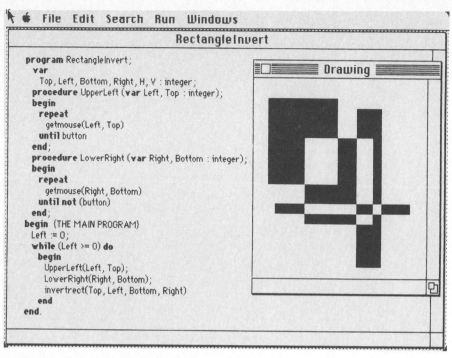

Figure 8.5   Program RectangleInvert with output.

Here is one more program using the function *button*.

```
program Slinky;
{USES THE MOUSE TO DRAW A SERIES OF OVALS}
var
  H,V,OvalType : integer;

procedure DrawAnOval(OvalType : integer);
{DRAWS ONE OF FOUR DIFFERENT KINDS OF OVAL.}
{OVALS ARE WIDER WHEN POINTER IS AT BOTTOM OF WINDOW.}
begin
  case OvalType of
   0 :
    frameoval(V,H,V + 80,H + V);
   1 :
    paintoval(V,H,V + 80,H + V);
   2 :
    invertoval(V,H,V + 80,H + V);
   3 :
    eraseoval(V,H,V + 80,H + V)
  end
end;
```

```
 {MAIN PROGRAM}
begin
 repeat
  getmouse(H,V);
  OvalType := H mod 4; {H mod 4 PRODUCES A NUMBER FROM 0 TO 3.}
  DrawAnOval(OvalType)
 until button
end.
```

Program Slinky draws ovals like the ones in **program** OvalDraw in Chapter 7. In this program you click the mouse button to terminate the oval-drawing loop. Slinky draws four different kinds of oval (see Figure 8.6).

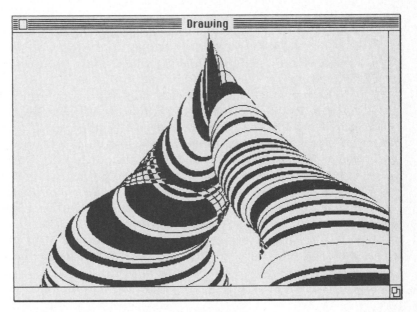

Figure 8.6   Sample output for **program** Slinky.

8.7 Logic and Computers

Type *boolean* is fundamental to computer science, because it is closely related to an important area of mathematics known as mathematical logic. This subject begins with the study of expressions built up from boolean variables and the logical operators **and**, **or**, and **not**. When is an expression true? This is the central question of mathematical logic.

Logic is important for computer science, because many basic questions in computing can be answered with certainty only by using mathematical logic. Here are three questions that computer people worry about every day:

1. Will a program do what we think it will do?
2. Does a program contain an infinite loop?
3. Will two programs that seem to do the same thing actually give identical output when we give them identical input?

Computer scientists have studied these questions intensely. Using mathematical logic, they have shown that for each of these questions, a "yes" answer can be given if a certain formula of mathematics can be proved. If a formula can be proved, we say it is a *theorem*. The formula is stated in the language of mathematical logic, so it involves boolean expressions built up from **and**, **or**, and **not**, as well as certain other symbols.

To see how this works, let's take as an example an enormous computer program, tens of thousands of lines long, that NASA uses to guide spacecraft. There is no margin for error in a guidance program, so NASA would like to know whether there is some set of inputs that will cause their program to go into an infinite loop.

Computer scientists give this answer: Transform your program into a giant formula. If you can prove it, your astronauts will have one less worry. No infinite loop in a guidance program will strand them in space.

But who's going to prove that the formula is a theorem? So far no one can come close to proving the kind of theorem that NASA would need to prove in order to certify that its guidance program is free from infinite loops. But some day computers may be able to do this. In an area of computer science known as *computational logic*, researchers are hard at work constructing programs to prove theorems.

This is why the type *boolean* is fundamental. It is Pascal's type for doing logic. Coming up is a very simple, very crude, cut-rate theorem prover. NASA would never buy it, but it will work.

8.8 The Truth Table

Suppose you are interested in the boolean expression p **or** q. When is it true and when is it false? The answers to this basic question of mathematical logic are usually reported in a *truth table*. Here is the truth table for the expression p **or** q.

p	q	p **or** q
False	False	False
False	True	True
True	False	True
True	True	True

The first row of the truth table says that, if p is false and q is false, then p **or** q is false. The table lists all the possible combinations for the values of p and of q, and for each combination it lists the value for the boolean expression p **or** q. You can write a truth table for any boolean expression.

EXERCISE 6   Complete the following truth table for p **and** (**not** q).

p	q	p **and** (**not** q)
False	False	False
False	True	?
True	False	?
True	True	?

Now let's use the computer to build a truth table for the boolean expression (**not** p) **or** (**not** q). To generate the four possible combinations of truth-table values for p and q, we will use a nested loop.

```
program TruthTable;
{PRINTS TRUTH TABLE FOR THE BOOLEAN EXPRESSION: (not p) or (not q)}
 var
 p,q,Answer : boolean;
begin
 writeln('p' : 10,'q' : 10,'Answer' : 10);
 writeln;
 for p := False to True do
  for q := False to True do
   begin
    Answer := (not p) or (not q);
    writeln(p : 10,q : 10,Answer : 10)
   end
end.
```

The first *writeln* statement prints the labels for the top line of the truth table. Next Pascal begins execution of the outer **for** loop. Because there is only one statement in its body—the inner **for** loop—the body of the outer loop does not need a **begin-end** pair. The first **for** statement initializes the boolean variable p to False. Then the computer comes to the inner loop, where the second **for** statement initializes q to False.

Now the computer gets to the line

```
Answer := (not p) or (not q);
```

First it evaluates the boolean expression on the right side of the assignment statement. Because both p and q are False during the first trip around the two loops, the formula is true. (Make sure you believe this!) So the value True is copied into the variable Answer. The *writeln* statement is then executed, printing the first row of the truth table:

```
False     False     True
```

The colon notation right-justifies the output in a field 10 spaces wide, keeping the rows of the truth table straight.

Next the inner loop is done again, this time with *q* holding the value True. Again Answer is true, and the next row in the truth table is printed:

```
False     True      True
```

This ends the first complete execution of the inner loop.

Now the outer loop variable, *p*, is set to True and the inner loop is executed again, printing the last two rows of the truth table. The complete output is shown in Figure 8.7.

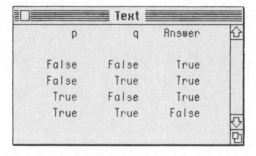

Figure 8.7   Output for **program** TruthTable.

8.9 Truth Tables and Theorems

A boolean expression is a *theorem* if, in each row of its truth table, the entry in the Answer column is True. For example, the expression

```
p or not(p)
```

is a theorem, because it is true no matter what value *p* has. Similarly, the expression

```
(p or q) or (not(p) and not(q))
```

is a theorem, because it is true for any combination of values for *p* and *q*.

We will build our theorem prover using the truth table for a boolean expression. If we ever find the value False in the Answer column, we will know we have a non-theorem on our hands (see Figure 8.8).

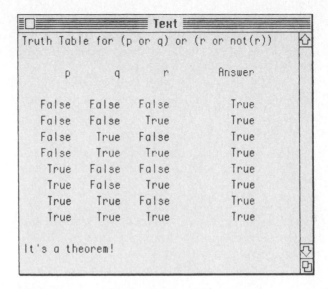

Figure 8.8 Output for **program** TheoremProver.

```
program TheoremProver;
{PROGRAM PRINTS A TRUTH TABLE FOR A BOOLEAN FORMULA}
{AND DECIDES WHETHER THE FORMULA IS A THEOREM.}
 var
  p,q,r,Answer,Theorem : boolean;
begin
 Theorem := True;
 writeln('Truth Table for (p or q) or (r or not(r))');
 writeln;
 writeln('p' : 8,'q' : 8,'r' : 8,'Answer' : 14);
 writeln;
 for p := False to True do
  for q := False to True do
   for r := False to True do
    begin
     Answer := (p or q) or (r or not(r));
     Theorem := Theorem and Answer;
     writeln(p : 8,q : 8,r : 8,Answer : 14)
     {PRINTS TRUTH TABLE}
    end;
 writeln;
 if Theorem then
  writeln('It''s a theorem!')
 else
  writeln('Not a theorem.')
end.
```

Let's see how the theorem prover decides whether a formula is a theorem. First the boolean variable Theorem is initialized to True: The program assumes that the formula it is working on is a theorem until the value False is found in the Answer column of the truth table.

As long as only the value True is found in the Answer column, the boolean variable Theorem remains true, because the formula

```
Answer and Theorem
```

is true as long as both Answer and Theorem are true.

But suppose a value False is found for Answer. Then the statement

```
Theorem := Theorem and Answer;
```

sets Theorem to False. Theorem will remain false, because the value of the boolean expression (Theorem and Answer) is false.

A Pascal curiosity: The line

```
writeln('It''s a theorem');
```

does *not* have a typo in it. In order to get Pascal to print an apostrophe, you must use two single quotation marks right next to each other.

Our theorem prover works fine, but it has two major limitations. First, it can attempt to prove theorems that have at most three boolean variables, and these variables must be named *p*, *q*, and *r*.

Second, the theorem prover is not interactive. When you try it out on a new formula, you must change the line in the program that lists the formula. For example, if you want to try to prove the theorem

```
p or (q or r)
```

you have to change the line of the program that reads

```
Answer := (p or q)and(r or not(r))
```

to

```
Answer := (p or q or r)
```

Now we come to an important point. An interactive program takes input data and applies a list of instructions to the data. Then it prints an answer. When you run it again on new data, the *same* instructions work on the new data to produce a new answer. The program's input is separate from the program itself.

Our theorem prover doesn't work this way. Every time you change the formula you want to prove—that is, every time you change the data that the program works on—you actually have to change one of the program's instructions. Changing an instruction every time you run a program can make program testing and debugging very difficult, so writing this kind of non-interactive program is generally not good programming practice.

Still, we have included the theorem prover because it is a good illustration of the type *boolean* in action. And for now, writing an interactive theorem prover, which completely separates data from instructions, would be too complex a project.

EXERCISE 7   **a.** How many rows in the truth table for the formula (*p* **or** *q*) **or** *r* have True entries in the Answer column? Check your answer using the theorem prover.

b. How many rows in the truth table for the formula (*p* **and** *q*) **and** *r* have True entries in the Answer column? Check your answer using the theorem prover. ▬▬

8.10 Subrange Types

Suppose you write a program to record your weekly activities, and the program includes the enumerated type DaysOfWeek:

```
DaysOfWeek = (Mon,Tue,Wed,Thur,Fri,Sat,Sun);
```

Now suppose that, in one part of the program, you want to calculate your weekday earnings. In Pascal you can identify the weekdays, Mon through Fri, and make them a separate type called a *subrange type*. To do this, you first declare the *parent type* DaysOfWeek, and then you declare the subrange:

```
type
  DaysOfWeek = (Mon,Tue,Wed,Thur,Fri,Sat,Sun);
  Weekdays = Mon..Fri;
```

Note the syntax: After the parent type has been defined, you name the subrange type (Weekdays). Then you define it by naming an element of the parent type (Mon), followed by two dots, followed by a later member of the same type (Fri).

Weekdays is now a genuine type, so you can declare a variable of type Weekdays:

```
var
  Workday : Weekdays;
```

Here are some other examples of subranges.

```
Letters = 'a'..'z'; {PARENT TYPE IS CHAR}
Digits = '0'..'9'; {PARENT TYPE IS CHAR}
SmallNumbers = 0..9; {PARENT TYPE IS INTEGER}
JulyDays = 1..31; {PARENT TYPE IS INTEGER}
TwentiethCentury = 1900..1999; {PARENT TYPE IS INTEGER}
Ovaltype = 0..3; {PARENT TYPE IS INTEGER}
```

Subranges are useful because they make programs more understandable. But subranges have several limitations. You can't have a subrange of type *real*. Also, elements from a subrange must run consecutively in the parent type. This means that the letters of the alphabet, which appear one after another in type *char*, can be represented by the subrange

```
'a'..'z'
```

But you *cannot* make a subrange of the vowels *a*, *e*, *i*, *o*, and *u*, because they don't appear one after the other within type *char*.

Program QuizScores reads in a list of ten quiz scores and then, using two subrange types, calculates and reports both the total score and the average score.

```
program QuizScores;
{YOU TYPE IN 10 QUIZ SCORES.}
{PROGRAM CALCULATES TOTAL SCORE AND AVERAGE SCORE.}
 const
  QuizCount = 10;
 type
  Quizzes = 1..QuizCount; {QUIZZES IS A SUBRANGE OF TYPE INTEGER.}
  ScoreRange = 0..100; {SCORERANGE IS SUBRANGE OF TYPE INTEGER.}
 var
  TotalScore : integer;
  Average : real;
  Quiz : Quizzes;
  Score : ScoreRange;
begin
 {LOOP READS IN THE SCORES & CALCULATES TOTAL SCORE}
 TotalScore := 0;
 for Quiz := 1 to QuizCount do
  begin
   writeln('Type in score from 0 to 100 on quiz number ',Quiz : 1);
   write('>');
   readln(Score);
   TotalScore := TotalScore + Score
  end;
 {CALCULATES AVERAGE SCORE}
 Average := TotalScore / QuizCount;
 {REPORTS TOTAL SCORE AND AVERAGE SCORE}
 writeln('The total score is ',TotalScore : 1);
 writeln('The average score is ',Average : 3 : 1)
end.
```

Note how the subranges make the program more readable. ScoreRange, for example, tells us how quizzes are graded—on a scale from 0 to 100. If we had made Score a variable of type *integer*, we would know less about the problem when we looked at the program.

The definition of the constant QuizCount and the declaration of the type Quizzes work together to make the program easy to modify. If the number of quizzes changes from 10 to 12, all you have to do is change the constant QuizCount.

EXERCISE 8   Suppose your instructor decides to give 5 bonus points on each quiz so that the highest score can now be 105. How would you alter **program** QuizScores to handle this change? ▬

_____**TEST YOURSELF**_____

1. What is *pred*(True)?
2. What is one of the basic questions of mathematical logic?
3. Give an example of a subrange type with parent type *integer*.
4. What is a boolean expression called when all entries in the Answer column of its truth table are True?
5. What is a flag?
6. When you write a program to check whether **begin-end** pairs match up properly, what area of computer science are you working in?
7. What are Pascal's logical connectives?
8. Can you make a subrange out of the digits 1 through 9?
9. Can you make a subrange that consists of the letters *A* through *Z and* the letters *a* through *z*?

_____**PROBLEMS**_____

1. Suppose Tall, Dark, and Handsome are boolean variables, and suppose Tall is false but Dark and Handsome are true. What are the values of the following boolean expressions?
   a. (Tall **or** Dark) **and** Handsome
   b. **not** (Tall) **and** (Handsome **or** Dark)
   c. Tall **and** (Handsome **and** Dark)
   d. **not** (Tall **and** (Dark **and** Handsome))
2. What does **program** Display print?
```
program Display;
  var
   p,q : boolean;
  begin
   for p := True downto False do
    for q := True downto False do
     writeln(p : 8,q : 8)
  end.
```

3. Suppose that H and V are the coordinates of a point in the Drawing window and that Top, Left, Bottom, and Right determine the boundaries of a rectangle. Write a boolean expression that is True when the point (H, V) lies inside (or on the border of) the rectangle and is False otherwise.

4. True or false: A boolean expression made up of boolean variables **and**'s and **or**'s—but no **not**'s—can never be a theorem.

5. Rewrite **program** DoubledChar using a **repeat**-**until** loop. (*Hint:* The **until** part of the loop should read as follows: **until** Found **or** (Ch = Period).

6. Write a program that reads in a sequence of characters interactively and prints ***acceptable*** if there are equal numbers of lowercase a's and lowercase b's.

7. **a.** Using pencil and paper, do the truth table for

       if p then q else r

   Remember: This expression means

   > if p is true
   >   then the value of q is the answer
   >   else the value of r is the answer

   Hint: For the row p = True, q = False, r = True, the value in the Answer column should be the value of q—False.

   b. Use **program** TheoremProver to print the truth table, using the expression

       if p then
         Answer := q
       else
         Answer := r

8. Change **program** TheoremProver so that it doesn't do extra loops once it has discovered a False row in the truth table.

9. Suppose **program** ParenCheck has the following bug in it. Instead of being declared as a variable parameter in the heading line of **procedure** ProcessCharacter, the formal parameter Acceptable is identified as a value parameter. Give an example of an illegal string that this faulty version of **program** ParenCheck would report as acceptable.

10. Write a program that reads in a sentence ending with a period and prints out the number of words in the sentence. Assume that (in addition to letters) only spaces, commas, and the period are allowed.

11. Write a program that reads in a sentence ending with a period and echoes the sentence to the Drawing window with all extra spaces between words deleted.

```
1
1   1
1   2   1
1   3   3   1
1   4   6   4   1
1   5  10  10   5   1
1   6  15  20  15   6   1
1   7  21  35  35  21   7   1
1   8  28  56  70  56  28   8   1
```

Arrays

9

Many computer programs process huge amounts of information. In order for them to read in, store, and process masses of data, the data need to be organized, or *structured*. In this chapter we will discuss one important way to organize information—the *array*.

9.1 The Rutland Street Survey: A First Look at Arrays

Suppose you are given a special assignment in your sociology class: You are to do a series of computer surveys of your street.

You live on Rutland Street, where the houses are numbered from 1 through 12. After you find out how many people live in each house, your assignment is to write a program that calculates the total number of people on the street, the average number of people per household, and the largest household. So you make a trip down Rutland Street, asking at each house how many people live there and recording the answers on paper in preparation for doing your programming assignment.

To do the required calculations in Pascal, you need a variable of type *integer* for each house on the block. Each variable will hold a value for the number of people living in a particular house.

You *could* declare the variables this way:

```
var
  RutlandSt1,RutlandSt2,RutlandSt3,RutlandSt4,
  RutlandSt5,RutlandSt6,RutlandSt7,RutlandSt8,
  RutlandSt9,RutlandSt10,RutlandSt11,
  RutlandSt12 : integer;
```

But writing out this giant declaration is tedious. And there's more trouble ahead. To enter the data, you need 12 groups of statements like these 3 for RutlandSt1:

```
writeln('How many people live at 1 Rutland St?');
write('>');
readln(RutlandSt1);
```

Imagine how painful things could get if Rutland Street had 50 or 100 houses!

This is where arrays come in. Using an array variable, you can declare the 12 Rutland Street variables all at once. They will be named RutlandSt[1], RutlandSt[2], RutlandSt[3], and so on, up to RutlandSt[12].

Each of the 12 variables is called a *component* of the array, or a *component variable*. And each of the components is identified by a number in square brackets, which is called the *index* of that variable.

Don't let the square brackets confuse you. The component variables—RutlandSt[1], RutlandSt[2], and so on—are legitimate variables that can be used in assignment statements, *writeln* statements, or any other kind of statement we've seen so far.

You must write RutlandSt[5] with *square* brackets when you refer to the fifth RutlandSt variable. No RutlandSt(5) allowed!

To create the array variable RutlandSt, you first give a type definition. Then you give the RutlandSt variable declaration.

```
type
  StreetSurvey = array[1..12] of integer;
var
  RutlandSt : StreetSurvey;
```

The StreetSurvey definition and the RutlandSt declaration instruct the Macintosh to create the 12 RutlandSt variables. The definition and declaration also command the Macintosh to set aside in memory 12 locations, or cells, indexed by the numbers 1 through 12. When you run the program, these cells hold the values of the component variables. The type definition specifies that only integer values can go in the cells. After it has been declared, the array will look like this in memory:

RutlandSt

cells												
indexes	1	2	3	4	5	6	7	8	9	10	11	12

The numbers that label the cells in this diagram are abbreviations for the full name of the component variable. The label 5, for example, is short for RutlandSt[5].

The index of an array variable—what's written between the brackets—can be a number, a variable, or even a complex expression. If the variable HouseNumber has the value 8, then

```
RutlandSt[HouseNumber]
```

refers to the eighth component variable of the array, or RutlandSt[8]. RutlandSt[HouseNumber + 1] is the component RutlandSt[9].

Now let's look at our first survey program, which merely reads in and then prints out the number of residents in each house on the street. The first loop reads in the number of people who live in each house. HouseNumber is the control variable for the loop *and* the index for the array. As HouseNumber advances from 1 to 12, the expression RutlandSt[HouseNumber] stands, in turn, for each of the component variables from RutlandSt[1] to RutlandSt[12]. The *readln* statement puts values into these 12 variables, one after another.

The second loop prints a table. Each row in the table lists a house number followed by the number of people at that house.

```
program Survey;
{YOU READ IN THE NUMBER OF PEOPLE THAT LIVE IN EACH HOUSE}
{ON RUTLAND ST. PROGRAM PRINTS A TABLE OF THE POPULATION DATA.}
 type
  StreetSurvey = array[1..12] of integer;
 var
  HouseNumber : integer;
  RutlandSt : StreetSurvey;

begin
 {DATA ENTRY LOOP}
 for HouseNumber := 1 to 12 do
  begin
   writeln('How many people live at ',HouseNumber : 1,' Rutland St?');
   write('>');
   readln(RutlandSt[HouseNumber])
  end;

 {PRINT TABLE HEADINGS}
 writeln;
 writeln('House Number  People');

 {PRINT SURVEY DATA}
 for HouseNumber := 1 to 12 do
  writeln(HouseNumber : 6,RutlandSt[HouseNumber] : 13)
end.
```

Here's what happens when you run **program** Survey. When the statement

```
readln(RutlandSt[HouseNumber]);
```

is first executed inside the data-entry loop, the value of HouseNumber is 1. So RutlandSt[1] receives the value you type, and that value is stored in the first cell in memory that has been created for the array.

During the second iteration of the loop, HouseNumber is 2, so you read in a value for RutlandSt[2]. The data entry process continues, filling each cell of the array, until the twelfth loop is completed.

Then the second **for** loop is executed. The first time

```
writeln(HouseNumber : 6,RutlandSt[HouseNumber] : 13)
```

is executed, the value of HouseNumber is 1. So a 1 is printed, followed by the value of RutlandSt[HouseNumber].

The Macintosh figures out the value of RutlandSt[HouseNumber] in two steps. First it looks up the value of HouseNumber to determine which of the component variables it is working on. It finds that HouseNumber is 1. So it looks up the value of RutlandSt[1], which is stored in the first cell set aside in memory for the array. There it finds the value that you typed in, and this is the value that's printed.

The loop goes through 12 iterations, each time printing a new house number, followed by the number of people who live in that house.

If you read in the values 3, 5, 7, 2, 4, 9, 1, 6, 4, 3, 4, and 5 for the number of residents in each house, the array RutlandSt will look like this in memory:

RutlandSt

cells	3	5	7	2	4	9	1	6	4	3	4	5
indexes	1	2	3	4	5	6	7	8	9	10	11	12

And here is what **program** Survey's output will look like:

```
┌──────────────────────────────┐
│ ▤□▬▬▬▬▬▬ Text ▬▬▬▬▬▬▬        │
│                          ⇧    │
│  House Number    People       │
│       1            3          │
│       2            5          │
│       3            7          │
│       4            2          │
│       5            4          │
│       6            9          │
│       7            1          │
│       8            6          │
│       9            4          │
│      10            3          │
│      11            4          │
│      12            5          │
│                          ⇩    │
└──────────────────────────────┘
```

EXERCISE 1   Assume that the array RutlandSt is filled as we have just indicated, and find the value of:

a. RutlandSt[10]

b. RutlandSt[7] + RutlandSt[3]

Answer: 8

c. RutlandSt[7 + 3]

Answer: 3

d. Suppose we change the second **for** loop in **program** Survey to the following:

```
HouseNumber := 12;
while (HouseNumber > 0) do
 begin
  writeln(RutlandSt[HouseNumber]);
  HouseNumber := HouseNumber - 1
 end
```

Tell what this change does. ▄

The array variable RutlandSt is set up to match the layout of the houses on the street: 12 houses, 12 variables, and 12 locations in memory. Whenever you write a program involving a group of related quantities (the number of people in each of 12 houses, the amount of money you earn each month, the distance from the sun to each of the planets), you will need to use an array. Getting an array declaration right, so that it matches an application, requires careful thinking, and this is what we want to talk about next.

9.2 The Blueprint for an Array—Array Type Definitions

Let's look at array declarations more closely. When you run **program** Survey, the Macintosh first takes note of StreetSurvey's type definition.

```
type
  StreetSurvey = array[1..12] of integer;
var
  RutlandSt : StreetSurvey;
```

Then it comes to the variable declaration for RutlandSt and sees that RutlandSt is of this type. So it looks back to the type definition, which it uses as a kind of blueprint. The blueprint tells the Macintosh to create 12 variables and set aside 12 cells in memory to hold their values. The blueprint also specifies that the variables and their cells in memory will be indexed by the numbers 1 through 12.

Component Type

In addition, the type definition tells what kinds of value can go in the cells. A component of an array variable of type StreetSurvey can hold integer values only. The type *integer* in the definition is called the *component type* for arrays of type StreetSurvey.

Index Type

The portion of the type definition in brackets,

```
1..12
```

is called the *index type*. The index type for StreetSurvey is a subrange of type *integer*. The values in the subrange—the numbers 1 through 12—identify, or index, the component variables created by an array declaration of type StreetSurvey. The index type also tells how many component variables there are.

What if Rutland Street has 15 houses numbered 11 through 25? Then we write

```
type
  StreetSurvey = array[11..25] of integer;
var
  RutlandSt : StreetSurvey;
```

Now StreetSurvey is a blueprint for arrays with 15 variables. The RutlandSt array declaration creates RutlandSt variables running from RutlandSt[11] through RutlandSt[25] and 15 cells in memory to hold the integer values of these variables. The notation 11..25 defines the index type, which is the subrange of type *integer* running from 11 through 25.

The component variables of an array do not have to be identified by numbers. You can use letters or elements of an enumerated type to identify components. This is a wonderful feature of Pascal: The components of an array can be labeled with characters, days of the week, months, states, countries, planets —you name it. The types *real* and *integer* won't work, however, because they don't have a fixed range. But subranges of type *integer* will work, and so will subranges of enumerated types and subranges of type *char*.

Suppose you were doing your survey in an apartment building at 34 Kellogg Avenue. If the apartments were labeled A through J, your array declaration would look like this:

```
type
  AptBldg = array['A'..'J'] of integer;
var
  ThirtyFourKellogg : AptBldg;
```

As before, the component type is *integer*, because the value of a component variable represents the number of people in an apartment. But the index type is the subrange of *char* 'A'..'J'. The component variable ThirtyFourKellogg[(A)] stands for the number of people living in apartment A. ThirtyFourKellogg[(B)] stands for the number of people living in apartment B, and so on.

When you are writing a type definition for an array, it often helps to tie the index type to concrete objects that are the subject of your program. Instead of imagining memory divided into abstract cells, imagine that the cells in memory are a street of houses numbered 1 through 12, a row of passenger seats in an airplane that are designated A through F, or planets in the solar system from Mercury to Pluto.

EXERCISE 2   For each of the following array declarations, give the component type, the number of component variables, and the index type.

    a. type
       ScoreByInnings = **array**[1..9] **of** integer;
      var
       Scores : ScoreByInnings;

    b. type
       LetterFrequency = **array**['a'..'z'] **of** integer;
      var
       LetterScore : LetterFrequency;

    c. type
       MonthlyRainfall = **array**[Jan..Dec] **of** real;
      var
       LastYearsRain : MonthlyRainfall;

What type do you need to define before you define the array type MonthlyRainfall? ▬

9.3   Keeping a Running Total—Program PeopleOnBlock

Now let's use an array to do a simple but very important kind of calculation. Your assignment asks for the total population and the average household size on Rutland Street. If you did this by hand, you might visit the houses on the street, adding in the number of residents in each house as you go. At the end of the block you would have the total population figure, which you could divide by 12 to get the average household size.

Program PeopleOnBlock works in just this way. After you fill the array RutlandSt with the number of people living in each house, the program "visits" each component of the array. It adds in the value of each component to the variable TotalPop, which keeps a running count of the street population. Here is **program** PeopleOnBlock.

```
program PeopleOnBlock;
{YOU READ IN NUMBER OF PEOPLE THAT LIVE IN EACH HOUSE ON STREET}
{PROGRAM PRINTS OUT TOTAL POPULATION AND AVERAGE SIZE OF HOUSEHOLD.}
  type
   StreetSurvey = array[1..12] of integer;
  var
   RutlandSt : StreetSurvey;
   TotalPop,HouseNumber : integer;
   AverageNumber : real;

begin
{READ IN NUMBER OF PEOPLE IN EACH HOUSE}
 for HouseNumber := 1 to 12 do
  begin
   writeln('How many people live in house number ',
            HouseNumber : 1,'?');
   readln(RutlandSt[HouseNumber])
  end;

{CALCULATE TOTAL POPULATION OF RUTLAND ST.}
TotalPop := 0;
HouseNumber := 1;
while (HouseNumber <= 12) do
  begin
   TotalPop := TotalPop + RutlandSt[HouseNumber];
   HouseNumber := HouseNumber + 1
  end;

{CALCULATE AVERAGE NUMBER OF PEOPLE PER HOUSE}
AverageNumber := TotalPop / 12;

{PRINT OUT TOTAL POPULATION AND AVERAGE SIZE OF HOUSEHOLD}
writeln('There are ',TotalPop : 1,' people on the block.');
writeln('Average number of people per house is ',
         AverageNumber : 4 : 2)
end.
```

As before, the first loop reads in the value for each of the 12 component variables for the array RutlandSt.

The second loop calculates the number of people living on the block by keeping a running total. First, TotalPop is initialized to zero. Then the loop adds the number of residents living in each house to the value of TotalPop. Each time through the loop, the value of the next array variable is added to TotalPop, and then the index of the variable is incremented by 1.

Finally, the average number of people per household is calculated, and the total number and the average are printed out.

EXERCISE 3   Suppose Rutland Street is numbered with the odd houses on the north side of the street and the even houses on the south side, like this:

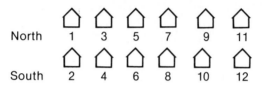

The following loop calculates the number of occupants on the south side.

```
TotalPop := 0;
HouseNumber := 2;
while (HouseNumber <= 12) do
  begin
   TotalPop := TotalPop + RutlandSt[HouseNumber];
   HouseNumber := HouseNumber + 2
  end;
```

Write a loop that calculates the number of occupants on the north side. ■

9.4 Finding the Largest Household

Suppose you want to find the largest household on Rutland Street. Finding the component of an array that holds the largest value is a very common and very important calculation. When you search for the largest household, you are looking for the index that identifies the component variable with the largest value. To find this index, you will need a new variable of type *integer* to represent the number of the house with the most residents. We'll call this variable MostFolks. The following piece of code tacked onto the body of **program** PeopleOnBlock will find the largest household.

```
{LARGEST HOUSEHOLD LOOP}
MostFolks := 1; {ASSUME LARGEST HOUSEHOLD IS AT # 1}
for HouseNumber := 1 to 12 do
 if RutlandSt[HouseNumber] > RutlandSt[MostFolks] then
   MostFolks := HouseNumber;
writeln('Biggest household is at ',MostFolks : 1,' Rutland Street.')
```

We start out by assuming that house number 1 has the most people:

```
MostFolks := 1
```

Then we loop through the houses, comparing the number of residents at the current largest household with the number of residents in each house. That is, we compare the value of RutlandSt[MostFolks] with the value of RutlandSt[2], RutlandSt[3], and so on. Whenever we find a house with more residents than the current MostFolks household, we change the value of MostFolks to the number of this house.

If the problem had asked for the *number of people* in the largest household, and not for the *address of the house*, the code would be the same except for the final statement, which would now read

```
writeln('Biggest household has ', RutlandSt[MostFolks] : 1,' residents')
```

EXERCISE 4   **a.** Will we get the right answer if the control line of the largest household loop looks like this?

```
for HouseNumber := 2 to 12 do
```

b. Suppose the RutlandSt array is filled with the values in the diagram on page 292. If you ran the Largest Household loop with these values in the array, MostFolks would initially have the value 1 and would end with the value 6. What other values would MostFolks have as it stepped through the loop?

c. What are the component type and the index type for the array type HouseKind given below? Explain what the variable RutlandHouseKind keeps track of.

```
type
ConstructionType = (WoodFrame,Brick,Cinderblock,Stone,Adobe);
HouseKind : array[1..12] of ConstructionType;
var
RutlandHouseKind : HouseKind;  ▬
```

9.5 The Scoreboard Principle

You can use an array to do more complicated kinds of record keeping. For example, you can use an array as a kind of scoreboard. Imagine a scoreboard during the fourth inning of a baseball game:

Home team runs	0	1	1	2					
Inning	1	2	3	4	5	6	7	8	9

Every time the home team scores a run in the fourth inning, the number in the fourth cell of the scoreboard is incremented by 1. If we were to represent the scoreboard with an array called HomeTeamRuns, we would show that the home team scored another run in the fourth inning by writing

```
HomeTeamRuns[4] := HomeTeamRuns[4] + 1;
```

When we use an array in this way to tally up data in a program, we are using the *scoreboard principle.*

Program QuestionDay

Let's see how the scoreboard principle can help with our Rutland Street survey. Suppose you want to write a program that reads in the day of the week that you visited each house on the block. Then the program prints the number of houses you visited on each day of the week.

If you wrote down the day you visited each house, you might come up with a chart something like this one:

Chart 1: When Visited

Day visited

Tue	Tue	Tue	Tue	Tue	Wed	Wed	Thur	Sat	Mon	Sun	Sun
1	2	3	4	5	6	7	8	9	10	11	12

House number

If you made this chart into an array, its type would be

array[1..12] **of** DaysOfWeek

Now suppose you use paper and pencil to calculate how many houses you visited each day. You might tally the information from the When Visited chart in a second chart like the following one, which serves as a scoreboard:

Chart 2: Surveys per Day

Number of houses visited	/	~~////~~	//	/		/	//
Day	Mon	Tue	Wed	Thur	Fri	Sat	Sun

If you declared the second chart as an array, it would have type

array[DaysOfWeek] **of** integer

Now let's create two arrays called WhenVisited and SurveysPerDay, and use them in a program called QuestionDay. **Program** QuestionDay stores the day you visited each house in WhenVisited, and tallies the number of houses visited each day in the scoreboard array SurveysPerDay. Here is the program:

```
program QuestionDay;
{TYPE IN THE DAY YOU VISITED EACH HOUSE ON RUTLAND STREET.}
{PROGRAM PRINTS TABLE OF THE NUMBER OF SURVEYS DONE EACH DAY.}
 type
  DaysOfWeek = (Mon,Tue,Wed,Thur,Fri,Sat,Sun);
  VisitDay = array[1..12] of DaysOfWeek;
  SurveyRecord = array[DaysOfWeek] of integer;
 var
  SurveysPerDay : SurveyRecord; {THE SCOREBOARD ARRAY}
  WhenVisited : VisitDay; {STORES DAY EACH HOUSE WAS VISITED}
  HouseNumber : integer;
  Day : DaysOfWeek;

begin
 {DATA ENTRY LOOP}
 for HouseNumber := 1 to 12 do
  begin
   writeln('Type in day of week you visited ',
             HouseNumber : 2,' Rutland Street.');
   write('>');
   readln(WhenVisited[HouseNumber]);
   writeln
  end;

 {INITIALIZE THE ARRAY SURVEYSPERDAY}
 for Day := Mon to Sun do
  SurveysPerDay[Day] := 0;

 HouseNumber := 1;
 {TALLY WHENVISITED INFORMATION IN SURVEYSPERDAY}
 while (HouseNumber <= 12) do
  begin
   Day := WhenVisited[HouseNumber];
   SurveysPerDay[Day] := SurveysPerDay[Day] + 1;
   HouseNumber := HouseNumber + 1
  end;

 {PRINT TALLY OF THE NUMBER OF SURVEYS DONE EACH DAY}
 writeln('DAY OF WEEK   SURVEYS DONE');
 for Day := Mon to Sun do
  writeln(Day : 8,SurveysPerDay[Day] : 10)
end.
```

The data-entry loop in **program** QuestionDay fills the array WhenVisited. Then the tally loop transfers this data to the array SurveysPerDay, the scoreboard array.

In the tally loop, the first statement assigns to the variable Day the day when a particular house is visited. In the second statement, the value of Day becomes an index for the array SurveysPerDay, and the variable with that index is incremented by 1.

This is an important part of the scoreboard principle. A value in the data-entry array has become an index in the scoreboard array. For example, in the tally loop of **program** QuestionDay, every time the value of WhenVisited [HouseNumber] is Tue, the value of SurveysPerDay[Tue] is incremented by 1.

Note that we initialized the components of the array SurveysPerDay before using it as a scoreboard. If we hadn't initialized the array, all of the SurveysPerDay component variables would be undefined or would hold arbitrary values when the program reached the tally loop. So the program might behave strangely the first time it tried to execute the statement:

```
SurveysPerDay[Day] := SurveysPerDay[Day] + 1;
```

9.6 Out-of-Range Errors: Program HowManyNeighbors

One kind of bug, called an *out-of-range* error, is very common in programs that include arrays. Out-of-range errors show up so often that you should look carefully for them before you run any program that contains an array. To see how these errors might get you into trouble, let's look at **program** HowManyNeighbors.

Program HowManyNeighbors calculates the number of next-door neighbors for each house on Rutland Street. All houses except houses 1 and 12 have neighbors on both sides. These two have neighbors on one side only. To distinguish the houses on the ends from the houses in the middle, we'll use a case statement.

```
program HowManyNeighbors;
{YOU TYPE IN THE NUMBER OF PEOPLE IN EACH HOUSE. PROGRAM}
{CALCULATES THE NUMBER OF NEIGHBORS THAT EACH HOUSE HAS.}
  type
    StreetSurvey = array[1..12] of integer;
  var
    RutlandSt : StreetSurvey;
    HouseNumber,Neighbors : integer;

begin
{DATA ENTRY LOOP}
  for HouseNumber := 1 to 12 do
    begin
      writeln('How many people live at ',
              HouseNumber : 1,' Rutland Street?');
      write('>');
      readln(RutlandSt[HouseNumber])
    end;
```

(continued)

```
HouseNumber := 1;
while(HouseNumber <= 12) do
 begin
  {CALCULATE NUMBER OF NEIGHBORS}
  case HouseNumber of
   1 :
    Neighbors := RutlandSt[HouseNumber + 1];
   12 :
    Neighbors := RutlandSt[HouseNumber - 1];
   otherwise
    Neighbors := RutlandSt[HouseNumber - 1] +
                 RutlandSt[HouseNumber + 1]
  end;
  {PRINT NUMBER OF NEIGHBORS}
  writeln('House number ',HouseNumber : 1,' has ',
          Neighbors : 1,' next-door neighbors.');
  HouseNumber := HouseNumber + 1
 end
end.
```

In **program** HowManyNeighbors we need to use a case statement so that houses with neighbors on only one side are treated differently from the others. We would get an out-of-range error if we treated all the houses the same and tried to do the neighbors calculation this way:

```
for HouseNumber := 1 to 12 do
 Neighbors := RutlandSt[HouseNumber - 1] + RutlandSt[HouseNumber + 1];
```

When HouseNumber is 1, RutlandSt[HouseNumber − 1] is out of range because the variable RutlandSt[0] doesn't exist. And RutlandSt[HouseNumber + 1] is out of range when HouseNumber is 12, because it refers to a nonexistent RutlandSt[13].

Referring to array variables that are out of range is one of the most common mistakes in programs with arrays, so watch out for this kind of error. One good way to make sure an array index is in range is to check the index value at the beginning and the end of a loop. In the **for** statement that we have just discussed, checking the body of the loop at the lower and upper loop limits (that is, when HouseNumber = 1 and HouseNumber = 12) reveals the two out-of-range errors.

EXERCISE 5   Suppose the word *neighbor* means not only those who live in a house right next door but also those who live two doors away. How would this new definition change **program** HowManyNeighbors? ■

9.7 Using an Array Variable as a Parameter for a Procedure

Programs in Pascal (except for the very simplest ones) are generally written in top-down fashion as a series of procedures. So it is important to know how to use procedures in programs that include arrays.

Program SurveyGraph, which draws a graph showing the number of people who live in each house on Rutland Street, consists of two procedures: **Procedure** GetStreetData reads in the number of people who live in each house, and **procedure** DrawLineGraph prints the graph. Each procedure is passed an array as a parameter.

Let's take a look at the program. Remember: Always read the main program first.

```pascal
program SurveyGraph;
{YOU READ IN NUMBER OF PEOPLE IN EACH HOUSE ON RUTLAND ST.}
{PROGRAM PRINTS LINE GRAPH OF STREET POPULATION.}
 const
  ScaleFactor = 10;
 type
  StreetSurvey = array[1..12] of integer;
 var
  HouseNumber : integer;
  RutlandSt : StreetSurvey;


 procedure GetStreetData(var Street : StreetSurvey);
  var
   HouseNumber : integer;
 begin
  for HouseNumber := 1 to 12 do
   begin
    writeln('How many people live at ',HouseNumber : 2,' Rutland St?');
    write('>');
    readln(Street[HouseNumber])
   end
 end;


 procedure DrawLineGraph(Street : StreetSurvey;
        Scale : integer);
  const
   Bottom = 175;
   Separation = 18;
   CharWidth = 4;
  var
   HouseNumber,Height,HPosition,Top : integer;
```

(continued)

```
begin
 moveto(20,20);
 writedraw('GRAPH OF STREET POPULATION');
 HPosition := 0;
 for HouseNumber := 1 to 12 do
  begin
 {DRAW LINE}
   HPosition := HPosition + Separation;
   Height := Scale * Street[HouseNumber];
   Top := Bottom - Height;
   drawline(HPosition,Top,HPosition,Bottom);
 {DRAW LABEL -- CENTER LABEL BY SUBTRACTING CHARWIDTH}
   moveto(HPosition - CharWidth, Bottom + 12);
   writedraw(HouseNumber : 1)
  end
 end;
       {MAIN PROGRAM}
begin
 GetStreetData(RutlandSt);
 DrawLineGraph(RutlandSt,ScaleFactor)
end.
```

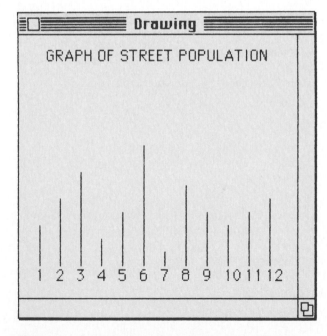

Figure 9.1 Typical output for **program** SurveyGraph.

The procedure heading line

```
procedure DrawLineGraph(Street: StreetSurvey; Scale : integer);
```

lists two formal parameters and their types. Street is of type StreetSurvey, our array type, and Scale is of type *integer*.

You can use an array variable as a parameter just the way you use a simple variable. When the main program calls DrawLineGraph, the Macintosh assigns the actual parameter RutlandSt to the formal parameter Street. Then the procedure is executed, and the Macintosh draws the graph that represents the number of people who live in each house on Rutland Street (see Figure 9.1).

9.8 Rotating an Array—Program VolleyBall

Let's look at another program in which we pass arrays to a procedure. Suppose you coach a volleyball team and you want to see a diagram of your players on the court. Here is your team

```
     Lee        Dana        Sandy
     Jan        Leslie      Jamie
     --------------------net-------------------
```

You also want to see the positions of your players after each clockwise rotation.

Program VolleyBall rotates your players through all six arrangements and prints diagrams of these arrangements in the Text window.

```
program VolleyBall;
{ROTATES MEMBERS OF VOLLEYBALL TEAM THROUGH 6 ARRANGEMENTS}
{OF PLAYERS AND PRINTS DIAGRAMS OF THE ARRANGEMENTS.}
 const
  Net = '--------------net------------';
 type
  Players = (Jan,Leslie,Jamie,Lee,Dana,Sandy);
  RowPositions = (Left,Center,Right);
  Row = array[RowPositions] of Players;
 var
  FrontRow,BackRow : Row;
  RotationNumber : integer;

 procedure MakeInitialTeam(var FrontRow,BackRow : Row);
 begin
  FrontRow[Left] := Jan;
  FrontRow[Center] := Leslie;
  FrontRow[Right] := Jamie;
  BackRow[Left] := Lee;
  BackRow[Center] := Dana;
  BackRow[Right] := Sandy
 end;
```

(continued)

```
procedure PrintTeam(FrontRow,BackRow : Row);
begin
 writeln(BackRow[Left] : 10,BackRow[Center] : 10,BackRow[Right] : 10);
 writeln(FrontRow[Left] : 10,FrontRow[Center] : 10,FrontRow[Right] : 10);
 writeln(Net)
end;

procedure RotateTeam(var FrontRow,BackRow : Row);
 var
  TempPosition : Players; {TEMPPOSITION IS A SCRATCHPAD VARIABLE}
begin
 TempPosition := BackRow[Right];
 BackRow[Right] := BackRow[Center];
 BackRow[Center] := BackRow[Left];
 BackRow[Left] := FrontRow[Left];
 FrontRow[Left] := FrontRow[Center];
 FrontRow[Center] := FrontRow[Right];
 FrontRow[Right] := TempPosition
end;
    {MAIN PROGRAM}
begin
 RotationNumber := 1;
 MakeInitialTeam(FrontRow,BackRow);
 PrintTeam(FrontRow,BackRow);
 writeln;
 repeat
  RotateTeam(FrontRow,BackRow);
  PrintTeam(FrontRow,BackRow);
  writeln;
  RotationNumber := RotationNumber + 1
 until(RotationNumber = 6)
end.
```

We have created two array variables, FrontRow and BackRow, each of type Row. The two arrays can be diagrammed this way:

```
       FrontRow                      BackRow
  ┌─────┬─────┬─────┐          ┌─────┬─────┬─────┐
  │     │     │     │          │     │     │     │
  └─────┴─────┴─────┘          └─────┴─────┴─────┘
  Left Center Right            Left Center Right
```

Procedure MakeInitialTeam assigns the initial arrangement of players to the rows. The formal parameters FrontRow and BackRow are variable parameters because the procedure alters the arrays. They come in empty and are passed back with the players in place.

Procedure PrintTeam, on the other hand, has value formal parameters. The procedure merely reports the members of the team on the screen.

Procedure RotateTeam is more interesting. Because it is passed one arrangement of players and passes back the next arrangement, both of its formal parameters, FrontRow and BackRow, are variable parameters. Inside the procedure, the local variable TempPosition holds the name of one player temporarily so that the others can be moved from position to position. TempPosition is a Scratchpad variable.

When RotateTeam is called, the name of the player in BackRow[Right] is copied into the variable TempPosition so that each of the other players can be rotated.

Then five assignment statements advance all the other players ahead one position. First an assignment statement copies the name of the player in BackRow[Center] into position BackRow[Right]. The assignment overwrites and destroys the name of the player in BackRow[Right]. This is not a problem, because we have saved a copy of that player's name in TempPosition.

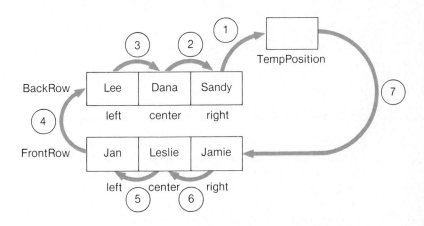

After the other players are rotated one position, the last assignment statement copies the player in TempPosition into FrontRow[Right]. The output for **program** VolleyBall is shown in Figure 9.2.

EXERCISE 6   Write an array-variable declaration for a basketball team, using this enumerated type for a team's players.

type
```
BBPositions = (guard1,guard2,forward1,forward2,center) ▬
```

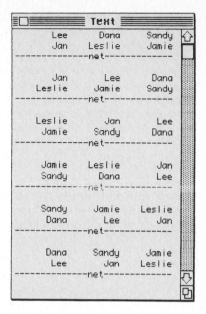

Figure 9.2   The output for **program** VolleyBall.

———9.9 Strings—Program TextEcho ————————

Because character processing is so important in computing, Macintosh Pascal has a special built-in kind of array called a *string* that makes character processing easy. To see how strings work, let's start with **program** TextEcho. **Program** Text-Echo reads in a text of up to 100 characters and then prints it out a few lines farther down in the Text window, as shown in Figure 9.3.

Program TextEcho begins with an array declaration:

```
var
  StringOfChar : string[100];
```

This declares StringOfChar to be a *string variable*. Note that the program has no type definition. You can think of this variable declaration as shorthand for

```
type
  CharString = array[1..100] of char;
var
  StringOfChar : CharString;
```

String variables are like regular array variables with component type *char*, but they have some special properties.

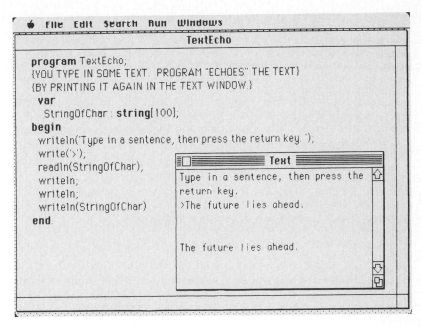

Figure 9.3 The output for **program** TextEcho.

Strings make it much easier for you to read in text, because you can read a sequence of characters into the component variables of a string all at once. You don't need to read in characters one at a time using a loop. The command

```
readln(StringOfChar)
```

keeps filling the cells of StringOfChar with the characters you type at the keyboard until you type a return. The return terminates the *readln* instruction. If you type in fewer than 100 characters before pressing the return key, the 100-cell string will be only partially filled, which is not a problem. If you type in *more* than 100 characters, however, you will get an error message.

Strings also make it easier to print out a sequence of characters. You don't need to put the *writeln* statement in a loop and print the contents of one component variable during each iteration. The single command

```
writeln(StringOfChar)
```

prints the whole string StringOfChar in the Text window, and the instructions

```
moveto(1,100);
writedraw(StringOfChar)
```

prints the string across the middle of the Drawing window.

The largest possible string declaration is **string**[255]. If you leave off the brackets entirely and simply write

```
var
   StringOfChar: string;
```

Macintosh Pascal assumes that you mean **string**[255]. Omitting the number in the brackets is a good idea unless you know that the string variable you declare will always hold far fewer than 255 characters. In that case you should declare a smaller size for your string variable. This will save space in the Macintosh's main memory so that there will be more room left for your program.

9.10 More on Strings—Program PrintBackward

Because strings are actually arrays, you can refer to the values of individual cells just as you can with other arrays. **Program** PrintBackward (see Figure 9.4) illustrates how this works. A text is read in, via a single *readln* statement, and then stored in a string variable called StringOfChar. StringOfChar[1] holds the first character you type in, StringOfChar[2] holds the second character, and so on.

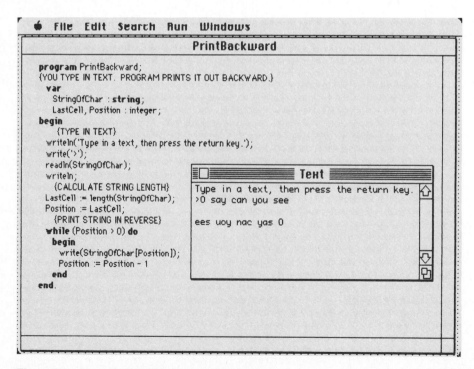

Figure 9.4   Program PrintBackward and its output.

To print the string in reverse, you need to know the position of the cell that contains the final character you typed. Macintosh Pascal has a standard function called *length* that does this calculation for you. The statement

```
LastCell := length(StringOfChar)
```

assigns to the integer variable LastCell the length of StringOfChar—that is, the number of cells in the string variable StringOfChar that are actually in use.

The length of a string is not the same as its size. A string's *size* is the number in square brackets in the variable declaration, or 255 if **string** is not followed by a number in brackets. When we write

```
StringOfChar : string[100]
```

StringOfChar has size 100. In the sample output for **program** PrintBackward, the length of StringOfChar is 17, because that is the number of characters typed before the return.

EXERCISE 7   What does **program** WonderWhat do?

```
program WonderWhat;
 var
  Position,StringLength : integer;
  StringOfChar : string;
begin
 writeln('Type in a string of characters.');
 write('>');
 readln(StringOfChar);
 StringLength := length(StringOfChar);
 Position := 1;
 while (Position <= StringLength) do
  begin
   writeln(StringOfChar[Position]);
   Position := Position + 1
  end
end.
```

9.11 An Array of Strings—Program RutlandStRoster

We have examined arrays whose components hold integers and enumerated types. Now we're going to show you an array that holds a string in *each* component variable. Let's go back to Rutland Street and create an interactive program that keeps track of the names of the people on the block.

In **program** RutlandStRoster, **procedure** EnterNames asks you to type in the name of the family living at each house. Then comes a question-and-answer loop: The program asks for a house number, you respond with the number, and then it gives you the name of the family at that address. This loop continues until you type a 0, which ends the **while** loop. Then the program prints "Session over." and execution ends. Figure 9.5 shows some typical output.

```
program RutlandStRoster;
 type
  NameList = array[1..12] of string[20];
 var
  WhoLivesAt : NameList;
  HouseNumber : integer;
 procedure EnterNames(var WhoLivesAt : NameList);
  var
   HouseNumber : integer;
 begin
  for HouseNumber := 1 to 12 do
   begin
    writeln('Who lives at ',HouseNumber : 1,' Rutland St?');
    write('>');
    readln(WhoLivesAt[HouseNumber])
   end
 end;
 procedure PrintPrompt;
 begin
  write('To find out who lives in house, type number from 1 to 12.');
  writeln('When you want to end the session, type a zero.');
  writeln
 end;
      {MAIN PROGRAM}
begin
 EnterNames(WhoLivesAt);
 PrintPrompt;
 HouseNumber := 1;
    {A QUESTION AND ANSWER LOOP}
 while (HouseNumber <> 0) do
  begin
   write('>');
   readln(HouseNumber);
   if (HouseNumber < 0) or (HouseNumber > 12) then
    writeln('Bad input -- try again.');
   if (HouseNumber >= 1) and (HouseNumber <= 12) then
    writeln(WhoLivesAt[HouseNumber],' lives at ',
            HouseNumber : 1,' Rutland St.')
  end;
 write('Session over.')
end.
```

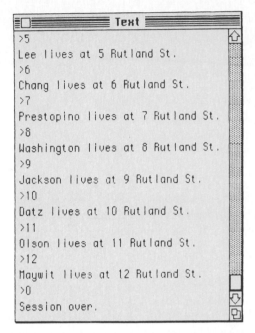

Figure 9.5 Typical output for **program** RutlandStRoster.

The one tricky part of the program is the following definition:

```
NameList = array[1..12] of string[20];
```

It is a blueprint for creating 12 cells in memory, where each cell can hold a string that is up to 20 characters long. When an array of type NameList is declared, each of its 12 cells is partitioned into 20 subcells. When you run **program** RutlandStRoster, each of these 12 cells will hold a string of up to 20 characters.

9.12 The Palindrome Problem

A man, a plan, a canal, Panama!

This phrase is a *palindrome;* the sequence of letters is the same whether you read forward or backward. When you read from right to left (ignoring spaces, capital letters, and punctuation), you encounter exactly the same words as when you read from left to right.

　　To check a phrase or a sentence to determine whether it is a palindrome, you must first change the uppercase letters to lowercase letters and delete all the punctuation and blank spaces. Then you must find out whether the first and the last characters are the same, whether the second and the next-to-last characters

---

Palindromes

Palindromes have been around for a long time. The earliest known palindrome in the English language is

Lewd did I live, & evil I did dwel.

(The word *dwell* was spelled differently then.)

---

are the same, and so forth. When all the characters match up with their opposites at the other end of the string, you've found a palindrome. If a string has an odd number of letters, as does

Madam, I'm Adam

the center letter doesn't pair up with anything. So you don't have to check it against any other letter.

Our palindrome program works this way: After you type in a possible palindrome, the program changes all uppercase letters to lowercase letters, using a procedure called MakeAllLowercase. (Remember that, in type *char*, capital and lowercase letters are *not* equal.) **Procedure** MakeAllLowercase works like **procedure** MakeLowercase in Chapter 7, except that MakeAllLowercase is passed an entire string, not just a character.

Next comes the problem of removing all spaces and punctuation so that a string such as

Sit on a potato pan, otis.

turns into

sitonapotatopanotis

We have created a procedure called Compress to do the job. Compress uses the standard procedure *delete*. Here's how *delete* works. Suppose we have a string called StringOfChar whose value is "I am undone." The command

```
delete(StringOfChar,6,2)
```

begins deleting at position 6 (the *u*) and deletes two characters (the *u* and the *n*). So the new value of StringOfChar is "I am done."

Important: The length of StringOfChar has changed. Before the *delete* procedure was applied, StringOfChar's length was 12. Now it is a different string, and its length is 10.

EXERCISE 8   Suppose StringOfChar has the value "Able was I, ere I saw Elba." What is the value of StringOfChar after each of the following delete operations?

    a. delete(StringOfChar,5,4)
    b. delete(StringOfChar,9,1)
    c. delete(StringOfChar,2,10)

In each case, what is the new length of StringOfChar? ■

Once the string is compressed, we check to determine whether it is a palindrome. If we create a variable called StringLength, which holds the value for the length of the string, we can compare

StringOfChar[1]	against	StringOfChar[StringLength]
StringOfChar[2]	against	StringOfChar[StringLength – 1]
StringOfChar[3]	against	StringOfChar[StringLength – 2]

and so on, until we get to the center of the string.

The program uses a procedure called PalCheck to determine whether it has been handed a palindrome. **Procedure** PalCheck is passed the compressed string and a boolean variable, OkSoFar, which has been initialized to True. The formal parameter, Ok, is a variable parameter. If the string is ever found to be a non-palindrome, the formal parameter Ok (and therefore the actual parameter OkSoFar) becomes False.

The variable parameter Ok is used as a flag inside the loop in PalCheck. Ok becomes False if a mismatch is ever found between paired characters, and this will end the loop. If no mismatch is found, Ok remains True and the program will report a palindrome as you can see in Figure 9.6

One final point. If a formal parameter in a procedure heading is of type **string**, then it must not be followed by a size value in brackets. Declarations such as **string**[100] or even **string**[255] are unacceptable in procedure headings; you will get an error message if you try them.

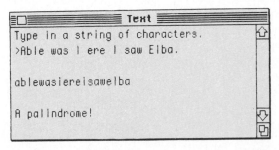

Figure 9.6   Typical output for **program** Palindrome.

```
program Palindrome;
{YOU TYPE IN A STRING OF CHARACTERS. PROGRAM DETERMINES}
{WHETHER STRING IS A PALINDROME.}
 var
  StringOfChar : string;
  Position,Center,StringLength : integer;
  OkSoFar : boolean;

procedure EnterString (var StringOfChar : string);
begin
 writeln('Type in a string of characters.');
 write('>');
 readln(StringOfChar);
 writeln
end;

procedure MakeAllLowercase (var StringOfChar : string);
 var
  Position,StringLength : integer;
  Ch : char;
begin
 Position := 1;
 StringLength := length(StringOfChar);
 while (Position <= StringLength) do
  begin
   Ch := StringOfChar[Position];
   if (Ch >= 'A') and (Ch <= 'Z') then
    StringOfChar[Position] := chr(ord(Ch) + 32);
   Position := Position + 1
  end
end;

procedure Compress (var StringOfChar : string);
 var
  Position : integer;
begin
 Position := length(StringOfChar);
 while (Position > 0) do
  begin
   if (StringOfChar[Position] < 'a') or
                  (StringOfChar[Position] > 'z') then
    delete(StringOfChar,Position,1);
   Position := Position - 1
  end
end;
```

```
procedure PalCheck (StringOfChar : string;
         var Ok : boolean);
  var
    Position,Center,StringLength : integer;
begin
  Position := 1;
  StringLength := length(StringOfChar);
  Center := StringLength div 2;
  while (Position <= Center) and Ok do
    begin
      if (StringOfChar[Position] <>
            StringOfChar[StringLength - Position + 1]) then
        Ok := False;
      Position := Position + 1
    end
end;
  {MAIN PROGRAM}
begin
  EnterString(StringOfChar);
  MakeAllLowercase(StringOfChar);
  Compress(StringOfChar);
  writeln(StringOfChar);
  writeln;
  OkSoFar := True;
  PalCheck(StringOfChar,OkSoFar);
  if OkSoFar then
    writeln('A palindrome!')
  else
    writeln('Not a palindrome.')
end.
```

Try running these:

> Step on no pets.
>
> Never odd or even.
>
> No evil Shahs live on.
>
> Able was I ere I saw Elba.
>
> Remarkable was I ere I saw Elba, Kramer.
>
> Live dirt up a sidetrack carted is a putrid evil.
>
> Straw? No! Too stupid a fad! I put soot on warts.
>
> Doc: Note I dissent. A fast never prevents a fatness—I diet on cod.
>
> Saippuakauppias (the Finnish word for soap salesman)

EXERCISE 9   **a.** How would you change **program** Palindrome so that it prints out the number of characters in the entry?

b. When you type in "No evil Shahs live on," how many iterations does the final **while** statement in **procedure** PalCheck do? ▬

9.13 A Universal Line Graph Procedure

Let's look again at **program** SurveyGraph (page 303) and the graphing procedure it includes, **procedure** DrawLineGraph. This procedure is quite limited: It will work only in programs that include the type definition for StreetSurvey.

We can alter **procedure** DrawLineGraph so that it can be used to graph the contents of *any* array with component type *integer* and an index type that is a subrange of type *integer*. This will make DrawLineGraph a *universal* graphing procedure—that is, a graphing procedure that will work in a wide variety of programs.

Here is **program** SurveyGraph with the new, universal **procedure** DrawLineGraph.

```
program SurveyGraphTwo;
{YOU READ IN NUMBER OF PEOPLE IN EACH HOUSE ON RUTLAND ST.}
{PROGRAM PRINTS LINE GRAPH OF STREET POPULATION.}
 const
  First = 1;
  Last = 12;
  ScaleFactor = 10;
 type
  NumberCells = array[First..Last] of integer;
 var
  CellPosition : integer;
  RutlandSt : NumberCells;

 procedure GetStreetData (var Street : NumberCells);
  var
   HouseNumber : integer;
 begin
  for HouseNumber := 1 to 12 do
   begin
    writeln('How many people live at ',HouseNumber : 2,' Rutland St?');
    write(')');
    readln(Street[HouseNumber]);
    writeln
   end
 end;
```

```
procedure DrawLineGraph(Numbers : NumberCells;
         Scale : integer);
{A UNIVERSAL LINE GRAPH PROCEDURE}
{FIRST AND LAST ARE GLOBAL CONSTANTS OF TYPE INTEGER.}
{NUMBERCELLS IS AN ARRAY[FIRST..LAST] OF INTEGER.}
 const
  Bottom = 175;
  Separation = 18;
  CharWidth = 4;
 var
  Position,Height,HPosition,Top : integer;
begin
 HPosition := 0;
 for Position := First to Last do
  begin
     {DRAW LINE}
   HPosition := HPosition + Separation;
   Height := Scale * Numbers[Position];
   Top := Bottom - Height;
   drawline(HPosition,Top,HPosition,Bottom);
      {DRAW LABEL -- SUBSTRACTING CHARWIDTH CENTERS LABEL}
   moveto(HPosition - CharWidth,Bottom + 12);
   writedraw(Position : 1)
  end
end;
```

```
{MAIN PROGRAM}
begin
 GetStreetData(RutlandSt);
 DrawLineGraph(RutlandSt,ScaleFactor)
end.
```

Note first that we have given StreetSurvey a more abstract name: Now it is NumberCells. The index type for the array is also as general as possible:

```
First..Last
```

In the declaration part of the program, we have defined First as 1 and Last as 12.

Given *any* array with component type *integer* and index type of the form First..Last, **procedure DrawLineGraph** will graph the array for you. By changing the definitions for First and Last, you can graph an array with any number of component variables.

This means you don't have to rewrite the procedure every time you want to include a graph in your program output. Instead, you simply write definitions for First and Last and for type NumberCells. Then you copy **procedure** DrawLineGraph from **program** SurveyGraphTwo into your new program. You can transfer a copy of the procedure from one program to another by using Copy and Paste. The Copy command saves a copy on the electronic Clipboard, and the copy remains there when you switch between MacPascal documents.

You now have a single instruction that will allow you to display any array of integers, indexed with any integer subrange, in graphic form *in any program you write*.

To see how convenient this can be, let's look at another example. Suppose you want to graph the number of complete miles you jog each day during the month of January. Using the universal graphing procedure **procedure** DrawLineGraph, you can easily create a program that displays your jogging record (see Figure 9.7).

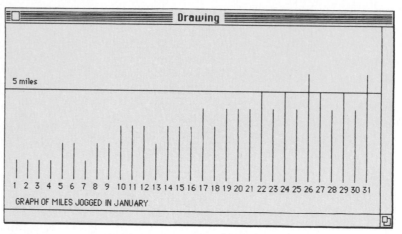

Figure 9.7   Typical output for **program** JanuaryJog.

```
program JanuaryJog;
 const
   First = 1;
   Last = 31;
   ScaleFactor = 20;
 type
   NumberCells = array[First..Last] of integer;
 var
   CellPosition : integer;
   JanJog : NumberCells;
```

```
procedure GetJoggingData(var Numbers : NumberCells);
 var
  Day : integer;
begin
 for Day := 1 to 31 do
  begin
   writeln('Type an integer for the number of miles
              jogged on Jan ',Day : 2);
   write('>');
   readln(Numbers[Day]);
   writeln
  end
end;
```

```
{THE UNIVERSAL LINE GRAPH PROCEDURE}
procedure DrawLineGraph(Numbers : NumberCells;
        Scale : integer);
{FIRST AND LAST ARE GLOBAL CONSTANTS OF TYPE INTEGER.}
{NUMBERCELLS IS AN ARRAY[FIRST..LAST]OF INTEGER.}
 const
  Bottom = 175;
  Separation = 15;
  CharWidth = 4;
 var
  Position,Height,HPosition,Top : integer;
begin
 HPosition := 0;
 for Position := First to Last do
  begin
   {DRAW LINE}
   HPosition := HPosition + Separation;
   Height := Scale * Numbers[Position];
   Top := Bottom - Height;
   drawline(HPosition,Top,HPosition,Bottom);
   {DRAW LABEL}
   moveto(HPosition - CharWidth,Bottom + 12);
   writedraw(Position : 1)
  end
end;
```

```
procedure LabelGraph;
begin
 drawline(0,75,500,75);
 moveto(10,70);
 writedraw('5 miles');
 moveto(15,205);
 writedraw('GRAPH OF MILES JOGGED IN JANUARY')
end;
```

(continued)

```
{MAIN PROGRAM}
begin
  GetJoggingData(JanJog);
  DrawLineGraph(JanJog,ScaleFactor);
  LabelGraph
end.
```

Note that First and Last are *global* constants. It is for precisely this reason that **procedure** DrawLineGraph is so easy to use. As long as the main program gives a type definition for NumberCells and constant definitions for First and Last, **procedure** DrawLineGraph can be used almost without alteration. In **program** JanuaryJog, the only change has been a reduction in the value of the constant Separation. Separation represents the distance between lines in the graph, and the reduction is necessary so that the graph will fit on the screen. (You also need to run the program using the small type size.)

BLAISE PASCAL

In 1635 a French boy named Blaise Pascal found a mistake in René Descartes's famous geometry book. Geometry fascinated young Pascal, but he had to study it secretly because his father thought he was too young to be learning math. By the time the boy was 16, he had written a scientific paper about sound and another about a difficult problem in geometry. Meanwhile the elder Pascal had been given an important job in the French province of Normandy. He was now responsible for deciding who should pay taxes and how much they should pay. This meant doing an enormous amount of paperwork, if his records were to be accurate and honest. He was a conscientious man—too conscientious, some people thought—and his strict tax collecting once caused disgruntled citizens to riot.

To help his father with all the necessary record keeping, 19-year-old Blaise Pascal invented a calculating machine. Called the Pascaline, it worked somewhat like an automobile odometer: Addition and subtraction were done by counting the revolutions of meshing wheels. In the next 10 years, Pascal built more than 50 improved versions of the Pascaline, which became the model for later adding machines, electric meters, and other measuring devices.

As a tribute to this early contribution to the science of mechanical computing, Niklaus Wirth, the creator of the programming language Pascal, named the language after Blaise Pascal.

One area of math that intrigued Pascal was a remarkable table of numbers that Greek and Chinese mathematicians had studied in ancient times. Pascal studied the table carefully, and he figured out how the table could be used in probability calculations and in about a dozen other ways. Soon people began calling the table Pascal's triangle. This table is still important in mathematics today.

A caution comes with this style of programming. When a procedure relies on global definitions, it becomes difficult to understand. If we hadn't included a comment, it would have been impossible to see the relationship between First and Last and the type NumberCells. When you write a universal procedure that relies on global values, be sure to include comments that explain the procedure's behavior without reference to a main program.

Pascal: Public and Private

For experienced programmers there are really two Pascals. First there is public Pascal. This is the language of the textbooks and manuals, and it includes all the standard Pascal and Macintosh Pascal instructions.

The second Pascal is private. As a seasoned programmer, you will accumulate an ever-growing collection of procedures (such as DrawLineGraph) that do a variety of important jobs. Using Copy and Paste, you can move "universal" procedure declarations from one program to another with ease, so that your invented instructions will almost seem built-in. As you enlarge your private stock of universal procedure instructions, the Pascal you use to solve problems will become increasingly powerful.

9.14 Pascal's Triangle

Let's use what we have learned about arrays to print a portion of *Pascal's triangle*. Here are the first nine rows, which we have numbered beginning with zero. (That way, the second entry in a row gives the row number in every row except the first one.)

Row 0	1								
Row 1	1	1							
Row 2	1	2	1						
Row 3	1	3	3	1					
Row 4	1	4	6	4	1				
Row 5	1	5	10	10	5	1			
Row 6	1	6	15	20	15	6	1		
Row 7	1	7	21	35	35	21	7	1	
Row 8	1	8	28	56	70	56	28	8	1

Beginning with row 1, each entry in the triangle is the sum of two numbers from the row above: the number directly above the entry and the number to the left of that number, if there is one. In the following triangle, the 3 with the arrow pointing to it is the sum of the two circled numbers.

Row 0	1			
Row 1	1	1		
Row 2	1	②	①	
Row 3	1	3	3↖	1

Pascal's triangle is more than a curiosity: It has great importance in probability theory and in other areas of mathematics. To see how Pascal's triangle relates to probability theory, look at row 3, which reads 1-3-3-1. The numbers in this row add up to 8.

The entries in the row (1-3-3-1), and the sum of the numbers in the row (8) have special significance. These numbers are related to the probability of getting a particular pattern of heads or tails when you flip three coins.

Suppose you toss three coins on the table. Each of the three coins can come up either heads (H) or tails (T), so there are $2 \times 2 \times 2 = 8$ possible outcomes of your toss.

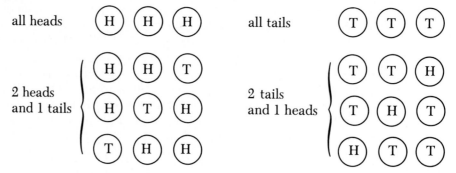

There is only *one* way a coin toss can come up all heads, and there is only *one* way a coin toss can come up all tails. These two "one's" correspond to the 1's on each end of the row: 1-3-3-1.

There are *three* ways that you can get two heads and one tails. The one tails could be the first coin, it could be the second coin, or it could be the third coin. Similarly, one heads and two tails can happen in three ways. So the 1-3-3-1 pattern in the row gives a profile of all possible head–tail outcomes when you toss three coins on a table.

Row 4 (1-4-6-4-1) gives you a profile of the possible outcomes when you toss *four* coins. The sum of the numbers in the row is *sixteen*, and there are sixteen possible outcomes. There's *one* way for you to get all heads and *one* way to get all tails. There are *four* ways to get one heads and three tails and *four* ways to get one tails and three heads. Finally there are *six* ways you can get two heads and two tails.

You can also use Pascal's triangle to compute probabilities. When you toss three coins, getting two heads can happen in three ways from among the eight possible outcomes. So the probability of getting two heads out of three is 3/8 = .375. And the probability of tossing four coins and getting three heads is 4/16 = .25.

EXERCISE 10   Suppose you toss five coins. What is the significance of each of the numbers in row 5: 1-5-10-10-5-1? ▬

Now let's use our standard think-plan-code-test-and-debug method to write a program that prints rows 0 through 8 of Pascal's triangle.

Thinking

The top row in Pascal's triangle, row 0, consists of a single 1. Each subsequent row can be calculated from the one before it. The Pascal's triangle problem can be solved by printing the first row and then repeatedly calculating each subsequent row and printing it out.

The rows are of different lengths, which is a problem if we want to use a single array variable to hold all the rows of the triangle. We can get around this difficulty by making all the rows the same length and putting zeros in the empty spots. When a row is printed, the program will simply skip over an entry if it is a zero.

Because the rows are the same length, we will be able to use the same array to hold the values of each row in the triangle. We'll call this array Row, and we'll call its type TriangleRow. The component type will be integer, and the index type will be the subrange 0..RowLength, where RowLength = 8.

We can use a variable called RowNumber to keep track of the number of the row we are working on from 0 up to HowManyRows, where HowManyRows has the value 8.

----------------- DATA TABLE -----------------

Input Variables	**Output Variables**	**Program Variables**
none	Row: TriangleRow;	RowNumber : integer;
		Row: TriangleRow;

Special formulas	**Loops**
none	the loop calculates and prints the triangle

Constant and Type Definitions
RowLength = 8;
HowManyRows = 8;
type TriangleRow = **array**[0..RowLength] **of** integer;

Planning

Here is our first plan:

1. Fill an array with values for the first row.
2. Print the first row.
3. Go through the remaining rows.
   Calculate a row.
   Print that row.

This rough plan identifies three actions that should be packaged as procedures: Fill the first row, which we'll call FillFirstRow; print a row, which we'll call PrintRow; and calculate the next row, which we'll name CalcRow. We can refine our plan to this:

1. FillFirstRow
2. PrintRow
3. while (RowNumber ⟨ = HowManyRows) do
    begin
        CalcRow
        PrintRow
        RowNumber : = RowNumber + 1
    end

Now let's clarify these three procedures.

Clarifying FillFirstRow

The first row is different from the other rows, because it is not calculated from the row above it. It consists of a 1 followed by eight 0's, and we want to use FillFirstRow to put this pattern of numbers in the cells of the array variable Row. FillFirstRow's formal parameter must be a variable parameter, because the procedure alters the array that it is passed: The array comes in empty and is passed back out filled. Here is our proposed heading line:

```
procedure FillFirstRow(var Row : TriangleRow);
```

Our paper check for FillFirstRow looks like this:

Clarifying PrintRow

PrintRow has the job of printing the contents of a row, except for the 0's, in a single line. Because it doesn't change the array, but only writes the contents on the screen, we'll use a value parameter in its heading line:

```
procedure PrintRow(Row : TriangleRow);
```

Here is our paper check for PrintRow:
Upon receiving the input

1	3	3	1	0	0	0	0	0

PrintRow prints

    1   3   3   1

Clarifying CalcRow

CalcRow is passed a row of Pascal's triangle and must pass back the next row. So it requires a variable parameter. Its proposed heading line is

```
procedure CalcRow(var Row : TriangleRow);
```

And here is our paper check:

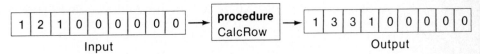

Now we know enough to code the top level.

```
begin
  FillFirstRow(Row);
  PrintRow(Row);
  RowNumber := 1;
  while (RowNumber <= HowManyRows) do
   begin
     CalcRow(Row);
     PrintRow(Row);
     RowNumber := RowNumber + 1
   end
end.
```

We have broken our problem into three simpler problems—writing the three procedures FillFirstRow, PrintRow, and CalcRow. The first two aren't hard, so we won't go over how to plan and code them. But let's work through CalcRow carefully.

Thinking through CalcRow

Remember that the first row is given and that each subsequent row is calculated from the one before it. The rule for calculating a row is this: Each entry in Pascal's triangle is the sum of two numbers—the number directly above it and the number to left of that number. When we calculate the next row in the triangle using a single array, we have to overwrite the old values in the array with new entries that will make up the next row in the triangle.

CalcRow is tricky. Working from left to right—the obvious way to create the new values in the array from the old values—won't work. To see why, let's take a typical row:

```
1 2 1 0 0 0 0 0 0
```

If we start at the left and add the first two values, we get 3. Now, if we put this sum in the second position of the array, our row becomes

```
1 3 1 0 0 0 0 0 0
```

So far so good. But what happens when we add the value in the second and third positions to get the new entry for the third position? We get 4, but we're supposed to get 3. This scheme didn't work because we should have added the *old* value in the second position, which is 2, to the 1 in the third position. Instead we used the *new* value in the second position.

So let's try another approach. This time we'll enter new values in the array working from *right to left*.

Suppose that we are filling cells from right to left and that we are working on the circled entry:

1   3   3   1   ⓪   0   0   0   0

The new entry in the circle will be the sum of the old entry in the circle and the entry to its left. So the sum will be 1.

Now we go to calculate the next entry:

1   3   3   ①   1   0   0   0   0

Its new value is the sum of 3 and 1, which are both *old* values. The new values are off to the right and out of the way. They won't affect future sums. So we get

1   3   3   4   1   0   0   0   0

If we continue in this way, we'll get the full row:

1   4   6   4   1   0   0   0   0

EXERCISE 11   To make sure you see how to get the correct row of numbers when working from right to left, write down the following sequence on a sheet of paper:

1   4   6   4   1   0   0   0   0

Now, beginning at the right, cross out each entry and write below each cross-out the sum of that number and the number to its *left*. When you're done, you will have the next row of the triangle. ▬

Once you have figured out how to do it, CalcRow turns out to be remarkably simple. The body of the procedure is this single **for** statement:

```
for Position := RowLength downto 1 do
  Row[Position] := Row[Position] + Row[Position - 1]
```

Row is of type TriangleRow, which has index type 0..RowLength. Because the **for** loop runs down to 1, *not* to 0, we won't be out of range the last time through the loop.

Here is the complete Pascal's triangle program:

```pascal
program PascalsTriangle;
{PRINTS OUT 8 ROWS OF PASCAL'S TRIANGLE}
 const
  HowManyRows = 8;
  RowLength = 8;
 type
  TriangleRow = array[0..RowLength] of integer;
 var
  Row : TriangleRow;
  RowNumber : integer;

 procedure FillFirstRow(var Row : TriangleRow);
  var
   Position : integer;
 begin
  Row[0] := 1;
  for Position := 1 to RowLength do
   Row[Position] := 0
 end;

 procedure PrintRow(Row : TriangleRow);
  var
   Position : integer;
 begin
  for Position := 0 to RowLength do
   if (Row[Position] > 0) then
    write(Row[Position]: 6);
  writeln
 end;

 procedure CalcRow(var Row : TriangleRow);
  var
   Position : integer;
 begin
  for Position := RowLength downto 1 do
   Row[Position] := Row[Position] + Row[Position - 1]
 end;
   {MAIN PROGRAM}
begin
 FillFirstRow(Row);
 PrintRow(Row);
 RowNumber := 1;
 while (RowNumber <= HowManyRows) do
  begin
   CalcRow(Row);
   PrintRow(Row);
   RowNumber := RowNumber + 1
  end
end.
```

EXERCISE 12   Change the values of RowPosition and BottomRow from 8 to 10 and see what you get. ▬

_____TEST YOURSELF _____

1. What is the component type of an array?
2. What is the index type?
3. Explain the scoreboard principle.
4. What is an out-of-range error?
5. What is a string?
6. What is a palindrome?
7. How can you transfer a procedure from one program to another electronically?
8. How are the rows in Pascal's triangle calculated?

_____PROBLEMS _____

1. Write a program that includes an array with 10 cells. Using a loop, the program stores the following pattern of numbers in the cells:

| 0 | 10 | 0 | 20 | 0 | 30 | 0 | 40 | 0 | 50 |

and then prints them, from last to first, in a column in the Text window.

2. Suppose your survey assignment includes calculating the percentage of houses on the street that have a garden. Write a declaration for an array variable called RutlandGardens, using the following two-element enumerated type:

```
type
    Garden = (HaveAGarden,NoGarden);
```

Use the variable RutlandGardens in a program that reads in the street's garden data and calculates the percentage of houses on the street that have a garden.

3. a. A freight train has 10 cars and there are 4 kinds of car—locomotives, coal cars, oil cars, and cattle cars. Define an array type called FreightTrain. What is the index type for FreightTrain? And what is the type of the components? _Hint:_ First declare an enumerated type for the 4 kinds of car.
   b. Now declare a variable called AltoonaLimited of type FreightTrain.
   c. Write a program that reads in the kind of each of the 10 cars in the Altoona Limited and prints out this information in a column.

d. Modify the program you wrote in part c so that it prints a table showing the number of each kind of car on the train. (*Hint:* Use the scoreboard principle.)

4. Your school has 3 outstanding sprinters, Jesse, Frankie, and Hilary, whom you have listed in an enumerated type:

```
type
   Runners = (Jesse,Frankie,Hilary);
```

They all run in the 50- and 100-yard dashes, and you want to compare their racing times (accurate to the nearest tenth of a second), using the following 2 array variables:

```
var
   Fifty,Hundred : SprintResults;
```

a. Give the type definition for SprintResults.
b. Write a program that reads in the time in seconds for each runner in each race and prints the name of the runner who has the best time in each race.

Hint: The prompt should look like this:

```
Give times for Jesse in the 50 and 100 yard dashes.
```

5. Write a program that fills a 10-cell array with the cubes of the numbers from 1 to 10—1, 8, 27, 64, and so on—and then prints these values out in a column.

6. Write a program that reads in Fahrenheit temperature data for a week in March. The data should be accurate to the nearest tenth of a degree, and they should be stored in an array. After you read in the temperatures, the program should convert them to Celsius and then print them in a table.

7. Modify the program you wrote in Problem 6 so that it prints out the average Fahrenheit temperature for the week.

8. Invent another universal line graph procedure, called DrawRealLine-Graph, that is passed an array with component type *real* instead of component type *integer*. Then use the procedure to graph the Celsius temperatures you found in Problem 6.

9. Write a program that includes an array called DigitPositions with the character subrange '0'..'9' as index type and component type *integer*. The program should fill this array with the *ord* of each digit and then print the contents of the array in a table in the Text window. The output should begin like this:

```
digit  ord value
  0        48
  1        49
```

10. You work for the Turnpike Authority. The Turnpike Authority has just bought automatic toll-collecting machines. Your job? Write an interactive program that takes the number of pennies, nickels, dimes, and quarters tossed into the machine and calculates whether the driver paid the correct toll. Your program should include a global constant called TollAmount for the amount of the toll, which will be less than one dollar. If the money deposited in the machine is less than TollAmount, the program should print a message asking for more cash. If the money deposited is equal to (or greater than!) the amount of the toll, the program should print the message "Thank you—drive carefully."

11. The Fibonacci numbers are a famous number sequence in mathematics that starts like this: 1, 1, 2, 3, 5, 8, 13, . . . beginning with the 2, each entry is the sum of the two numbers that precede it: 8 = 5 + 3, for example. Write a program that calculates the first 20 Fibonacci numbers, stores them in an array, and prints them out in a column in the Text window.

12. Write **program** DietRecord. You read in the number of calories in the food you consume each day for a month, and this information is stored in an array. You also enter a "cut-off" figure—the maximum number of calories you wish to eat in a day. For output, the program should print a line graph of the calories you have eaten. It should also print the total number of calories you ate in a month, your average daily caloric intake, and the percentage of days on which the number of calories you consumed was less than your "cut-off" figure.

13. Invent a universal bar graph procedure, and change **program** DietRecord so that it prints a bar graph of your daily caloric intake.

Functions and Random Numbers

10

When you use Pascal to solve a complicated problem, you divide the problem into manageable pieces and create a procedure to handle each piece. Each procedure is a little subprogram. Now we're going to tell you about another subprogram instruction, the *function*.

Functions, like procedures, are instructions that do some special job. The main difference between functions and procedures is that a function gives you a single value as output. We say that a function *returns* a single value.

Just as Pascal has standard procedures, it has *standard functions*, many of which we introduced in Chapter 4. We will first review how these standard functions work. Then we'll show you how to make up your own functions and how to use them in your programs. Finally, we will tell you how to use a special function called *random*, which generates random numbers.

10.1 Standard Functions: A Review

Round, *sqrt*, and *odd* are standard functions. Each one returns a single value as an answer. For example,

```
round(3.14) = 3
sqrt(4.0) = 2.0
odd(3) = True
```

Round rounds off a real number and gives you the closest integer as its single answer. *Sqrt* gives the square root of a number as its single answer. And *odd* checks whether an integer is odd and gives True or False as its answer.

When the assignment statement

```
Number := round(3.14)
```

is executed, the right side is evaluated first. Then the value that the function returns is assigned to the variable Number. When the Macintosh evaluates *round*(3.14), it is doing a *function call*. The number inside the parentheses, 3.14, is called the *actual parameter* of the function. It is sometimes called the *argument* of the function.

As a rule, the actual parameter of a function must be of a particular type. For example, the argument of the function *odd* must be an integer. *Odd*(4) makes sense—it returns the value False. But *odd*(98.6) is nonsense.

There are some exceptions to the rule that the parameter of a function can be of one type only. For example, *sqrt* behaves properly with either a real *or* an integer argument. So both *sqrt*(2.0) and *sqrt*(2) are acceptable.

The value a function returns is always of a particular type, too. *Round* returns an answer of type *integer*. *Odd* returns an answer of type *boolean*. And *sqrt* returns an answer of type *real*. The type of the value that a function returns is called the *result type*.

Now here's something interesting. *Sqrt* can take a real number as input, and it will give a real number as output. This means you can put a *sqrt* function call inside another *sqrt* function call. For example, the following expression takes the square root of the square root of 2—that is, it takes the fourth root of 2.

```
sqrt(sqrt(2.0))
```

This is known as a *nested* function call.

The Macintosh evaluates nested function calls from the inside out. Here it evaluates *sqrt*(2.0) first and returns a real-number value, 1.414. Then it uses 1.414 as the actual parameter for the outer function call and takes the square root of this value.

When you put a function call inside a function call, you must be sure that the type of the answer from the inner function will work as a parameter for the outer function. For example,

```
writeln(sqrt(odd(6)))
```

won't work. The *odd* function returns the value False, and you can't take the square root of False.

EXERCISE 1   Which of the following nested function calls will work?

    a. sqrt(sqrt(9.9))

    b. sqrt(round(9.9))

    c. sqrt(odd(9.9))

    d. round(sqrt(9.9))

    e. round(round(9.9))

f. `round(odd(9.9))`

g. `odd(odd(9))`

h. `odd(round(9.9))`

i. `odd(sqrt(4))`

Try them in the Instant window to test your hypotheses. ▬

Odd, *round*, and *sqrt* are built-in, standard functions because the jobs they do are so important that everybody uses them. We have also used other standard functions in this book, such as *abs*, *sqr*, *chr*, *ord*, *pred*, and *succ*. *Length* is a standard function too, but it appears only in Macintosh Pascal and not in most other versions of the language.

We will need one other standard function in this chapter, the function *copy*. *Copy* is a MacPascal standard function with three parameters—a **string** value followed by two integers. The function call

```
copy(AString,Position,NumberOfChars)
```

returns a string value. This value is a substring of AString that begins at location Position in AString and is NumberOfChars long. The function call

```
Copy('Hi there',4,3)
```

returns the value *the*.

Inside the front cover you will find a list of all the standard functions we use in this book.

10.2 Creating Your Own Functions

When you are working on a programming problem, you often identify a subproblem that requires a single-value answer, but no standard function gives the answer you need. This is the time to create your own Pascal function. For example, you can make up functions that will

- Take a capital letter and return a lowercase letter
- Take a number and give its cube root
- Take two numbers and give the average of the two
- Take a word and give the word with the letters printed in reverse
- Take a principal, an interest rate, and a number of years in the bank, and return the money accumulated

Creating your own functions helps you break complex problems into easy-to-code subproblems. Functions clarify a program in the same way that procedures do. And once you make up a useful function, you can often reuse it in other programs.

10.3 How to Declare Your Own Functions

How do you make up a function? Suppose you are writing a program and you need to know whether a number falls between two other numbers. That is, you need to know whether it's the same as or larger than the first and whether it's the same as or smaller than the second. This problem calls for a single answer: True or False. So this is a job for a function.

Suppose we create one called Between. If we pass **function** Between three numbers, it will tell us whether the middle number is between the other two. Here is the heading line for the function:

```
function Between(Smaller,Middle,Larger : integer) : boolean;
```

A function declaration starts with the word **function**, which is followed by the name of the function. Then comes a formal parameter list, which in this case has three entries called Smaller, Middle, and Larger. These are all value formal parameters. (Variable parameters are possible with functions, but they are seldom used.)

The word *integer* specifies that the parameters must be of type *integer*. And the word *boolean* at the end of the heading line specifies the result type of the function—the type of the single value that the function returns. In the case of **function** Between, a boolean answer is returned.

Now let's look at the complete function declaration:

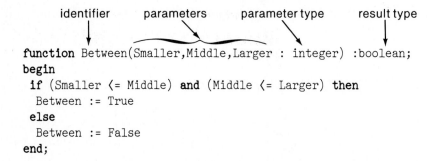

```
function Between(Smaller,Middle,Larger : integer) :boolean;
begin
  if (Smaller <= Middle) and (Middle <= Larger) then
    Between := True
  else
    Between := False
end;
```

The body of the function says this: If the value of Smaller is less than or equal to the value of Middle, and the value of Middle is less than or equal to the value of Larger, then the function returns the value True; otherwise it returns the value False.

All this makes good sense. But there is something peculiar about the body of a function. The name of the function is actually used *inside* the function definition. When the name Between shows up in the body of the function, it acts almost like an ordinary variable of type *boolean*, and it gets assigned a value—either True or False. This value is the answer that the function returns.

Important: For now, the name of the function can appear only on the left side of an assignment statement inside the function definition. We will tell you about an important exception to this rule later.

EXERCISE 2   What is the value of each of the following function calls?

a. Between(5,7,9)

b. Between(5,10,9)

c. Between(5,5,9)

d. Between(10,11,5)

Answers: Only a and c are True. ■

10.4 Program PointInRec—Preparing for Mouse Control

Here is an intriguing use for **function** Between in a program called PointInRec. You read in a point and a rectangle, and the program tells you whether the point is inside the rectangle. Then it draws the point and the rectangle in the Drawing window (see Figure 10.1).

Program PointInRec is more than just an interesting novelty. The principle used in the program is an important part of the program that operates the Macintosh's menus. Think about what happens when you pull down a menu, drag the pointer to a row, and release the mouse button. How does the computer know what menu choice you've made? It decides by taking the position of the tip of the arrow when you release the button—a point—and checking to see inside which of the rectangular menu bars the point lies.

The check we are about to do in **program** PointInRec is exactly the same kind of test the Macintosh does when it figures out which menu item you've chosen. In the next chapter, we'll show you how to create your own rectangular menu items. And we'll show you how to control programs by placing the pointer in one of these menu items and clicking the mouse.

Here is **program** PointInRec.

Figure 10.1   Typical output for **program** PointInRec.

```
program PointInRec;
{PROGRAM DECIDES IF POINT IS INSIDE RECTANGLE. IT ALSO}
{DRAWS THE RECTANGLE AND THE POINT.}
 var
  Top,Left,Bottom,Right : integer; {WALLS OF RECTANGLE}
  HPoint,VPoint : integer;
 function Between(Smaller,Middle,Larger : integer) : boolean;
 begin
  if (Smaller <= Middle) and (Middle <= Larger) then
   Between := True
  else
   Between := False
 end;
 procedure DrawPoint(Horizontal,Vertical : integer);
 begin
  moveto(Horizontal,Vertical);
  lineto(Horizontal,Vertical)
 end;
 procedure EnterRectangle(var Top,Left,Bottom,Right : integer);
 begin
  writeln('Type in values for the top, left, bottom,
           and right sides of a rectangle.');
  write('>');
  readln(Top,Left,Bottom,Right);
  writeln
 end;
 procedure EnterPoint(var HPoint,VPoint : integer);
 begin
  writeln('Type in the horizontal and then the vertical
           position of a point.');
  write('>');
  readln(HPoint,VPoint)
 end;
   {MAIN PROGRAM}
begin
 EnterRectangle(Top,Left,Bottom,Right);
 EnterPoint(HPoint,VPoint);
 if Between(Left,HPoint,Right) and Between(Top,VPoint,Bottom) then
  writeln('Yes! Point is inside rectangle.')
 else
  writeln('Point is not inside rectangle.');
   {DRAWS POINT, THEN RECTANGLE}
 DrawPoint(HPoint,VPoint);
 framerect(Top,Left,Bottom,Right)
end.
```

And here's how **function** Between works in **program** PointInRec. In the function call

```
Between(Left,HPoint,Right)
```

the variables Left, HPoint, and Right are actual parameters. They hold the values that you have entered interactively. The actual parameters are passed to the function, where the formal parameters— Smaller, Middle, and Larger—take on these values. Then Between returns a value—True or False. Next comes a second function call, and Between is passed another set of values—Top, VPoint, and Bottom. If *both* function calls return the value True, the program reports

```
Yes! Point is inside rectangle.
```

If one or the other or both of the function calls return the value False, the program prints

```
Point is not inside rectangle.
```

A function includes *formal parameters* in the heading line of its declaration and *actual parameters* or *arguments* in the function call. When the call is made, the values of the actual parameters in the call are assigned to the formal parameters in the heading line. As with procedures, it doesn't matter what names you pick for the parameters, although it is sensible to choose names that suggest their use.

Important: The actual parameters in a function call must be listed in the same order as the formal parameters in the function heading line. Accordingly, if you write a function with more than one formal parameter, make sure that the order of the arguments in a call agrees with the order in the heading.

```
function Between(Smaller,Middle,Larger :integer) : boolean;
                      ↕        ↕        ↕
         Between(Left,HPoint,Right);
```

Note where we placed the declaration for **function** Between. It is in the declaration part of the program after the variable declarations. Function declarations, like procedure declarations, always come at the end of the declaration part of a program just before the body.

EXERCISE 3   **a.** How would you declare **function** InBetween, which returns the value True if Smaller is *strictly* less than Middle (rather than less than or equal to) and Middle is *strictly* less than Larger?

b. What will **program** PointInRec report when the point lies exactly on the edge of the rectangle? What happens when the point lies exactly on a corner of the rectangle?

c. What do you think **function** Tomorrow does? What is the formal parameter? What is the type of the parameter? What is the result type?

```
function Tomorrow(Today : DaysOfWeek) : DaysOfWeek;
  begin
    if Today = Sun then
      Tomorrow := Mon
    else
      Tomorrow := succ(Today)
  end;
```

d. Write a companion function called Yesterday. ■

Now let's work through two more examples of made-up functions, one with result type *char* and the other with result type *integer*.

—— 10.5 Function Capitalize ————————————————————————

Function Capitalize capitalizes lowercase letters and returns other characters unchanged. It has result type *char*.

```
function Capitalize(Ch : char) : char;
{FUNCTION CAPITALIZES LOWERCASE LETTERS AND LEAVES OTHERS UNCHANGED.}
  const
    OffSet = 32; {EACH CAPITAL LETTER COMES 32 POSITIONS EARLIER}
                 {IN TYPE CHAR THAN ITS LOWERCASE EQUIVALENT}
  begin
    if (Ch >= 'a') and (Ch <= 'z') then
      Capitalize := chr(ord(Ch) - OffSet)
    else
      Capitalize := Ch
  end;
```

When the function call passes a character to Capitalize, the value of the character is assigned to the formal parameter Ch. If Ch is a lowercase letter, the function returns the uppercase equivalent, which appears 32 elements earlier in type *char*. Otherwise, Capitalize returns the original value of Ch. The function *will always return a value*, no matter what character it is passed.

This last point is an important one. A function *must* return a value for every value it is passed. If you write a function that returns a value for only some of the actual parameters it can be passed, you incur the risk of a run-time error.

EXERCISE 4   What is the value of each of the following calls to Capitalize?

    a. `Capitalize('A')`

    b. `Capitalize('a')`

    c. `Capitalize('#')`

    d. `Capitalize('3')` ■

Note that Capitalize has a local constant, OffSet. Function declarations can include constants, variables, type definitions, and even procedures and other functions. Like a procedure, a function is a complete subprogram that can be every bit as complex as many programs.

Let's look at Capitalize in action. Suppose you have a summer job doing layout work for a publisher. Some of your work involves titles and headings, and, in this particular publisher's books, the first letter of each word in a title or heading is capitalized. Let's use the function we have just written in a program that capitalizes words for you.

Program TitlesAndHeadings reads in a text and then prints the text with the first letter of every word capitalized, as you can see in Figure 10.2. (As you examine **program** TitlesAndHeadings, remember to start by reading the main program.)

```
program TitlesAndHeadings;
{YOU TYPE A TITLE OR HEADING.}
{PROGRAM CAPITALIZES FIRST LETTER OF EVERY WORD.}
 var
  CharString : string;


 function Capitalize(Ch : char) : char;
  {FUNCTION CAPITALIZES LOWERCASE LETTERS AND LEAVES OTHERS UNCHANGED.}
  const
   OffSet = 32; {EACH CAPITAL LETTER COMES 32 POSITIONS EARLIER}
               {IN TYPE CHAR THAN ITS LOWERCASE EQUIVALENT}
 begin
  if (Ch >= 'a') and (Ch <= 'z') then
   Capitalize := chr(ord(Ch) - OffSet)
  else
   Capitalize := Ch
 end;
```

(continued)

```
procedure CapFirstLetters(var CharString : string);
{PROCEDURE CAPITALIZES FIRST LETTER OF EACH WORD IN CHARSTRING}
{AND LEAVES OTHER CHARACTERS UNCHANGED.}
 const
  Blank =' ';
 var
  StringLength,Position : integer;
begin
 StringLength := length(CharString);
 if (StringLength > 0) then
  begin
   CharString[1] := Capitalize(CharString[1]); {FUNCTION CALL}
   Position := 2;
   while (Position <= StringLength) do
    begin
     if (CharString[Position - 1] = Blank) then
      CharString[Position] := Capitalize(CharString[Position]);
     Position := Position + 1
    end
  end
end;

procedure EnterString(var CharString : string);
begin
 writeln('Type in a title or a heading, followed by a return.');
 write('>');
 readln(CharString)
end;

{MAIN PROGRAM}
begin
 EnterString(CharString);
 CapFirstLetters(CharString);
 writeln;
 writeln(CharString)
end.
```

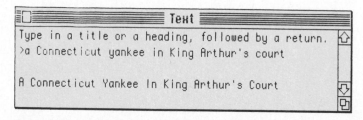

Figure 10.2   Typical output for **program** TitlesAndHeadings.

After you type in a string of characters, **procedure** CapFirstLetters is called with the actual parameter CharString. It capitalizes the first letter in the string, and thereafter it capitalizes any letter that is preceded by a blank. To capitalize a letter, it makes a call to **function** Capitalize.

Notice that **procedure** CapFirstLetters checks to determine whether CharString has length greater than zero before it goes to work capitalizing. This is necessary because you might type a carriage return immediately after the prompt. A carriage return would end the *readln* statement without filling the first cell of the string, so CharString would have length 0. When the procedure attempted to capitalize the character in CharString[1], it would find an undefined value, and a run-time error would occur.

One final reminder: The declaration for **function** Capitalize comes *before* the declaration for **procedure** CapFirstLetters. You would get an error if you declared them in the opposite order.

A function or procedure that is called by another function or procedure must be declared *before* the calling function or procedure. That is, it must be declared *above* the calling subprogram in the declaration part of the program.

EXERCISE 5   What would **program** TitlesAndHeadings do if Position were initialized to 1 instead of 2 in **procedure** CapFirstLetters?

Hint: The indexes for the components of a string variable begin at 1, not at 0. ■

10.6 Another Math Puzzle—Finding Perfect Numbers

Now let's look at a function with result type *integer*. We will use it in a program that does a calculation that has fascinated mathematicians for thousands of years. **Program** Perfect will tell you whether a number is a perfect number. A *perfect number* is a positive integer that's the sum of all its *proper divisors*. That is, it is the sum of all the numbers (except the number itself) that divide it evenly. Because the numbers 1, 2, and 3 are the proper divisors of 6, and the sum of 1, 2, and 3 is 6, 6 is a perfect number.

EXERCISE 6   What is the sum of the proper divisors of each of the following numbers?

a. 11
Answer: 1

b. 15
Answer: 9

c. 24
Answer: 36 ■

The ancient Greek mathematician Euclid knew about perfect numbers in the third century B.C., but mathematicians still do not completely understand them. Nobody knows whether a largest perfect number exists or whether there are infinitely many of them. And, though the perfect numbers that have been found so far are all even numbers, there may be odd ones that nobody knows about.

Program Perfect checks each of the numbers from 1 to 500 to determine whether it is a perfect number, and prints out any perfect numbers it finds. The function called ProperDivisorSum calculates the sums of the divisors of a number. Note that **function** ProperDivisorSum has its own private or local variables, Divisor and Sum. Sum accumulates the sum of the divisors of the value of the formal parameter Number. Then, in the last statement in the function declaration, the function identifier ProperDivisorSum is assigned the value of Sum, and this value becomes the value returned by the function.

```
program Perfect;
{PRINTS PERFECT NUMBERS FROM 1 TO 500}
 const
  Limit = 500;
 var
  Number : integer;

 function ProperDivisorSum(Number : integer) : integer;
 {CALCULATES THE SUM OF THE PROPER DIVISORS OF A NUMBER}
  var
   Divisor,Sum : integer;
 begin
  Divisor := 1;
  Sum := 0;
  while (Divisor <= Number div 2) do
   begin
    if (Number mod Divisor = 0) then
     Sum := Sum + Divisor;
    Divisor := Divisor + 1
   end;
  ProperDivisorSum := Sum
 end;
     {MAIN PROGRAM}
 begin
  for Number := 1 to Limit do
   if (Number = ProperDivisorSum(Number)) then
    writeln(Number : 1,' is a perfect number.')
 end.
```

For each value of Number, ProperDivisorSum checks only values that are less than or equal to half the value of Number. No number greater than this value can be a proper divisor. Even though this cuts in half the number of values to be checked, the program takes a long time to run. When execution is over, you will see in the Text window the four perfect numbers from 1 to 500: 1, 6, 28 and 496.

What would happen if, instead of using Sum to accumulate the sum of the divisors, we used the identifier ProperDivisorSum inside the function as though it were a regular variable and wrote the loop this way?

```
Divisor := 1;
ProperDivisorSum := 0;
while (Divisor <= Number div 2) do
 begin
  if Number mod Divisor = 0 then
   ProperDivisorSum := ProperDivisorSum + Divisor;
  Divisor := Divisor + 1
end;
```

It wouldn't work. ProperDivisorSum can't appear on the right side of an assignment statement inside the function declaration the way a regular variable can. For now, it can appear only on the left side of an assignment statement.

10.7 Passing an Array to a Function—Program ReportHottestDay

The functions we have created so far use characters or integers as parameters. Arrays can also be used as parameters. Let's see how this works.

Suppose you keep weather records and you want to find the hottest day in July. You can invent a function called HottestDay that will find the day with the highest temperature. The program passes the function a 31-component array with a real number temperature in each cell, and the function passes back the number of the cell that holds the highest temperature. (The principle here is the same one that we used in **program** LargestHousehold in Chapter 9.)

Here is the complete program:

```
program ReportHottestDay;
{YOU TYPE IN THE HIGHEST TEMPERATURE FOR EACH DAY IN JULY.}
{PROGRAM REPORTS THE HOTTEST DAY IN JULY.}
 type
  MonthlyTemp = array[1..31] of real;
 var
  JulyTemp : MonthlyTemp;
  Scorcher,HottestDay : integer;
```

(continued)

```
procedure EnterTemperatures(var Temp : MonthlyTemp);
 var
  Date : integer;
begin
 for Date := 1 to 31 do
   begin
   writeln('Type in the highest temperature on July ', Date : 1);
   write('>');
   readln(Temp[Date])
   end
end;


function FindHottestDay(Temperature : MonthlyTemp): integer;
 var
  Date : integer;
begin
 Date := 1;
 HottestDay := 1;
 while (Date <= 31) do
   begin
   if (Temperature[Date] > Temperature[HottestDay]) then
    HottestDay := Date;
   Date := Date + 1
   end;
 FindHottestDay := HottestDay
end;


{MAIN PROGRAM}
begin
 EnterTemperatures(JulyTemp);
 Scorcher := FindHottestDay(JulyTemp);
 writeln('The hottest day of the month was July ', Scorcher : 1)
end.
```

The formal parameters in a function declaration can be any type we have seen so far: *integer, real, char, boolean,* an enumerated type, an array, or a string (as long as string is not followed by a size value in brackets). However, there are restrictions on the result type of a function. A function's result type cannot be an array or a string with a size qualifier.

_____ 10.8 A Planning Example—Program LetterFrequency _____

Now that you understand how to create your own functions, we can examine how to use them in top-down programming. The next two programs depend on many nested functions and procedures to divide up programming tasks. Each program solves a complex character analysis problem.

Every writer has a characteristic style and uses a characteristic vocabulary. This fact can sometimes be used to solve mysteries about who wrote certain ancient texts. Even knowing how often an author uses each letter of the alphabet can sometimes help investigators decide whether that author wrote a particular work.

Let's write a program called **program** LetterFrequency that prints a line graph of the letter frequencies in a text you type in. Using procedures and functions, we can transform this complicated programming problem into a series of manageable subproblems.

Thinking

The program will read in a text. Then it will calculate the letter frequencies, and finally it will print out a line graph representing the frequency with which each letter shows up in the text.

Let's start by building a data table. We'll need an input variable of type **string**, which we'll call CharString. The output is a graph with 26 vertical lines representing the frequencies in the text of the letters of the alphabet.

It will help our analysis of the problem to identify the most important typical action the program will take: The program will examine a single character in a string. If that character is a letter, the program will record this occurrence in a scoreboard of the letter frequencies. This means we should develop our program around the scoreboard principle, and we must therefore include a scoreboard array in our data table.

The scoreboard array will be indexed by the letters of the alphabet. Each component will have an integer value that represents the number of times a particular letter appears in the text. Let's call the array variable Scoreboard and define an array type called LetterChart:

```
type
   LetterChart = array['A'..'Z'] of integer;
var
   Scoreboard : LetterChart;
```

When a *C* turns up in the text, the computer will update the scoreboard with this statement:

```
Scoreboard['C'] := Scoreboard['C'] + 1;
```

The main loop of the program will cycle through CharString character by character, and every time it comes to a letter, it will increment by 1 a cell in the scoreboard. Here is our data table.

―――――――――――――――――――――― DATA TABLE ――――――――――――――――――――――

Input Variable	Output Variable	Program Variable
CharString : **string**	a line graph	Scoreboard : LetterChart;

Constants	Formulas
none	none so far

Main Loop

cycles through Charstring, filling Scoreboard in the process

Type Definitions

type
   LetterChart = **array**['A'..'Z'] **of** integer;

――

Planning

Our first plan for **program** LetterFrequency is just a restatement of the problem.

Plan I
1. Enter the text.
2. Calculate the letter frequencies.
3. Print out a graph.

We can make each of these steps into a procedure. When we do, our second plan looks like this:

Plan II
1. EnterString
2. CalcFrequency
3. PrintGraph

When we calculate the letter frequencies, we will use a scoreboard array. Because of the way a scoreboard works, it's important to initialize the scoreboard before it is passed to a procedure. Here is the third version of our plan.

Plan III
1. EnterString
2. InitScoreboard
3. CalcFrequency
4. PrintGraph

Now let's clarify the procedures by writing their heading lines and doing paper checks

procedure EnterString(**var** CharString : **string**);

CharString with empty cells

procedure EnterString

CharString with full cells

procedure InitScoreboard(**var** Scoreboard : LetterChart);

Scoreboard with 26 empty cells

procedure InitScoreboard

Scoreboard with 26 cells containing 0's

procedure CalcFrequency(CharString : **string**;
        var Scoreboard : LetterChart)

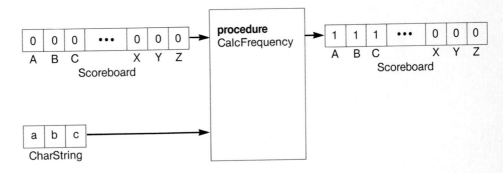

Scoreboard

procedure CalcFrequency

Scoreboard

CharString

procedure PrintGraph(Scoreboard : LetterChart; Scale : **integer**);

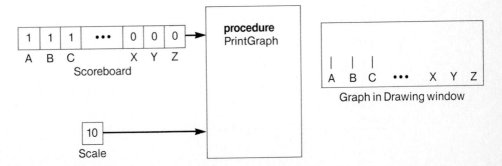

Scoreboard

procedure PrintGraph

Graph in Drawing window

Scale

Now that we have clarified the procedures, we can code the top level.

```
{MAIN PROGRAM}
begin
  ReadString(CharString);
  InitScoreboard(Scoreboard);
  CalcFrequency(CharString,Scoreboard);
  PrintGraph(Scoreboard,Scale)
end.
```

Next we need to go back and plan the procedures. EnterString and InitScoreboard are easy to code. So is PrintGraph: It's like the universal line graph procedure we wrote in Chapter 9, except that it graphs an array whose index is made up of letters instead of integers. **Procedure** CalcFrequency is the heart of the program, so let's plan it next.

Thinking About CalcFrequency

The inputs to **procedure** CalcFrequency are the string CharString and the array Scoreboard. The output is the variable parameter Scoreboard. Typically, CalcFrequency takes a character from CharString and, if the character is a letter, tallies that letter in the array Scoreboard. The tally is done by incrementing by 1 the component variable that has that letter as its index. So the main loop of CalcFrequency moves down the string, checking for letters and scoring them on the scoreboard.

To loop through CharString we'll need a control variable for the loop—Position—and we'll need an upper limit for the loop—StringLength = length(CharString). We can create the following data table for CalcFrequency.

_____ **DATA TABLE** _____

Input	Output	Program Variables
Scoreboard, CharString	Scoreboard	Position, StringLength

Types	Formulas	Constants
none	none	none

Loops

loop moves down CharString, letter by letter, tallying letters in Scoreboard

---

Planning Procedure CalcFrequency

Plan I

```
loop through CharString
    if CharString[Position] is a letter then
    record it in Scoreboard
```

Plan II

```
Position := 1;
StringLength := length(CharString);
while (Position <= StringLength) do
begin
    if CharString[Position] is a letter then
    add 1 to the appropriate component of Scoreboard
end;
```

We're almost there—except that we have to change all letters to uppercase, because the uppercase letters are the index type of Scoreboard. We can use **function** Capitalize to make this change.

In order to make the code more readable, we have added a new program variable called ThisChar, which we use to store the value of Capitalize—the capital-letter version of CharString[Position]. If ThisChar is a capital letter, not a blank space or a punctuation mark, we can use it as an index for Scoreboard, which has index type 'A'..'Z'.

Plan III

```
Position := 1;
StringLength := length(CharString);
while (Position <= StringLength) do
begin
    ThisChar := Capitalized version of CharString[Position];
    if ThisChar is a capital letter then
    add 1 to Scoreboard[This Char]
end;
```

Let's farm out to a function we'll call IsCapitalLetter the job of checking whether ThisChar is a capital letter. The function will return a boolean value. When IsCapitalLetter(ThisChar) is True, we'll increment the value of Scoreboard[ThisChar] by 1.

Now we are ready to code **procedure** CalcFrequency.

```
procedure CalcFrequency(CharString : string;
        var Scoreboard : LetterChart);
 var
  StringLength,Position : integer;
  ThisChar : char;
begin
 Position := 1;
 StringLength := length(CharString);
 while (Position <= StringLength) do
  begin
   ThisChar := CharString[Position];
   ThisChar := Capitalize(ThisChar);
   if IsCapitalLetter(ThisChar) then
    Scoreboard[ThisChar] := Scoreboard[ThisChar] + 1;
   Position := Position + 1
  end
end;
```

Next we need to code **function IsCapitalLetter**. The input for the function is a character, so let's call its formal parameter Ch. The output will be *boolean*. Here is the function declaration.

```
function IsCapitalLetter(Ch : Char) : boolean;
begin
 if (Ch >= 'A') and (Ch <= 'Z') then
  IsCapitalLetter := True
 else
  IsCapitalLetter := False
end;
```

And here is the full **program LetterFrequency**. See Figure 10.3 for sample output.

```
program LetterFrequency;
{TYPE TEXT OF UP TO 255 CHARACTERS. PROGRAM GRAPHS LETTER FREQUENCY.}
 const
  Scale = 10; {SCALING FACTOR FOR LINE GRAPH}
  Period ='.';
 type
  Letters = 'A'..'Z';
  LetterChart = array[Letters] of integer;
 var
  CharString : string;
  Scoreboard : LetterChart;
```

```pascal
procedure PrintGraph(Scoreboard : LetterChart;
        Scale : integer);
 const
  Bottom = 180;
  Separation = 16;
  CharWidth = 4; {USED TO CENTER LABEL UNDER LINE.}
 var
  Ch : Letters;
  HPos : integer; {HORIZONTAL POSITION OF LINE}
  Height : integer;
begin
 HPos := 0;
 for Ch := 'A' to 'Z' do
  begin
   HPos := Hpos + Separation;
   Height := Bottom - (Scale * Scoreboard[Ch]);
   drawline(HPos,Bottom,HPos,Height);
   moveto(HPos - CharWidth, Bottom + 15); {PLACE PEN UNDER LINE}
   drawchar(Ch) {WRITE LETTER LABEL}
  end;
 moveto(10,20);
 writedraw('LETTER FREQUENCY CHART')
end;



procedure EnterString(var CharString : string);
begin
 writeln('Type in a text of up to 255 characters.
         Then type a carriage return.');
 write('>');
 readln(CharString)
end;



procedure InitScoreboard(var Scoreboard : LetterChart);
 var
  Ch : char;
begin
 for Ch := 'A' to 'Z' do
  Scoreboard[Ch] := 0
end;
```

(continued)

```
function Capitalize(Ch : char) : char;
begin
 if (Ch )= 'a') and (Ch <= 'z')then
  Capitalize := chr(ord(Ch) - 32)
 else
  Capitalize := Ch
end;

function IsCapitalLetter(Ch : char) : boolean;
begin
 if (Ch )= 'A') and (Ch <= 'Z') then
  IsCapitalLetter := True
 else
  IsCapitalLetter := False
end;

procedure CalcFrequency(CharString : string;
        var Scoreboard : LetterChart);
 var
  StringLength,Position : integer;
  ThisChar : char;
begin
 Position := 1;
 StringLength := length(CharString);
 while(Position <= StringLength) do
  begin
   ThisChar := CharString[Position];
   ThisChar := Capitalize(ThisChar);
   if IsCapitalLetter(ThisChar) then
    Scoreboard[ThisChar] := Scoreboard[ThisChar] + 1;
   Position := Position + 1
  end
end;
 {MAIN PROGRAM}
begin
 EnterString(CharString);
 InitScoreboard(Scoreboard);
 CalcFrequency(CharString,Scoreboard);
 PrintGraph(Scoreboard,Scale)
end.
```

EXERCISE 7   Does the output of the program change if we make CharString a variable
parameter in **procedure CalcFrequency**? ■

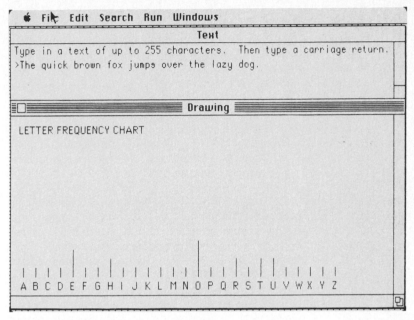

Figure 10.3 Typical output for **program** LetterFrequency.

Your private version of Pascal has begun to grow. It now includes three valuable functions: IsCapitalLetter, Between, and Capitalize.

10.9 Program WordFrequency

Let's look at a program that Mosteller and Wallace could have used in their study (see boxed discussion of disputed authorship on page 356). **Program** WordFrequency reads in a text of up to 255 characters that ends with a period. Then it reads in a single word and prints out the number of times this word occurs in the text as you can see in Figure 10.4.

Program WordFrequency consists of many nested functions and procedures. The top level does five separate jobs: **Procedure** EnterString reads in a text; **procedure** EnterWord reads in the word you want to search for; **function** ChangeToLowercase converts the input string to lowercase letters; **function** CountOccurrences counts the number of occurrences of the word in the string; and finally, a *writeln* statement prints out this count.

Disputed Authorship and Computers

Should the United States stay united? That question was almost answered "No!" in July of 1788, when New York had to vote on whether to accept the newly written American Constitution. Many New Yorkers were against acceptance, which would unite the former colonies in a federation of states. What could persuade them to vote in favor of federation? Perhaps newspaper articles and pamphlets could do the trick. So three prominent men—Alexander Hamilton, John Jay, and James Madison—decided to publish their arguments in favor of accepting the Constitution. The pieces (which were signed simply "Publius") were very well written, and there is no doubt that they influenced many people. New York voted "Yes" for federation.

All the pieces were finally put together in a book called *The Federalist.* Then arguments began. Which man had written which piece? It was agreed that Jay was the author of five and that Hamilton and Madison had collaborated on some. But there were twelve that caused dispute. Some people said Hamilton alone wrote them. Others gave the credit to Madison. The argument might have died if the papers themselves had not been important; lawyers have often cited them in cases that involve interpretations of the Constitution. But for almost 200 years there seemed to be no way to settle the question of authorship. Now computer studies have almost certainly given us the answer.

According to F. Mosteller and D. Wallace, identifiable patterns recur in most writers' use of certain common words, such as *on, of, enough, also, while,* and *upon.* So these two men wrote a program that analyzed material known to have been written by each of the *Federalist* authors. Hamilton, they discovered, used the word *upon* five times more often than did Madison. This and other clues led Mosteller and Wallace to conclude that the author of all twelve disputed papers was very probably Madison.

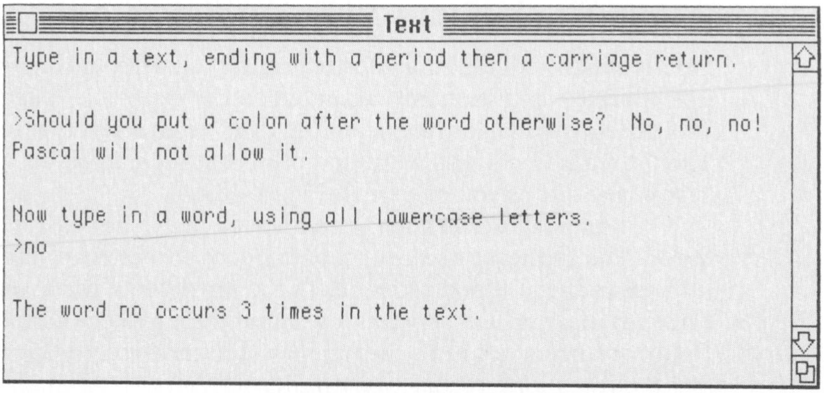

```
▤▢▤▤▤▤▤▤▤▤▤▤▤▤▤▤▤ Text ▤▤▤▤▤▤▤▤▤▤▤▤▤▤▤▤
Type in a text, ending with a period then a carriage return.     ⇧

>Should you put a colon after the word otherwise?  No, no, no!
Pascal will not allow it.


Now type in a word, using all lowercase letters.
>no


The word no occurs 3 times in the text.                          ⇩
                                                                 ⬒
```

Figure 10.4   Typical output for **program** WordFrequency.

```pascal
program WordFrequency;
{YOU TYPE IN A TEXT AND A WORD. PROGRAM REPORTS THE NUMBER}
{OF TIMES THE WORD OCCURS IN THE TEXT.}
 var
  Count : integer;
  Word : string;
  CharString : string;

 function Lowercase(Ch : char) : char;
 begin
  if (Ch )= 'A') and (Ch <= 'Z') then
   Lowercase := chr(ord(Ch) + 32)
  else
   Lowercase := Ch
 end;

 function IsALetter(Ch : char) : boolean;
 begin
  if ((Ch )= 'A') and ((Ch <= 'Z')) or
                      ((Ch )= 'a') and (Ch <= 'z')) then
   IsALetter := True
  else
   IsALetter := False
 end;

 function ChangeToLowercase(CharString : string) : string;
  var
   Position,StringLength : integer;
 begin
  StringLength := length(CharString);
  Position := 1;
  while (Position <= StringLength) do
   begin
    CharString[Position] := Lowercase(CharString[Position]);
    Position := Position + 1
   end;
  ChangeToLowercase := CharString
 end;

 function CountOccurrences(Word,CharString : string) : integer;
{THE DECLARATION PART OF FUNCTION COUNTOCCURRENCES HAS LOCAL}
{DECLARATIONS FOR THE NESTED FUNCTIONS OKONENDS AND MATCH.}
  var
   Position,StringLength,WordLength,Count : integer;
```

(continued)

```
function Match (Word : string;
        CharString : string;
        Position : integer) : boolean;
 var
  SubPiece : string;
begin
 SubPiece := copy(CharString,Position,length(Word));
 Match := (SubPiece = Word)
end;


function OkOnEnds(Word : string;
        CharString : string;
        Position : integer) : boolean;
{THE DECLARATION PART OF FUNCTION OKONENDS CONTAINS DECLARATIONS}
{FOR TWO NESTED FUNCTIONS -- OKONFRONT AND OKONBACK.}


 function OkOnFront(CharString : string;
         Position : integer) : boolean;
  const
   Blank = ' ';
 begin
  if (Position = 1) then
   OkOnFront := True
  else
   OkOnFront := (CharString[Position - 1] = Blank)
 end;


 function OkOnBack(CharString : string;
         PositionAfterWord : integer) : boolean;
 begin
  if IsALetter(CharString[PositionAfterWord]) then
   OkOnBack := False
  else
   OkOnBack := True
 end;


{BODY OF FUNCTION OKONENDS}
begin
 OkOnEnds := OkOnFront(CharString,Position) and
             OkOnBack(CharString, Position + length(Word))
end;
```

```
{BODY OF FUNCTION COUNTOCCURRENCES}
begin
 Count := 0;
 StringLength := length(CharString);
 WordLength := length(Word);
 Position := 1;
 while (Position <= (StringLength - WordLength)) do
  begin
   if (Match(Word,CharString,Position) and
       OkOnEnds(Word,CharString,Position)) then
    Count := Count + 1;
    Position := Position + 1
  end;
 CountOccurrences := Count
end;


procedure EnterWord(var Word : string);
begin
 writeln('Now type in a word, using all lowercase letters.');
 write('>');
 readln(Word);
 writeln
end;


procedure EnterString(var CharString : string);
begin
 writeln('Type in a text, ending with a period
          then a carriage return.');
 writeln;
 write('>');
 readln(CharString);
 writeln
end;
     {MAIN PROGRAM}
begin
 Count := 0;
 EnterString(CharString);
 EnterWord(Word);
 CharString := ChangeToLowercase(CharString);
 Count := CountOccurrences(Word, Charstring);
 writeln('The word ',Word,' occurs ',Count : 1,' times in the text.')
end.
```

The workhorse of the program is **function** CountOccurrences, which has several other functions nested inside it. Let's examine how it works. The following diagram illustrates the structure of the functions that are used inside **function** CountOccurrences.

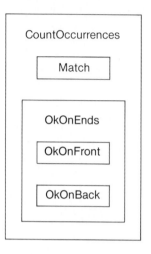

CountOccurrences "slides" the word along the string, looking for a match. But checking for a match is not done directly inside the body of the function. Instead, this job is handed to another function called Match with result type *boolean*. Match uses yet another function, the standard function *copy*, to extract the characters from the string that the word is checked against.

A successful match does not guarantee that the word has been found. If you are looking for the word *up*, you don't want to count the *up* in *upon*. So you must make sure the character after the *p* is not a letter. You must also rule out the *up* in *stirrup*, because it is not preceded by a blank.

CountOccurrences requires that the word match a piece of CharString *and* that the matching piece from CharString be both preceded by a blank space and not followed by a letter. Once again, **function** CountOccurrences passes along a job to another function. A function called OkOnEnds checks the character that comes before the matching substring and the character that comes after it.

Even **function** OkOnEnds has its own private functions, OkOnFront and OkOnBack. OkOnFront checks whether the string is preceded by a blank. And OkOnBack makes sure the string is not followed by a letter. (The program assumes that the last character in the input string is a period.)

When you write a function such as CountOccurrences, and you encounter a complex part that will require more than two or three statements, you can keep the body of the function from getting too complicated by packaging the complex part as a separate function or procedure subprogram. We've been able to keep the body of **function** CountOccurrences simple by farming out the two main pieces of its job to **functions** Match and OkOnEnds.

ChangeToLowercase is another function that gives part of its job to a simpler function. It takes in a string of characters and returns the string with all the letters changed to lowercase letters. As it loops through the characters, **function** ChangeToLowercase calls **function** Lowercase, which actually changes each capital letter to a lowercase letter.

We have placed the declaration for Lowercase *outside* **function** ChangeToLowercase in order to make Lowercase available to other functions and procedures in the program, as well as to ChangeToLowercase. Lowercase is a fairly general function; if we add to **program** WordFrequency, we might want to use it in our addition.

Note that the variable Count has both a *global* definition in the declaration part of the program and a *local* declaration inside **function** CountOccurrences. Global and local variable declarations work exactly the way global and local constant definitions do. When a variable is used inside a function or procedure, the Macintosh first checks locally for its value. If it can't find one, it looks up a level for a more global value. The variable Count is declared in the **function** CountOccurrences, so inside the function the Macintosh uses the local value of Count rather than the one that appears in the main program.

10.10 Sorting and Alphabetizing

An astronomer prints out a list of the meteorites found on earth this year, in order of increasing weight. A businesswoman brings up her list of employees and prints out their names in alphabetical order. A sports writer prints out a listing, in order, of the top 50 hitters in the major leagues.

In each case, a list of items has been *sorted*—that is, put in numerical or alphabetical order—by a computer program. Sorting is one of the most important operations in computing.

First we will examine how we can sort numbers. Then we'll write a program that puts a list of names in alphabetical order.

Suppose we want to sort five numbers in an array, putting the smallest first.

51	32	44	18	20
1	2	3	4	5

First we'll locate the smallest number in the array. It is 18, in position 4. Then we'll swap the numbers in positions 1 and 4.

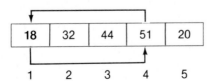

We have made some progress: The number 18 is in the right place. Now we can focus our attention on the part of the array that runs from position 2 through position 5. This is called a tail of the array. A *tail* can start anywhere in the array, and it goes all the way to the end.

If we look at the tail that starts at position 2, we find that the smallest number is 20, in position 5. So we exchange the number in position 2 for the 20 in position 5.

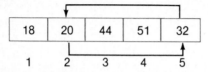

18	20	44	51	32
1	2	3	4	5

Now the first two numbers are in place. So we search once again for the smallest number, this time looking in the tail that starts at position 3. If we continue comparing numbers in the tail and swapping their positions, we can sort *any* list of numbers.

One of the great features of Pascal is that we can use exactly the same swapping technique for alphabetizing a list of words or names. Macintosh Pascal allows us to use relational operators to compare strings. For example, if you type in the Instant window

```
writeln('money' < 'monkey')
```

and click on Do It, the Macintosh will print True in the Text window because *e* comes before *k*. And if you try

```
writeln('bake' < 'baker')
```

it will also print True. MacPascal's rules for putting strings in alphabetical order using relational operators are similar to those used in telephone books or dictionaries. This way of ordering strings is called *lexicographic* ordering, and it is built into MacPascal. Note: 'Bill' < 'bill' and 'Bill' < 'aardvark', because 'B' < 'b' and 'B' < 'a' in type *char*.

Let's look at a program that alphabetizes names.

```
program NameSort;
{YOU READ IN 8 NAMES. PROGRAM PRINTS THEM IN ALPHABETICAL ORDER.}
  const
    Size = 8; {THE NUMBER OF NAMES TO BE SORTED}
  type
    ListOfWords = array[1..Size] of string[30];
  var
    NameList : ListOfWords;
```

```pascal
procedure EnterNames(var NameList : ListOfWords);
 var
  NameNumber : integer;
begin
 for NameNumber := 1 to Size do
  begin
   writeln('Type in a name.');
   write('>');
   readln(NameList[NameNumber]);
   writeln
  end
end;


procedure SortNames(var NameList : ListOfWords);
 var
  StartPosition,PositionOfNextName : integer;
{DECLARATION PART OF PROCEDURE SORTNAMES CONTAINS}
{FUNCTION NEXTNAMEINTAIL AND PROCEDURE SWAP.}


 function NextNameInTail(StartPosition : integer;
         NameList : ListOfWords) : integer;
 {RETURNS POSITION IN THE TAIL OF THE NAME THAT SHOULD COME NEXT}
  var
   Position : integer;
   PositionOfNextName : integer; {INDEX OF NAME THAT SHOULD COME}
                       {NEXT IN THE ALPHABETIZED ARRAY}
 begin
  PositionOfNextName := StartPosition; {ASSUME THAT THE NAME}
                {INDEXED BY STARTPOSITION SHOULD COME NEXT}
  Position := StartPosition + 1;
  while (Position <= Size) do
   begin
    if (NameList[Position] < NameList[PositionOfNextName]) then
     PositionOfNextName := Position;
    Position := Position + 1
   end;
  NextNameInTail := PositionOfNextName
 end;
```

(continued)

```
procedure Swap(StartPosition,PositionOfNextName : integer;
          var NameList : ListOfWords);
{USES THE SCRATCHPAD PRINCIPLE TO EXCHANGE NAME AT POSITION}
{STARTPOSITION WITH NAME AT POSITION POSITIONOFNEXTNAME}
  var
   TempName : string[30]; {THE SCRATCHPAD VARIABLE}
  begin
   TempName := NameList[StartPosition];
   NameList[StartPosition] := NameList[PositionOfNextName];
   NameList[PositionOfNextName] := TempName
  end;
  {BODY OF PROCEDURE SORTNAMES}
 begin
  for StartPosition := 1 to (Size - 1) do
   begin
    PositionOfNextName := NextNameInTail(StartPosition,NameList);
    Swap(StartPosition,PositionOfNextName,NameList)
   end
 end;


procedure PrintNames(NameList : ListOfWords);
  var
   NameNumber : integer;
 begin
  for NameNumber := 1 to Size do
   writeln(NameList[NameNumber])
 end;
     {MAIN PROGRAM}
 begin
  EnterNames(NameList);
  SortNames(NameList);
  PrintNames(NameList)
 end.
```

Program NameSort has been organized around three procedures: EnterNames, SortNames, and PrintNames. **Procedure** SortNames is the interesting part of the program, so let's see how it works.

After **procedure** EnterNames reads eight names into the array NameList, **procedure** SortNames is called and is passed this array of strings. Using a single **for** statement with two functions as its body, **procedure** SortNames arranges the names alphabetically. **Function** NextNameInTail finds the position of the name that should come next. And **function** Swap swaps the name at this position for the name at the beginning of the tail.

The loop in **procedure** SortNames advances the control variable StartPosition from 1 to Size – 1. With StartPosition equal to 1, **function** NextNameInTail locates the position of the name you want to put first. This value is stored in the variable PositionOfNextName. Then **function** Swap exchanges the name in that position for the name in StartPosition. This swap moves to position 1 the name that should appear first.

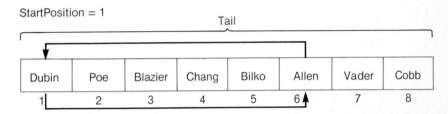

StartPosition = 1

Then StartPosition is advanced to 2, and the body of the loop in SortNames works on the tail of the array that begins at position 2. The position of the name that should come next is found. Then that name is swapped for the name in position 2.

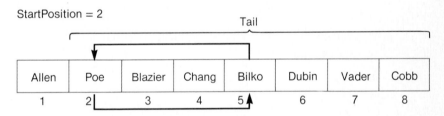

StartPosition = 2

Procedure SortNames continues in this fashion until the whole array has been sorted. **Procedure** PrintNames then prints the names in alphabetical order, as you can see in Figure 10.5.

Figure 10.5   Output for **program** NameSort.

EXERCISE 8   **a.** Why does the loop in the body of **procedure** SortNames have Size – 1 instead of Size as its upper limit?

b. Why is NameList a variable parameter in **procedure** Swap? ▬

10.11 A Brief Look at Recursion

Many problems in computing and mathematics can be solved by using the following general approach: *Find a solution to a smaller version of the problem. Then use this solution to solve the original problem.* When you solve a problem in this way, you have given a *recursive solution.* Recursive problem solving is easy to do in Pascal, and we will show you how it is done in a moment. But first let's look at a simple example of recursive problem solving from mathematics.

When you raise a number to a power, you multiply the number by itself some number of times:

$$x^n = \underbrace{x \times x \times x \times \cdots \times x}_{n \text{ times}}$$

You can calculate the value of a number raised to a power by using the following two equations.

$$x^0 = 1$$
$$x^n = x \times x^{n-1} \text{ if } n > 0$$

The two equations say, "If the exponent of x is 0, x^n is equal to 1. Otherwise, x^n equals x times x raised to the power $n - 1$."

We can turn these two equations into an algorithm that recursively calculates the value of a number raised to a power. To find a value for x^n, we calculate a value for x raised to a smaller power: x^{n-1}. That is, we create a simpler problem to solve. When the simpler problem is solved, we multiply its answer by x. This solves the original problem. Let's use two equations to calculate recursively the value of 5^3.

Because the exponent in 5^3 is greater than zero, the second equation applies, yielding

$$5^3 = 5 \times 5^2$$

We have made progress because the exponent is smaller: Now it's 2. Next we apply the second equation again, this time to the 5^2 term. We get

$$5^3 = 5 \times 5 \times 5^1$$

Now we use the second equation for the last time and get

$$5^3 = 5 \times 5 \times 5 \times 5^0$$

The first equation now applies, and yields

$$5^3 = 5 \times 5 \times 5 \times 1 = 5 \times 5 \times 5 = 5 \times 25 = 125$$

This method for calculating the value of a number raised to a power is called a *recursive method*, because instances of the problem that become progressively simpler *recur* over and over.

Now let's see how Pascal handles recursion. Unlike many other programming languages, Pascal allows this recursive style of calculation in a function. The resulting function is called a *recursive function*. We'll show you how this works by turning our two equations for calculating powers into a Pascal recursive function that does exponentiation inside a program called **program Expo**.

```
program Expo;
{YOU TYPE AN INTEGER AND A NON-NEGATIVE INTEGER POWER, THE EXPONENT.}
{PROGRAM PRINTS THE VALUE OF THE FIRST INTEGER RAISED TO THE POWER.}
 var
  X : integer; {THE NUMBER TO BE RAISED TO A POWER}
  N : integer; {THE EXPONENT}
  Answer : integer;

 function Power(X,N : integer) : integer;
 {CALCULATES RECURSIVELY THE VALUE OF A NUMBER RAISED TO A POWER}
 {IF THE EXPONENT IS NEGATIVE OR ZERO, POWER RETURNS THE VALUE 1.}
 begin
  if (N <= 0) then
   Power := 1
  else
   Power := X * Power(X,N - 1)
 end;
   {MAIN PROGRAM}
begin
 writeln('Type in an integer followed by a non-negative exponent');
 write('>');
 readln(X,N);
 Answer := Power(X,N);
 writeln;
 writeln(Answer)
end.
```

When **program** Expo calculates the value of 5^3, it makes this function call: Power(5,3). Inside the function declaration, X will be equal to 5 and N equal to 3. Because N is positive, the **else** part of the body of the function is followed. The **else** part says that the value of Power is $5 \times$ Power(5,2).

We have something new here. Inside the function, the name of the function appears on the *right* side of an assignment statement. Power has actually called itself. This is a *recursive* function call.

What happens when Power calls itself? The original function call, Power(5,3), isn't over yet; it has just been suspended. The answer to the original call will be 5 times the result of the internal call to Power. Note that the internal function call now has the actual parameters 5 and 2.

Now Power(5,2) is computed. Again the **else** part of the **if** statement is executed, and the function call Power(5,2) is also suspended. It is set aside with an answer equal to 5 times the result of another computation: Power(5,1). In the same way, Power(5,1) is executed, and then suspended, with a value of $5 \times$ Power(5,0).

We are almost done. Power(5,0) returns a definite value: 1. So we can now calculate Power(5,1). The value of Power(5,1) is $5 \times$ Power(5,0) $= 5 \times 1 = 5$. Power(5,2) can now be calculated. Its value is $5 \times$ Power(5,1) $= 25$. Finally, we can compute Power(5,3). Its value is $5 \times$ Power(5,2) $= 125$.

As you can see, calculation by recursion has a different flavor from the looping techniques we have seen so far. Many problems that can be solved with looping can also be solved with recursive functions and recursive procedures. And, because the recursive description of a problem is often especially clear and succinct, a recursive solution can be very pleasing. On the other hand, recursive functions and procedures often require extra memory when they are executed, and this can be a problem if you aren't careful.

10.12 Random Numbers

Suppose you open the Instant window and type

```
writeln(random)
```

When you click on Do It, the Macintosh chooses an element of type *integer* at random. That is, it chooses a number from −32767 to 32767. Then it prints its choice in the Text window. *Random*, like *button*, is a built-in function with no parameters. Its result type is *integer*.

If you click on Do It ten times in a row, you will get a list of ten numbers chosen at random, such as that shown in Figure 10.6.

What does "random" *really* mean? You can't actually say that a single number, such as 5, is random. But you can talk about a random sequence. A sequence

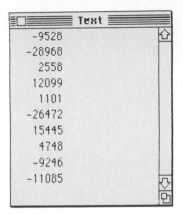

Figure 10.6   Ten random numbers produced by the standard function random.

is random when the numbers in the sequence have nothing to do with each other:
Looking at the first few numbers of a random sequence doesn't help you guess the
next number. This sequence is definitely *not* random:

    10,20,30,40

If you cover up the last number and ask a friend to guess what it is, you will almost certainly hear the right answer.

Random numbers have many applications in computing. In the rest of this
chapter we will tell you about three of them. First we will talk about using random numbers to simulate events in real life. Then we'll look at "Monte Carlo"
methods, which are used for estimating the values of important numbers in
mathematics. Finally, we'll show how random numbers can be used for program testing.

10.13 Simulating a Coin Toss

Random numbers are often used in computing to help perform *simulations* of
events that occur in real life. Suppose you want to simulate a coin toss. Because
the **function** *random* produces numbers at random, it is just as likely to produce
an odd number as it is to produce an even number. When you compute

    random **mod** 2

you will get 0 if the number is even and 1 if the number is odd. Therefore (*random* **mod** 2) is just as likely to give you a 0 as a 1. If we use 1 to represent heads
and 0 to represent tails, (random **mod** 2) simulates a coin toss. This is what we've
done in **program** TossOneCoin.

```
program TossOneCoin;
{PROGRAM SIMULATES THE TOSS OF A COIN. YOU TYPE IN FLIP}
{AND THE PROGRAM REPORTS EITHER HEADS OR TAILS.}
 type
  Commands = (Flip,Quit);
  Toss = (Heads,Tails);
 var
  Command : Commands;
  Number : integer;
  TossResult : Toss;

 procedure EnterCommand(var Command : Commands);
 begin
  writeln('Type in a command: Flip or Quit.');
  write('>');
  readln(Command)
 end;

 procedure PrintResult(TossResult : Toss);
 begin
  writeln(TossResult);
  writeln
 end;
   {MAIN PROGRAM}
begin
 EnterCommand(Command);
 while (Command <> Quit) do
  begin
   Number := random mod 2;
   case Number of
    0 :
     TossResult := Tails;
    1 :
     TossResult := Heads
   end;
   PrintResult(TossResult);
   EnterCommand(Command)
  end
end.
```

When you run **program** TossOneCoin, the prompt asks you to type in either *Flip* or *Quit*. If you type *Flip, random* **mod** 2 is calculated. When a 0 is returned, the variable TossResult is assigned Tails. When a 1 is returned, TossResult is assigned Heads. In either case, the result is printed and you are prompted to give another command—Flip or Quit.

The principle we used to simulate coin flipping also works for simulating a throw of dice. Because dice have six sides, we need an expression that will produce each of the numbers 1 through 6 with equal likelihood. The expression *random* **mod** 6 produces the numbers 0, 1, 2, 3, 4, and 5 with equal likelihood, so

```
(random mod 6) + 1
```

is equally likely to return any value from among the values 1, 2, 3, 4, 5, and 6.

EXERCISE 9   **a.** Write an expression that chooses at random a number from 1 to 3.
     Answer: (*random* **mod** 3) + 1

    b. Give an expression that chooses at random a number from 10 to 20.

    c. What range of values can Number hold after the following assignment statement has been executed?
      `Number := (random/32768)`
    Answer: −1 < Number < +1

    d. What range of values can Number hold after the following assignment statement has been executed?
      `Number := abs(random)/32768` ▬

A Coin Toss Experiment

Let's write a program that does a more ambitious simulation using random numbers. **Program** CoinFlip uses the **function** *random* to simulate tossing 8 coins some large number of times—say 1000. Each time the 8 coins are tossed, we will get between no heads and 8 heads. The program will keep track of the number of times out of the 1000 tosses that we get no heads, 1 heads, 2 heads, and so on. The program's output will be a graph that displays how the tosses have come out.
  We can obtain the theoretical probabilities for the outcomes of the 8 coin tosses from row 8 of Pascal's triangle, which is

  1 8 28 56 70 56 28 8 1

Each of the 8 coin flips has 2 possible outcomes: heads or tails. So each time you flip 8 coins, $2 \times 2 \times 2 \times 2 \times 2 \times 2 \times 2 \times 2 = 256$ outcomes are possible. The probability distribution has the following profile:

  0 heads = 1/256 = .0039 = .39%
  1 heads = 8/256 = .0312 = 3.12%
  2 heads = 28/256 = .1094 = 10.94%
  3 heads = 56/256 = .2187 = 21.87%
  4 heads = 70/256 = .2734 = 27.34%
  5 heads = 56/256 = .2187 = 21.87%
  6 heads = 28/256 = .1094 = 10.94%
  7 heads = 8/256 = .0312 = 3.12%
  8 heads = 1/256 = .0039 = .39%

This table shows that, when you flip 8 coins, you should get no heads and 8 tails about .39% of the time and that you should get 4 heads and 4 tails about 27% of the time. If you flip 8 coins 1000 times, you can expect this output profile on average:

0 heads = .0039 × 1000 ~ 4 times
1 heads = .0312 × 1000 ~ 31
2 heads = .1094 × 1000 ~ 109
3 heads = .2187 × 1000 ~ 219
4 heads = .2734 × 1000 ~ 273
etc.

In other words, you should get no heads and all tails about 4 times, and you should get 4 heads and 4 tails about 273 times. Figure 10.7 shows a graph of the theoretical profile.

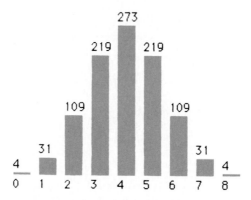

Figure 10.7   The approximate theoretical profile of the outcome of flipping 8 coins 1000 times.

Now let's look at **program** CoinFlip. When you run it, you type in the number of times you want to toss 8 coins. The program simulates these tosses, and then graphs the distribution of the number of heads.

The body of **program** CoinFlip consists of five statements that divide the program into five subjobs. First, EnterTossCount reads in the number of tosses you want to make and stores this value in the variable TossCount. Then InitScoreboard initializes the scoreboard array that tallies the result of each toss. FlipAndTally does the real work of the program: It tosses 8 coins TossCount number of times, and it records the result of each round of 8 tosses in the scoreboard. Then **function** CalcScale calculates a scaling factor for the bar graph output, and finally **procedure** PrintGraph draws the graph in the Drawing window. Here is **program** CoinFlip.

```pascal
program CoinFlip;
{YOU READ IN HOW MANY TIMES YOU WANT 8 COINS TO BE FLIPPED. PROGRAM}
{PRINTS GRAPH OF THE NUMBER OF TIMES THE OUTCOME WAS NO HEADS,}
{1 HEADS, 2 HEADS, AND SO ON UP TO 8 HEADS.}
 const
  NumberOfCoins = 8;
 type
  Chart = array[0..NumberOfCoins] of integer;
 var
  TossCount : integer;
  Scoreboard : Chart;
  Scale : real;
 function RandomToss(NumberOfCoins : integer) : integer;
  var
   CoinNumber,Count,Flip : integer;
 begin
  Count := 0;
  for CoinNumber := 1 to NumberOfCoins do
   begin
    Flip := (random mod 2);
    if (Flip = 1) then {FLIP = 1 MEANS THE OUTCOME WAS HEADS}
     Count := Count + 1 {ADD ONE TO THE NUMBER OF HEADS}
   end;
  RandomToss := Count
 end;
 procedure PrintGraph(Scale : real;
         Numbers : Chart);
  const
   Bottom = 180;
   Thickness = 20;
   Separation = 10;
  var
   Top,Left,Right,Height,BarNumber : integer;
 begin
  Right := 0;
  for BarNumber := 0 to NumberOfCoins do
   begin
   {DRAW BARS}
    Height := round(Numbers[BarNumber] * Scale);
    Top := Bottom - Height;
    Left := Right + Separation;
    Right := Left + Thickness;
    paintrect(Top,Left,Bottom,Right);
   {DRAW LABELS}
    moveto(Left, Top - 5);
    writedraw(Numbers[BarNumber] : 1);
    moveto(Left,Bottom + 13);
    writedraw(BarNumber : 1)
   end
 end;
```

(continued)

```pascal
procedure EnterTossCount(var TossCount : integer);
begin
 writeln('Type in the number of times you want ',NumberOfCoins : 1,
         ' coins to be tossed.');
 write('>');
 readln(TossCount)
end;
procedure InitScoreboard(var Scoreboard : Chart);
 var
  Outcome : integer;
begin
 for Outcome := 0 to NumberOfCoins do
  Scoreboard[Outcome] := 0
end;
procedure FlipAndTally(TossCount : integer;
        var Scoreboard : chart);
 var
  TossNumber,Outcome : integer;
begin
 TossNumber := 1;
 while (TossNumber <= TossCount) do
  begin
   Outcome := RandomToss(NumberOfCoins);
   Scoreboard[Outcome] := Scoreboard[Outcome] + 1;
   TossNumber := TossNumber + 1
  end
end;
function CalcScale(Scoreboard : Chart) : real;
 const
  CenterBar = 150; {THE HEIGHT OF THE CENTER BAR WILL ALWAYS BE 150}
 var
  MidPosition,MiddleValue : integer;
begin
 MidPosition := (NumberOfCoins div 2);
 MiddleValue := Scoreboard[MidPosition];
 if (MiddleValue <> 0) then
  CalcScale := CenterBar / MiddleValue
 else
  CalcScale := 0.0
end;
  {MAIN PROGRAM}
begin
 EnterTossCount(TossCount);
 InitScoreboard(Scoreboard);
 FlipAndTally(TossCount,Scoreboard);
 Scale := CalcScale(Scoreboard);
 PrintGraph(Scale,Scoreboard)
end.
```

374

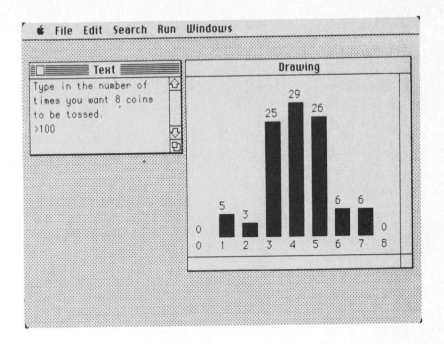

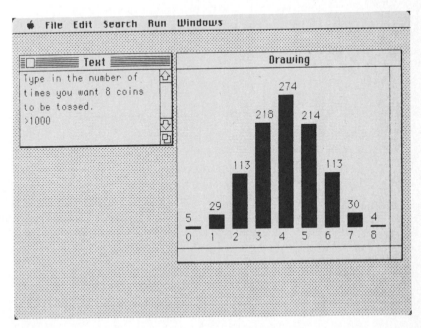

Figure 10.8 Two sample outputs for **program** CoinFlip.

Look carefully at **function** RandomToss. It returns a value from 0 to 8. This figure represents the number of heads in a round of 8 tosses. RandomToss uses a **for** loop to do 8 coin flips and counts the number of heads that turn up. Note that the values 0 through 8 are *not* equally likely to occur. **Function** RandomToss will return 4's much more often than 0's or 8's. This is because, according to the laws of probability, we are likely to get 4 heads about 27% of the time, whereas we expect no heads or 8 heads only about .39% of the time.

In **program** CoinFlip we have a tougher scaling problem than in previous graphing programs. If we had used a constant value for the scaling factor, as we have done before, the bars would be too tall when we flip the coins 1000 times or too small when we flip them 100 times. So we have created **function** CalcScale to make the bars about the same height no matter how many times the coins are tossed.

Function CalcScale makes the center bar 150 units high no matter how many coins are tossed. Then it returns a value using the following formula:

```
CenterBar/MiddleValue
```

This value is assigned to the variable Scale in the main program, and Scale is then passed to **procedure** PrintGraph. PrintGraph uses Scale to adjust the heights of the bars. Figure 10.8 shows two examples of output from **program** CoinFlip, each with a different number of coin flips.

Each time you run the program, you get a slightly different distribution of heads and tails. The more times you flip the coins, the more closely the graph should resemble the graph of the theoretical probability of getting from no heads to 8 heads (Figure 10.7).

10.14 The Monte Carlo Method

Monte Carlo applications have nothing to do with gambling. They involve using random numbers and the laws of chance to calculate some result in mathematics—square roots, for example.

Suppose we want to calculate the square root of 2. We know that the square root of 2 lies between 1 and 2, because 1 squared equals 1, which is less than 2, and 2 squared equals 4, which is greater than 2. Suppose we pick at random 1000 values between 1 and 2. Imagine that each number is a point that lies between 1.0 and 2.0 on a line.

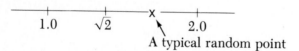

A typical random point

Somewhere along the line there is a point that represents the square root of 2. If we take any one of the 1000 points, we can tell, just by squaring its value, whether it falls to the left or to the right of the square root of 2. For example, $(1.5)^2 = 2.25$, so 1.5 is greater than the square root of 2.

Now here's the interesting part: If the 1000 numbers are chosen truly at random, they should be distributed *uniformly* between 1 and 2. Therefore, we should get a reasonable estimate for the square root of 2 from the proportion of the 1000 random values that lie to the left of the square root of 2. The square root of 2 is about 1.414. If we pick 1000 numbers at random between 1 and 2, on average 414 of them should fall to the left of the root.

Figure 10.9 shows the program that estimates the square root of 2 using random numbers. Each time we run the program, we will probably get a slightly different answer, because the random numbers will be different. If we change the constant Sample to a number larger than 1000, the program will take longer to run, but the program's estimate of the square root of 2 should be more accurate.

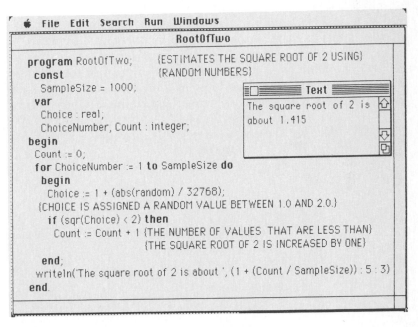

Figure 10.9   Program RootOfTwo and its output.

10.15 Estimating Pi with the Monte Carlo Method

We can use random numbers to do a Monte Carlo application that is even more intriguing—estimating the value of π. We'll do this problem using random points. If we choose two numbers between 0 and 199, we can put them together and interpret the pair as the random point (H, V).

```
H := random mod 200;
V := random mod 200
```

Now suppose we draw a quarter-circle with radius 200 in the Drawing window.

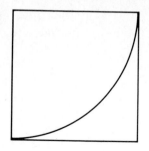

The area of the quarter-circle is $1/4\pi \times \text{Radius}^2 = 1/4 \times \pi \times (200)^2 = 10,000\pi$. The area of the standard Drawing window, which is a square 200 units on a side, is 40,000, so the ratio of the area of the quarter-circle to the area of the square is $\pi/4$. When we choose points at random inside the square, on average $\pi/4$ of them should fall inside the arc of the circle.

We can approximate the value of $\pi/4$ by dividing the number of random points inside the arc by the total number of points in the Drawing window. To get an estimate for π, we multiply this value by 4.

A randomly chosen point (H,V) lies inside the quarter circle when the distance from that point to point $(0,0)$—the center of the circle—is less than or equal to the radius of the circle. To find this distance we can use the distance formula we derived in Section 4.14. A point (H,V) lies inside the arc if $\sqrt{H^2 + V^2}$ $\langle= 200$. But there is no need to take the square root: We may as well just ask whether $H^2 + V^2 \langle= 40,000$.

Here is **program** CalculatePi. Its output is shown in Figure 10.10.

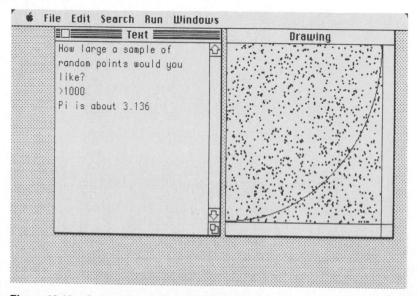

Figure 10.10   Output for **program** CalculatePi.

```pascal
program CalculatePi;
{ESTIMATES THE VALUE OF PI USING RANDOM NUMBERS}
 var
  H,V,Score,SampleSize,Test : integer;
  SqrOfDistance : longint; {SQUARE OF DISTANCE FROM (H,V) TO (0,0)}
  PiOverFourRatio : real;

 procedure FrameCircle(X,Y,Radius : integer);
 begin
  frameoval(Y - Radius,X - Radius,Y + Radius,X + Radius)
 end;

 procedure MakePoint(H,V : integer);
 begin
  paintcircle(H,V,1)
 end;

 procedure ReadSampleSize(var SampleSize : integer);
 begin
  writeln('How large a sample of random points would you like?');
  write('>');
  readln(SampleSize)
 end;
     {MAIN PROGRAM}
 begin
 ReadSampleSize(SampleSize);
 FrameCircle(0,0,200);
 Score := 0;
 for Test := 1 to SampleSize do
  begin
   H := random mod 200;
   V := random mod 200;
   MakePoint(H,V);
   SqrOfDistance := H * H + V * V;
   if (SqrOfDistance <= 40000) then
    Score := Score + 1
  end;
 PiOverFourRatio := Score / SampleSize;
 writeln('Pi is about ',4 * PiOverFourRatio : 5 : 3)
 end.
```

There are much better ways to estimate π, and Monte Carlo estimates of the number are rarely done. The Monte Carlo method is most often used when a problem is so "messy" and uncommon that no one has worked out a more effective way to find a solution.

___ 10.16 Using Random Numbers to Test Programs _____

There is a third major use for random numbers in computer programming. Suppose you are part of a programming team that is developing a new piece of software. You have been assigned the job of testing the program.

As program tester, your chores are different from those of the coders on your software development team. They write code; you take their code and try to "break" it. That is, you try to get the program to crash, to give wrong answers, to go into an infinite loop, or to perform poorly in any way you can think of. You are a detective snooping for bugs.

There are some obvious, crude things you can do to try to make bugs show up. For example, you can type with your elbows. If the program responds with

```
Bad command, try again.
```

it's doing fine. If it crashes, you know it's not idiot-proof.

You can also try the code out on extreme values. If the program prints the prompt

```
Type in a real number that is greater than 10.0
```

for example, try typing 10.0001 and see what happens. Programs often fail when you give them values that are at or near the upper or lower limits of allowable inputs.

Another effective way to test a program is to use a barrage of random values as test data. Let's see how to use random data to test a sorting procedure.

Suppose your software team has asked you to test a procedure called **procedure** SortList, which puts in order, from smallest to largest, a list of integers that have been stored in an array. You must determine whether the procedure (which is similar to the alphabetizing procedure in **program** NameSort) reliably puts numbers in order.

You can test **procedure** SortList by inserting it into a program that will pass it an array of random numbers. An interactive program called **program** SortTest will do the job. When you run it, you type in the number of times you want to test the procedure. For each test, the program passes **procedure** SortList a list of 6 random numbers to be sorted. After the sort has been performed, another procedure checks whether it was done successfully.

```
program SortTest;
{YOU READ IN THE NUMBER OF TIMES YOU WANT TO TEST PROCEDURE}
{SORTLIST. FOR EACH TEST PROGRAM GENERATES 6 RANDOM NUMBERS FOR}
{SORTLIST TO TEST AND REPORTS WHETHER THE SORT WAS SUCCESSFUL.}
  const
    Size = 6; {THE NUMBER OF VALUES TO BE SORTED}
  type
    Numbers = array[1..Size] of integer;
  var
    TestCount,TestNumber : integer;
    NumberList : Numbers;
```

(continued)

```pascal
procedure GenerateList(var NumberList : Numbers);
 var
  Position : integer;
begin
 for Position := 1 to Size do
  NumberList[Position] := random
end;


procedure SortList(var NumberList : Numbers);
 var
  StartPosition, PositionOfNextNumber : integer;
{DECLARATION PART OF PROCEDURE SORTLIST CONTAINS}
{FUNCTION NEXTNUMBERINTAIL AND PROCEDURE SWAP.}


 function NextNumberInTail(StartPosition : integer;
          NumberList : Numbers) : integer;
{RETURNS POSITION OF THE NUMBER IN THE TAIL THAT SHOULD COME NEXT}
  var
   Position,PositionOfNextNumber : integer;
 begin
  PositionOfNextNumber := StartPosition;
  Position := StartPosition + 1;
  while (Position <= Size) do
   begin
    if (NumberList[Position] < NumberList[PositionOfNextNumber]) then
     PositionOfNextNumber := Position;
    Position := Position + 1
   end;
  NextNumberInTail := PositionOfNextNumber
 end;


procedure Swap(StartPosition,PositionOfNextNumber : integer;
          var NumberList : Numbers);
{USES THE SCRATCHPAD PRINCIPLE TO EXCHANGE THE NUMBER AT POSITION}
{STARTPOSITION WITH THE NUMBER AT POSITION POSITIONOFNEXTNUMBER}
  var
   TempNumber : integer; {THE SCRATCHPAD VARIABLE}
 begin
  TempNumber := NumberList[StartPosition];
  NumberList[StartPosition] := NumberList[PositionOfNextNumber];
  NumberList[PositionOfNextNumber] := TempNumber
 end;
```

(continued)

```
{BODY OF PROCEDURE SORTLIST}
begin
 for StartPosition := 1 to (Size - 1) do
  begin
   PositionOfNextNumber := NextNumberInTail(StartPosition,NumberList);
   Swap(StartPosition,PositionOfNextNumber,NumberList)
  end
end;
procedure PrintList(LineLabel : string;
        NumberList : Numbers);
 var
  Position : integer;
begin
 write(LineLabel : 15);
 for Position := 1 to Size do
  begin
   write(NumberList[Position])
  end;
 writeln
end;
procedure CheckList(NumberList : Numbers);
 var
  Position : integer;
  OkSoFar : boolean; {FLAG}
begin
 OkSoFar := True;
 Position := 1;
 while (Position <= (Size - 1)) and OkSoFar do
  begin
   if (NumberList[Position] > NumberList[Position + 1]) then
    OkSoFar := False;
   Position := Position + 1
  end;
 if OkSoFar then
  begin
   writeln;
   writeln('The list of ',Size : 1,
           ' numbers has been sorted successfully.');
   writeln
  end
 else
  begin
   writeln;
   writeln('The list of ',Size : 1,
           ' numbers has not been sorted properly');
   writeln('There is a bug in procedure SortList');
   writeln
  end
end;
```

```
{MAIN PROGRAM}
begin
 writeln('How many times would you like to test procedure SortList?');
 write('>');
 readln(TestCount);
 for TestNumber := 1 to TestCount do
  begin
   GenerateList(NumberList);
   PrintList('test list:',NumberList);
   SortList(NumberList);
   PrintList('sorted list:',NumberList);
   CheckList(NumberList)
  end
end.
```

The main loop of **program** SortTest consists of five procedure calls. First **procedure** GenerateList generates 6 random values and copies them into the array NumberList. Then **procedure** PrintList prints this array of random numbers. Next **procedure** SortList puts in order the numbers in the array. Then PrintList is called again. This time it prints the array of sorted numbers. Finally **procedure** CheckList checks whether the array has been sorted correctly and reports the result. Figure 10.11 shows some typical output for **program** TestSort.

If you do a large number of test runs and the lists of numbers have all been properly arranged, you can conclude only that **procedure** SortList probably works right. But using random numbers to test a program is not 100% foolproof. To be absolutely certain that **procedure** SortList works correctly, you would need to prove the kind of theorem we talked about in Section 8.7.

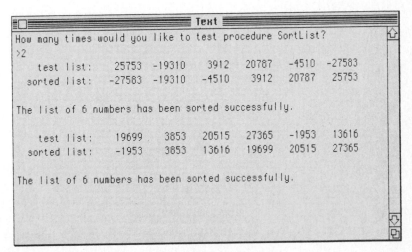

Figure 10.11   Sample output for **program** TestSort.

We have now seen three of the most important applications of random numbers in computer programming: simulations, Monte Carlo mathematics, and program testing. Random-number techniques are one of the most fascinating areas in computing. You can spend a lifetime exploring them and never lose interest.

TEST YOURSELF

1. What are the values of the following expressions?
   a. ('up' < 'down')
   b. ('fish' = 'Fish')
   c. ('McDonald' > 'MacDonald')
2. What does a function do?
3. Give another name for the argument of a function.
4. Can a function have no arguments?
5. What restrictions are there on the type of a formal parameter for a function?
6. What restrictions are there on a function's result type?
7. Where in a program should you put the declaration for a function?
8. What is a recursive function call?
9. How does Pascal evaluate a nested function call?
10. Write an expression that will produce a number from 100 to 200 at random.
11. What are three important uses for random numbers in computing?
12. What is a Monte Carlo method?

PROBLEMS

1. Write a function called OneOver that takes an integer argument and returns a real value, the reciprocal of the input value. For example, OneOver(4) = 0.25. On input 0, have your function declaration return 0.0 as the value of OneOver. Then use the function in a program that adds 1/2, 1/4, 1/8, and so forth, up to 1/256. What do you think the answer will be?
2. Write a function called InsideCircle that tests whether a point lies inside a circle. Then write an interactive program that uses the function. The program should read in a point, then read in a circle (a point and a radius), and then report whether the point is inside the circle.
3. Write **function** CompoundInterest, which takes as input a principal, an interest rate, and a number of years and returns the amount of money accumulated during the specified time interval. Use the function in an interactive program that reads in a principal, an interest rate, and a number of years and prints out the money accumulated. Then the program asks you to quit or to submit another set of figures.

4. Write a function called IPower that raises a real number to some integer power. For example, IPower(2.0,5) = 32.0. *Note*: Any number raised to the power 0 is 1, so IPower(10.0,0) = 1.0.

5. The factorial function is defined this way: factorial(0) = 1, and factorial(N) = N × (N − 1) × (N − 2) × . . . × 2 × 1, where N ⟩ 1. Factorial(5) = 5 × 4 × 3 × 2 × 1. Write a recursive function that calculates the factorial function in Pascal. Then put it inside an interactive program and test it.

6. Now write and test a Pascal function that calculates factorial without using recursion.

7. Two positive integers are *amicable* numbers if the sum of the proper divisors of the first number equals the second number and if the sum of the proper divisors of the second number equals the first number. Find all amicable pairs in which one of the numbers is less than or equal to 1200.

8. Write a program like **program** CoinFlip that simulates tossing dice.

9. Write a program that reads in ten real numbers, puts them in numerical order from largest to smallest, and prints the sorted list of numbers.

10. The *integer square root* of a positive integer is the integer part of the number's square root: IntegerSqrt(10) = 3, and IntegerSqrt(16) = 4. *Without* using the *sqrt* function, create a function that calculates the integer square root of a positive integer. Then put the function inside an interactive program and test it.

11. Write a function that calculates batting averages.

12. Write **program** RandomRollBall, which races six balls across the Drawing window.

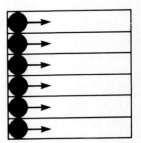

The program chooses at random which ball to advance next. Announce the winner in the Text window.

13. Write a program called LetterPairs, which works this way: You type in a text and a sequence of two letters, and the program reports how many times in the text the two letters appear in sequence.

14. Redesign **function** RandomToss in **program** CoinFlip so that the coin that is tossed is biased and will come up heads two times out of three, on the average. Be sure to modify CalcScale so that your graph will remain inside the Drawing window.

15. Use random numbers to estimate the cube root of 10.

16. To get out of the rain, a drunk steps into the opera house and ends up in the cloakroom just as a performance is ending. He cheerfully hands out umbrellas at random to the opera buffs (they all brought umbrellas). Mathematicians have shown that *no one* will get his or her own umbrella about 37% of the time, no matter how many people are at the opera (as long as there are at least a few). Use the *random* function to verify this surprising figure experimentally.

(*Hint*: Write an interactive program. You type in a number of trials, say 100, and the program should simulate the drunk's umbrella handout 100 times. Then the program should report the number of times no one got his or her umbrella. Use a global constant called NumberOfPatrons to stand for the number of patrons attending the opera.)

Advanced Topics: The Mouse, Records, and Files

11

Now we are ready to look at several advanced topics. We will begin with a large program that's based on the Macintosh application program MacPaint. Our program, which is called MiniPaint, allows you to draw pictures with the mouse.

In this chapter we will also discuss a new way to organize information called a record type. A variable of type *record* can have several components, and the components can be of different types.

Finally we will discuss files. A *file* is a collection of data that a program stores on a disk rather than in main memory. Files allow you to save permanently information that you create or organize in a program. The data remain intact even when the Macintosh is turned off.

11.1 Program MiniPaint

Program MiniPaint is an interactive program that uses the mouse and a menu of labeled rectangles to control program execution. The program brings together several important topics that we have developed over the last few chapters: functions and procedures, the mouse, and the notion of a *private* Pascal—a personal collection of functions and procedures that you can recycle in any program you write. It's important that you study this program carefully. We will reuse parts of it later in the chapter.

Program MiniPaint creates its own menu. The menu, which is shown in Figure 11.1, consists of rectangles at the top of the Drawing window labeled with MiniPaint commands—Quit, Circle, and MakeLine. When you run MiniPaint, you choose a command by clicking the mouse button inside one of the rectangular menu boxes.

To get MiniPaint to work properly, you must set up the Drawing and Text windows in the arrangement you see in Figure 11.1. When you run it, the menu appears at the top of the Drawing window. Using the mouse to operate the menu, you can produce drawings like the one shown in Figure 11.2.

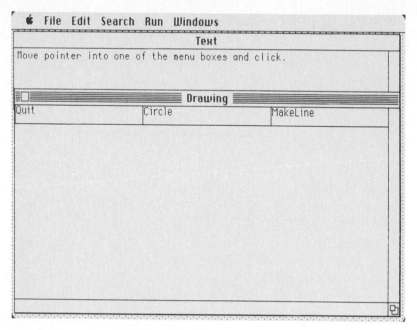

Figure 11.1   The **program** MiniPaint menu.

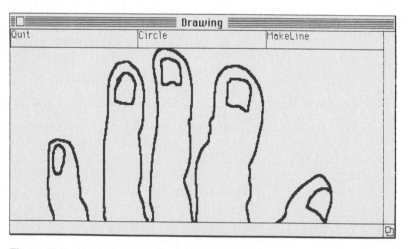

Figure 11.2   Typical output for **program** MiniPaint.

After you click on Go, the MiniPaint menu appears and you are ready to begin painting. If you click in the box labeled Circle, the program executes a procedure called ExplodeCircle. First a prompt appears in the Text window at the top of the screen, asking you to type in a radius. Then you click the mouse in the Drawing window, and a circle is "exploded" where you clicked. The circle grows until its radius equals the radius you typed in.

If you click on MakeLine, you can use the mouse to draw a line in the Drawing window. Just hold the button down and slide the pointer around the window. Releasing the button ends the drawing loop.

When you click on Quit, program execution ends.

MiniPaint is the longest program we've seen so far. Although it is complex, each of the many nested procedures and functions is understandable and is built on ideas that we have seen before. Let's start by looking at the main program. As you read the next few pages, you may find it helpful to look ahead to the diagram of the program in Figure 11.3. (The complete program appears on page 390.)

```
{BODY OF PROGRAM MINIPAINT}
begin
 writeln('Move pointer into one of one menu boxes and click.');
 LayOutMenu;
 ClickPoint(H,V);
 Command := ChooseCommand(H,V);
  while (Command <> Quit) do
   begin
    DoCommand(Command);
    ClickPoint(H,V);
    Command := ChooseCommand(H,V)
   end
end.
```

First **procedure** LayOutMenu draws the boxes for the menu and inserts the labels. Then you click the mouse button in one of the menu boxes—MakeLine, for example. **Procedure** ClickPoint reports the position of the pointer, using the variables H and V. **Function** ChooseCommand uses the values of H and V to determine that you've clicked in the MakeLine box. Then it assigns the command MakeLine to the variable Command.

Now **procedure** DoCommand is called with MakeLine as its parameter. The body of DoCommand is the program's "switchboard."

```
{BODY OF PROCEDURE DOCOMMAND}
begin
 case Command of
  Bad :
   begin
    sysbeep(10);
    writeln('Bad command -- enter another.')
   end;
  Circle :
   ExplodeCircle;
  MakeLine :
   Lines
 end
end;
```

Procedure DoCommand takes the command you select by clicking and connects it to the procedure that does the command. When you click on MakeLine, DoCommand calls **procedure** Lines, which allows you to draw lines in the Drawing window.

Procedure Lines uses a MacPascal standard procedure called *pensize*, which sets the width of the lines drawn on the screen. Ordinarily, when you draw a line, each point on the line is a tiny square 1 unit high by 1 unit wide. The procedure call *pensize*(3,3) sets the Macintosh's electronic pen for a thicker line made up of points 3 units high by 3 units wide.

Procedure Lines draws lines with the standard procedure *lineto*, which we discussed in Problem 6 of Chapter 3. *Lineto*(H,V) draws a line from the current position of the pen to the point (H,V), moving the pen as it goes. If the pen is at the point (0,0), then *lineto*(200,200) draws a diagonal across the Drawing window. After *lineto*(200,200) is executed, the pen is at the position (200,200).

Clicking on MakeLine lets you draw a line 3 units wide in the Drawing window as you drag the pointer with the button depressed. To stop drawing, you release the mouse button.

When you click again in the MakeLine or the Circle box, the **while** loop in the body of the main program will do another iteration.

The commands Quit, Circle, and MakeLine are all members of the enumerated type Commands, which is declared in the declaration part of the program:

```
type
  Commands = (Bad,Quit,Circle,MakeLine);
```

There is another element in the type—Bad. When you click outside the menu boxes, the command Bad is chosen, and the Macintosh signals with a beep to let you know that you have clicked in the wrong place.

Here is **program** MiniPaint.

```
program MiniPaint;
{ALLOWS YOU TO USE THE MOUSE TO DRAW LINES AND EXPLODE CIRCLES}
 const
  CommandCount = 4;
  BoxHeight = 20;
  WindowWidth = 500;
 type
  Commands = (Bad,Quit,Circle,MakeLine);
 var
  H,V : integer;
  Command : Commands;
```

```
 procedure ClickPoint(var H,V : integer);
 begin
  repeat
{DO NOTHING}
  until button;
  repeat
   getmouse(H,V)
  until not (button)
 end;


 procedure LayOutMenu;
  var
   BoxWidth : integer;


  procedure DrawAndLabelBoxes(BoxWidth,BoxCount : integer);
   var
    BoxNumber,Position : integer;
    Command : Commands;


   procedure PrintLabel(Position : integer;
            Command : Commands);
 {LABEL STARTS A LITTLE IN FROM LINE, HALFWAY DOWN MENU BOX}
    begin
     moveto(Position + 1, BoxHeight div 2);
     writedraw(Command)
    end;


 {BODY OF DRAWANDLABELBOXES}
  begin
   Command := Bad;
   BoxNumber := 0;
   Position := 0;
   repeat
    Command := succ(Command);
    BoxNumber := BoxNumber + 1;
    drawline(Position,0,Position,BoxHeight);
    PrintLabel(Position,Command);
    Position := Position + BoxWidth
   until (BoxNumber = BoxCount)
  end;
```

(continued)

```
{BODY OF LAYOUTMENU}
begin
 drawline(0,BoxHeight,WindowWidth,BoxHeight);
 BoxWidth := WindowWidth div (CommandCount - 1);
{THE COMMAND "BAD" DOESN'T GET A BOX}
 DrawAndLabelBoxes(BoxWidth,CommandCount - 1)
end;

function ChooseCommand(H,V : integer) : Commands;
 {FUNCTION CHOOSECOMMAND CONTAINS 3 OTHER FUNCTIONS}
 var
  BoxNumber : integer;

 function VerticalOk(V : integer) : boolean;
 begin
  if (V )= 0) and (V < BoxHeight) then
   VerticalOk := True
  else
   VerticalOk := False
 end;

 function HorizontalOk(H : integer) : boolean;
 begin
  if (H )= 0) and (H < WindowWidth) then
   HorizontalOk := True
  else
   HorizontalOk := False
 end;

 function SelectCommand(BoxNumber : integer): Commands;
  var
   Box : integer;
   CommandChoice : Commands;
 begin
  Box := BoxNumber;
  CommandChoice := Quit;
   while (Box > 0) do
    begin
     Box := Box - 1;
     CommandChoice := succ(CommandChoice)
    end;
   SelectCommand := CommandChoice
 end;
```

```
{BODY OF FUNCTION CHOOSECOMMAND}
begin
 if VerticalOk(V) and HorizontalOk(H) then
  begin
   BoxNumber := ((CommandCount - 1)*H) div WindowWidth;
   ChooseCommand := SelectCommand(BoxNumber)
  end
 else
  ChooseCommand := Bad
end;


procedure DoCommand(Command : Commands);

 procedure ExplodeCircle;
  var
   H,V,Radius,BigRadius : integer;
 begin
  writeln('Type in a maximum radius.');
  write('>');
  readln(BigRadius);
  writeln('Now click in the Drawing window.');
  ClickPoint(H,V);
  for Radius := 1 to BigRadius do
   paintcircle(H,V,Radius)
 end;


 procedure Lines;
  var
   H,V : integer;
 begin
  pensize(3,3);
  writeln('To draw a line, depress button and drag pointer.');
  writeln('Release the mouse button to quit drawing.');
  repeat
   getmouse(H,V)
  until button;
  moveto(H,V);
  repeat
   getmouse(H,V);
   lineto(H,V)
  until not (button)
 end;
```

(continued)

```
{BODY OF PROCEDURE DOCOMMAND}
begin
 case Command of
  Bad :
   begin
    sysbeep(10);
    writeln('Bad command -- enter another.')
   end;
  Circle :
   ExplodeCircle;
  MakeLine :
   Lines
 end
end;

{BODY OF PROGRAM}
begin
 writeln('Move pointer into one of the menu boxes and click.');
 LayOutMenu;
 ClickPoint(H,V);
 Command := ChooseCommand(H,V);
 while (Command <> Quit) do
  begin
   DoCommand(Command);
   ClickPoint(H,V);
   Command := ChooseCommand(H,V)
  end
end.
```

Program MiniPaint is quite long and complex, but it's worth typing in and trying. Be sure to save it. We'll be using parts of it later in the chapter.

Figure 11.3 is a diagram of the procedures and functions in the program. Examining this diagram will help you understand the structure of MiniPaint. Note that the procedures and functions are more deeply nested than in any previous program. For example, **procedure** PrintLabel is nested three levels down from the top level.

Adding to Program MiniPaint

Program MiniPaint is structured so that new painting commands are easy to add. Note how general the main program is. It doesn't mention any commands related to painting circles or drawing lines. All of the graphics instructions are relegated to nested procedures within **procedure** DoCommand. So, when you

```
program Minipaint
   ┌──────────────────────────────────────────┐
   │ procedure ClickPoint                     │
   └──────────────────────────────────────────┘

   ┌──────────────────────────────────────────┐
   │ procedure LayOutMenu                     │
   │    ┌───────────────────────────────────┐ │
   │    │ procedure DrawAndLabelBoxes       │ │
   │    │   ┌────────────────────────────┐  │ │
   │    │   │ procedure PrintLabel       │  │ │
   │    │   └────────────────────────────┘  │ │
   │    │                                   │ │
   │    └───────────────────────────────────┘ │
   └──────────────────────────────────────────┘

   ┌──────────────────────────────────────────┐
   │ function ChooseCommand                    │
   │    ┌───────────────────────────────────┐ │
   │    │ function VerticalOk               │ │
   │    └───────────────────────────────────┘ │
   │                                          │
   │    ┌───────────────────────────────────┐ │
   │    │ function HorizontalOk             │ │
   │    └───────────────────────────────────┘ │
   │                                          │
   │    ┌───────────────────────────────────┐ │
   │    │ function SelectCommand            │ │
   │    └───────────────────────────────────┘ │
   └──────────────────────────────────────────┘

   ┌──────────────────────────────────────────┐
   │ procedure DoCommand                       │
   │    ┌───────────────────────────────────┐ │
   │    │ procedure ExplodeCircle           │ │
   │    └───────────────────────────────────┘ │
   │                                          │
   │    ┌───────────────────────────────────┐ │
   │    │ procedure Lines                   │ │
   │    └───────────────────────────────────┘ │
   └──────────────────────────────────────────┘
```

Figure 11.3 Diagram of the procedures and functions in **program** MiniPaint.

add another command, you will need to adjust the declarations in the main program and alter DoCommand, but LayOutMenu and ChooseCommand aren't changed at all. Let's see how simple this addition will be.

Suppose you want to add an erase command. You can use the command to erase a square 10 units on a side, which you can drag around the Drawing window using the mouse. See Figure 11.4. Here is the procedure you need to include:

```
procedure Erase;
 const
  EraserSize = 10;
 var
  Top,Left,Bottom,Right : integer;
begin
 repeat
     {DO NOTHING}
 until button;
     {BUTTON IS NOW DOWN}
 repeat
  getmouse(Left,Top);
  eraserect(Top,Left,Top + EraserSize,Left + EraserSize)
 until not (button)
end;
```

To include Erase in **program** MiniPaint, you must make the following changes:

1. Add 1 to CommandCount, changing it from 4 to 5. CommandCount is a constant that specifies the number of commands in the enumerated type Commands. The program uses CommandCount to divide the menu into the proper number of equal-sized boxes.
2. Add Eraser to the type definition for Commands.
3. Insert the declaration for **procedure** Erase into the declaration part of DoCommand, and add the command Eraser to the case statement in DoCommand.

And you're done. You have now added an eraser to your mouse-driven MiniPaint program—and you have changed only DoCommand and the declaration part of the main program.

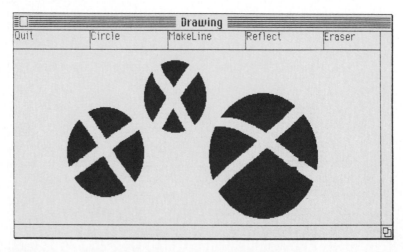

Figure 11.4   Program MiniPaint's output using the eraser.

EXERCISE 1   Add a fifth command called Reflect to MiniPaint. When you choose Reflect, you draw using the mouse. As you draw, the line you make is reflected on the opposite side of the window, creating a horizontal mirror image of your sketch. Here is the procedure that draws reflected lines:

```
procedure ReflectLines;
 var
  H,V,LeftLastH,RightLastH,LastV : integer;
begin
 pensize(3,3);
 repeat
  getmouse(H,V)
 until button;
 repeat
  LastV := V;
{RECORDS PREVIOUS LOCATIONS OF PEN ON THE LEFT AND ON THE RIGHT}
  LeftLastH := H;
  RightLastH := WindowWidth - H;
{REPORTS PRESENT LOCATION OF POINTER}
  getmouse(H,V);
{DRAWS LINE FROM LAST LEFT POINT TO NEW LEFT POINT}
  moveto(LeftLastH,LastV);
  lineto(H,V);
{DRAWS LINE FROM LAST RIGHT POINT TO NEW RIGHT POINT}
  moveto(RightLastH,LastV);
  lineto(WindowWidth - H,V)
 until not (button)
end;
```

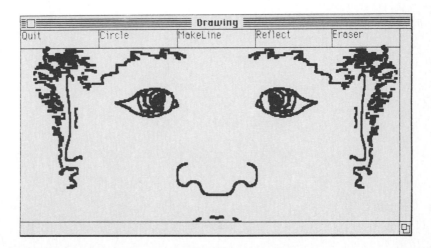

Figure 11.5   Output of **program** MiniPaint using Reflect.

Figure 11.5 shows the output of **program** MiniPaint using Reflect. **Procedure** ReflectLines works on the following principle: If the mouse pointer is at the point (H,V), the horizontal reflection of the pointer is at the point(WindowWidth $- H,V$). Type it in and try it. ▬

After you understand how **program** MiniPaint works, you'll be able to create your own menus to use in any interactive program. The procedures that create the menu in **program** MiniPaint will be part of your growing private collection of Pascal functions and procedures. The phone book program that we present at the end of the chapter will use the MiniPaint style, so be sure to study the program carefully before reading on.

11.2 Records

So far in our study of Pascal, the idea of the value of a variable has had a very simple meaning. It is a number, character, string, element of an enumerated type, or true/false value that is written in the location in memory assigned to that variable. Now we will look at a new kind of variable that enables you to keep track of more complex units of information.

Suppose we want to invent a variable that represents a baby's weight. (We will use the English system of weight—pounds and ounces.) When we say, "John and Sheila's baby weighs 9 pounds, 12 ½ ounces," we are actually using *two* values to describe the baby's weight: one for the pounds and one for the ounces. It would be handy to have one variable, called Weight, to hold both pieces of information.

This is where Pascal's *record* type comes in. Using a record type, we can create a variable called Weight that comes with two separate components, one for pounds and the other for ounces. The cell in memory that holds the value of the record variable Weight will be divided into two separate parts, one for the value of pounds (an integer value) and the other for the value of ounces (a real value).

pounds | 9 |

ounces | 12.5 |

record variable Weight

Here is the type definition that sets up the two-part memory cell:

```
type
  EnglishWeight = record
    Pounds : integer;
    Ounces : real
  end;
```

EnglishWeight is the name of the record type. Now we can declare variable Weight of type EnglishWeight:

```
var
 Weight : EnglishWeight;
```

The type definition for the record EnglishWeight is a blueprint for the declaration of the record variable Weight. When the computer sets aside a location in memory for Weight, the location is divided into a part for pounds and a part for ounces, each part with its own type.

We can now use one assignment statement to fill the pounds part and another to fill the ounces part of the record variable. The statement

```
Weight.Pounds := 9;
```

assigns the value 9 to the pounds part of Weight. The dot between Weight and Pounds (no spaces allowed) tells where the 9 goes—into the pounds part. Similarly, the following assignment statement copies 12.5 into the ounces part.

```
Weight.Ounces := 12.5
```

Now let's use the record type EnglishWeight in a program that reads in a weight in kilograms and prints out this weight in pounds and ounces.

```
program KilogramsToPounds;
{TYPE WEIGHT IN KILOS. PROGRAM PRINTS WEIGHT IN LBS AND OUNCES.}
 const
  OzPerKg = 35.28;
 type
  EnglishWeight = record
    Pounds : integer;
    Ounces : real
   end;
 var
  Weight : EnglishWeight;
  Kilograms : real;
  TotalOunces : real;
begin
 writeln('Type in a number of kilograms.');
 write('>');
 readln(Kilograms);
 TotalOunces := OzPerKg * Kilograms;
 Weight.Pounds := trunc(TotalOunces/16);
 Weight.Ounces := TotalOunces - (Weight.Pounds * 16);
 writeln('English weight is ',Weight.Pounds : 3,' pounds ',
         Weight.Ounces : 4 : 1,' ounces.')
end.
```

When you run **program** KilogramsToPounds, a two-part memory cell is set aside for Weight. After you type in a value for Kilograms, the statement

```
TotalOunces := OzPerKg * Kg
```

converts kilograms to ounces. Next comes this statement:

```
Weight.Pounds := trunc(TotalOunces/16)
```

First the right side of the assignment calculates the number of whole pounds. TotalOunces/16 gives the number of pounds as a real number. The function *trunc* takes this number, throws away the decimal-fraction part, and gives a whole-number answer. This integer answer is then assigned to the pounds part of the record variable Weight.

Now the program does the following assignment statement:

```
Weight.Ounces := TotalOunces - (Weight.Pounds * 16)
```

After the right side of the assignment statement calculates the number of ounces, that value is assigned to the ounces subcell of the record variable Weight.

Finally the *writeln* statement prints out the values of the two subcells of the record variable Weight. If you read in 65.0 kilograms, it will print the output shown in Figure 11.6.

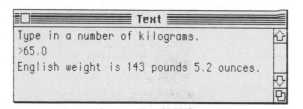

Figure 11.6   Sample output of **program** KilogramsToPounds.

11.3 Record Syntax

A type definition for a record always begins with the name of the record, an equal sign, and the reserved word **record**. A record definition always ends with the word **end**. Between the word **record** and the word **end** are the *fields* of the record. The first field in the definition of EnglishWeight is this line:

```
Pounds : integer;
```

A record field consists of an identifier called a *field selector*, followed by a colon and a type definition for the selector.

When the Macintosh reaches the variable declaration for Weight in **program** KilogramsToPounds, the record type definition for EnglishWeight tells the computer how to lay out the memory cell assigned to Weight. The definition also specifies what type restrictions govern the values that will appear in the subcells.

11.4 Program Checks

Using a somewhat more complicated record variable, **program** Checks can help you keep track of your checking account. At the end of the month you read in information about each check: to whom you wrote it, for how much, and whether the payment is tax-deductible. The program prints the total amount of money paid out that month and how much of it is tax-deductible, along with a list of the people to whom you wrote checks and the amount of each check (see Figure 11.7). Here is **program** Checks.

```
program Checks;
{FOR EACH CHECK, YOU READ IN WHO IT IS TO, HOW MUCH IT IS FOR,}
{AND WHETHER IT IS DEDUCTIBLE. PROGRAM PRINTS TOTAL AMOUNT}
{PAID OUT FOR THE MONTH AND DEDUCTIBLE AMOUNT.}
 const
  StartHeightForTable = 10;
 type
  ACheck = record
    WhoTo : string;
    Amount : real;
    Deductible : boolean
   end;
 var
  Check : ACheck;
  TotalAmount : real;
  DeductibleAmount : real;
  Done : boolean;
  HeightOfRow : integer; {OUTPUT IS SERIES OF ROWS IN DRAWING WINDOW}

 procedure GatherInfo(var Check : ACheck;
           var Done : boolean);
 begin
  writeln('Type in amount of check,
          or type negative number to end entry loop.');
  write('>');
  readln(Check.Amount);
  if (Check.Amount < 0.0) then
   Done := True
  else
   begin
    writeln('Who is check to?');
    write('>');
    readln(Check.WhoTo);
    writeln('Is check deductible? Type True or False.');
    write('>');
    readln(Check.Deductible)
   end
 end;
```

(continued)

```
procedure PrintEntry(Check : ACheck;
        var Height : integer);
 const
  SeparationBetweenLines = 15;
begin
 moveto(1,Height);
 writedraw(Check.WhoTo);
 moveto(150,Height);
 writedraw(Check.Amount : 6 : 2);
 Height := Height + SeparationBetweenLines
end;

procedure UpdateTotals(Check : ACheck;
        var TotalAmt,DeductibleAmt : real);
begin
 TotalAmt := TotalAmt + Check.Amount;
 if Check.Deductible then
  DeductibleAmt := DeductibleAmt + Check.Amount
end;

procedure ReportTotals(TotalAmount,DeductibleAmount : real);
begin
 writeln;
 writeln('Amount paid out this month is $',TotalAmount : 6: 2);
 writeln('Deductible amount paid out this month is $',
         DeductibleAmount : 6 : 2)
end;
    {MAIN PROGRAM}
begin
 TotalAmount := 0.0;
 DeductibleAmount := 0.0;
 Done := False;
 HeightOfRow := StartHeightForTable;
 while not (Done) do
  begin
   GatherInfo(Check,Done);
   if not (Done) then
    begin
     UpdateTotals(Check,TotalAmount,DeductibleAmount);
     PrintEntry(Check,HeightOfRow)
    end
  end;
 ReportTotals(TotalAmount,DeductibleAmount)
end.
```

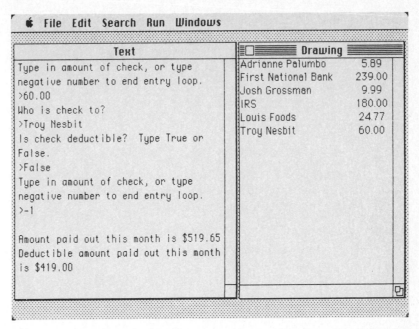

Figure 11.7   Typical output for **program** Checks. When you type a negative number, the program reports your checking totals.

The data you enter is collected by the **procedure** GatherInfo. When you type the amount of a check, the program stores this value in the Amount field of the variable Check. If the amount is greater than zero, the procedure fills the WhoTo and Deductible fields. Then Check is passed to **procedure** UpdateTotals, where the contents of the record are added into the monthly totals. Next Check is passed to **procedure** PrintEntry, which prints the contents of the variable in the Drawing window.

The main loop in the body of the program continues as long as you keep entering positive values for Check.Amount. After you end the loop by typing a negative value, **procedure** ReportTotals reports the values of TotalAmount and DeductibleAmount, and program execution ends.

Program Checks gives you a glimpse of the importance of records for business computing. If you work at a bank, or if you want to keep small business records or personal banking records on a computer, using records is an ideal way for you to organize data. Because a record can have any number of fields, you can define types that are completely tailored to your needs. For example, you could easily keep a more extensive record for your checks that includes the following information:

Check Records

who to
check number
amount
deductible
month
day
year
canceled check returned

An important point: Be careful when you use a field selector such as Month that has for its type an enumerated type. You must define this type *before* you use Month in the definition for ACheck.

EXERCISE 2   Complete this revised type definition for ACheck by filling in the types for the field selectors.

```
type
 ACheck = record
  WhoTo : string;
  CheckNumber : [_____];
  Amount : real;
  Deductible : boolean;
  Month : Months;
  Day : 1..31;
  Year : [_____];
  CanceledCheckBack : [_____]
 end;  ■
```

11.5 Employee Records

Let's look at another illustration of a record structure in business computing. Suppose you are hired by Aristotle Software Company to computerize its employee information records. Here is a table of the kinds of information about each employee the firm would like to have.

Name	Lilly French-Smith
Social Security number	177-36-3810
Employee number	133
Salary	24950.00
Married	True
Years with company	6

Work schedule	10	10	10	5	0
	Mon	Tue	Wed	Thur	Fri

You could use the following record structure to organize this information:

```
type
  Employee = record
    Name : string;
    SocSecNumber : string[11];
    EmployeeNumber : integer;
    Salary : real;
    Married : boolean;
    YearsWithCompany : integer;
    Hours : array[Mon..Fri] of integer
  end;
```

The last field of the record is an array. If you declared a record variable called Worker of type Employee, you could refer to the Hours field using an assignment statement such as

```
Worker.Hours[Tue] := 7
```

Worker.Hours is an array with index type DaysOfWeek, and Worker.Hours[Tue] is the Tues component of the array.

EXERCISE 3   Consider the declaration

```
    var
      Worker : Employee;
```

a. Write a statement that assigns the name Alvin Bosco to the name field of Worker.

b. Tell what the following statement does.

```
      Worker.Married := not (Worker.Married);
```

c. Write a statement that increases by 1 the number of years Bosco has been with the firm.

d. Tell what the following program fragment does.

```
      Total := 0;
        for Day := Mon to Fri do
          Total := Total + Worker.Hours[Day]; ▰
```

11.6 Arrays of Records

Records are a powerful way to organize data. With a record, you collect related pieces of information of *different* types and tie them together with a single variable. Arrays organize data differently. An array collects related pieces of data of the *same* type and enables you to give these data a common name.

Records and arrays are two *data structures* that are built into Pascal. They make organizing complex data easy and convenient. We will introduce another data structure, the *file*, in a moment. But first we want to explore an important hybrid structure that combines records and arrays.

Let's look at an example of a collection of records of the same type, which have been combined into an array. Suppose Aristotle Software has 50 employees. To calculate the company's monthly payroll, we can write a program that uses an array of 50 elements of type Employee. Here is the declaration part of the program.

```
const EmployeeCount = 50;
type
 Employee = record
   Name : string;
   Age : integer;
   MonthlySalary : real;
   SocSecNumber : string[11]
  end;

PayrollRecords = array[1..EmployeeCount] of Employee;
var
 Roster : PayrollRecords;
 NumberOfEmployee : integer;
```

The array variable, which we have called Roster, has index type 1..EmployeeCount and component type Employee. Each component has four subcells. Here is a diagram of the array variable Roster.

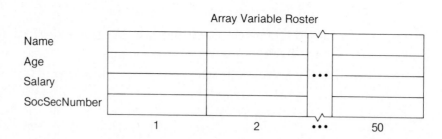

Array Variable Roster

To print a list of the employees along with their monthly salaries, we can use this loop:

```
for NumberOfEmployee := 1 to EmployeeCount do
 writeln(Roster[NumberOfEmployee].Name,
         Roster[NumberOfEmployee].Salary : 10 : 2);
```

Suppose we want to find the oldest employee. The following loop uses an integer variable called Oldest to do the trick.

```
Oldest := 1;
NumberOfEmployee := 1;
while (NumberOfEmployee <= EmployeeCount) do
  begin
    if (Roster[NumberOfEmployee].Age > Roster[Oldest].Age) then
    Oldest := NumberOfEmployee;
    NumberOfEmployee := NumberOfEmployee + 1
  end;
writeln(Roster[Oldest].Name,' is the oldest employee.');
writeln('Age: ',Roster[Oldest].Age)
```

EXERCISE 4   **a.** Using the array variable Roster, write a loop that prints a list of employees and their Social Security numbers.

b. Using the array variable Roster, write a loop that prints the names of the employees under 25 who earn more than $2000 per month. ■

11.7 Program ReflectOvals

Our next example is a complete program called ReflectOvals, which uses an array of records. **Program** ReflectOvals builds on **program** OvalDraw from Section 7.12. In that program we used the mouse to draw a pattern of ovals in the Drawing window. We will draw a pattern of ovals in **program** ReflectOvals, too. This time, however, we will store the ovals as we draw them in an array consisting of 100 records. After 100 ovals have been drawn, the program will print the reflection of the pattern in the Drawing window, as shown in Figure 11.8.

The data used to frame an oval are stored in a record of type Oval, which is declared as follows:

```
type
  Oval = record
    Top : integer;
    Left : integer;
    Bottom : integer;
    Right : integer
  end;
```

We will use an array variable called Picture of type Drawing to hold the information needed to draw the reflection of the original drawing.

Each of Picture's 100 components has 4 subcells labeled Top, Left, Bottom, and Right. The component type for Picture is Oval, and the index type is the subrange of *integer* 1..Size (Size is a constant whose value is 100).

Here is program ReflectOvals.

```
program ReflectOvals;
 const
  Size = 100;
  WindowWidth = 500;
 type
  Oval = record
     Top : integer;
     Left : integer;
     Bottom : integer;
     Right : integer
    end;
  Drawing = array[1..Size] of Oval;
 var
  Picture : Drawing;
  H,V,OvalNumber : integer;


procedure Reflect(var Pix : Drawing;
         Last : integer);
  var
   NewLeft,NewRight,OldTop,OldBottom,OvalNumber : integer;
 begin
  for OvalNumber := Last downto 1 do
   begin
    OldTop := Pix[OvalNumber]. Top;
    OldBottom := Pix[OvalNumber].Bottom;
    NewLeft := WindowWidth - Pix[OvalNumber].Left;
    NewRight := WindowWidth - Pix[OvalNumber].Right;
    if (NewLeft < NewRight) then
     frameoval(OldTop,NewLeft,OldBottom,NewRight)
    else
     frameoval(OldTop,NewRight,OldBottom,NewLeft)
   end
 end;


procedure StoreOval(H,V,OvalNumber : integer;
         var Picture : Drawing);
 begin
  Picture[OvalNumber].Top := V;
  Picture[OvalNumber].Left := H;
  Picture[OvalNumber].Bottom := V + 80;
  Picture[OvalNumber].Right := H + V;
 end;
```

```
        {MAIN PROGRAM}
begin
 OvalNumber := 1;
 while (OvalNumber <= Size) do
  begin
   repeat
    {DO NOTHING}
   until button;
   while (OvalNumber <= Size) and button do
    begin
     getmouse(H,V);
     frameoval(V,H,V + 80,H + V);
     StoreOval(H,V,OvalNumber,Picture);
     OvalNumber := OvalNumber + 1
    end
  end;
 Reflect(Picture,Size)
end.
```

The program includes two procedures: **procedure** StoreOval, which is inside the **while** loop, and **procedure** Reflect, which comes at the end of the program. The procedure call

```
StoreOval(H,V,OvalNumber,Picture)
```

passes to the procedure the parameters *H* and *V*—the coordinates for the upper-left corner of the rectangle that frames the oval you have just drawn. It also passes the number of the oval and the array variable Picture, which holds the

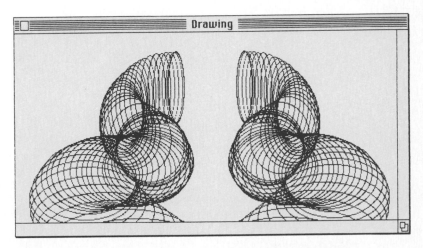

Figure 11.8   A typical picture drawn using **program** ReflectOvals.

ovals. Each time StoreOval is called, the procedure fills 1 more component of the array Picture, until each of the 100 components is filled with the 4 pieces of information needed to frame an oval.

Picture is a variable parameter. Each time **procedure** StoreOval is called, the procedure changes the value of the actual parameter Picture by copying into the next component of the array the 4 walls that frame the most recent oval you've drawn.

After all 100 ovals have been drawn and stored in the array, the **while** loop ends and **procedure** Reflect draws reflected ovals, starting with the *last* oval in the array. The procedure call

```
Reflect(Picture,Size)
```

passes the array variable Picture and the constant Size, which is the index of the last element in the array.

The parameter list for Reflect is peculiar. Reflect does not change the array in any way, yet we have made Picture a variable rather than a value parameter. Why?

Picture is a large array; it has 100 cells that hold 4 integers each. We can make the array even larger simply by increasing the value of the constant Size. The Macintosh's main memory is limited, so we have declared Picture as a variable parameter because it takes up less memory than a value parameter would. Here's why.

When Reflect is called, the procedure's formal parameter Pix becomes a second name for the array Picture. At all times there is just one copy in memory of the array.

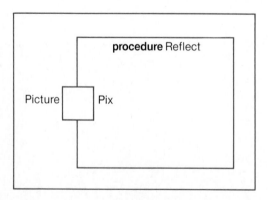

If Pix had been a value parameter, the computer would have made a complete second copy of the array in main memory each time **procedure** Reflect is called, and the second copy of the array might use up so much space in memory that the program wouldn't run.

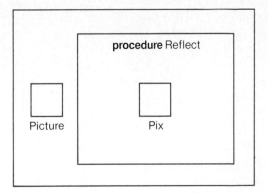

When a program passes to a procedure a large array, especially a large array of records, it's a good idea to make the formal parameter a variable parameter even if the procedure is not supposed to change the array. Using a variable parameter saves space in main memory. However, when you use a variable parameter in this way, be careful: If the procedure *does* alter the contents of the array, a bug might be created that would be difficult to track down.

When you type in **program** ReflectOvals, you will quickly discover that keying in the four statements that involve

```
Pix[OvalNumber]
```

is particularly tedious. Pascal offers a way around this problem by streamlining references to record variables, as we will see in the next section.

11.8 The With Statement

Pascal's **with** statement makes typing in record variables easier and makes programs with records more readable. Let's see how we can use a **with** statement to simplify **procedure** GatherInfo from **program** Checks.

```
procedure GatherInfo(var Check : ACheck;
        var Done : boolean);
begin
 writeln('Type in amount of check,
         or type negative number to end entry loop.');
 write('>');
 readln(Check.Amount);
 if (Check.Amount < 0.0) then
  Done := True
 else
```
(continued)

```
      begin
       writeln('Who is check to?');
       write('>');
       readln(Check.WhoTo);
       writeln('Is check deductible? Type True or False.');
       write('>');
       readln(Check.Deductible)
      end
    end;
```

Procedure GatherInfo includes several occurrences of the record variable Check along with a record field selector. Using the **with** statement, we can rewrite the procedure this way:

```
   procedure GatherInfo(var Check : ACheck;
            var Done : boolean);
   begin
    with Check do
     begin
      writeln('Type in amount of check,
               or type negative number to end entry loop.');
      write('>');
      readln(Amount);
      if (Amount < 0.0) then
       Done := True
      else
       begin
        writeln('Who is check to?');
        write('>');
        readln(WhoTo);
        writeln('Is check deductible? Type True or False.');
        write('>');
        readln(Deductible)
       end
     end {END OF WITH STATEMENT}
   end;
```

Inside the scope of the **with** statement, you don't have to identify the variable Check. Whenever the computer encounters a field selector for Check inside the **with** statement, it assumes you mean to preface that selector with "Check."

Inside the **with** statement, Amount is short for Check.Amount, WhoTo is short for Check.WhoTo, and Deductible means Check.Deductible.

The **with** statement can also help simplify **procedure** Reflect from **program** ReflectOvals. The procedure has four assignment statements involving Pix[OvalNumber]. Remember: Pix is an array of ovals, and Pix[OvalNumber] is a component variable of the array. The component is of type Oval, which is a record.

```
procedure Reflect(var Pix : Drawing;
        Last : integer);
 var
  NewLeft,NewRight,OldTop,OldBottom,OvalNumber : integer;
begin
 for OvalNumber := Last downto 1 do
  begin
   OldTop := Pix[OvalNumber].Top;
   OldBottom := Pix[OvalNumber].Bottom;
   NewLeft := WindowWidth - Pix[OvalNumber].Left;
   NewRight := WindowWidth - Pix[OvalNumber].Right;
   if (NewLeft < NewRight) then
    frameoval(OldTop,NewLeft,OldBottom,NewRight)
   else
    frameoval(OldTop,NewRight,OldBottom,NewLeft)
  end
end;
```

Using the **with** statement, we can clarify the procedure considerably by eliminating all of the Pix[OvalNumber] references in the body of the **with**:

```
procedure Reflect(var Pix : Drawing;
        Last : integer);
 var
  NewLeft,NewRight,OldTop,OldBottom,OvalNumber : integer;
begin
 for OvalNumber := Last downto 1 do
  with Pix[OvalNumber] do
   begin
    OldTop := Top;
    OldBottom := Bottom;
    NewLeft := WindowWidth - Left;
    NewRight := WindowWidth - Right;
    if (NewLeft < NewRight) then
     frameoval(OldTop,NewLeft,OldBottom,NewRight)
    else
     frameoval(OldTop,NewRight,OldBottom,NewLeft)
   end
end;
```

The **with** statement has the following syntax:

```
with RecordVariable do
  <statement>
```

EXERCISE 5   Rewrite **procedure** StoreOval using a **with** statement. ■

11.9 Files

All the programs we have seen so far have suffered from one shortcoming: Any data that are generated while a program is running disappear from main memory as soon as you turn off the Macintosh. Your program is stored permanently on the disk, but data produced by the program are lost from the computer forever.

You can get around this limitation by using a data structure called a *file*. Files make it possible to save large amounts of data permanently on a disk. Once you run a program that creates a file, you can write other programs that read the information stored in that file.

A file consists of a sequence of entries called *components*. The components must be of the same type. Files can be very large because they are not stored in main memory. A file can hold, in principle, up to *maxlongint*, or 2,147,483,647, data items.

While you are running a program that uses a file, the program is in main memory but the file is still on the disk. You can copy data from the file into your program one entry at a time. But the file as a whole is never in main memory. For this reason files are often referred to as *external files*. (In this book we will assume that external files are on the Pascal disk, but this is not always true in MacPascal. For example, it is possible to use file commands to send data to a printer or modem.)

Macintosh Pascal has two facilities for working with files, a *sequential file* facility and a *random-access file* facility. Each consists of a set of commands for working with external files. Sequential file commands are part of every Pascal system. Pascal systems that include random-access file commands are less common.

Sequential file commands are adequate for saving, or *archiving*, large bodies of information that you don't expect to change. If you want to keep a record of the distance you jog every day, for example, sequential file commands are sufficient: You probably won't want to go back and change any of the figures. Using sequential file commands is awkward, however, if you want to alter the data that you have stored in a file.

Random-access file commands do not share this limitation. They are easy to use both for archiving data and for storing data that you expect to change frequently. Because of this flexibility, the random-access file system is a much more powerful file structure. Accordingly, in our brief introduction to files, we will present material on random-access file commands only.

11.10 Random-Access File Commands

To see how random-access files work, let's look at **program** Temperatures. When you run **program** Temperatures for the first time, a file command creates a file called JulyHighTemps on the Pascal disk; JulyHighTemps is the *title* of the file. Then, in a data entry loop, you enter the 31 high temperatures for the month of

July. These values are sent one by one to the file on the disk. Next the program reads back the values from the file, one by one, and prints them in the Text window. After program execution is over, JulyHighTemps is a Macintosh document, which is permanently on the disk. Here is **program** Temperatures:

```
program Temperatures;
{YOU TYPE IN THE HIGH TEMPERATURES FOR EACH DAY IN JULY. PROGRAM}
{SENDS THIS DATA TO A FILE. THEN IT READS THE DATA FROM THE FILE}
{AND PRINTS IT IN THE TEXT WINDOW.}
 const
  DaysInMonth = 31;
 var
  Date : integer;
  Temperature : real;
  TemperatureData : file of real;
begin
 open(TemperatureData,'JulyHighTemps');
  {DATA ENTRY LOOP}
 for Date := 1 to DaysInMonth do
  begin
   writeln('Give temperature for July ',Date : 1,
            ' in degrees Fahrenheit.');
   write('>');
   readln(Temperature);
   write(TemperatureData,Temperature)
  end;
 reset(TemperatureData);
  {DATA DISPLAY LOOP}
 Date := 1;
 while not (eof(TemperatureData)) do
  begin
   read(TemperatureData,Temperature);
   writeln('The temperature for July ',Date : 1,
            ' was ',Temperature : 4 : 1);
   Date := Date + 1
  end;
 close(TemperatureData)
end.
```

The declaration

```
var
 TemperatureData : file of real;
```

creates a file variable called TemperatureData that will act as a link between the program and a file on the disk. Because TemperatureData is declared to be a file of real values, all the components in an external file associated with TemperatureData must be of type *real*.

When you run **program** Temperatures for the first time, the *open* command

```
open(TemperatureData, 'JulyHighTemps')
```

creates the file JulyHighTemps on the disk. The *open* command also links the file JulyHighTemps with the file variable TemperatureData.

The file variable comes with a *file pointer*—an imaginary arrow (you never see it) that "points to," or specifies, a particular component in the external file. The components of a file hold positions that are numbered consecutively beginning with zero. Just after the *open* command is executed, the pointer points to position 0 at the beginning of the external file.

When the *open* command is finished, the computer comes to the data entry loop. The *writeln* statement prompts you for the temperature on July 1 and you type in a value, say 91.0. The *readln* statement reads 91.0 into the variable Temperature.

Next comes the statement that sends the value of Temperature to the external file:

```
write(TemperatureData,Temperature)
```

The first parameter of the *write* command, TemperatureData, directs the *write* statement to send, or write, the value of Temperature, 91.0, to the external file associated with TemperatureData. When a *write* statement has a file variable as its first parameter, the value of the second parameter is sent to the file variable's associated external file and *not* to the Text window.

The value of Temperature is sent to the position in JulyHighTemps that is indicated by the file pointer. The pointer starts out at the beginning of the file. Therefore the temperature for July 1 is stored in position 0. After the *write* statement writes a value to a file, it advances the pointer to position 1. See Figures 11.9(a) and (b).

When the first iteration of the loop is over, thirty more iterations are done. After the thirty-first entry is read in, main memory and the disk look as shown in Figure 11.9(c). There is nothing in the external file JulyHighTemps except a sequence of real-number values—no program, or any part of a program.

Now the program has finished writing to the file and is about to start reading back from it. First the command

```
reset(TemperatureData)
```

is executed. The standard procedure *reset* repositions TemperatureData's file pointer at the beginning of the file.

Next comes the **while** statement, which reads each component from the file and then prints the component in the Text window. The **while** loop is controlled

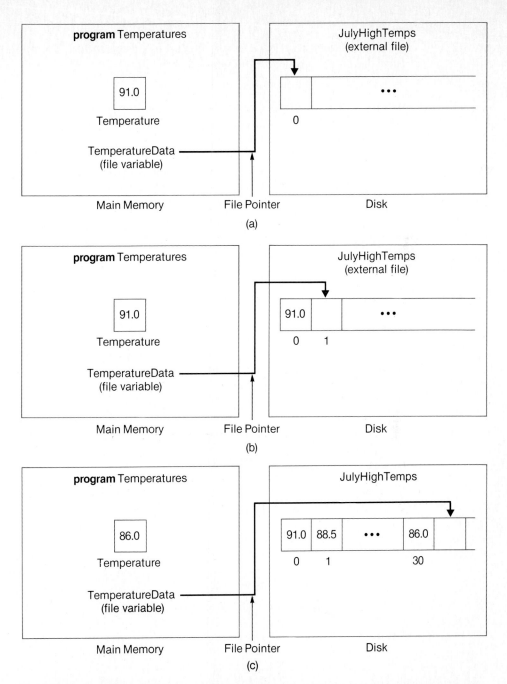

Figure 11.9 (a) Main memory and the Pascal disk after you type the first value for Temperature but before the statement *write*(TemperatureData, Temperature) is executed. (b) Main memory and the Pascal disk after the statement *write*(TemperatureData, Temperature) is executed. (c) Main memory and the MacPascal disk after 31 entries have been written to JulyHighTemps.

by the standard function *eof,* which stands for *end of file.* The function *eof* returns a *boolean* value. In the **while** control line

```
while not(eof(TemperatureData)) do
```

the expression *not(eof(*TemperatureData)) is true as long as the file pointer for TemperatureData points to a component in the file. It becomes false once the pointer advances past the last entry.

After the *reset* command is executed, TemperatureData's file pointer points to the first of the 31 entries in JulyHighTemps. Hence *not(eof(*TemperatureData)) is true, and the loop is executed beginning with the *read* statement:

```
read(TemperatureData,Temperature)
```

The first parameter of the *read* statement, TemperatureData, instructs the computer to read from TemperatureData's associated external file, JulyHighTemps. The *read* statement reads into the variable Temperature the value of the component specified by TemperatureData's file pointer. Then the *read* statement advances TemperatureData's pointer to the next entry in the external file.

Next the *writeln* statement prints the value of Temperature in the Text window, completing one iteration of the loop. The file pointer now points to the second entry. We have not yet reached the end of the file, so the **while** test *not(eof(*TemperatureData)) is still true, and a second iteration is executed.

After the thirty-first execution of the *read* statement copies the last entry of the file into Temperature, the pointer advances past the last entry, and *not(eof(*TemperatureData))becomes false. This terminates the loop. A portion of the output of this loop is printed in the Text window as is shown in Figure 11.10.

Finally, the *close* statement,

```
close(TemperatureData)
```

is executed. The *close* statement breaks the association between the file variable TemperatureData and the external file JulyHighTemps.

```
Text
The temperature for July 23 was 94.0
The temperature for July 24 was 96.0
The temperature for July 25 was 99.0
The temperature for July 26 was 99.0
The temperature for July 27 was 86.0
The temperature for July 28 was 85.0
The temperature for July 29 was 93.0
The temperature for July 30 was 85.0
The temperature for July 31 was 86.0
```

Figure 11.10   A portion of the output for **program** Temperatures.

JulyHighTemps is now a Macintosh document. It is represented by an icon in the Pascal disk window. But you cannot open JulyHighTemps by clicking on the icon and choosing Open from the File menu. You can, however, create other programs that will read the data from JulyHighTemps, as we shall see in the next section.

EXERCISE 6   Suppose you want to keep monthly records of the number of laps you swim each day at your community pool. In a program you are writing to record and report the data, you create a file variable called MonthlySwim, with the declaration

```
var
 MonthlySwim : file of integer;
```

a. How would you open the file variable MonthlySwim and associate it with an external file called JuneLaps?

b. The following program fragment prints the entries in JuneLaps in a column, using the variable Laps. What command goes in the box?

```
reset(MonthlySwim);
Date := 1;
while not (eof(MonthlySwim)) do
begin
  ┌─────────────────────────────┐
  └─────────────────────────────┘
 writeln(Date : 1, Laps : 3);
 Date := Date + 1
end; ▬
```

The Seek Command

Now suppose you want to go back to the data in the external file JulyHighTemps and find out how hot it was on the fourth of July (or any other day of the month). You can get this information using **program** ReportTemperatures. When you run the program, you type in a date, and the program responds by printing the high temperature for that July day.

Program ReportTemperatures locates data in the external file using the *seek* command. The command

```
seek(FileVariable,Position)
```

places FileVariable's file pointer at location Position in a file. If Position is larger than the number of components in the file, the pointer is placed at the end of the file, just after the last entry.

```
program ReportTemperatures;
 var
  Date : integer;
  Temperature : real;
  TemperatureData : file of real;
begin
open(TemperatureData,'JulyHighTemps');
Date := 1;
    {QUESTION AND ANSWER LOOP}
 while(Date <> 0) do
 begin
   writeln('For which day do you want to know the high temperature?');
   writeln('Type a number from 1 to 31, or type a 0 to quit.');
   write('>');
   readln(Date);
   if (Date < 0) or (Date > 31) then
    writeln('Bad date -- try again.')
   else if (Date > 0) then
    begin
     seek(TemperatureData,Date - 1);
     read(TemperatureData,Temperature);
     writeln('The high temperature on July ', Date : 1,' was ',
             Temperature : 4: 1,'.');
     writeln
    end
   end;
 close(TemperatureData)
end.
```

When you run **program** ReportTemperatures, the *open* command opens the external file JulyHighTemps, which is now permanent on the Pascal disk. The command associates this file with the file variable TemperatureData.

Next comes a question and answer loop, which prompts you for a date. Suppose you type 4. The *readln* statement reads 4 into the variable Date. Then the command

```
seek(TemperatureData, Date-1)
```

positions TemperatureData's file pointer at position Date − 1 = 3. The entry for July 4 is at position 3 because file components are numbered beginning with 0.

Next *read*(TemperatureData, Temperature) reads the value at position 3 into the variable Temperature. Then the *writeln* statement prints the high temperature for the fourth of July, as you can see in Figure 11.11. Finally, the *close* statement breaks the link between TemperatureData and JulyHighTemps.

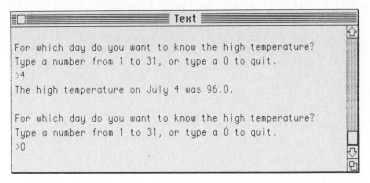

Figure 11.11   Typical output for **program** ReportTemperatures.

Passing a File to a Procedure

Program HotDays illustrates how to pass a file to a procedure. Using monthly temperature data from an external file such as JulyHighTemps, the program reports the number of days in a month that were hotter than a particular cutoff temperature (see Figure 11.12).

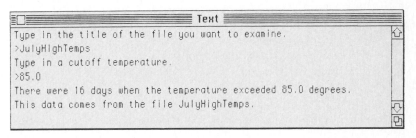

Figure 11.12   Typical output for **program** HotDays.

```
program HotDays;
{YOU TYPE IN A CUTOFF TEMPERATURE. PROGRAM REPORTS THE NUMBER OF}
{DAYS IN THE MONTH THAT WERE HOTTER THAN THE CUTOFF TEMPERATURE.}
  type
   FileOfReals = file of real;
  var
   CutOff : real;
   FileName : string;
   TemperatureData : FileOfReals;
```

(continued)

```
procedure ReportHotDays(var TempData : FileOfReals;
        CutOff : real);
{WHEN YOU PASS A FILE TO A PROCEDURE, THE FORMAL PARAMETER MUST BE A}
{VARIABLE PARAMETER AND ITS TYPE MUST BE DEFINED EARLIER IN PROGRAM.}
  var
   HotCount : integer;
   Temperature : real;
 begin
 HotCount := 0;
 reset(TempData);
 while not (eof(TempData)) do
  begin
   read(TempData,Temperature);
   if (Temperature > CutOff) then
    HotCount := HotCount + 1
  end;
 writeln('There were ',HotCount : 2,' days when the temperature exceeded ',
         Cutoff : 3 : 1,' degrees.');
 writeln('This data comes from the file ',FileName,'.')
 end;
      {MAIN PROGRAM}
begin
 writeln('Type in the title of the file you want to examine.');
 write ('>');
 readln(FileName);
 open(TemperatureData,FileName);
 writeln('Type in a cutoff temperature.');
 write('>');
 readln(CutOff);
 ReportHotDays(TemperatureData,CutOff);
 close(TemperatureData)
end.
```

When you run **program** HotDays, you type in the name of an external file, such as JulyHighTemps. If you had already created other files of monthly temperature data such as MayHighTemps or JuneHighTemps, you could type in one of these file names and the program would examine the data in that file.

The procedure call passes the file variable TemperatureData and the cutoff temperature to **procedure** ReportHotDays. Let's examine the heading line to see how to pass a file to a procedure:

```
procedure ReportHotDays(var TempData : FileOfReals; CutOff : real);
```

The formal parameter TempData is declared to be of type FileOfReals, which we have declared in the declaration part of the program. We were

Summary of Random-Access File Commands and Concepts

Open

The *open* command associates a file variable with an external file. It opens the file for reading or writing. A file must be open before data can be sent to it or read from it. The open command has two parameters, a file variable and an external file name or title. The title has type **string**.

```
open(FileVariable,TitleOfExternalFile)
```

Close

The *close* command breaks the association between a file variable and an external file, and it closes the external file. It has only one parameter:

```
close(FileVariable)
```

File Pointer

Every file variable comes with a file pointer. When a file variable becomes associated with an external file, the file variable's pointer points to some entry in the file or to the end of the file. Immediately after an *open* or *reset* command is executed, the file variable pointer points to the first position in the file, position 0.

Reset

The command *reset*(FileVariable) positions FileVariable's file pointer at the beginning of the file variable's associated external file.

Eof

Eof is a function with one parameter, a file variable. The function returns a *boolean* value. *Eof*(FileVariable) is True if the file variable's pointer is past the last component in the file.

Seek

Seek(FileVariable,n) positions the file variable's pointer at position n in the file variable's associated external file. The entries in the file are numbered beginning at 0. If the position of the last component is less than n, *seek*(FileVariable,n) positions the pointer just past the last entry in the file—even if n greatly exceeds the position of the last entry in the file. Files can have up to *maxlongint* entries, so the command *seek*(FileVariable,*maxlongint*) will always place the pointer just past the last entry.

Passing a File to a Procedure or Function

When a file is used as a parameter for a procedure or function, it must be a variable parameter. Furthermore the type of the formal parameter must be defined not in the parameter list but at some higher level of the program.

required to create type FileOfReals because the type of a formal parameter must be either a type that has been defined in the declaration part of the program or a standard type.

You would get an error message if you tried to use the following heading line for **procedure** ReportHotDays:

```
procedure ReportHotDays(var TempData : file of real; CutOff : real);
```

This would not work because TempData's type is defined inside the parameter list of the procedure.

Note that TempData is a variable parameter, although the procedure does not alter the external file in any way. When the formal parameter for a procedure or function is a file, it must *always* be a variable parameter. If it were possible to pass a file as a value parameter, the procedure would have to make a copy of the entire file. But there is not enough space in main memory to accommodate a large file. For this reason Pascal requires that files be passed as variable parameters.

Files that hold entries of type *real* or *integer* are not uncommon. But file applications most often involve files of records. A corporation's employee payroll file, an inventory file for an auto parts store, the membership file of a union local—all of these files involve complex data items, making a file of records the appropriate data structure. For our last example, we will show you how to work with a file of records.

11.11 The Last Program—Program PhoneBook

We will end this book with a final program that creates an electronic telephone book. **Program** PhoneBook creates a file of names and phone numbers. Each entry is stored as a record. After you type in your entries, you can list the whole directory or look up a phone number by searching for a particular name. Because the names and numbers are stored in a random-access file, you can easily change old entries or add new ones.

All this is accomplished using the menu procedures we introduced in **program** MiniPaint. There are five menu items in this program, as you can see in Figure 11.13.

If you click on Directory, the program lists all the telephone book entries. Clicking on AddEntry lets you add a new name and number to the phone book. Search enables you to search for a particular name. And Alter allows you to change a name or number. If you make several entries and then click on Directory, your screen will look something like the screen in Figure 11.13.

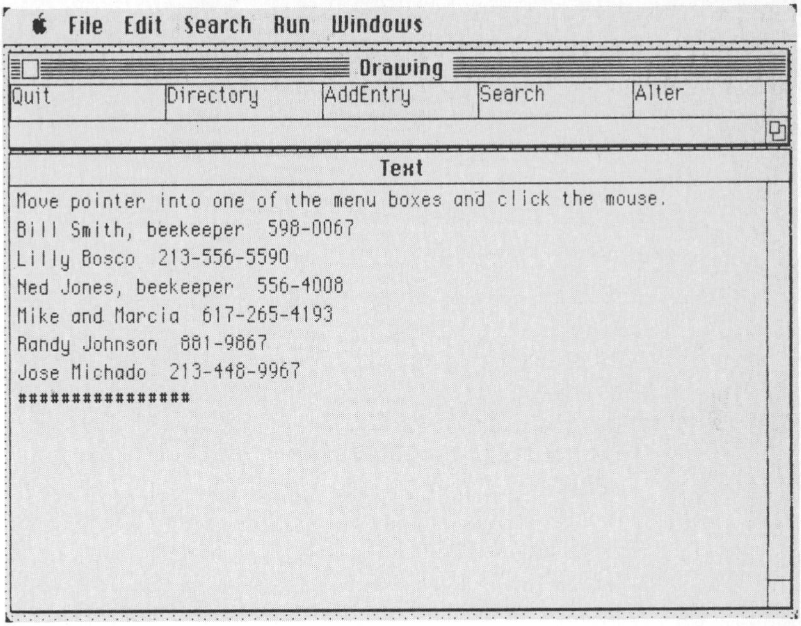

Figure 11.13 **Program** PhoneBook's menu in the Drawing window, along with a sample directory in the Text window.

Program PhoneBook uses a file of records as its principal data structure. The record data structure is called PhoneBookEntry, and it has the following definition:

```
PhoneBookEntry = record
  Name : string;
  PhoneNumber : string[20]
end;
```

The Main Program

The main program uses the mouse and menu body from **program** MiniPaint, with two additions—an *open* command at the beginning of the main program and a *close* statement at the end. The first statement in the body of the program,

```
open(NameList,'NamesAndNumbers')
```

opens the file variable NameList and associates it with the external file NamesAndNumbers. The last statement in the body,

```
close(NameList)
```

closes the file.

The four commands in the menu—Directory, AddEntry, Search, and Alter—are implemented as procedures and are included inside **procedure** DoCommand.

Directory

Directory is the simplest command. When you click on Directory, **procedure** ListEntries lists all names and numbers that appear in the external file.

```
procedure ListEntries;
 var
   Entry : PhoneBookEntry;
begin
 reset(NameList);
 while not(eof(NameList)) do
  begin
   read(NameList,Entry);
   PrintContentsOf(Entry)
  end
end;
```

First, *reset* positions the pointer at the beginning of the external file NamesAndNumbers. Then the **while** loop is executed until the pointer reaches the end of the file. During each iteration, the *read* statement reads an entry from the external file into the variable Entry. PrintContentsOf is a one-line procedure that prints out Entry.Name followed by Entry.PhoneNumber in the Text window.

AddEntry

When you click on AddEntry, **procedure** AddAnEntry is called. You are prompted for a name and a phone number. Then the name and number you type in are sent to the external file.

```
procedure AddAnEntry;
 var
   Entry : PhoneBookEntry;
begin
 seek(NameList,maxlongint);
 PromptAndRead_String('Enter a name.',Entry.Name);
 PromptAndRead_String('Enter a phone number.',Entry.PhoneNumber);
 if (length(Entry.Name) > 0) then
   write(NameList,Entry)
end;
```

First, the command

```
seek(NameList,maxlongint)
```

advances the file pointer to the end of the file, just after the last entry. Next you enter a name and a number. These are stored in the local record variable Entry. Then the value of Entry is written out to the external file. Because NameList's pointer points to the end of the file NamesAndNumbers, the contents of Entry are placed at the very end of the file.

Search

When you click on Search, **procedure** HuntForAllOccurrences is called, and a prompt appears in the Text window asking you to type in a name or phrase. After you type one in, the procedure looks for your entry in the file.

HuntForAllOccurrences works like **procedure** ListEntries, except that, instead of printing every component of the file, it prints only those components that contain the name or phrase you have entered.

To identify entries that contain the name or phrase you entered, the procedure uses the MacPascal string function *pos*, which has result type *integer*. In the function call

```
pos(SubString,CharString)
```

the variable Substring has as its value the name or phrase you entered. If SubString occurs as a part of the string CharString, *pos* returns the position of the character in CharString where the match begins. So *pos*('ab','abcd') = 1, and *pos*('cd','abcd') = 3. *Pos* returns 0 if SubString is not a substring of CharString. For example, *pos*('ac', 'abcd') = 0.

When the name or phrase you have entered occurs in the Name field of any of the entries, the *pos* function returns a value greater than zero and the procedure prints those entries out. This means that you don't have to type a complete name or even a complete last name to look up someone's number. You can list all the Walters in your telephone book, along with their numbers, just by typing *Walter*.

The Search command also enables you to do keyword searches. Suppose your phonebook entries include not only names, but also short descriptions for some or all of the entries. For example, you might include the entry

```
Bill Smith, beekeeper  598-0067
```

If you click on the Search command and then type *bee*, all entries that include the substring *bee* in the Name field will be printed out, and you will get a listing of all the beekeepers in your telephone book, as you can see in Figure 11.14.

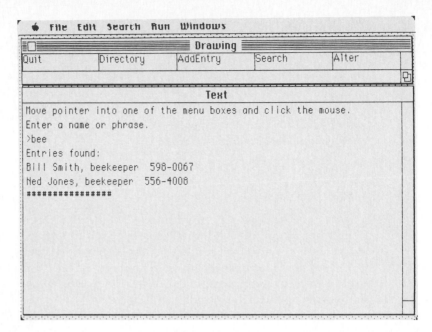

Figure 11.14 The output windows after a search has been done for the word *bee.*

Here is the code for **procedure** HuntForAllOccurrences.

```
procedure HuntForAllOccurrences;
 var
  NameOrPhrase : string;
  ThisEntry : PhoneBookEntry;
begin
 PromptAndRead_String('Enter a name or phrase.',NameOrPhrase);
 reset(NameList);
 writeln('Entries found:');
 while not(eof(NameList)) do
  begin
   read(NameList,ThisEntry);
   if (pos(NameOrPhrase,ThisEntry.Name) > 0) then
    PrintContentsOf(ThisEntry)
  end
end;
```

Alter

When you click on Alter, the **procedure** ChangeEntry is executed. ChangeEntry first asks for a name or phrase to use in locating the entry you want to change. Then the Find function is called. Find returns the file position of the *first* entry that contains the name or phrase you entered, if it can find one. Otherwise it returns − 1, and ChangeEntry asks you to try again.

Find uses the standard function *filepos* to locate the entry you are looking for. *Filepos* has one argument, a file variable. It returns the position of the file variable's pointer in its associated external file.

If Find does turn up an entry, the *seek* command positions the pointer there, and the contents of that entry are printed out. Then you supply a replacement entry.

Next, because the *read* statement has advanced the pointer 1 position, another *seek* command repositions the file pointer back 1 position.

Finally, the *write* statement writes your alternative entry out to the file. The record variable NewEntry holds the altered entry you want to insert, and the statement

```
write(NameList,NewEntry)
```

overwrites the entry you want to change.

Here is the code for ChangeEntry.

```
procedure ChangeEntry;
 var
  NameOrPhrase : string;
  Location : integer;
  OldEntry,NewEntry : PhoneBookEntry;
 begin
 reset(NameList);
 PromptAndRead_String('Whose number do you want to look
                       for? ',NameOrPhrase);
 Location := Find(NameOrPhrase);
 if (Location < 0) then
  writeln('Name or phrase not found -- try again.')
 else
  begin
   seek(NameList,Location);
   read(NameList,OldEntry);
   PrintContentsOf(OldEntry);
   PromptAndRead_String('Type in a new name.',NewEntry.Name);
   PromptAndRead_String('Type a new number.',NewEntry.PhoneNumber);
   seek(NameList,Location);
   write(NameList,NewEntry)
  end
 end;
```

Here is the complete program, the last program in the book.

```pascal
program PhoneBook;
 const
  CommandCount = 6;
  BoxHeight = 20;
  WindowWidth = 500;
 type
  Commands = (Bad,Quit,Directory,AddEntry,Search,Alter);
  PhoneBookEntry = record
    Name : string;
    PhoneNumber : string[20]
   end;
 var
  H,V : integer;
  Command : Commands;
  NameList : file of PhoneBookEntry;

 procedure PromptAndRead_String(Prompt : string;
          var WhatIsRead : string);
 begin
  writeln(Prompt);
  write('>');
  readln(WhatIsRead)
 end;

 procedure ClickPoint(var H,V : integer);
 begin
  repeat
   getmouse(H,V)
  until button;
  repeat
   getmouse(H,V)
  until not (button)
 end;

 procedure LayoutMenu;
  var
   BoxWidth : integer;

  procedure DrawAndLabelBoxes(BoxWidth,BoxCount : integer);
   var
    BoxNumber, Position : integer;
    Command : Commands;
   procedure PrintLabel(Position : integer;
          Command : Commands);
```

```
  begin
   moveto(Position + 1,BoxHeight div 2);
   writedraw(Command)
  end;
{BODY OF DRAWLABELSANDBOXES}
begin
 Command := Bad;
 BoxNumber := 0;
 Position := 0;
 repeat
  Command := succ(Command);
  BoxNumber := BoxNumber + 1;
  drawline(Position,0,Position,BoxHeight);
  PrintLabel(Position,Command);
  Position := Position + BoxWidth
 until (BoxNumber = BoxCount)
end;
{BODY OF LAYOUTMENU}
begin
 drawline(0,BoxHeight,WindowWidth,BoxHeight);
 BoxWidth := WindowWidth div (CommandCount - 1);
 DrawAndLabelBoxes(BoxWidth,CommandCount - 1)
end;


function ChooseCommand(H,V : integer) : Commands;
 var
  BoxNumber : integer;


 function VerticalOk(V : integer) : boolean;
 begin
  if (0 <= V) and (V < BoxHeight) then
   VerticalOk := True
  else
   VerticalOk := False
 end;


 function HorizontalOk(H : integer) : boolean;
 begin
  if (0 <= H) and (H < WindowWidth) then
   HorizontalOk := True
  else
   HorizontalOk := False
 end;
```

(continued)

```pascal
function SelectCommand(BoxNumber : integer) : Commands;
 var
  Box : integer;
  CommandChoice : Commands;
 begin
 Box := BoxNumber;
 CommandChoice := Quit;
 while (Box > 0) do
  begin
   Box := Box - 1;
   CommandChoice := succ(CommandChoice)
  end;
 SelectCommand := CommandChoice
 end;
{BODY OF PROCEDURE CHOOSECOMMAND}
begin
 if VerticalOk(V) and HorizontalOk(H) then
  begin
   BoxNumber := ((CommandCount - 1)*H) div WindowWidth;
   ChooseCommand := SelectCommand(BoxNumber)
  end
 else
  ChooseCommand := Bad
end;

procedure DoCommand(Command : Commands);

 procedure PrintContentsOf(ThisEntry : PhoneBookEntry);
 begin
  writeln(ThisEntry.Name,' ', ThisEntry.PhoneNumber)
 end;

 procedure ListEntries;
  var
   Entry : PhoneBookEntry;
 begin
  reset(NameList);
  while not (eof(NameList)) do
   begin
    read(NameList,Entry);
    PrintContentsOf(Entry)
   end
 end;

 procedure AddAnEntry;
  var
   Entry : PhoneBookEntry;
```

```
begin
 seek(NameList,maxlongint);
 PromptAndRead_String('Enter a name.',Entry.Name);
 PromptAndRead_String('Enter a phone number.',Entry.PhoneNumber);
 if (length(Entry.Name) > 0) then
  write(NameList,Entry)
end;


procedure HuntForAllOccurrences;
 var
  NameOrPhrase : string;
  ThisEntry : PhoneBookEntry;
begin
 PromptAndRead_String('Enter a name or phrase.',NameOrPhrase);
 reset(NameList);
 writeln('Entries found:');
 while not (eof(NameList)) do
  begin
   read(NameList, ThisEntry);
   if (pos(NameOrPhrase,ThisEntry.Name) > 0) then
    PrintContentsOf(ThisEntry)
  end
end;


function Find(NameOrPhrase : string) : integer;
{FIND REPORTS THE FIRST OCCURRENCE OF NAMEORPHRASE IN THE PHONEBOOK}
 var
  Position : integer;
  Found : boolean;
  ThisEntry : PhoneBookEntry;
begin
 reset(NameList);
 Found := False;
 while not (eof(NameList)) and not (Found) do
  begin
   read(NameList, ThisEntry);
   if (pos(NameOrPhrase,ThisEntry.Name) > 0) then
    begin
     Found := True;
     Position := filepos(NameList) - 1
{FILEPOS IS A STANDARD FUNCTION THAT RETURNS THE POSITION}
{OF THE FILE POINTER.}
    end
  end;
 if Found then
  Find := Position
 else
  Find := -1
end;
```

(continued)

```pascal
procedure ChangeEntry;
 var
  NameOrPhrase : string;
  Location : integer;
  OldEntry,NewEntry : PhoneBookEntry;
begin
 reset(NameList);
 PromptAndRead_String('Whose number do you want to look for?',
                      NameOrPhrase);
 Location := Find(NameOrPhrase);
 if (Location < 0) then
  writeln('Name or phrase not found -- try again.')
 else
  begin
   seek(NameList,Location);
   read(NameList,OldEntry);
   PrintContentsOf(OldEntry);
   PromptAndRead_String('Type in a new name.',NewEntry.Name);
   PromptAndRead_String('Type in a new number.',
                        NewEntry.PhoneNumber);
   seek(NameList, Location);
   write(NameList, NewEntry)
  end
end;
  {BODY OF DOCOMMAND}
begin
 case Command of
  Bad:
   begin
    sysbeep(20);
    writeln('Bad command -- enter another')
   end;
  Directory:
   ListEntries;
  AddEntry:
   AddAnEntry;
  Search:
   HuntForAllOccurrences;
  Alter :
   ChangeEntry
 end;
 writeln('###############')
end;
```

```
 {BODY OF PROGRAM}
begin
 open(NameList,'NamesAndNumbers');
 writeln('Move pointer into one of the menu boxes
          and click the mouse.');
 LayoutMenu;
 ClickPoint(H,V);
 Command := ChooseCommand(H,V);
 while (Command <> Quit) do
  begin
   DoCommand(Command);
   ClickPoint(H,V);
   Command := ChooseCommand(H,V)
  end;
 close(NameList)
end.
```

Program PhoneBook is long and complex, but it's worth studying until you understand it completely. Using it as a model, you can write programs that balance your checkbook, manage inventories, or keep track of data in a scientific experiment. Some of these projects are outlined in the problems at the end of this chapter.

You have now seen most of the programming language Pascal. After you have mastered files and records, which enable you to store almost unlimited amounts of structured data on disks, you will be able to write programs that are truly useful.

TEST YOURSELF

1. What is a record field?
2. What is a field selector?
3. What does the command *seek* do?
4. Where are data in an external file stored?
5. What does the string function *pos* do?
6. What does the MacPascal standard procedure *pensize* do?
7. What does *eof* test for?
8. What does the command *open* do?

PROBLEMS

1. Add a straight line instruction to MiniPaint: You click twice in the Drawing window, and the program draws a line between the two points where you clicked.

2. The Reflect command we presented in Exercise 1 on page 397 reflects any line you draw horizontally in the Drawing window. Change the command so that it reflects any line you draw both horizontally and vertically, like this:

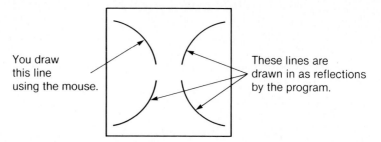

You draw this line using the mouse.

These lines are drawn in as reflections by the program.

3. Change **program** Survey in Chapter 9 so that RutlandSt is an array of records. Each component in the array should record the number of people in a house and the day you made your visit. The output of the program should be a table that shows (1) the household size for each house on the street and (2) the day you visited the house.

4. Define a point to be a record consisting of two integers. Then define an array of points with index type 1..20, and write a program that generates the points in the array randomly. The program should then draw a picture that consists of lines connecting all the points.

5. Suppose you have a special telephone service that allows you to call to an adjacent area code inexpensively. The first hour of calls is free each month, and each additional minute costs 6 cents. Write a program that calculates how much you owe for the special service each month. Every day you type in the number of minutes you talk. At the end of a month, the program prints how much you owe the phone company. The program should use a random-access file to keep track of your phone records.

6. Write a program that keeps track of two health statistics for a month—say, daily weight and hours of sleep. The program stores this information in an external file. One part of the program should allow you to add new data to the external file. The entries in the file should be of this type:

```
type
  HealthInfo = record
    Weight : integer;
    Sleep : real
  end;
```

Each morning you should be able to get up, weigh yourself, count the hours you slept, and then enter these data in your health information file.

Another part of the program should display the data in the file as two line graphs—one for Weight, the other for Sleep, like this:

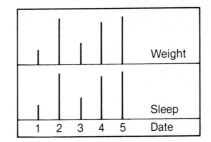

(*Hint:* Don't write the whole program at once. The program should include a procedure called DisplayData. In your first version of the program, DisplayData should print the data in a simple table. Once you get this simpler version of the program running, you can change **procedure** DisplayData so that it prints the output as a graph.)

7. Write a program that keeps track of the checks you write during the year, using a random-access file. A check has record type ACheck.

```
type
 ACheck = record
    Month : Months;
    Date : 1..31;
    CheckNumber : integer;
    Amount : real;
    WhoTo : string;
    Returned : boolean
 end;
```

Use the MiniPaint functions and procedures in your program, and include the following commands:

■ AddCheck. AddCheck adds a check entry to the file.

■ CheckNumberInfo. You type a check number, and the program prints all information about that check.

■ ListAllSince. You type a date, and the program lists all checks written since that date.

■ AmtInMonth. You type a month, and the program prints the amount of money you spent by check during the month.

Glossary

Actual parameter The variable or expression in a procedure or function call that is actually passed to a procedure or function. *See also* parameter.

Algorithm A step-by-step plan for solving a problem or writing a program.

Argument An actual parameter.

Array A group of related variables that are declared with a common name in a single variable declaration. The variables all have the same type, which is called the *component type* of the array. Each variable is identified by an *index*, which is given in square brackets after the name of the variable. The index indicates the position of the variable in the array.

Assignment statement A statement that assigns a value to a variable. The left side of an assignment statement must be a variable.

Body of a program The main part or statement part of a program. Everything that follows the declaration part of a program.

Boolean One of Pascal's standard types. There are only two members of type *boolean*, true and false. *See also* type.

Boolean expression An expression made up of boolean variables and the boolean operators **and, or,** and **not.** A boolean expression has a boolean value. That is, it is either true or false.

Boolean variable A variable that is declared to be of type *boolean*. The value of a boolean variable is either true or false.

Braces The symbols { }, which are used to enclose comments.

Bug A mistake in a program. When you correct a mistake, you debug the program.

Case statement A statement that allows selection of one of several possible actions. A single **case** statement can often do the job of a series of nested **if** statements.

Cell A location in memory.

Central processing unit The "brain" of the computer. It controls how the computer does arithmetic and logic, and it fetches and executes machine-language instructions that are stored in memory. Abbreviated as CPU.

Char One of Pascal's standard types. Type *char*, which is short for *character*, includes letters, digits, punctuation, and every other symbol on the keyboard. *See also* type.

Code To convert an algorithm into a Pascal program.

Comment A note inserted in a program that explains something about the program. A comment is surrounded by braces and does not affect program execution.

Compiler After a program is typed in, Pascal commands must be translated into machine language—a binary code that tells the computer what actions to take. With most versions of Pascal, a program called a compiler does this translation step. Only after the whole program has been compiled (a process that can take several minutes), is it ready to be executed. With Macintosh Pascal, the translation into machine language is done by a program called an interpreter, which translates Pascal commands, line by line, during program execution. Because MacPascal programs are interpreted, they are ready to run as soon as they are typed in. *See also* interpreter.

Component of an array One of a group of related variables, all of the same type, that make up an array. The position that each component occupies in the array is specified by the component's index.

Component of a file An entry in an external file.

Compound statement A sequence of statements separated by semicolons and listed between the word **begin** and the word **end.** Pascal treats compound statements as a single statement.

Computational logic The area of computer science that deals with formal reasoning by computer. Theorem proving by computer is part of this field.

Conditional statement An **if-then** or **if-then-else** statement.

Constant An identifier that has been given a fixed value.

Control line of a for statement The first line in a **for** statement. It sets the number of times the loop is to be executed.

Control line of a *while* statement The first line in a **while** statement. The control line contains a test, and looping continues until the test becomes false.

CPU *See* central processing unit.

Dangling else The **else** part of an **if-then-else** statement that has been nested inside an **if-then** statement.

Data structure An organizing scheme for data in a program. Arrays, records, and files are data structures.

Data table A table that includes information about input variables, output variables, program variables, loops, constants, type definitions, and special formulas used in a program. Making up a data table is useful in the thinking stage of program writing.

Debug To fix an error in a program. *See also* bug.

Declaration part of a program The part of a program that comes before the statement part and consists of declarations for variables, procedures and functions, and definitions for constants and types. Procedures and functions also have declaration parts. *See also* statement part.

Disk A platter that the computer uses to store programs and files. The Macintosh can use both floppy disks and larger hard disks. Unlike main memory, disks store data and programs permanently.

Divide-and-conquer strategy An approach that involves breaking a large problem into small parts and then solving the parts one by one. *See also* top-down programming.

Echoing Reading in a text and then printing it out unchanged in one of the output windows.

Empty statement A nonexistent statement, which is considered to exist when two separator symbols, such as a semicolon and an **end,** appear next to each other in a program. The empty statement tells the computer to take no action.

Enumerated type A type that a programmer makes up. An enumerated type consists of an ordered collection of identifiers listed in a type definition.

Execute To carry out an instruction or a series of instructions.

Expression A grouping of values, constants, variables, or functions. Number, 5, (5 * Number), and *sqrt*(5 * Number) are all expressions.

External file A Macintosh document that holds data generated by a Pascal program.

Field selector The identifier for a field of a record variable.

Field width When MacPascal prints out a value, it allots a space, or field width, for the value. It right-justifies the value in the allotted space, leaving any extra spaces to the left of the value. The field width for a parameter of a *writeln* or *write* statement can be specified by a colon followed by the number of spaces to be allotted for the value.

File A collection of data that a program stores permanently on a disk. *See also* external file.

File pointer An imaginary pointer that comes with a file variable and identifies a specific location in an external file.

File variable A variable of type *file* that links a program with an external file. A file variable comes with a file pointer.

Flag A boolean variable that is part of a test in a loop. A flag is used to end looping early when some special condition is met.

Floppy disk *See* disk.

Formal parameter An identifier that is declared in the heading line of a procedure or function. *See also* actual parameter, variable parameter, and value parameter.

Function A kind of subprogram that always returns a single value.

Function call A statement that tells the computer to execute a function subprogram. The function call can pass actual parameters to the function declaration.

Generate and test method A problem-solving method that uses a loop to generate a set of values and to apply some test to each element in that set of values.

Global identifier An identifier that has meaning throughout a program, not merely in one section of it. A global constant, for example, is a constant whose value can be used in the main program as well as in any procedure or function defined in the program. Global identifiers are defined in the declaration part of the main program.

Heading line The first line of a program, function, or procedure.

Identifier Any word that you use as a name for a program, variable, constant, function, or procedure. An identifier cannot be a reserved word.

Idiot-proofing Protecting a program against inappropriate input values.

Increment To increase the value of a variable.

Index A value that identifies a component of an array. The index follows the name of the array and is enclosed in square brackets. The index type of an array specifies how the components of an array are identified. *See also* array.

Infinite loop A loop that repeats forever because the condition that terminates the loop is never met.

Initialize To give a beginning value to a variable.

Input Data that are given to a program while the program is running. Input can be supplied interactively (typed in while the program is running) or it can be supplied from an external file.

Integer One of Pascal's standard types. Type *integer* consists of the whole numbers from $-32,767$ to $32,767$. *See also* maxint.

Interactive program A program that receives values for some of its variables directly from the keyboard during program execution.

Interpreter A program that translates Pascal commands into machine language, instruction by instruction, while a program is running. Macintosh Pascal is interpreted, which means that programs are ready to run as soon as they are typed in; most other versions of Pascal are compiled. *See also* compiler.

Iteration One repetition of a looping statement.

Local identifier A constant or variable that is declared inside a procedure or function. *See also* global identifier.

Longint One of Macintosh Pascal's standard types. It includes all the whole-number values from $-2,147,483,647$ to $2,147,483,647$. *See also* maxlongint.

Loop A command that instructs the computer to repeat an instruction or group of instructions over and over. There are three looping commands in Pascal: the **for** loop, the **repeat-until** loop, and the **while** loop.

Machine language A primitive code that uses patterns of zeros and ones to control a computer. Programs written in Pascal and other high-level programming languages must be translated into machine language before the computer can execute them.

Main memory   The storage locations inside the Macintosh where a program is stored temporarily while it is being written or used. When the Macintosh is turned off, main memory goes blank.

Main program   The statement part, or body, of a program. Everything that comes after the declaration part of a program.

Maxint   The largest value in type *integer*: 32767.

Maxlongint   The largest value in type *longint*: 2,147,483,647.

Mixed-mode expression   An expression in which both real and integer values or variables are used.

Monte Carlo method   A method that uses the laws of chance to calculate results in mathematics.

Nesting   Placing one kind of statement inside another statement of the same kind, as in a nested **for** loop.

Operator   A symbol or word used in mathematical calculations. The arithmetic operators are +, −, *, /, **div**, and **mod**. Another group of operators, called the relational operators, are = , <, >, < >, < = , and > = . Pascal also uses logical operators that work only with boolean expressions. The logical operators are **and**, **or**, and **not**.

Parameter   A special kind of variable used in a procedure or function.

Parent type   *See* subrange type.

Pretty printing   Macintosh Pascal style for displaying programs. Reserved words are automatically printed in boldface, and the lines in a program are automatically indented to follow the logical structure of the program.

Procedure   A subprogram that does part of the work of a program. A procedure has two parts: a declaration part and a statement part. A procedure declaration lists the instructions that the procedure will carry out. A procedure statement tells the computer to execute the instruction in the procedure declaration.

Procedure call   Execution of a procedure statement.

Prompt   A message printed in the Text window that tells a person who is using an interactive program to type in some information.

Random-access file   Macintosh Pascal's file system includes random-access-file commands. These commands make it possible to access file components in any order. The *seek* command advances a file variable's pointer directly to a particular component in a file. This is not possible with sequential files. *See also* file and sequential file.

Random number   A number with an unpredictable value. The MacPascal function *random* generates random numbers.

Real   One of Pascal's standard types. The type consists of numbers that are decimal fractions.

Record   A data structure with component variables that need not be of the same type.

Recursion   A calculating technique in which a function or procedure calls itself.

Relational operator   A symbol that tests the relationships between values. The relational operators are = , <, >, < >, < = , and > = . *See also* operator.

Reserved word   Words such as **program, var, begin,** and **end** that have special meanings in Pascal. A complete list of reserved words is given inside the back cover of this book. These words may not be used as identifiers.

Result type   The type of the value returned by a function.

Run   To execute a program.

Run-time error   A bug that shows up during program execution.

SANE   An abbreviation that stands for Standard Apple Numerics Environment. SANE is a system for doing arithmetic with real numbers. Macintosh Pascal's arithmetic operators are part of SANE.

Scientific notation   A system that represents real numbers using exponents. Macintosh Pascal output is printed in scientific notation unless colon notation is used to specify the number of digits to the right of the decimal point. Scientific notation is also called *floating-point* notation.

Scoreboard principle   A method of using an array to keep a running tally of data generated in a program.

Scratchpad principle A programming technique in which a "scratchpad" variable is used to hold a value temporarily while values of two or more variables are exchanged.

Sequential file Pascal's traditional file system uses sequential file commands exclusively. With the sequential file facility, the components of a file must be read sequentially, begining with the first component. It is not possible to advance a file variable's pointer directly to a particular location in a file. This feature makes it inconvenient to alter data entries in a sequential file. *See also* random-access file.

Standard function A predefined function, such as *round* or *sqrt*, that is built into MacPascal. Like other functions, a standard function returns a single value.

Standard procedure A predefined procedure, such as *writeln* or *paintcircle*, that is built into Macintosh Pascal.

Standard type The Macintosh Pascal standard types are *integer*, *longint*, *real*, *char*, *string*, and *boolean*. *See also* type.

Statement part of a program The program body or main program, which comes after the declaration part of the program; the series of statements that make up the action part of a program. *See also* declaration part of a program.

String A sequence of characters. The standard type **string** allows you to manipulate a sequence of characters directly.

Subprogram A Pascal procedure or function.

Subrange type A type that consists of a number of consecutive elements from another type, called the parent type. The parent type can be *integer*, *char*, an enumerated type, or even another subrange type.

Syntactic analysis The study of the techniques and algorithms that are needed to analyze the syntax of a program.

Syntax The rules that determine the proper arrangement of symbols and words that make up a command or program.

Syntax diagram A diagram used to specify the syntax rules that govern Pascal commands. Sometimes called a bubble diagram.

Test An expression that can be either true or false. *See also* boolean expression.

Theorem A boolean expression that is always true, no matter what values its boolean variables have. *See also* boolean expression and boolean variables.

Top-down programming A method for writing programs that consists of breaking a big programming problem into small, manageable parts and solving each part separately.

Truth table A table that lists the possible values of a boolean expression. *See also* boolean expression.

Type In Pascal all variables must be declared to be of a specific type. Numbers are of type *integer*, type *longint*, or type *real*. Letters, symbols, and the digits 0 to 9 are of type *char*. Type *boolean* consists of the two values true and false. *Integer*, *longint*, *real*, *char* and *boolean* are standard types. The type **string** is also considered a standard type. Enumerated types are types made up by a programmer.

Value parameter A formal parameter of a procedure or function that is assigned the value of the actual parameter when a procedure or function is called. The value of an actual parameter associated with a value parameter cannot change during execution of the subprogram. *See also* variable parameter.

Variable An identifier whose value changes as a program runs. Every variable has an associated location in memory, where the variable's value is stored.

Variable parameter A formal parameter in a procedure or function that becomes a second name for an actual parameter. The value of both a formal value parameter and its corresponding actual parameter can change during execution of the subprogram. For this reason, an actual parameter that corresponds to a variable formal parameter must be a variable rather than a fixed value or expression.

Solutions to Exercises and Selected Problems

Chapter 1

Exercises

1. **a.** (100,100)

2. **a.** diagonal   **b.** diagonal   **c.** vertical   **d.** horizontal   **e.** slanted

3. `paintcircle(100,100,100)`

Problems

3. **a.** 2.   **b.** 3   **c.** 1   **d.** 2   **e.** 3

9. a triangle

13. **b.** `program ThreeCircles;`
    ```
    begin
      invertcircle(100,66,66);
      invertcircle(66,134,66);
      invertcircle(134,134,66)
    end.
    ```

14.
    ```
    program OverAndOver;
     var
      PledgeNumber : integer;
     begin
      for PledgeNumber := 1 to 500 do
       begin
        writeln(PledgeNumber);
        writeln('I will not talk in class.')
       end
     end.
    ```

15. **a.** program RollDownLine;
```
   var
     Position : integer;
   begin
    writeln('The First Cartoon!');
    drawline(99,0,99,200);
    for Position := 20 to 180 do
     begin
      paintcircle(120,Position,20);
      invertcircle(120,Position,20)
     end
   end.
```

b. program Perpendicular;
```
   var
     Position : integer;
   begin
    for Position := 20 to 180 do
     begin
      drawline(99,0,99,200);
      drawline(0,100,200,100);
      paintcircle(120,Position,20);
      invertcircle(120,Position,20);
      paintcircle(Position,80,20);
      invertcircle(Position,80,20)
     end
   end.
```

Chapter 2

Exercises

1. **a.** 4   **b.** 0

2. **a.** 2   **b.** 0   **c.** 47

3. **b.** program FirstLoopOne;
```
   var
     Number : integer;
   begin
    for Number := 1 to 4 do
     begin
      writeln(3 * Number)
     end
   end.
```

```pascal
program FirstLoopTwo;
 var
  Number : integer;
begin
 for Number := 0 to 3 do
  begin
   writeln(3 * Number)
  end
end.

program FirstLoopThree;
 var
  Number : integer;
begin
 for Number := -1 to 2 do
  begin
   writeln(2 * Number)
  end
end.

program FirstLoopFour;
 var
  Number : integer;
begin
 for Number := -4 to -1 do
  begin
   writeln(2 * Number)
  end
end.
```

4. (4 * LeapYear)

Problems

1. **b.** 1038 **div** 12 = 86

5. **b.**
```pascal
program NotSure_b;
 var
  Point : integer;
begin
 for Point := 0 to 10 do
  begin
   drawline(0,200,200,20 * Point)
  end
end.
```

8.
```pascal
program OffCenterDiamond;
  var
   MeetingPoint : integer;
 begin
  for MeetingPoint := 0 to (200 div 4) do
   begin
    drawline(0,100,50,4 * MeetingPoint);
    drawline(200,100,50,4 * MeetingPoint)
   end
 end.
```

13. d.
```pascal
program NumberColumn_d;
   var
    Number : integer;
  begin
   for Number := 9 downto 5 do
    begin
     writeln(Number * 10)
    end
  end.
```

g.
```pascal
program NumberColumn_g;
   var
    Number : integer;
  begin
   for Number := 0 to 8 do
    begin
     writeln(Number div 3)
    end
  end.
```

17. a.
```pascal
program RailRoadTracks;
   var
    Position : integer;
  begin
   drawline(0,80,200,80);
   drawline(0,120,200,120);
   for Position := 1 to 5 do
    begin
     drawline((40 * Position) - 20,80,(40 * Position) - 20,120)
    end
  end.
```

_____Chapter 3_____

Exercises

1. Eliminate the **begin** and **end** that surround the *drawline* statement.

3. **a.** The loop prints "Polly want a cracker?" 200 times.

4. **a.** Change the value of the constant Radius to 30 and the value of Line-Height to 175.
   b. Change Radius to 45 and LineHeight to 195.

5. The program reads in two numbers, adds them, and then prints their sum. The first two *writeln* statements are prompts. The program would produce unreliable output if you moved the last *writeln* statement from the end to the beginning of the body of the program, because the two variables in the *writeln* statement would have arbitrary values.

6. The answer is (a). To get the output in (b), reverse the order of the *writeln* statements.

7. **a.** Be there or be square.
   b. Be there or be square.
   c. Be there or
   be square.

8. **b.** 19.95
   -126.0
   0.0
   0.342
   0.25
   3.96e5 or 396000.0

9. **a.** `writeln(5/7 : 12 : 10)`
   b. `writeln(100/7 : 9 : 6)`
   c. `writeln('My bucket of night crawlers costs $', 2.98 : 4 : 2)`

Problems

3. ```
   program Grid;
     var
       LineNumber : integer;
     begin
     for LineNumber := 1 to 20 do
       begin
         drawline(0,10 * LineNumber,200,10 * LineNumber);
         drawline(10 * LineNumber,0,10 * LineNumber,200)
       end
     end.
   ```
   ```

7.
```
program Line2;
  var
   V : integer;
  begin
  moveto(0,0);
  writeln('Type in a vertical position.');
  readln(V);
  lineto(200,V);
  lineto(0,200)
  end.
```

8.
```
program Line3;
  var
   V : integer;
  begin
  moveto(0,0);
  for V := 0 to 4 do
   begin
    lineto(200,20 + (40 * V));
    lineto(0,40 + (40 * V))
   end
  end.
```

12. Little equals 4 and Big equals 5.

13. The program prints 21-14-7-24-16-8-27-18-9 in a column.

14.
```
program TimesTable;
  var
   M,N : integer;
  begin
  writeln('    The times table');
  writeln;
  for N := 1 to 10 do
   begin
    for M := 1 to 10 do
     write(M * N : 4);
    writeln
   end
  end.
```

```
15. program CrossHatch;
      const
        Separation = 40;
      var
        Width : integer;
      begin
        for Width := 0 to 10 do
          drawline(Separation * Width,0,0,Separation * Width);
        for Width := -5 to 5 do
          drawline(Separation * Width,0,200,200 - Separation * Width)
      end.
```

-----------------**Chapter 4**-----------------

Exercises

5. **a.** The program prints 2-4-6-8 in a column.

   b. The program prints 2-4-8 in a column.

7. **a.** The program prints 3-6-9-12-15.

   b. When Number reaches the value 32,766, the Macintosh will be unable to execute the assignment statement Number : = Number + 3. To print out just 5 numbers, change the test to (Number = 18).

   c. It draws horizontal lines ten units apart across the standard Drawing window.

8. **a.** The program goes into an infinite loop, or it crashes if V eventually becomes smaller than $-maxint$ or larger than $maxint$.

   b. The ball leaves at the bottom of the Drawing window.

   c. HChange must be some positive even integer, and VChange must be $-(\text{Hchange } \textbf{div } 2)$. For example, if HChange is 2 and VChange is -1, the ball will leave the window at the corner.

9. **c.** 1   **d.** 1   **e.** 1

10. If the two points lie on a vertical line, then $(H_2 - H_1) = 0$ and DistanceApart is assigned the value of $V_2 - V_1$. If the points lie on a horizontal line, $(V_2 - V_1) = 0$ and the variable DistanceApart is assigned the value of $H_2 - H_1$.

11. Instead of following the lower semicircle of its orbit, the planet moves from right to left, retracing the path it followed in the first part of the program.

Problems

1. **a.** −5   **b.** 4

5. **a.** ```program``` PrintNumbers_while; {PRINTS NUMBERS IN LAST COLUMN.}

```
  var
   Number : integer;
  begin
  Number := 30;
  while (Number )= 6) do
   begin
    writeln(Number);
    Number := Number − 6
   end
  end.
```

    b. ```program``` PrintNumbers_repeat; {PRINTS NUMBERS IN LAST COLUMN.}

```
  var
   Number : integer;
  begin
  Number := 30;
   repeat
    writeln(Number);
    Number := Number − 6
   until (Number < 6)
   end.
```

7. ```program``` CrossHairs;

```
  var
   HPosition,VPosition,Radius : integer;
  begin
  writeln('Specify the horizontal and vertical position
          of a point.');
  readln(HPosition,VPosition);
  writeln('Now specify the radius of a circle.');
  readln(Radius);
  drawline(HPosition,0,HPosition,200);
  drawline(0,VPosition,200,VPosition);
  invertcircle(HPosition,VPosition,Radius)
  end.
```

8. ```program``` CompoundInterest;

```
  var
   Years,Schedule,TimesCompounded : integer;
   Principal,Rate,Amount : real;
```

```
begin
  writeln('Type in the starting principal.');
  readln(Principal);
  writeln('Type in the interest rate.');
  readln(Rate);
  writeln'(Type in the number of years in bank.');
  readln(Years);
  writeln('Type number of times interest is compounded per year.');
  readln(Schedule);
  Amount := Principal;
  for TimesCompounded := 1 to (Schedule * Years) do
    Amount := Amount + Amount * (Rate / Schedule);
  writeln('Amount after ',Years : 1,' years is $',Amount : 4 : 2)
end.
```

11. 23

13.
```
program TriangleArea;
  var
    a,b,c,s,Area : real;
    Hpos1,Vpos1,Hpos2,Vpos2,Hpos3,Vpos3 : integer;
  begin
    writeln('Type position of first corner of triangle.');
    readln(Hpos1,Vpos1);
    writeln('Type position of second corner of triangle.');
    readln(Hpos2,Vpos2);
    writeln('Type position of third corner of triangle.');
    readln(Hpos3,Vpos3);
  {DISTANCE BETWEEN (Hpos1,Vpos1) & (Hpos2,Vpos2) IS a}
  {DISTANCE BETWEEN (Hpos2,Vpos2) & (Hpos3,Vpos3) IS b}
  {DISTANCE BETWEEN (Hpos3,Vpos3) & (Hpos1,Vpos1) IS c}
    a := sqrt(sqr(Hpos2 - Hpos1) + sqr(Vpos2 - Vpos1));
    b := sqrt(sqr(Hpos3 - Hpos2) + sqr(Vpos3 - Vpos2));
    c := sqrt(sqr(Hpos1 - Hpos3) + sqr(Vpos1 - Vpos3));
    s :=(a + b + c)/2;
    drawline(Hpos1,Vpos1,Hpos2,Vpos2);
    drawline(Hpos2,Vpos2,Hpos3,Vpos3);
    drawline(Hpos3,Vpos3,Hpos1,Vpos1);
    Area := sqrt(s * (s - a) * (s - b) * (s - c));
    writeln('Area of triangle is ',Area : 6 : 1,' square units.')
  end.
```

14.
```
program AngleRoll;
  const
    Radius = 20;
  var
    H,V,Hstart,Vstart,Hchange,Vchange : integer;
```

(continued)

```
begin
  HStart := 0;
  writeln('Type vertical starting position of ball.');
  readln(Vstart);
  write('Type in horizontal change and vertical change. ');
  write('Horizontal change must be a positive integer,but ');
  writeln('vertical change can be either positive or negative.');
  readln(Hchange,Vchange);
  H := Hstart;
  V := Vstart;
  repeat
    paintcircle(H,V,Radius);
    invertcircle(H,V,Radius);
    H := H + Hchange;
    V := V + Vchange
  until (H > 180)
end.
```

_____**Chapter 5**_____

Exercises

1. **a.** The first *writeln* statement would print the smaller number, and the second *writeln* statement would print the larger number.
   b. The larger number is 5.
   The smaller number is 5.
   c. All three variables will get the original value of FirstNumber.

2. **a.** 5,2,1,0,3
   b. The program prints 1-2-3-4-0-1-2-3-4-0 in a column.

5. **a.** `paintrect(0,0,200,200)`
   b. `invertrect(75,0,125,200);`
   `invertrect(0,75,200,125)`

6. **a.** Define the constants this way:
   BarCount = 12;
   Separation = 8;
   Thickness = 8;
   b. Use these values for the constants Left and Right:
   Left = 100;
   Right = 200;

7. **a.** `paintoval(0,75,200,125);`
   `framerect(0,75,200,125)`
   b. `paintoval(0,0,100,200);`
   `paintoval(100,0,200,200);`
   `drawline(0,100,200,100)`

```
c. paintoval(0,0,100,200);
   paintoval(100,0,200,200);
   invertoval(50,0,150,200)
```

8. Grow is always even, so the **then** part of the **if-then-else** statement is never executed and only rectangles are drawn.

Problems

3.
```pascal
program Cube;
begin
  framerect(75,25,175,125);
  framerect(25,75,125,175);
  drawline(25,75,75,25);
  drawline(25,175,75,125);
  drawline(125,175,175,125);
  drawline(125,75,175,25)
end.
```

4. 1038 **mod** 12 = 6

7.
```pascal
program DrawPoint;
  var
    Horizontal,Vertical : integer;
begin
  writeln('Type in horizontal and vertical position of point.');
  readln(Horizontal,Vertical);
  paintcircle(Horizontal,Vertical,2);
  moveto(Horizontal,Vertical + 12);
  writedraw('(',Horizontal : 1,',',Vertical : 1,')')
end.
```

8.
```pascal
program IsPointInRectangle;
  var
    Horiz,Vert,Top,Left,Bottom,Right : integer;
begin
  writeln('Type in horizontal and vertical position of point.');
  readln(Horiz,Vert);
  writeln('Type top,left,bottom and right sides of rectangle.');
  readln(Top,Left,Bottom,Right);
  paintcircle(Horiz,Vert,2);
  framerect(Top,Left,Bottom,Right);
  if (Horiz >= Left) and (Horiz <= Right)
    and (Vert >= Top) and (Vert <= Bottom) then
    writeln('The point is inside the rectangle!')
  else
    writeln('The point is not inside the rectangle.')
end.
```

11.
```
program RectangleToSquare;
  var
   Top,Left,Bottom,Right,SideOfSquare,Number,Area : integer;
  begin
   writeln('Type in top,left,bottom and right sides of a rectangle.');
   readln(Top,Left,Bottom,Right);
   framerect(Top,Left,Bottom,Right);
   for Number := 1 to 1000 do
    ;
   {FOR LOOP DELAYS FLIP BY EXECUTING THE EMPTY STATEMENT 1000 TIMES.}
   Area := (Bottom - Top) * (Right - Left);
   SideOfSquare := round(sqrt(Area));
   Top := 200 - SideOfSquare;
   Right := SideOfSquare;
   framerect(Top,0,200,Right)
  end.
```

12. No.

13. 46.7%

Chapter 6

Exercises

1. a. **Program** Lines draws parallel lines that slant upward from left to right.
   b. The lines would slant at a 45° angle. The last line drawn would be the diagonal from the lower left to the upper right corner.

2. a.
```
begin
  HPosition := 20;
  VPosition := 20;
  while (VPosition <= 180) do
   begin
    Flicker(HPosition,VPosition);
    VPosition := VPosition + 1
   end
end.
```
   b.
```
begin
  HPosition := 20;
  VPosition := 20;
  while (HPosition <= 180) do
   begin
    Flicker(HPosition,VPosition);
    HPosition := HPosition + 1
   end
end.
```

3.
```
program FallingPlanet;
  const
   Horizontal = 100;
  var
   Vertical,Radius : integer;

  procedure BigFlicker(Horizontal,Vertical,Radius : integer);
  begin
   paintcircle(Horizontal,Vertical,Radius);
   invertcircle(Horizontal,Vertical,Radius)
  end;
 {BODY OF THE PROGRAM}
 begin
  Radius := 0;
  for Vertical := 20 to 200 do
   begin
    BigFlicker(Horizontal,Vertical,Radius);
    Radius := round(Vertical div 2)
   end
 end.
```

4.
```
if (Top < 10) then
   Top := 10;
```

5.

6. Eliminate the **else** part of the **if** statements that begin:
   "**if** odd(CurrentStripe) ..."

Problems

2.
```
program TicTacToe;

  procedure DrawLineTwo(H1,V1,H2,V2 : integer);
  begin
   moveto(H1,V1);
   lineto(H2,V2)
  end;
```

(continued)

```
begin
 DrawLineTwo(66,0,66,200);
 DrawLineTwo(133,0,133,200);
 DrawLineTwo(0,66,200,66);
 DrawLineTwo(0,133,200,133)
end.
```

3. ```
program Curves;
  var
   Radius : integer;

  procedure FrameCircle(H,V,Radius : integer);
   var
    Top,Left,Bottom,Right : integer;
  begin
   Top := V - Radius;
   Left := H - Radius;
   Bottom := V + Radius;
   Right := H + Radius;
   frameoval(Top,Left,Bottom,Right)
  end;

begin
 Radius := 50;
 while (Radius <= 250) do
  begin
   FrameCircle(0,0,Radius);
   Radius := Radius + 50
  end
end.
```

6. ```
program Yoyo;
  var
   Position,YoyoCount,YoyoBounce : integer;

  procedure Flicker(Horizontal,Vertical : integer);
   const
    Radius = 20;
  begin
   paintcircle(Horizontal,Vertical,Radius);
   invertcircle(Horizontal,Vertical,Radius)
  end;
```

```
begin
 writeln('How many yoyo drops would you like to see?');
 readln(YoyoCount);
 for YoyoBounce = 1 to YoyoCount do
  begin
   for Position := 20 to 170 do   {YO YO DROPS.}
    begin
     drawline(100,0,100,Position);
     Flicker(100,Position)
    end;
   for Position := 170 downto 20 do  {YO YO RETURNS.}
    begin
     drawline(100,0,100,Position);
     Flicker(100,Position)
    end
  end
end.
```

11.
```
program BrickUp;
  const
   WindowSize = 200;
  var
   Height,Width,Left,Top,RowNumber,BricksPerRow : integer;


   procedure DrawRow(Width,Height,BricksPerRow,
                     LeftEdge,Top : integer);
    var
     BrickNumber,LeftSide,RightSide,Bottom : integer;
   begin
    BrickNumber := 1;
    LeftSide := LeftEdge;
    RightSide := LeftSide + Width;
    Bottom := Top + Height;
     while (BrickNumber <= BricksPerRow) do
      begin
       framerect(Top,LeftSide,Bottom,RightSide);
       LeftSide := LeftSide + Width;
       RightSide := LeftSide + Width;
       BrickNumber := BrickNumber + 1
      end
   end;
```

(continued)

```
        {BODY OF PROGRAM}
begin
 writeln('How many units wide are the bricks?');
 readln(Width);
 writeln('How high are the bricks?');
 readln(Height);
 BricksPerRow := WindowSize div Width + 1;
 RowNumber := 0;
 Top := 0;
 repeat
  RowNumber := RowNumber + 1;
  if odd(RowNumber) then
   Left := 0
  else
   Left := -Width div 2;
  DrawRow(Width,Height,BricksPerRow,Left,Top);
  Top := Top + Height
 until (RowNumber * Height > 200)
end.
```

─────── Chapter 7 ───────────────────────

Exercises

1. ```
   program pmMeals;
     type
      meals = (breakfast,lunch,dinner,midnightsnack);
     var
      Meal : meals;
   begin
    for Meal := lunch to midnightsnack do
    writeln(Meal)
   end.
   ```

2. **a.** It does nothing.
   b. Change the *moveto* instruction to
   ```
   moveto(Hpos + (Width div 2),HeightOfLabels)
   ```

3. **a.** False   **b.** True   **d.** B   **e.** False

4. **a.** After the statement *drawchar*(Ch) add another identical *drawchar*(Ch) statement.
   b. After the *drawchar* statement add the statement:
   ```
   drawchar(Blank)
   ```
   ```

Problems

1. **a.** `program WhichWay;`

```
  type
    Directions = (North,NorthEast,East,SouthEast,South,
                  SouthWest,West,NorthWest);
  var
    Direction : Directions;
  begin
    for Direction := North to NorthWest do
    writeln(Direction)
  end.
```

b. `program WhichWayBackwards;`

```
  type
    Directions = (North,NorthEast,East,SouthEast,South,
                  SouthWest,West,NorthWest);
  var
    Direction : Directions;
  begin
    for Direction := NorthWest downto North do
    writeln(Direction)
  end.
```

5. The procedure takes the four sides of a rectangle and changes them to form the sides of a new rectangle. The new rectangle is the reflection of the old one across the diagonal that goes from the upper-left corner of the Drawing window to the lower-right corner. Any square with its upper-left corner on this diagonal is left unchanged by the procedure. A square with this property is called a *fixed point* of the procedure.

6. `program ThreeSort;`

```
  var
    First,Second,Third : real;

  procedure SwapNumbers(var First,Second : real);
  var
    Temp : real;
  begin
    Temp := First;
    First := Second;
    Second := Temp
  end;
```

(continued)

```
begin
  writeln('Type in three real numbers, separated by spaces.');
  write('>');
  readln(First,Second,Third);
  if (First < Second) then
   SwapNumbers(First,Second);
  if (First < Third) then
   SwapNumbers(First,Third);
  if (Second < Third) then
   SwapNumbers(Second,Third);
  writeln(First : 10 : 2,Second : 10 : 2,Third : 10 : 2)
end.
```

9. ```
   program DrawCompass;
   {FACE OF COMPASS IS A CIRCLE OF RADIUS 60.}
   {POINTS ON THE CIRCLE THAT STAND FOR NE, SE, SW}
   {AND NW ARE 58 UNITS FROM THE CLOSEST WALL.}
    const
     DistanceToWall = 58;
    type
     Directions = (North,NorthEast,East,SouthEast,
                   South,NorthWest,West,SouthWest);
    var
     Direction : Directions;

    procedure EnterDirection(var Direction : Directions);
    begin
     writeln('Type in a direction.');
     write('>');
     readln(Direction)
    end;

    procedure DrawBackground;
    begin
     frameoval(40,40,160,160);
      {DRAWS CIRCLE OF RADIUS 60}
     moveto(100,20);
     writedraw('N');
     moveto(100,180);
     writedraw('S');
     moveto(20,100);
     writedraw('W');
     moveto(180,100);
     writedraw('E')
    end;
   ```
   ```

```pascal
procedure DrawNeedle(Direction : Directions);
begin
 case Direction of
  North :
   drawline(100,100,100,40);
  West :
   drawline(100,100,40,100);
  South :
   drawline(100,100,100,160);
  East :
   drawline(100,100,160,100);
  NorthWest :
   drawline(100,100,DistanceToWall,DistanceToWall);
  NorthEast :
   drawline(100,100,200 - DistanceToWall,DistanceToWall);
  SouthWest :
   drawline(100,100,DistanceToWall,200 - DistanceToWall);
  SouthEast :
   drawline(100,100,200 - DistanceToWall,200 - DistanceToWall)
  end
 end;
    {MAIN PROGRAM}
begin
 EnterDirection(Direction);
 DrawBackground;
 DrawNeedle(Direction)
end.
```

11.
```pascal
program Calendar;
{MAKE DRAWING WINDOW EXTEND ACROSS SCREEN}
 const
  StartHeight = 20;
  Separation = 25;
  ColumnWidth = 50;
  LeftStart = 10;
 type
  Months = (Jan,Feb,Mar,Apr,May,Jun,Jul,Aug,Sept,Oct,Nov,Dec);
  DaysOfWeek = (Mon,Tue,Wed,Thur,Fri,Sat,Sun);
 var
  MonthName : Months;
  Day,StartDay : DaysOfWeek;
  Date,DaysInMonth,Height,Row : integer;

 procedure TypeMonth_DayCount_Day(var Name : Months;
         var DaysInMonth : integer;
         var StartDay : DaysOfWeek);
```

(continued)

```pascal
begin
 writeln('Type in name of month.');
 write('>');
 readln(Name);
 writeln('Type in number of days in month.');
 write('>');
 readln(DaysInMonth);
 writeln('Type in first day of week in month.');
 write('>');
 readln(StartDay)
end;
procedure PrintRow(var Date : integer;
         var StartDay : DaysOfWeek;
         Height : integer);
 var
  HPos : integer;
  Day : DaysOfWeek;
begin
 Hpos := LeftStart;
 moveto(HPos,Height);
 for Day := Mon to Sun do
  begin
   if (Day >= StartDay) and (Date <= DaysInMonth) then
    begin
     writedraw(Date : 2);
     Date := Date + 1
    end;
   HPos := HPos + ColumnWidth;
   moveto(HPos,Height)
  end
end;

procedure PrintDaysOfWeek(Height : integer);
 var
  HPos : integer;
  Day : DaysOfWeek;
begin
 HPos := LeftStart;
 for Day := Mon to Sun do
  begin
   moveto(HPos,Height);
   writedraw(Day);
   HPos := HPos + ColumnWidth
  end
end;
```

```
procedure PrintNameOfMonth(Name : Months;
        Height : integer);
 const
   Center = 160;
 begin
 moveto(Center,Height);
 writedraw(Name)
 end;
  {BODY OF PROGRAM}
begin
 TypeMonth_DayCount_Day(MonthName,DaysInMonth,StartDay);
 Day := StartDay;
 Date := 1;
 Height := StartHeight;
 PrintNameOfMonth(MonthName,Height);
 Height := Height + Separation;
 PrintDaysOfWeek(Height);
 Height := Height + Separation;
 for Row := 1 to 6 do
  begin
   PrintRow(Date,Day,Height);
   Height := Height + Separation;
   Day := Mon
  end
end.
```

Chapter 8

Exercises

1. **a.** FirstNumberIsGreater has the value False, so the program prints "The first number is less than or equal to second."

3. **a.** Invalid. There are more left parentheses than right parentheses.
   b. Invalid. The second right parenthesis is not preceded by its matching left parenthesis.
   c. Valid.

4. ***accept***

5. If you drag in any other direction, top would be greater than or equal to bottom, or left would be greater than or equal to right, so no rectangle would be drawn.

6. False
   True
   False

7. **a.** 7   **b.** 1

8. You must change the definition of the ScoreRange subrange type to:

   ```
   ScoreRange = 0..105;
   ```

   You must also change the prompt in the main loop so that it reads:

   ```
   "Type in score from 0 to 105 ..."
   ```

Problems

4. True. The value of a boolean expression that doesn't use the operator **not** must be false when all the boolean variables in the expression are false.

5.
```
program DoubledChar;
{YOU TYPE IN A SENTENCE. PROGRAM REPORTS}
{FIRST PAIR OF DOUBLED LETTERS.}
 const
  Period = '.';
  Blank = ' ';
 var
  Ch,PreviousChar : char;
  Found : boolean; {THE FLAG}
begin
 Ch := Period;
 PreviousChar := Period;
 Found := False; {THE FLAG IS INITIALIZED TO FALSE.}
 writeln('Type a sentence ending with a period.');
 write('>');
 repeat
  read(Ch);
  if (Ch <> Period) then
   if (PreviousChar = Ch) then
    Found := True; {IF FOUND BECOMES TRUE, LOOP ENDS EARLY.}
   PreviousChar := Ch
 until Found or (Ch = Period);
 writeln;
 if Found then
  writeln('The character ',PreviousChar,
          ' is doubled in the sentence.')
 else
  writeln('There are no doubled characters in the sentence.')
end.
```

9. The program would accept any sequence with an equal number of left and right parentheses. For example, the program would accept the string   )))(((.

11.
```
procedure DeleteExtraSpaces;
  const
    Blank = ' ';
    Period = '.';
    DollarSign = '$';
  var
    PreviousCh,Ch : char;
begin
  moveto(5,100);
  PreviousCh := DollarSign; {INITIALIZE PreviousCh TO ARBITRARY
                                          CHARACTER}
  writeln('Type in a sentence ending with a period.');
  write('>');
  while (Ch <> Period) do
    begin
      read(Ch);
      if (PreviousCh <> Blank) or (Ch <> Blank) then
        drawchar(Ch);
      PreviousCh := Ch
    end
end.
```

Chapter 9

Exercises

1. **a.** 3

   d. It lists the number of people in each house on the street, beginning with house 12 and ending with house 1.

2. **a.** The component type is *integer*, and there are 9 component variables. The index type is the subrange of *integer* 1..9.

   b. The component type is *integer*. There are 26 component variables. The index type is the *char* subrange 'a'..'z'.

   c. The component type is *real*. There are 12 component variables. The index type is an enumerated type that consists of the months of the year. We would have to define a type called Months before we gave the definition for the array type MonthlyRainfall.

3. The loop would be the same, but HouseNumber should be initialized to 1 instead of 2.

4. **a.** Yes.   **b.** 2,3

    c. The component type is the enumerated type ConstructionType. The index type is the subrange of integer 1..12. The variable RutlandHouse-Kind keeps track of the construction type for each house on the street.

5.
```
case HouseNumber of
  1 :
   Neighbors := RutlandSt[HouseNumber + 1] +
       RutlandSt[HouseNumber + 2];
  2 :
   Neighbors := RutlandSt[HouseNumber - 1] +
       RutlandSt[HouseNumber + 1] + RutlandSt[HouseNumber + 2];
  12 :
   Neighbors := RutlandSt[HouseNumber - 1] +
       RutlandSt[HouseNumber - 2];
  11 :
   Neighbors := RutlandSt[HouseNumber - 2] +
       RutlandSt[[HouseNumber - 1] + RutlandSt[HouseNumber +1];
  otherwise
   Neighbors := RutlandSt[HouseNumber - 1] +
       RutlandSt[HouseNumber + 1] + RutlandSt[HouseNumber - 2] +
       RutlandSt[HouseNumber + 2]
end;
```

6. Assume there is an enumerated type called Names consisting of players' names. Then this type definition for Team defines the basketball team:

```
Team = array[BBPositions] of Names;
```

7. **Program** WonderWhat reads in a string and then prints this string vertically in the Text window.

8. **a.** Able I, ere I saw Elba.   23 characters.
    b. Able wasI, ere I saw Elba. 26 characters.
    c. A ere I saw Elba.   17 characters.

9. **a.** Add the statement *writeln*(*length*(StringOfChar)) as the second statement in the body of the program.
    b. 8

10. The 1's on the ends represent the number of ways you can get all heads or all tails. The 5's represent the ways you can get exactly 1 heads or exactly 1 tails. The 10's represent the ways you can get 2 heads or 2 tails.

Problems

3. c.
```pascal
program RailRoad;
   type
    CarType = (Locomotive,CoalCar,OilCar,CattleCar);
    FreightTrain = array[1..10] of CarType;
   var
    AltoonaLimited : FreightTrain;
    Number : integer;
  begin
   for Number := 1 to 10 do
    begin
     writeln('Type in Locomotive,CoalCar,OilCar or CattleCar.');
     writeln('What kind of car is number ',Number : 1,'?');
     write('>');
     readln(AltoonaLimited[Number])
    end;
   for Number := 1 to 10 do
    writeln(AltoonaLimited[Number])
  end.
```

   d.
```pascal
program RailRoad;
   type
    CarType = (Locomotive,CoalCar,OilCar,CattleCar);
    FreightTrain = array[1..10] of CarType;
    CarsPerType = array[Locomotive..CattleCar] of integer;
   var
    AltoonaLimited : FreightTrain;
    Number : integer;
    NumberOfCars : CarsPerType;
    WhichCar : CarType;
  begin
   for Number := 1 to 10 do
    begin
     writeln('What kind of car is number ',Number : 1,'?');
     writeln('Type in Locomotive,CoalCar,OilCar or CattleCar.' );
     write('>');
     readln(AltoonaLimited[Number])
    end;
   Number := 1;
   while (Number <= 10) do
    begin
     WhichCar := AltoonaLimited[Number];
     NumberOfCars[WhichCar] := NumberOfCars[WhichCar] + 1;
     Number := Number + 1
    end;
```

(continued)

```
        writeln;
        writeln(' LOCOMOTIVE  COALCAR  OILCAR  CATTLECAR');
        write(NumberOfCars[Locomotive] : 13);
        write(NumberOfCars[CoalCar] : 13);
        write(NumberOfCars[OilCar] : 13);
        write(NumberOfCars[CattleCar] : 13)
      end.

4. program Races;
   type
    Runners = (Jesse,Frankie,Hilary);
    SprintResults = array[Runners] of real;
   var
    Fifty,Hundred : SprintResults;
    Name,Winner : Runners;

   procedure RecordRaceResults(var Fifty,Hundred : SprintResults);
    var
     Name : Runners;
   begin
    for Name := Jesse to Hilary do
     begin
      writeln('Give time for ',Name,' in 50 and 100 yard dashes.');
      write('>');
      readln(Fifty[Name],Hundred[Name])
     end
   end;

   procedure FindWinner(RaceTime : SprintResults;
           var Winner : Runners);
    var
     Runner : Runners;
   begin
    Winner := Jesse;
    for Runner := Jesse to Hilary do
     if (RaceTime[Runner] < RaceTime[Winner]) then
      Winner := Runner
   end;
       {MAIN PROGRAM}
begin
 RecordRaceResults(Fifty,Hundred);
 FindWinner(Fifty,Name); {Name WILL HOLD NAME OF 50 YD DASH WINNER}
 writeln('The winner of the 100 yard dash is ',Name);
 FindWinner(Hundred,Name); {Name WILL HOLD NAME OF 100 YD DASH WINNER}
 writeln('The winner of the 50 yard dash is ',Name)
end.
```

9.
```pascal
program DigitDisplay;
  type
   Digits = '0'..'9';
   DigitValues = array[Digits] of integer;
  var
   DigitPositions : DigitValues;
   Digit : Digits;
 begin
  for Digit := '0' to '9' do
   DigitPositions[Digit] := ord(Digit);
  writeln('digit' : 8,'ord value' : 12);
  writeln;
  for Digit := '0' to '9' do
   writeln(Digit : 6,DigitPositions[Digit] : 10)
 end.
```

10.
```pascal
program Turnpike;
  const
   TollAmount = 65;
  type
   CoinType = (penny,nickel,dime,quarter);
   CoinChart = array[CoinType] of integer;
  var
   TollPayment : CoinChart;
   AmountDeposited : integer;

 procedure ReadPayment(var TollPayment : CoinChart);
   var
    Coin : CoinType;
 begin
  writeln('Type in coins deposited in a toll booth transaction.');
  writeln;
  for Coin := penny to quarter do
   begin
    writeln('Type in ',Coin,' count.');
    write('>');
    readln(TollPayment[Coin])
   end;
  writeln
 end;

 procedure CalcPayment(TollPayment : CoinChart;
         var AmountDeposited : integer);
   var
    Coin : CoinType;
```

```
begin
 AmountDeposited := 0;
 for Coin := penny to quarter do
  case Coin of
   Penny :
    AmountDeposited := AmountDeposited + TollPayment[Coin];
   Nickel :
    AmountDeposited := AmountDeposited + 5 * TollPayment[Coin];
   Dime :
    AmountDeposited := AmountDeposited + 10 * TollPayment[Coin];
   Quarter :
    AmountDeposited := AmountDeposited + 25 * TollPayment[Coin]
  end
end;
    {MAIN PROGRAM}
begin
 ReadPayment(TollPayment);
 CalcPayment(TollPayment,AmountDeposited);
 if (AmountDeposited)= TollAmount) then
  writeln('Thank you -- drive carefully.')
 else
  begin
   write('Please deposit ');
   writeln(TollAmount - AmountDeposited : 2,' cents more.')
  end
end.
```

11. ```
    program Fibonacci;
     type
      Numberlist = array[1..20] of integer;
     var
      Fibo : NumberList;
      Number : integer;
    begin
     for Number := 1 to 20 do
      Fibo[Number] := 0;
     Fibo[1] := 1;
     Fibo[2] := 1;
     for Number := 3 to 20 do
      Fibo[Number] := Fibo[Number - 1] + Fibo[Number - 2];
     for Number := 1 to 20 do
      writeln(Fibo[Number])
    end.
    ```
    ```

_____**Chapter 10**_____

Exercises

1. a, b, d, e, h

3. **a.**
```
function InBetween(Smaller,Middle,Larger : integer) : boolean;
  begin
    if (Smaller < Middle) and (Middle < Larger) then
    Between := True
    else
    Between := False
  end;
```

   b. In both cases, the program reports that the point lies inside the rectangle.

   c. **Function** Tomorrow takes a variable of type DaysOfWeek as its argument, and it returns the next day. Today is the formal parameter; it has type DaysOfWeek. The result type is also DaysOfWeek.

   d.
```
function Yesterday(Today : DaysOfWeek) : DaysOfWeek;
  begin
    if (Today = Mon) then
    Yesterday := Sun
    else
    Yesterday := pred(Today)
  end;
```

4. **a.** A   **b.** A   **c.** #   **d.** 3

5. The test (CharString[Position − 1] = Blank) in **procedure** CapFirstLetters would cause an out-of-range error.

7. No.

8. **a.** If the upper limit were Size, the final iteration of the loop would involve a tail of length 1, and with a tail that has only one element further rearrangement would be unnecessary.

   b. **Procedure** Swap alters NameList.

9. **b.** (*random* **mod** 11) + 10

   d. $0 \leq$ Number < 1

Problems

1.
```
program OneOverTest;
  var
   Number : integer;
   Sum : real;
```

(continued)

```pascal
function OneOver(Number : integer) : real;
begin
 if (Number = 0) then
  OneOver := 0.0
 else
  OneOver := 1 / Number
end;
     {MAIN PROGRAM}
begin
 Sum := 0.0;
 Number := 2;
 while (Number <= 256) do
  begin
   Sum := Sum + OneOver(Number);
   Number := 2 * Number
  end;
 writeln('Sum is ',Sum : 6 : 4)
end.
```

5.
```pascal
program FacTest;
  var
   Number : longint;

  function Factorial(N : integer) : longint;
  {A RECURSIVE FUNCTION}
  begin
   if (N <= 0) then
    Factorial := 1
   else
    Factorial := N * Factorial(N - 1)
  end;
      {MAIN PROGRAM}
begin
 writeln('Type in a non-negative integer value.');
 write('>');
 readln(Number);
 writeln('Factorial of ',Number : 2,' is');
 writeln(Factorial(Number) : 2)
end.
```

10.
```pascal
program IntegerSquareRoot;
  var
   Number : integer;

  function IntegerRoot(N : integer) : integer;
   var
    Root : integer;
```

```
      begin
       if (N <= 0) then
        IntegerRoot := 0
       else
        begin
         Root := 0;
         while (sqr(Root + 1) <= N) do
         {BODY OF WHILE STATEMENT IS A SIMPLE STATEMENT.}
          Root := Root + 1;
         IntegerRoot := Root
        end
      end;
       {MAIN PROGRAM}
      begin
      writeln('Type in a non-negative integer.');
      write('>');
      readln(Number);
      write('The integer square root of ',Number : 2,' is ');
      writeln(IntegerRoot(Number) : 1,'.')
      end.
```

12.
```
    program BallRace;
     const
      BallCount = 6;
      WindowSize = 200;
     type
      BallRecord = array[1..BallCount] of integer;
     var
      BallNumber,ChosenBall,Separation,Radius : integer;
      HPos : BallRecord;
     {KEEPS TRACK OF HORIZONTAL POSITION OF EACH BALL}
      VPos : BallRecord;
     {KEEPS TRACK OF VERTICAL POSITIONS OF EACH BALL}

     procedure InitializeVPositions(var VPos : BallRecord);
      var
        VCenter,BallNumber : integer;
     begin
      VCenter := Separation div 2;
      BallNumber := 1;
      while (BallNumber <= BallCount) do
       begin
        VPos[BallNumber] := VCenter;
        VCenter := VCenter + Separation;
        BallNumber := BallNumber + 1
       end
     end;
```

(*continued*)

```pascal
procedure DrawBackGround;
 var
  Number : integer;
begin
 Number := 0;
 repeat
  Number := Number + Separation;
  drawline(0,Number,WindowSize,Number)
 until (Number )= WindowSize)
end;


procedure StartRace(var HPos : BallRecord);
 var
  BallNumber : integer;
begin
 for BallNumber := 1 to BallCount do
  begin
   HPos[BallNumber] := Radius;
   paintcircle(HPos[BallNumber],VPos[BallNumber],Radius)
  end
end;


function PickABall : integer;
begin
 PickABall := (random mod BallCount) + 1
end;


procedure Advance(ChosenBall : integer;
       var HPos : BallRecord);
 const
  Speed = 5;
 begin
{ERASE THE BALL THAT'S BEING ADVANCED}
  invertcircle(HPos[ChosenBall],VPos[ChosenBall],Radius);
{UPDATE THE POSITION OF THE BALL BEING ADVANCED}
  HPos[ChosenBall] := HPos[ChosenBall] + Speed;
{PAINT THE NEW POSITION OF THE BALL THAT WAS MOVED}
  paintcircle(HPos[ChosenBall],VPos[ChosenBall],Radius)
 end;


function ABallIsDone(HPos : BallRecord) : boolean;
 var
  BallNumber : integer;
```

```
  begin
   ABallIsDone := False;
   for BallNumber := 1 to BallCount do
    if (HPos[BallNumber] >= (WindowSize - Radius)) then
      ABallIsDone := True
  end;
  {MAIN PROGRAM}
  begin
   Radius := WindowSize div (2 * BallCount);
   Separation := 2 * Radius;
   InitializeVPositions(VPos);
   DrawBackGround;
   StartRace(HPos);
   repeat
    ChosenBall := PickABall;
    Advance(ChosenBall,HPos);
    DrawBackGround
   until ABallIsDone(HPos)
  end.

17. program DrunkAtOpera;
    const
     NumberOfPatrons = 6;
    type
     UmbrellaHolders = array[1..NumberOfPatrons] of integer;
    var
     UmbrellaNumber,WhichPosition,TrialNumber : integer;
     TrialCount,Score : integer;
     People : UmbrellaHolders;

    function PickUmbrella(UmbrellaNumber : integer;
             People : UmbrellaHolders) : integer;
     var
      Umbrella,N,Position : integer;
    begin
     Umbrella := random mod (NumberOfPatrons - UmbrellaNumber + 1) + 1;
     N := 1;
     Position := 1;
     while (Umbrella > 0) and (Position <= NumberOfPatrons) do
      begin
       if (People[Position] = 0) then
        Umbrella := Umbrella - 1;
       if (Umbrella > 0) then
        Position := Position + 1
      end;
     PickUmbrella := Position
    end;
```

(continued)

```
procedure Place(WhichUmbrella,Position : integer;
        var People : UmbrellaHolders);



begin
 People[Position] := WhichUmbrella
end;



function NoPatronGetsOwnUmbrella(People : UmbrellaHolders) : boolean;
 var
  SomeoneGetsHerOwn : boolean;
  N : integer;
begin
 SomeoneGetsHerOwn := False;
 N := 1;
 while (N <= NumberOfPatrons) and not (SomeoneGetsHerOwn) do
  begin
   if (People[N] = N) then
    SomeoneGetsHerOwn := True;
   N := N + 1
  end;
 NoPatronGetsOwnUmbrella := not (SomeoneGetsHerOwn)
end;



procedure InitializeHandout(var People : UmbrellaHolders);
 var
  UmbrellaNumber : integer;
begin
 for UmbrellaNumber := 1 to NumberOfPatrons do
  People[UmbrellaNumber] := 0
end;



procedure DoDrunkenHandOut(var People : UmbrellaHolders);
 var
  UmbrellaNumber,WhichPosition : integer;
begin
 for UmbrellaNumber := 1 to NumberOfPatrons do
  begin
   WhichPosition := PickUmbrella(UmbrellaNumber,People);
   Place(UmbrellaNumber,WhichPosition,People)
  end
end;
```

```
      {MAIN PROGRAM}
begin
 write('Type in the number of times ');
 writeln('you want to simulate umbrella handout.');
 write('>');
 readln(TrialCount);
 Score := 0;
 for TrialNumber := 1 to TrialCount do
  begin
    InitializeHandOut(People);
    DoDrunkenHandOut(People);
    if NoPatronGetsOwnUmbrella(People) then
     Score := Score + 1
  end;
 write((Score / TrialCount) * 100 : 4 : 2, '% of the time ');
 writeln('no one gets her own umbrella.')
end.
```

Chapter 11

Exercises

2.
```
CheckNumber : integer;
Year : integer;
CanceledCheckBack : boolean
```

3. a. `Worker.Name := 'Alvin Bosco';`

b. It changes the marital status of Worker from married to not married, or from not married to married.

c.
```
if (Worker.Name := 'Alvin Bosco') then
   Worker.YearsWithCompany := Worker.YearsWithCompany + 1;
```

d. It calculates the total number of hours that Worker works in a week.

4. a.
```
NumberOfEmployee := 1;
while (NumberOfEmployee <= EmployeeCount) do
 begin
   write(Roster[NumberOfEmployee].Name : 25);
   writeln(Roster[NumberOfEmployee].SocSecNumber : 20);
   NumberOfEmployee := NumberOfEmployee + 1
 end;
```

b.
```
NumberOfEmployee := 1;
while (NumberOfEmployee <= EmployeeCount) do
 begin
  if (Roster[NumberOfEmployee].Age < 25) and
   (Roster[NumberOfEmployee].MonthlySalary) > 2000.00) then
   writeln(Roster[NumberOfEmployee].Name);
   NumberOfEmployee := NumberOfEmployee + 1
 end;
```

5.
```
procedure StoreOval(H,V,OvalNumber : integer;
         var Picture : Drawing);
begin
 with Picture[OvalNumber] do
  begin
   Top := V;
   Left := H;
   Bottom := V + 80;
   Right := H + V
  end
end;
```

6. **a.** `open(MonthlySwim,'JuneLaps')`

b. `read(MonthlySwim,Laps)`

Problems

1.
```
procedure DrawStraightLine;
{A NEW MINIPAINT INSTRUCTION}
  var
   H1,VI,H2,V2 : integer; {THE POINTS (H1,V1) AND (H2,V2)}
begin
 ClickPoint(H1,V1);
 ClickPoint(H2,V2);
 drawline(H1,V1,H2,V2)
end;
```

4.
```
program ConnectRandomPoints;
{TO RUN, FILL ENTIRE SCREEN WITH DRAWING WINDOW}
 const
  Size = 20;
 type
  Point = record
    H : integer;
    V : integer
   end;
  ListOfPoints = array[1..Size] of Point;
 var
  PointList : ListOfPoints;

 procedure GeneratePoints(var List : ListOfPoints);
  var
   PointNumber : integer;
```

```
begin
 for PointNumber := 1 to Size do
  begin
   List[PointNumber].H := random mod 501;
   List[PointNumber].V := random mod 301
  end
end;


procedure ConnectPoints(List : ListOfPoints);
 var
  StartPoint,EndPoint : integer;
begin
 for StartPoint := 1 to (Size - 1) do
  for EndPoint := (StartPoint + 1) to Size do
   begin
    moveto(List[StartPoint].H,List[StartPoint].V);
    lineto(List[EndPoint].H,List[EndPoint].V)
   end
end;
   {MAIN PROGRAM}
begin
 GeneratePoints(PointList);
 ConnectPoints(PointList)
end.
```

7.
```
program CheckRecords;
 const
  CommandCount = 6;
  BoxHeight = 20;
  WindowWidth = 500;
 type
  Commands = (Bad,Quit,AddCheck,CheckNumberInfo,
             ListAllSince,AmtInMonth);
  Months = (Jan,Feb,Mar,Apr,May,Jun,Jul,Aug,Sept,Oct,Nov,Dec);
  ACheck = record
    Month : Months;
    Date : integer;
    CheckNumber : integer;
    Amount : real;
    WhoTo : string;
    Returned : boolean
   end;
```

(continued)

```
var
 H,V : integer;
 Command : Commands;
 Check : ACheck;
 CheckFile : file of ACheck;

procedure ClickPoint(var H,V : integer);
begin
 repeat
{DO NOTHING}
 until button;
 repeat
  getmouse(H,V)
 until not (button)
end;

procedure PromptAndRead_Month(Prompt : string;
        var MonthName : Months);
begin
 writeln(Prompt);
 write('>');
 readln(MonthName)
end;

procedure PromptAndRead_Integer(Prompt : string;
        var Number : integer);
begin
 writeln(Prompt);
 write('>');
 readln(Number)
end;

procedure PromptAndRead_Real(Prompt : string;
        var Number : real);
begin
 writeln(Prompt);
 write('>');
 readln(Number)
end;

procedure PromptAndRead_String(Prompt : string;
        var Str : string);
begin
 writeln(Prompt);
 write('>');
 readln(Str)
end;
```

```pascal
procedure PromptAndRead_Boolean(Prompt : string;
        var Test : boolean);
begin
 writeln(Prompt);
 write('>');
 readln(Test)
end;

procedure LayOutMenu;
 var
  BoxWidth : integer;

 procedure DrawAndLabelBoxes(BoxWidth,BoxCount : integer);
  var
   BoxNumber,Position : integer;
   Command : Commands;

  procedure PrintLabel(Position : integer;
          Command : Commands);
{LABEL STARTS A LITTLE IN FROM LINE, HALFWAY DOWN MENU BOX}
  begin
   moveto(Position + 1,BoxHeight div 2);
   writedraw(Command)
  end;

 {BODY OF DRAWANDLABELBOXES}
 begin
  Command := Bad;
  BoxNumber := 0;
  Position := 0;
  repeat
   Command := succ(Command);
   BoxNumber := BoxNumber + 1;
   drawline(Position,0,Position,BoxHeight);
   PrintLabel(Positon,Command);
   Position := Position + BoxWidth
  until (BoxNumber = BoxCount)
 end;

{BODY OF LAYOUTMENU}
begin
 drawline(0,BoxHeight,WindowWidth,BoxHeight);
 BoxWidth := WindowWidth div (CommandCount - 1);
{THE COMMAND "BAD" DOESN'T GET A BOX}
 DrawAndLabelBoxes(BoxWidth,CommandCount - 1)
end;
```

(continued)

```pascal
function ChooseCommand(H,V : integer) : commands;
{FUNCTION CHOOSECOMMAND CONTAINS 3 OTHER FUNCTIONS}
var
 BoxNumber : integer;

 function VerticalOk(V : integer) : boolean;
 begin
  if (V >= 0) and (V < BoxHeight) then
   VerticalOk := True
  else
   VerticalOk := False
 end;

 function HorizontalOk(H : integer) : boolean;
 begin
  if (H >= 0) and (H < WindowWidth) then
   HorizontalOk := True
  else
   HorizontalOk := False
 end;

 function SelectCommand(BoxNumber : integer) : Commands;
  var
   Box : integer;
   CommandChoice : Commands;
 begin
  Box := BoxNumber;
  CommandChoice := Quit;
  while (Box > 0) do
   begin
    Box := Box - 1;
    CommandChoice := succ(CommandChoice)
   end;
  SelectCommand := CommandChoice
 end;

{BODY OF FUNCTION CHOOSECOMMAND}
begin
 if VerticalOk(V) and HorizontalOk(H) then
  begin
   BoxNumber := ((CommandCount - 1) * H) div WindowWidth;
   ChooseCommand := SelectCommand(BoxNumber)
  end
 else
  ChooseCommand := Bad
end;
```

```
procedure DoCommand(Command : Commands);

 procedure PrintEntry(Check : ACheck);
 begin
  writeln('Recipient: ',Check.WhoTo);
  writeln('Date:', Check.Month : 8, Check.Date : 3);
  writeln('Number ',Check.CheckNumber);
  writeln('For: ',Check.Amount : 6 : 2);
  writeln('Returned?: ',Check.Returned)
 end;

procedure AddACheck;
  var
   Check : ACheck;
 begin
  seek(CheckFile,maxlongint);
  PromptAndRead_Month('Type in month of check.',Check.Month);
  PromptAndRead_Integer('Type in day of check.',Check.Date);
  PromptAndRead_Integer('Type in check number.',Check.CheckNumber);
  PromptAndRead_Real('Type in amount of check.',Check.Amount);
  PromptAndRead_String('Type in who check is to.',Check.WhoTo);
  PromptAndRead_Boolean('Type in if check has been returned.',
                        Check.Returned);
  write(CheckFile,Check)
 end;

procedure ListSinceDate;
 var
  Check : ACheck;
  SinceMonth : Months;
  SinceDay : integer;
 begin
  PromptAndRead_Month('Type in cut off month.',SinceMonth);
  PromptAndRead_Integer('Type in cut off day.',SinceDay);
  reset(CheckFile);
  while not (eof(CheckFile)) do
   begin
    read(CheckFile, Check);
    if (Check.Month > SinceMonth) or ((Check.Month = SinceMonth)
        and (Check.Date >= SinceDay)) then
     PrintEntry(Check)
   end
 end;
```

(continued)

```pascal
procedure NumberInfo;
 var
  Number : integer;
  Found : boolean;
  Check : ACheck;
begin
 reset(CheckFile);
 Found := False;
 PromptAndRead_Integer('Type in number of check.',Number);
 while not (eof(CheckFile)) and not (Found) do
  begin
   read(CheckFile,Check);
   if (Check.CheckNumber = Number) then
    begin
     PrintEntry(Check);
     Found := True
    end
  end;
 if not (Found) then
  writeln('Check not found')
end;


procedure MonthAmt;
 var
  Mo : Months;
  Amt : real;
  Check : ACheck;
begin
 PromptAndRead_Month('Type in a month.',Mo);
 reset(CheckFile);
 Amt := 0.0;
 while not (eof(CheckFile)) do
  begin
   read(CheckFile, Check);
   if (Check.Month = Mo) then
    Amt := Amt + Check.Amount
  end;
 writeln('Amount spent in ',Mo : 5,' is:$',Amt : 6 : 2)
end;
```

```
         {BODY OF PROCEDURE DOCOMMAND}
begin
 case Command of
  Bad :
   begin
    sysbeep(10);
    writeln('Bad command -- enter another.')
   end;
  AddCheck :
   AddACheck;
  ListAllSince :
   ListSinceDate;
  CheckNumberInfo :
   NumberInfo;
  AmtInMonth :
   MonthAmt
 end
end;
     {BODY OF PROGRAM}
begin
 open(CheckFile, 'Checks84');
 writeln('Move pointer into one of the menu boxes and click.');
 LayOutMenu;
 ClickPoint(H,V);
 Command := ChooseCommand(H,V);
 while (Command <> Quit) do
  begin
   DoCommand(Command);
   writeln('#################');
   ClickPoint(H,V);
   Command := ChooseCommand(H,V)
  end;
 close(CheckFile)
end.
```

Index
to Programs

Index